T0246265

A TRIBUTE TO
ZHONG NANSHAN

www.royalcollins.com

A TRIBUTE TO
ZHONG NANSHAN

The Man Who Saved Millions of Lives

YE YI

Books Beyond Boundaries

ROYAL COLLINS

A Tribute to Zhong Nanshan:
The Man Who Saved Millions of Lives

By Ye Yi

First published in 2023 by Royal Collins Publishing Group Inc.
Groupe Publication Royal Collins Inc.

Headquarters: 550-555 boul. René-Lévesque O Montréal (Québec) H2Z1B1 Canada

Original Edition © Guangdong Education Publishing House

ISBN: 978-1-4878-1073-3

To find out more about our publications, please visit www.royalcollins.com.

CONTENTS

PART 2   THE DOCTORS

PART 3   AN EXTRAORDINARY LIFE

THE LIGHT OF AN EMBLEM OF THE PARTY

"Person-to-person transmission can now be confirmed."

On January 20, 2020, on behalf of the high-level panel of experts from the National Health Commission (NHC), Dr. Zhong Nanshan decisively informed the nation on the facts of the situation. Two days earlier, the NHC had sent word to Dr. Zhong Nanshan that he must rush to Wuhan that very day and conduct a thorough investigation and evaluate the epidemic in Wuhan. Dr. Zhong conscientiously carried out his duty, leaving no room for error to slip into the work.

By this time, the entire country was immersed in the festive atmosphere of welcoming the Chinese New Year. Everyone was busy visiting friends and family, traveling, and gathering.

When the announcement of person-to-person transmission of the novel coronavirus came, it put the whole country on alert. The city of Wuhan was closed down, masks were donned, homes were closed, residential areas fortified, hospitals expanded, and suspected cases quarantined. Pandemic prevention and control quickly became an issue of vital importance for every Chinese person.

It was a race against the clock. At 84 years old, Dr. Zhong forgot all about eating, and he had no time to rest. Without hesitation or letting up the slack, he boarded the northbound high-speed train to Wuhan. With his decades of in-depth knowledge of research into respiratory medicine and an insight acquired through years of study and experience, he had an idea of the potential danger that lay ahead.

The Communist Party of China (CPC), the Chinese government, and all the Chinese people loaded all their anticipation onto the ship of history. Dr. Zhong was well aware of what his mission was in Wuhan. He knew that behind the fact of the pandemic was the question of life or death, existence or extinction – it was a matter that would determine the fate of the country, and of the world.

Faced with this urgent mission, he had only one thought – *take action!* Action had to be taken immediately.

"Thank you, Dr. Zhong." Through word of mouth, it had become widely known that Dr. Zhong was the one who uncovered the truth about the atypical pneumonia pathogen in 2003. After having sounded the alarm for SARS all those years ago, he was now faced with a rapidly spreading epidemic. His clarion call was, "Send all the critical patients to me." He fought on the front line day and night, bringing patients back from the brink of death.

What if the world had learned of Covid-19 a day or even a few days later? Or what if Dr. Zhong had made an incorrect evaluation? What would the threat to everyone's life have been then? What would have become of China? Anyone can ask these "what ifs." Not everyone is grateful, but I urge that you cherish what has been achieved in this battle against Covid-19. It is easy to forget as the pandemic drags on, but will history also forget? The world does not have room for so many "what ifs."

Having come to the end of 2019, the Chinese people were undergoing a severe test for which there was no precedent. With the Party emblem on their chest, the vast number of frontline medical workers fighting against the pandemic were not afraid of the hardships ahead. They well knew that this was the mission bestowed on them by the Party and the country, and they knew that the people were putting great trust in them. The words on the Party emblem Dr. Zhong wore on his chest glittered, *Serving the People.* Dr. Zhong was a pragmatic, truth-seeking person, and he took these words as a solemn, sacred commitment, which was as heavy as a mountain and as long as a great river.

"Fighting for Communism with my life, and being ready to sacrifice everything for the Party and the people," he recited firmly, leading the oath.

The light of the Party emblem would illuminate the world. From early in the morning until deep in the night, the light from the chest badges of thousands of people would converge into the energy of salvation. Seeing China rally like this was a source of great pride.

The Chinese people were amazed by the way Dr. Zhong always prioritized truth. He placed the people's safety above his own life, because he lived up to his own conscience and expectations. When facing the Party and the people, he followed the spirit of science and persistently pursued the truth.

It was evident that with an epidemic once again on Dr. Zhong's shoulders, weighing down on him like a mountain just as SARS had done before, he was no longer walking as swiftly, now that he was 84 years old. But he remained as calm and steady as ever.

His greatest joy was the recovery of the patients he was treating. At the same time, any misfortune his patients suffered was like an incurable wound for him. He stepped forward over and over, always speaking the truth, sometimes shedding tears of compassion as he did. His patients' lives were heavier than Mount Tai, a point reflected in his words, "In my opinion, the most important thing is my patients' lives."

It was so natural for Dr. Zhong to integrate the aim of serving the people into his entire being. It was only in this way that anyone could dedicate himself so thoroughly to his mission, and this spirit of dedication would accompany him throughout his life. It was not easy to achieve this state. But for Dr. Zhong, it was not a difficult thing, as the word "self" was not in his vocabulary. His courage in speaking the truth gave hope to the people.

Any patient who was saved from death was naturally very grateful, and the heroes who brought this salvation were commended. Such heroes extended a trustworthy helping hand when others were in crisis and needed assistance. This was why Zhong Nanshan's name gained universal appreciation and admiration in the hearts of the Chinese people.

Covid-19 renewed the Chinese people's respect for medical workers and revealed the familial relationship that develops between medical workers and patients. The pandemic allowed Chinese medical workers to inscribe the words, *Serving the People* all across the land.

The global fight against the pandemic caused the world to put aside its arrogance and condescension, finally providing a yardstick to measure success. China's name was emblazoned on that yardstick.

The Chinese people's unanimous rapid response to the pandemic and Dr. Zhong's approach of "early detection, early quarantine, early diagnosis, and early treatment" was a valuable contribution to the world, and it was shared all around the world. The principle Dr. Zhong always lived by was, *Not for fame, but only for the truth.* As a scientist, he held up the arms of the community with his vision for a shared future for humankind. Equality and respect were not a matter of words, and the modest, gentle Chinese people built up the pride of China.

The glow from his chest and its undying power was all only for the people. The glow and the power were contagious, a driving force, and they filled homes, societies, and peoples with love.

What was this power that allowed us to continue living unharmed and enabled us to enjoy such peace and prosperity in China? What was the power that made China rise so completely in the eyes of the people of the world? It was the goal of "putting the interests of the people above all else" that was embodied in the shining Party emblem. Only those who were wholehearted in their work would have no regrets and regard that aim as their faith and their life's goal.

Dr. Zhong once noted, "I won't retire. I can't imagine how life would be with no work or scientific research." He added frankly, "I have never thought of taking a break or going somewhere to relax. Achieving things in my academic work is what makes me happy." He encouraged his team, saying, "We may not get anything in return for our diligence and the way we quietly save human lives, but seeking the happiness of all humankind has always been what I believed in." He ended by saying that being wholeheartedly committed to his patients was his habit.

The Nanshan Spirit had penetrated, driven, and affected the people from all walks of life in Guangdong since 2003. In the hearts of the Chinese people, Zhong Nanshan's truthfulness represented the scientific spirit of seeking truth from facts and the voice of the general public, so he was respected as a champion of the truth. He was such a truthful, pragmatic scientist who not only made outstanding contributions in the field of medicine, but who had always been praised throughout China for his refusal to report only good news while omitting the bad, and for his willingness to offer negative or unpopular advice. His credibility as an "ordinary doctor" and his almost instinctive self-consciousness in "fighting for life" won him great praise from the Party and the government.

The pandemic made us look back. On every page, this volume unfolds the stories behind the historical facts.

With the approach of the 100th anniversary of the founding of the CPC, I can't help but reflect on what the image of an excellent Communist Party member should be. When SARS came, what compelled Dr. Zhong Nanshan to speak the truth? It was because, beneath the falsehoods, his was a conscience that could not be appeased. The fact was that thousands of patients' lives were at stake. It was a matter of life and death.

Unlike Dr. Zhong's truthful speech, the falsehoods are disrespectful to the reality of our world. The pandemic is not terrible, nor is any true speech. What is terrible is to have a lack of direction in one's mind.

Some call him a cannon who dares to speak the truth. Some say he is trying to make a name for himself. Some call him the embodiment of truth. This book seeks only to convey the truth. Out of the most fundamental pursuit of conscience, I have made this my mission.

Now, I am holding the manuscript of this book and reading the legend of Dr. Zhong's bumpy life once again, and I am again overwhelmed by emotion. The sun rises as usual, just as I firmly believed in my heart. The people must work hard and do well, because our will is indestructible

Now, in the world that I can see, the waves on the sea are bowing to the morning sun. At this moment, as I look on the book I have written, the golden sun shines all over the world.

On January 18, Zhong Nanshan in the dining car on the train heading to Wuhan. (photo by Su Yueming)

Dr. Zhong Nanshan stated in an interview that with the help of the whole country, the heroic city of Wuhan would be able to pull through. (photo by Liu Dawei, Xinhua News Agency)

Dr. Zhong Nanshan is busy working. (photo by Su Yueming)

A special press briefing held by the Office of Public Press of the General Affairs Office of the Guangzhou Municipal People's Government on February 27, 2020, at Guangzhou Medical University. (Photo: Visual China Group)

February 27, 2020, Dr. Zhong Nanshan states at a special press briefing on the prevention and control of the epidemic that Covid-19 first appeared in China, but may not have originated there. (Photo: Visual China Group)

On March 2, 2020, Zhong Nanshan leads the oath-taking ceremony for two frontline medical workers from the First Affiliated Hospital of Guangzhou Medical University.

April 22, 2020, at the First Affiliated Hospital of Guangzhou Medical University, Zhong Nanshan greets the medical team as they return from assisting Hubei, expressing appreciation for their contributions. (Photo: Visual China Group)

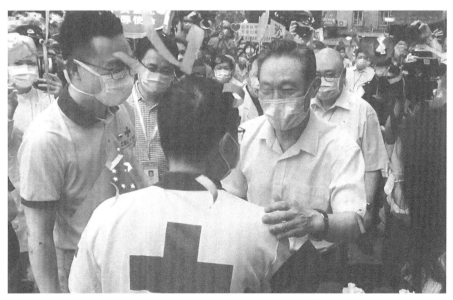

The First Affiliated Hospital of Guangzhou Medical University warmly welcomes two experts returning from their mission to assist Iraq; Dr. Zhong embraces them with a smile and expresses appreciation for their successful mission. (Photo: Visual China Group)

March 18, 2020 Cao Xinwen presents her painting and best wishes to Dr. Zhong Nanshan after the press briefing on epidemic prevention and control. (Photo: Visual China Group)

April 15, 2020, at the 78th press briefing on epidemic prevention and control held by the Office of Public Press of the General Affairs Office of the Guangzhou Municipal People's Government, Dr. Zhong Nanshan poses for a selfie with a foreign student after an exchange with nineteen foreigners working and studying in Guangzhou. (Photo: Visual China Group)

March 25, Zhong Nanshan's team participates in a video conference with European experts, discussing the fight against the pandemic and sharing China's treatment plans and its approach to prevention and control.

Zhong Nanshan and his wife at the birthday party.

Zhong Jiabin, grandson of Zhong Nanshan.

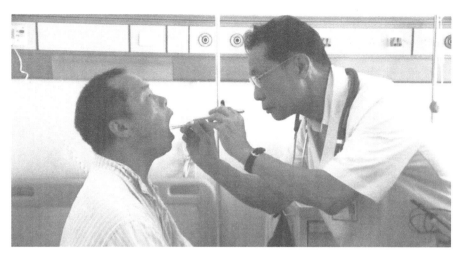

Dr. Zhong in consultation with a patient.

After an 18-floor climb, Dr. Zhong, calm and collected.
During the Two Sessions in March 2003, the residence of the members of the National Committee of the Chinese People's Political Consultative Conference was surrounded on all sides as usual. Journalists from a wide range of agencies waited in groups around the perimeter, hungry for interviews. As the conference on the afternoon of March 6 concluded, Dr. Zhong snuck into the building, preparing to go up a flight of stairs to avoid the journalists. I caught him in the act. It wasn't easy to conduct an interview in the stairwell, so I joined him on an 18-floor climb up the stairs. I was barely breathing when we arrived on the 18th floor, and my hands were shaking with exhaustion. However, as soon as I saw Dr. Zhong's smile, I knew I had to pick up my camera and snap this picture.

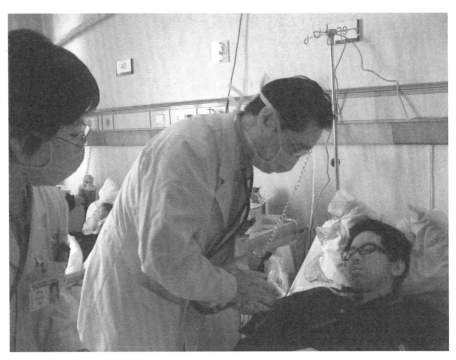

Warming up his stethoscope for a patient.

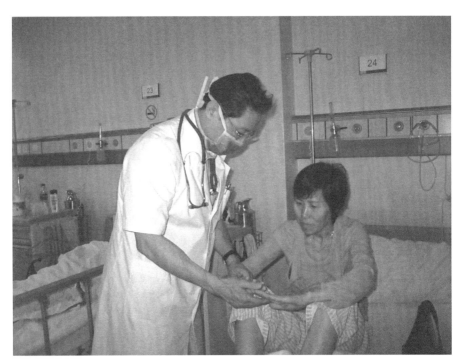

Palpating a patient.

Making exercise a habit.

Dr. Zhong showing off his muscular physique.

Interviewed as a NPC deputy at the Two Sessions in 2017.

Announcing the methods of prevention and treatment of COPD at the launching ceremony of the China Health Knowledge Dissemination Incentive Program.

The cover of Erke Jibing Jianbie Zhenduan.

Photo of Dr. Zhong Nanshan's parents.

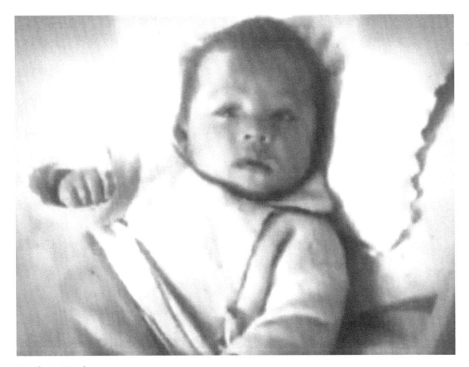

Newborn Nanshan.

12-year-old Nanshan.

18-year-old Nanshan.

Photo of Zhong family, Nanshan, his parents and his younger sister.

Boating on the Pearl River. "My mother only allowed me to go boating when I reached Grade 8." Zhong Nanshan is second to the left.

Hanging out with friends during Grade 11. Zhong Nanshan is the first on the left.

1959, breaking the national record in the men's 400 meter hurdles during the selection stage of the first National Games.

Playing on the PMU basketball court, the shooter is Zhong Nanshan.

Dating.

Getting married.

The Zhong family.

Dr. Zhong Nanshan and his lovely grandson.

Studying in the UK.

Reunion with Prof. Truman (Front row, middle).

Reunion of professors and friends.

❨ PART 1 ❩

GUARDIAN OF THE NATION

"My pressure comes from the patients' lives.
My greatest aim is to save their lives."

—Zhong Nanshan

A NEW VIRUS

An epidemic never makes an appointment. Dr. Zhong Nanshan was truly born to be the great defender of a great nation in an unexpected time of emergency.

It can be safely assumed that on January 18, 2020, almost every medical conference in China discussed the same topic. An ominous storm thundered overhead, calling to mind the early days of 2003.

It was a cold winter day in Guangzhou, and everyone was clad in a down jacket. Even the sun looked sickly, as if hinting at something untoward.

Slightly after eleven that morning, Su Yueming, secretary of the medical researcher Zhong Nanshan, received an urgent phone call from China's National Health Commission (NHC). The news was disturbing. "The situation regarding the novel coronavirus remains unclear. We urge Dr. Zhong to travel to Wuhan today."

It was precisely the "inevitable call" Su had been worried about. Dr. Zhong was still in relatively good health, but he certainly was not as young as he had been when SARS struck the region seventeen years earlier.

Since December 2019, information regarding an "unknown pneumonia" had continually come from Wuhan, making Dr. Zhong feel quite concerned. On January 8, 2020, experts from the NHC issued preliminary confirmation that the pathogen causing this unknown pneumonia had been determined to be a novel coronavirus, making it a top priority for Dr. Zhong's team. The entire province of Guangdong was caught up in a silent rush to prepare to fight against this new viral threat.

On January 17, Dr. Zhong had just concluded a medical conference at the Third People's Hospital of Shenzhen, which he had attended with his former comrade-in-arms in the fight against SARS years before, Professor Li Yimin, Secretary of the Party Committee of the First Affiliated Hospital of Guangzhou Medical University, when news came that there was a suspected case of the novel coronavirus in Shenzhen.

"There will be another meeting at the Health Commission of Guangdong Province (HCGP)," Dr. Zhong said. "Could we fly to Wuhan tomorrow morning?"

The response from NHC came quickly. "Please hold while we discuss the possibility."

Su began scrambling to check for all available flights and trains to Wuhan that day.

Within an hour, NHC called back with their response. After extensive discussion, it had been decided that Dr. Zhong was indeed needed in Wuhan that very day. Su immediately informed them that all plane and train tickets were sold out.

The person on the other end of the line said sternly, "Just go to the train station. We'll sort out the ticketing."

At noon, Zhong Nanshan rushed out of the meeting room, calling to Su, "I got a call from NHC. I must reach Wuhan today. It's a critical situation. Our nation needs us. We have to go right away."

A critical situation for the nation! These words filled Su with great ardor.

After a quick lunch, Dr. Zhong wasted no time in rushing to the HCGP for yet another conference regarding the novel coronavirus. Many experts had gathered to present analysis and plans for the response effort.

During the meeting, Su received a call from the staff at the Guangzhou South Railway Station informing him that he and Dr. Zhong would be aboard the G-class train to Wuhan. The staff would improvise and come up with a seating plan for the pair.

The meeting ended at 4:30 that afternoon, and Dr. Zhong and Su rushed to the railway station. "We managed to pull through SARS in 2003," Dr. Zhong mumbled in the car. "Who would have imagined that something like this would happen again just seventeen years later?"

It was five days before the Chinese New Year, which fell on January 23 that year. This was typically the time that preparations were made for the festivities, but this year's Chinese New Year was destined to be very different from the norm.

It was 5:30 in the afternoon, and the Guangzhou South Railway Station was filled with the happy faces of those who were returning home for the holiday. At the time, no one was wearing a face mask.

An energetic doctor and his young secretary rushed through the crowd to board the G1022 train to Wuhan. Fortunately, two seats had been reserved for them in the dining car, a special arrangement made by the conductor.

It was a long journey from Guangzhou to Wuhan. There was a strange sense of unease in the air as the train left the station. The attendants in the dining car showed the old doctor great care, and their curiosity about him was equally evident.

"Doctor, would you mind if I ask your age?" one young attendant asked, smiling. "I only ask because I can't really tell. You have a youthful air about you."

"I'll be 84 soon," Dr. Zhong replied.

"No way!" she blurted out. "You look like you're in your 60s."

Because it was a train journey of several hours, Su began to worry that spending such a long period in the dining car seat would put a strain on Dr. Zhong. He started to call a train attendant over, but Dr. Zhong waved him off, stopping him from making a fuss. "There's no need for that," he said. "What's wrong with the dining car? All that matters is that we get to Wuhan. We can't demand that someone else give up their seat just because we've boarded the train."

He smiled gently to the attendant as he spoke, expressing a wish that no one else be disturbed. He seemed relieved that nobody in the dining car recognized him.

It was clear that the NHC team had asked him and his team to travel to Wuhan on such short notice because they needed to quickly define the illness that was caused by the novel coronavirus. Dr. Zhong had been watching it closely since it first started to spread.

Zhang Jixian, Director of the Department of Respiratory and Critical Care Medicine in Hubei Provincial Hospital of Integrated Chinese and Western Medicine, had been the first to report a case of "unknown pneumonia." On the morning of December 26, 2019, Dr. Zhang had seen an elderly female patient who presented symptoms of fever, coughing, and difficulty breathing. The patient was later admitted to the inpatient ward. The following day, the hospital's department of neurology invited Dr. Zhang to a joint consultation for an elderly male patient. This patient was suffering from asthenia, and a CAT scan showed there were large areas with inflammation. He was immediately transferred to the Respiratory Department.

After the two patients had been admitted into wards of the pneumology department, Dr. Zhang noticed that they were a married couple and that their symptoms and CAT scans were similar. This made her suspicious, so she asked the couple to have their son come in for a checkup as well. The son did not display any symptoms of coughing or fever, but his CAT scan revealed a similar pattern of inflammation in the lungs. By this time, Dr. Zhang began to feel that the situation was quite serious. That same afternoon, she reported the matter to the hospital, which in turn reported the cases to the District Center for Disease Control and Prevention (CDC). The CDC of Jianghan District then conducted an epidemiological investigation. On December 28 and 29, the outpatient department saw another four cases of patients from the Huanan Seafood Wholesale Market, all with similar symptoms. An expert team from the Wuhan City Health Commission (WCHC), conducted a follow up investigation and issued two departmental notices, at 3:10 pm and 6:50 pm, on December 30. One of the notices was entitled "Urgent Notice on the Report of a Viral Pneumonia with Unknown Cause."

The virus had reared its ugly head. Before long, it bared its teeth to the entire world.

Dr. Zhong wasted no time, turning on his laptop and checking through the relevant files and literature as soon as he was situated in the dining car. As around 8:00 in the evening, Su went to pay for their train ticket. He returned with two boxed meals.

Smiling and respectful, the conductor came to greet Dr. Zhong. "Dr. Zhong, you're making this trip for the sake of the nation. How could we charge you for a meal?"

Su tried to pay for the food, but the conductor insisted that they enjoy the food free of charge.

It was 9:00 pm when Dr. Zhong finished his dinner. It was the first short break he had had during the entire hectic day. He wanted to make full use of every minute, but he knew that even a few minutes of sleep would go a long way toward preparing him for what was coming. He settled a little deeper into his seat and leaned his head back on the narrow headrest.

Unbeknownst to those around him, a sense of exhaustion overcame him. But he knew he had to force himself to be energetic as soon as this fleeting moment of rest was gone.

Even at the age of 83, Dr. Zhong was still actively participating in medical research and clinical work, and he led a national-level research team with his inspiration and his pursuit of science. His movements were as swift as the wind, and when he sat, he was as still as a mountain. Most importantly, when he pondered a problem, it was with the deliberation of a wise scholar. Anyone who knew him was familiar with both his practicality and his integrity. He never bombarded his listeners with flamboyant language, but always gave off an inherent sense of class. He was down to earth, and he was a skilled listener. He was always greatly admired for his charisma, which led those around him to love and respect him. This was especially true of his patients.

At 9:15 pm on January 18, 2020, seeing that Dr. Zhong was resting, Su was so moved with feelings of respect and admiration for this tireless giant of a man that he snapped a photo of the sleeping doctor. *He must be exhausted, but we'll never hear a word of it. Never,* Su thought.

Dr. Zhong first came to the public's attention during the 2003 SARS outbreak. In the years since, he had never ceased being an object of interest, and journalists in Guangdong had followed him everywhere he went.

On the morning of January 21, 2020, the photo was featured in the newspaper alongside reports that Dr. Zhong was heading to Wuhan. As he swam against the stream of other travelers toward the frontline in the battle against the virus, the *People's Daily* posted commentary on its Weibo account, which circulated rapidly online to the enthusiastic response of the public. This demonstrated not only the nation's respect for Dr. Zhong, but also the gratitude the people felt toward all the frontline medical workers who had gone to help. The article noted, "Just like seventeen years ago when he fought against SARS, the now 84-year-old medical researcher Zhong Nanshan has arrived at the frontline in the battle against this virus. We believe that we are in good hands, because he is armed with the professionalism of a scientist, the courage of a warrior, and the resolute spirit of a hero. Embarking on this herculean journey, he has devoted heart and soul to this nation and its people. We salute him with utmost respect. We would like to thank Dr. Zhong Nanshan, the medical workers, and all those who have contributed to our fight against this disease. With all of our total might combined, we will brave the tempest, and we will triumph over this virus."

It is often said that to live is to serve. This sentiment sums up why Dr. Zhong still took the time for regular physical exercise, despite his busy schedule. He lived a tireless pursuit of medical science, and his greatest satisfaction came from the health of his patients. He would gladly give up everything he had to bring about a world without pain or illness.

At 10:00 that night, the train was just half an hour from its destination. As it approached the city, darkness was banished by the urban lights.

At 10:20 pm, the train reached Wuhan. The winter night greeted Dr. Zhong with a nagging cold. With only a thin shirt under his brown checked blazer, he braved the harsh weather with stern determination.

The smells of Wuhan floated on the air, and the city lights were resplendent. Though it created a scene of prosperity, danger lurched in the shadows. The crowds continued to go about their business, oblivious to the looming epidemic.

Forty minutes later, the bus arrived at the Wuhan Conference Center. It was then that Dr. Zhong realized how heavy a responsibility he was shouldering. A grim seriousness was etched on his face, and his mind was plunged into a deep concentration – a sight rarely seen since the end of the SARS epidemic in 2003.

On the morning of January 19, NHC's high-level national team of six senior medical and disease control experts arrived at the conference center, where WCHC briefed Dr. Zhong's team on the latest news of the epidemic. The team included Dr. Yuan Guoyong, Dr. Li Lanjuan, Dr. Gao Fu, Dr. Zeng Guang, and Dr. Du Bin. So many mysteries remained to be unraveled.

As the briefing concluded, the experts hurried to the Wuhan Jinyintan Hospital, where the novel coronavirus patients were being treated. Another briefing was conducted by the directors of the hospital once the team arrived, followed by a joint consultation with the patients.

In the early afternoon, the team of experts held a closed-door meeting to discuss the situation. After hours of consideration and discussion, a preliminary conclusion was drawn: the source of the infection was most likely the wild animals in the Huanan Seafood Wholesale Market.

At this point, no one imagined that the entire country would soon be caught up in a fight against the virus, and they certainly never dreamed that a global pandemic would rampage across the world. Or, almost no one – Dr. Zhong alone grasped this fact.

At 5:00 pm, the team boarded a flight to Beijing. At around 6:00 pm, the in-flight dinner was served. The exhausted doctor laid down his files. Su knew that the doctor usually ate a light dinner. Seeing the far from fancy meal now being served, he could not help but worry.

"Doctor, will this really be enough for you?"

"Not a problem," Dr. Zhong replied breezily.

Upon arriving in Beijing, the team rushed to the NHC for a report and discussion on the field survey. They drew a general conclusion regarding the situation and prepared for the panel with central government officials the following day. The meeting started at 11:00 pm and lasted well into the night.

At 6:00 am on January 20, Dr. Zhong was once again up early preparing the material for the panel, mainly focused on the latest updates and advice for prevention and control. A few critical points lingered in Dr. Zhong's mind. *How should I tell the public? Human to human transmission is a big deal. What will we do if there is human to human transmission? Through what pathways, and who is most susceptible? How bad is the spread? How will this situation develop? How can we cure those who have been infected? How long will the treatment take? How high is the risk of death?*

Dr. Zhong did not hesitate. He proposed that communication should be transparent. Despite all the pressure and risk, he insisted that the public be made aware of the situation so that greater effort could be made and measures for disease prevention and control could be taken on the national level.

It was during this meeting that the team of experts suggested that "the public must be advised immediately not to enter or leave Wuhan." The NHC Leading Group on Responding to the Novel Coronavirus Pneumonia Outbreak issued an urgent warning, urging hospitals to immediately call for briefings and distribute PCR test kits. On that day, the WCHC reported seventeen newly confirmed cases to the NHC.

On January 20, the State Council approved the team's advice and listed the novel coronavirus pneumonia as a Category B Infectious Disease, as defined by the Law of the People's Republic of China on Prevention and Treatment of Infectious Diseases. They further adopted prevention and control measures for Category A Infectious Diseases and applied management measures as stated in the Frontier Health and Quarantine Law of the People's Republic of China. That same evening, Dr. Zhong was interviewed by Bai Yansong, the host of *News 1+1* on China Central Television (CCTV). Given his tight schedule, Dr. Zhong's staff arranged for a videoconference connection between Dr. Zhong's hotel room and the livestream studio in CCTV's offices.

At 9:20 pm, Dr. Zhong started preparing for the livestream. He was feeling a little dizzy after several days of sleep deprivation, but at 9:30 sharp, when all the cameras were pointed at him, he appeared sharp and vigorous on countless screens of various sizes across the nation. Even so, Su was worried, knowing Dr. Zhong must be exhausted.

This was probably one of the most watched livestreams in China's history. The entire nation listened intently to every single word.

Bai Yansong's direct question to Dr. Zhong was met with a concise answer: *Yes, there is human to human transmission of the novel coronavirus, and fourteen members of the medical team have been infected.*

These words carried the explosive power of an atomic bomb. The coronavirus that had seemed so far away to people outside Wuhan had barged into everyone's life now.

Shortly after this interview, Dr. Zhong's warnings circulated all over China: *Prevent the spread of the disease; do not enter or leave Wuhan; avoid crowded places; try to stay at home; wear a mask; wash your hands often.*

Within two days, face masks were sold out all over China, while anti-flu medication, both traditional and modern, became scarce. Cities were empty, and countryside villages were quiet. *Don't go out.* This message spread to every corner of China, just because it had come from Dr. Zhong. *If Dr. Zhong said it, I believe it.* Like magic, this sentence became the new Internet catchphrase.

This was the second time, with the SARS epidemic being the first, that the people of China felt such great gratitude toward Dr. Zhong, because once again, he had told the hard truth. Many people expressed their thanks to the elderly doctor for rushing into danger, telling the truth, and raising the warning level from municipal to national. The Party, the military, and the people were now united in the battle against the virus.

The situation developed quickly. On January 23, Wuhan issued the order that the city was to be locked down. With the Spring Festival travel rush, more than five million workers had left Wuhan, dispersing throughout the nation. The authoritative definition offered by Dr. Zhong brought the nation's attention to the city. This later proved to be one of the most critical turning points during the pandemic.

Beginning at 10:00 am on January 23, 2020, all urban and intercity bus, metro, and ferry services were suspended in Wuhan and nearby cities such as Ezhou, Xiantao, Qianjiang, Huanggang, and Jingmen, while all exit points, such as airports, train stations, and highways, were closed in an effort to contain the spread of the novel coronavirus. Medical researcher Li Lanjuan was very concerned about the situation, and in an exclusive interview with a China Media Group journalist, Dong Qian, she explained that Wuhan had been placed under quarantine because the fight to contain the virus had reached a critical point. Only with strict quarantine at the source could the virus be prevented from becoming a nationwide epidemic.

The swift quarantine of infected patients was another critical part of the containment of the disease. During the SARS epidemic in 2003, the Xiaotangshan Hospital was built in Beijing specifically to receive and cure patients who contracted SARS. In an effort to similarly cure patients of this new illness, the government of Wuhan decided to follow the example that had been set in 2003, building two dedicated hospitals, the Huoshenshan and Leishenshan Hospitals. This measure played a significant role in stopping the spread of the virus. The construction of the Wuhan Huoshenshan Hospital began on January 23, 2020. By January 29, wards were being installed. On the morning of February 2, the hospital was operational. After taking only ten days to go from design to final delivery, the hospital stood as a shining example of the world renowned "China speed." Similarly, design of the Wuhan Leishenshan Hospital was begun on January 25, 2020, and delivery came on February 5. Dr. Zhong found great comfort in these achievements.

2

PRIDE AND COMPASSION

The tears shed by heroes are like rain soothing the earth.

On January 24, Dr. Zhong did not go home for the traditional family reunion on the eve of Chinese New Year. The patients of the coronavirus who were hospitalized at the First Affiliated Hospital of Guangzhou Medical University were in critical condition. He was studying the virus's characteristics and patterns and developing treatment plans. The sudden torrential epidemic had him very worried.

He had not changed his clothes for days, and the short curly hair on the top of his head had lost its usual fluffiness, now lying flat instead. A sheen of oil and sweat blanketed his forehead.

Dr. Zhong's credibility was like a monument in the people's hearts. His every word was an immediate headline, and they influenced the actions of the entire society, functioning as a weather vane for the epidemic. The news media kept a close eye on everything he said and did. Dr. Zhong had been pursued by both Chinese and foreign journalists during the 2003 SARS epidemic, a familiar scene that returned now. For multiple reasons, the hospital added a door to the building in which his office was located.

Though there was a need to release information about the virus, especially about individual health and the prevention of an epidemic, Dr. Zhong instructed his office to try to decline press interviews, because he had little time or mood to deal with them. Most importantly, he was not interested in self-promotion, as if he were the greatest. He could not accept that sort of attention.

Countless people spontaneously wrote songs about him, and there were expressions of admiration of his heroism everywhere. Plagued by the virus, the Chinese people looked to Dr. Zhong as a spiritual pillar in the time of crisis.

Dr. Zhong's colleagues cherished all of this praise, and they felt it in their own hearts too. They did not want to bother him, not wishing to add to the pressure he was under. He was never afraid to meet any challenge, but they could not help but worry about his health.

Dr. Zhong seldom had time to keep up with the news online or on television, and this was especially true during the busy, intense days of the pandemic. On January 27, the third night of Chinese New Year, he was still busy at his office when one of his students in Wuhan sent him a video that captured his attention. In the video, an old man wearing a mask hobbled in the street, singing the national anthem. In the background, the residents of Wuhan opened their windows and sang the national anthem with him. The singing spread from one building to another, instantly becoming loud and uplifting.

Standing alone in front of the window and facing the sporadic light illuminating the Pearl River, Dr. Zhong felt tears in his eyes. The quarantined residents of Wuhan opened their windows and sang the national anthem together, cheering for themselves.

Mr. Wang, whose family lived downtown, had first thought that tales of people opening their windows and singing the national anthem was just a rumor, but at 8:00 that night, one of his neighbors in a building opposite his opened the window and stretched out it with a karaoke mic in hand, shouting, "Hey, quarantined Wuhanians! We're going to organize a large-scale event tonight, singing the national anthem together. Join us!"

Many neighborhoods in Wuhan spontaneously began singing patriotic songs, such as "March of the Volunteers" and "My Motherland and I." As if on command, the residents in these neighborhoods opened their windows and sang along heartily, their loud, clear voices echoing from building to building.

"Go, Wuhan! Go!" many residents shouted. The national anthem and shouts of, "Go, Wuhan," were heard from different areas of the city, such as Wuchang, Hongshan, Hanyang, Hankou, and East-West Lake.

"Wuhan is a heroic city," Dr. Zhong said excitedly and with tears in his eyes during a press interview the following day, "and we are confident and capable of winning the battle ground against this virus." The entire country supported Wuhan and contributed to the battle. He believed that Wuhan would certainly overcome the difficulties and win the fight against the virus under the leadership of the Party.

Dr. Zhong was a compassionate, benevolent doctor. At this historic moment, a powerful flood of comfort surged from him to his patients, and to all the people who were full of expectations. Yet he himself felt helpless and anxious in the face of it all.

"Dr. Zhong wept!" The video instantly spread across the country. His tears touched the nation. A silent force was formed, accelerating the assistance to Wuhan.

On January 28, according to the NHC press conference, there were 1,771 newly confirmed cases on the previous day, which was equivalent to 60% of the total previously confirmed cases (then numbering 2,774). Nearly 30% (515) of the new cases were critical cases, and there were an additional 1,291 newly confirmed cases and 24 newly reported deaths in other parts of Hubei.

It was clear that there was no end in sight in the battle of prevention and control of this virus. Even worse, according to Dr. Zhong's estimations at that time, the epidemic would reach a peak in a week or ten days. Wuhan's hospitals were already overcrowded, and the protective gear for medical workers, medical equipment, and hospital space were all facing severe shortages.

On January 23, the country declared a lockdown of severely affected regions. Assisting Wuhan was a race against the clock. The epidemic was a call to action. By January 24, the Air Force Medical University team was ordered to send urgent aid to Wuhan. On January 24, a total of 136 medical workers from Shanghai arrived in Wuhan.

Dr. Sang Ling, a former student of Dr. Zhong and now Deputy Chief Physician of the Intensive Care Unit at the hospital where he worked, the First Affiliated Hospital of Guangzhou Medical University, was selected to work on the frontline in the fight against the epidemic in Wuhan. On the Chinese New Year Eve, Dr. Sang traveled on his own from Guangzhou to Wuhan, where he plunged himself into the work in the ICU at Wuhan Jinyintan Hospital the moment he arrived. Before leaving Guangzhou, he wrote, "We will definitely win this fireless, smokeless battle. We can do it. Go China!"

The five medical workers who formed the team led by Dr. Zhong arrived in Wuhan on Chinese New Year's Eve, January 24. One of the team members, Li Yingxian, a woman in her 20s, was as a nurse in the Department of Endocrinology at the First Affiliated Hospital of Guangzhou Medical University. On Chinese New Year's Eve, she left her family and went to Wuhan to join the medical team the hospital had formed. When she reached Wuhan, she began working in the Hankou Hospital.

The battlefield upon which war was waged against the virus was not limited to Hubei; it extended to Guangzhou as well, where Dr. Zhong's team had no easy time fighting the epidemic. Xu Yonghao, Deputy Chief Physician of the Intensive Care

Unit, had gone to the Linzhi People's Hospital in Tibet in June 2019, as a member of the ninth team of cadres sent to carry out medical support and assistance missions for one year. He submitted his application to join the Communist Party of China in December 2019. On the first day of the Chinese New Year, he returned to Guangzhou from Linzhi, and he then remained on the front line in the fight against the epidemic. Guided by Dr. Zhong and others, he led his team to complete the transfer of the first Covid-19 patient supported with extracorporeal membrane oxygenation (ECMO), commonly known as an "artificial lung," in Guangzhou and successfully removed the tracheal intubation for a patient in severe condition. He participated in many remote video consultations organized by the Health Commission of Guangdong Province.

The first medical team arrived at the front line, bringing hope and confidence to the medical workers who were holding on in Wuhan. The local medical workers had been working round the clock. As they embraced this team who had come from so far away to help them, many feelings welled up inside them.

The medical workers who came to Wuhan and those who had already been holding on there for some time joined together, sharing the hardships as they faced the problems of providing clinical treatments and shortages of various medical supplies, especially protective gear. Since January 29, restrictions on entering and leaving the country had gradually increased, and the public made conscious efforts to achieve an unprecedented level of cooperation with the relevant departments. A large-scale, high-level battle to defend public health through strict prevention and control measures had been launched.

"Let's go, Wuhan! Let's go, China!" These words echoed all over the nation as TV stations, radio stations, official websites, We-Media, and more than a billion Chinese people expressed their fervent support for the military and various regional medical teams who rushed to the front line to assist Wuhan. People from every sector of society donated funds and supplies to aid in these efforts.

The Ministry of Industry and Information Technology (MIIT) continued to urge various provinces to organize the relevant enterprises to immediately resume work and production in order to produce protective medical equipment to fulfill the demand in Wuhan. On January 30, all government departments across the country implemented the decision handed down from the central government and fully mobilized epidemic prevention and control procedures.

Although the Guangzhou Eighth People's Hospital was the designated hospital with the greatest number of patients who had been infected with the novel coronavirus in the city, most of those in critical condition were sent to the First Affiliated Hospital of Guangzhou Medical University, which was downstairs from Dr. Zhong's office.

On Saturday, February 1, the atmosphere in Dr. Zhong's office in Guangzhou was tense, but all the people who busily worked there maintained an inner calm. In the evening, Dr. Zhong walked out of the conference room and headed for his office. On the other side of the corridor, the sunlight tilted into the length of the hallway, making it seem like a path through time – a path that was not long, but each step taken on it was pivotal.

The light did not shine on Dr. Zhong as he walked, slower and less nimbly than before, and he seemed to carry a heavy weight on his shoulder. His head was lowered, and his back was slightly hunched. His steps were heavy, and he held a phone in his hand, walking and talking quickly and calmly. It was clear he had lost weight, but fortunately, his heart did not revolt against the extra stress put on it, and he was not often suffering from stomach ailments. The only real problem was that he was not sleeping well. When a friend asked after his health, he replied, "Sometimes I can sleep at night, but sometimes I can't." He smiled as he spoke, but there was a somber look beneath the smile, prompting his secretary to add in a whisper, "I'm very worried about him."

Even at the age of 84, Dr. Zhong worked as hard as he ever had. When his friends and family saw how insistent he was even in the face of his exhaustion, they silently prayed that he would soon return to his hale, hearty look, but that would only happen when the burden of this illness was lifted from China.

It was important to establish a good foundation at this time, while the virus was just beginning to spread. This was always Dr. Zhong's conviction, especially now, when faced with the sudden outbreak of the novel coronavirus. Dr. Zhong and his team had begun conducting a nationwide clinical survey of patients with the virus over the past several days, obtaining data from a clinical study of 1,099 patients from 522 hospitals. Based on the analysis of the data obtained, several countermeasures were settled on. On the front line, where the battle against the virus was in full swing, it was not easy to collect data while also treating patients, but pathological research and observation was still conducted on each patient. Dr. Zhong then needed to understand the data collected. He always respected science and facts, and for him, everything needed a scientific, factual foundation. This rigorous attitude had become a habit for him, to the point that it was as instinctive for him now as were eating and sleeping.

On the afternoon of February 1, a second group of medical workers departed for Wuhan from the First Affiliated Hospital of Guangzhou Medical University. They were all Dr. Zhong's key personnel and some of his best students. They expressed their determination, telling him to rest assured in the knowledge that they would do the best they could to fight the virus. Dr. Zhong saw them off, embracing each in turn, like a father.

When the second medical team arrived, the families of the patients flocked around them. The team was assigned to deal with patients who were very ill, some even in critical condition, and the working conditions were very tough. Wuhan was in danger. Scientific research was in demand, and the need was urgent. No matter how anxious or restless they felt, these medical workers had to make adjustments and remain calm. Human lives were at stake. Central to every action was the need to make an accurate judgment of the path that needed to be taken.

Dr. Zhong repeatedly emphasized that he did not want to be personally high-lighted, reminding that clinical treatment and scientific research were always a team effort, and never the work of any individual. He repeatedly said that he did not have the heart or the time to give interviews. There was an epidemic raging, and time saved was a life saved. His time – his entire life – was dedicated to saving people.

Despite his wishes, countless people, limitless praise, and numerous tributes appeared in the media, especially the flourishing We-Media. The praise and tributes were touching.

When spring comes and the virus fades
We will join you
To recite these words of praise!

"Things are tough for Dr. Zhong! He's amazing," people everywhere said, offering both praise and support. At the same time, many worried about him. Even those who had never met him felt that he was like a member of the family.

When the Central Military Commission issued an order on February 2, the Air Force immediately dispatched eight large transport aircraft in the early morning. They departed from Shenyang, Lanzhou, Guangzhou, and Nanjing, airlifting 795 military forces to support Hubei's medical workers and delivering 58 tons of supplies to Wuhan. All arrived at the Wuhan Tianhe Airport at 9:30 am on that day. This was the second largest humanitarian aid effort the Air Force had undertaken, trailing only the disaster relief work following the Wenchuan and Yushu earthquake.

Resolute, every department of the local government quickly implemented the decision and deployment of the CPC Central Committee under Xi Jinping's leader-ship. From the highest levels down, the Chinese people fought with all their might to stop the spread of the virus. Everyone was united in a concerted push to aid Wuhan.

Human resources, supplies, and equipment for protection and treatment, which now faced a severe shortage, reached Wuhan and other virus-stricken parts of Hubei.

The NHC updated its reports and issued data on the diagnosis and treatment of the disease and its plans for prevention and control of the spread of the virus. It improved its nationwide "daily report and zero report" system and tightened measures for monitoring, pre-examination, and quarantining of patients with a fever.

With the support of the NHC, Dr. Zhong and his team analyzed and drew conclusions regarding the characteristics of the more than one thousand confirmed cases nationwide. Samples of 1,099 confirmed patients were taken from 552 hospitals in thirty provinces and municipalities across China. The patients had all presented symptoms by January 29, with the majority dating from January 1, 2020. The study proved that the median incubation period of the virus was four days. Cases with positive lab tests and normal medical imaging were called infections, and pneumonia developed only in a severe infection. Of the non-critical cases whose medical imaging was normal, 17.9% were normal at first diagnosis, while only 2.9% of critical cases were normal.

In the course of this study, Dr. Zhong made clear the importance of distinguishing between infections and pneumonia patients. This line of thinking was critical to the overall decisive victory in Wuhan's fight against the virus. Dr. Zhong called the pneumonia resulting from the novel coronavirus Covid-19, indicating patients who had tested positive in lab testing and who had some symptoms, but had no obvious issues in their medical imaging. They did not necessarily present symptoms of pneumonia. This was the sort of rational foundation urgently needed in the frontline effort.

The study also indicated that clinicians needed to identify patients at an earlier stage, before the disease progressed, and to treat them accordingly. The results of the study further verified Dr. Zhong's initial inclination toward achieving "four early steps" for people infected with the virus. These included early prevention, early detection, early diagnosis, and early quarantine.

A surprising finding rose from the study as well. It was discovered that among the thousand confirmed cases nationwide (including those in Wuhan), only 1.9% had a history of direct contact with wild animals within the two weeks prior to infection. Among the confirmed cases of patients outside Wuhan, 31.3% had been to Wuhan, and 72.3% had been in contact with people from Wuhan. Among the more than one thousand cases studied, 43.9% were Wuhan residents. This confirmed that the virus spread rapidly from person to person.

The average age of patients was 47. There were more male than female patients, with only 41.9% of all patients being female. The prevalence was highest among middle aged and elderly males with underlying conditions such as hypertension or chronic obstructive pulmonary disease.

The study led to the determination of a quarantine period for close contacts of a patient infected with the virus. The results of the study confirmed related reports, indicating a likelihood of spread among family clusters, including infection by asymptomatic patients. The existence of super-spreaders could not be ruled out. The study also proved that respiratory droplets were one of the main factors in the rapid transmission of the virus.

The study reported that 15% of patients admitted to the hospital were in critical condition. Compared with those patients in non-critical condition, this group was on average seven years older and the rate of underlying conditions was higher. However, there was no difference detected in the infections of the two groups.

On February 28, the results of the study were officially published in *The New England Journal of Medicine*. This was a significant contribution made by Dr. Zhong and the 552 hospitals across China who had cooperated with the study.

Dr. Zhong advocated the use of traditional Chinese medicine (TCM) in conjunction with other methods of treatment. He believed that TCM could relieve and treat mild cases, especially during the early onset of illness. Though he was a professional in the field of Western medicine, he had strongly recommended the use of Chinese medicines such as *banlangen, lianhuaqingwen,* and *yupingfeng* for many years. He also had great respect for TCM's approach to diagnosis and treatment.

As the epidemic raged, Wuhan quickly established isolation hospitals in a key move to deal with the surge of patients during this critical period. Beginning on February 3, the NHC announced emergency mobilization of all equipment across the country, ordering it sent to hospitals for use in treating patients of the novel coronavirus. The equipment came to Wuhan in batches, and the first group of 600 medical workers had been put in place as well. In addition, 1,400 nurses were mobilized in Wuhan. The National Emergency Medical Rescue Team dispatched ten vehicles which were the equivalent of a small hospital. These included medicine and equipment vehicles, life support vehicles, power support vehicles, troop carriers, inspection vehicles, and similar equipment. On February 5, the isolation hospitals began to take in Covid-19 patients with mild pneumonia symptoms. These hospitals were located in various parts of Wuhan, including Caidian, Jiangxia, and Huangpi.

The isolation hospitals established in China settled Dr. Zhong's most urgent concerns, which centered around effectively separating mild and critical patients. As a result, many TCM doctors rushed to Wuhan and began to treat patients with mild symptoms who had been admitted to the isolation facilities. This was an effective way of keeping these patients from developing more serious symptoms.

From that time, patients with mild symptoms were mostly treated with TCM, while treatment of critical cases was targeted and collective. Though it required considerable human and material resources to save a critically ill patient, the belief in China was that human life was the most important thing. Even mild cases of Covid-19 were difficult to cure. Saving the life of a critically ill patient was so much more challenging.

From the evening of February 6 to the early morning of the 7th, countless Chinese people were much too sad to sleep. A message first published by a 34-year-old ophthalmologist from Wuhan, Li Wenliang and forwarded to numerous WeChat groups read, *Seven cases of SARS have been confirmed at the South China Fruit and Seafood market.* Li reminded people to guard against infection, but sadly, he himself was stricken by the virus and died after treatment proved ineffective. Despite the prayers many people offered on his behalf, he was taken much too early. The NHC and three other government departments commended various advanced collectives and individuals in the national health system for their work in the prevention and control of the virus, and 34 individuals received posthumous awards. Li Wenliang was among them, receiving an award for "advanced individual effort in the national health system's prevention and control of Covid-19." Li was among the 14 people who had died on the front line that were declared martyrs by the People's Government of Hubei Province on April 2.

Dr. Zhong spoke highly of Li, saying, "I think most Chinese doctors regard Li Wenliang as a national hero, and I agree with them. I am proud of him." When speaking with a journalist from Reuters, Dr. Zhong said in fluent English, "He is a hero." He could not help but cry as he praised Li Wenliang.

Dr. Zhong told the foreign journalist that Li had told people the truth from late December. "And as you know, he died," Dr. Zhong said. He recounted a unanimous decision by medical workers on the morning that they learned of Li's death. "Wuhan and other cities held simple memorials to mourn him," Dr. Zhong said. "They turned on the lights on their mobile phones and held up the devices for several minutes before going back to work. They did not have time to stop and really think about his passing, but they admired him and believed he was a hero. I think so too."

Dr. Zhong never concealed his feeling for all of China's angels in white, like Li Wenliang. "This is a Chinese doctor. I believe most Chinese doctors are like him."

Many people commented on Dr. Zhong's compassion. The people had such high expectations of him. What sort of burden did he bear? In the early days, the information was incomplete, which resulted in many lost opportunities and many people being caught off guard, which led to poor protection of the frontline workers, who really needed to keep up their morale. Dr. Zhong felt great sorrow over Li Wenliang's misfortune and the burden carried by all the frontline workers. He constantly worried about the suffering of the people.

Heroes understand one another. Both Li Wenliang and Zhong Nanshan just wanted to be ordinary doctors, but what was it that made these ordinary doctors heroes? Simply put, it was that they told the truth, when the conscience is not covered in dust and the mind remains as clear in the days of youth, telling the truth comes naturally, a direct expression of what is in the heart and a breeze that dispels the haze. Telling the truth allows people to enjoy peace and happiness, and it guides all the people in the same direction. The truth is a hardy thing. Even in the crevice of a rock, it will stand tall.

Seventeen years earlier, Dr. Zhong had been commended by the people. They called him a cannon who dared to speak the truth. In facing the facts without regard for any obstructions, he boldly told the truth, driven by the conscience of a scientist. Now, his true words were once again a voice for the world at a time when a pandemic had begun to rage.

3

A MATTER OF SCIENCE

On the afternoon of February 6, Dr. Zhong finished a joint consultation. As he left the meeting room, he sent a short message to his family. *I'm fine, just very busy.*

On the 13th day of the Chinese New Year, February 7, he was interviewed after a meeting hosted by HCGP. He said, "There has been no sudden spike in the number of cases. This is good, but does it mean we've reached a turning point? It's still too early to tell."

A Covid-19 Global Research and Innovation Forum was held in the WHO headquarters in Geneva, ending on February 12. During the media conference that followed the forum, a Western journalist asked, "Did the Chinese government insist that it should be praised by the WHO?"

Dr. Tedros Adhanom Ghebreyesus, Director-General of the WHO, replied, "The pathogen was identified in record time, and the sequence was shared immediately. When they shared the sequence, it helped other countries prepare the diagnostic tools to test the cases of infection. By implication, China has helped prepare other countries to prevent the further growth of this problem because if you can't test or diagnose cases, many infections will be missed, and local transmission will begin."

Dr. Tedros raised an example in which the Chinese and German Departments of Health worked together to quickly identify and quarantine infected patients in Germany. As Dr. Tedros saw it, the openness, transparency, and responsibility demonstrated by China helped Germany "take action immediately and prevent serious issues" as they "got things under control."

Dr. Tedros reminded the journalists gathered that while they had been in the same boardroom, nearly all the members of the WHO Executive Board commended China during the 146th board session. They stated that "China undertook massive action at the epicenter of the outbreak in the lockdown of the city of Wuhan, and that helped prevent cases from spreading to other provinces in China and throughout the rest of the world. I remember a board member from the UK describing the effort as heroic, to use his exact words [...] The actions of China are making us all safer."

Dr. Tedros admitted that "the WHO faces great pressure when we express our appreciation of China, but we should not let that pressure keep us from telling the truth. We must tell the truth, and that is the truth. China does not need to ask us for praise, and I don't expect any country to make such a request. That has not happened and is not happening. It's the truth, the whole truth, and my colleagues and I speak with one voice, because we have seen these actions, and we appreciate them."

When asked why the WHO praised China's efforts, Dr. Tedros explained, "We don't say anything just to appease someone [...] This assembly gave them recognition because they said and did the right things. This helps in two ways. First, it helps them keep doing the right things they are doing. And second, it helps other countries recognize their good practices so that they can learn from them. That's all there is to it."

On Friday, February 14, Dr. Zhong replied to a friend via text message, "I'll keep this brief. I'm fine, just very busy. It's good that I managed to do a few things, and some of the urgently needed medical equipment can now be manufactured. This brings me great comfort."

In addition to the medical equipment, Dr. Zhong's team had also published many research results regarding the virus, among which was the prediction of the curve of the spread of Covid-19, developed by combining artificial intelligence with the traditional epidemiological prediction model, summed up as Susceptible-Exposed-Infectious-Removed (SEIR). Since the epidemic had broken out in China, the Chinese people had put their faith in Dr. Zhong, and he had not let them down. To the general public, he was highly experienced and skilled in dealing with epidemics. Some even believed he had "psychic powers." But above all, they trusted him because of his truthfulness, his fearlessness, and his scientific spirit.

The traditional SEIR model had previously been applied in other countries to predict and control the community spread of infectious diseases. However, if the model was applied without modification in China, it would not be accurate enough, as its functions were limited by the collection process of natural data. The outbreak of the novel coronavirus was abrupt and unpredictable, and the risk of infection and a rapid spread were both high. Combined with the significant increase in the flow of travel among students and workers during China's Spring Festival travel rush, the potential for serious challenges to arise in prevention and control efforts was very high. Based on the on-the-ground situation in China, Dr. Zhong's team took some extra factors into consideration when applying the model. China's government at both the central and regional levels applied strong intervention measures. The Chinese people united in their efforts. Distribution of goods and materials was prompt, and supplies were thus abundant. Self-quarantine was quickly and broadly applied. In addition, due consideration was given to the characteristics of the asymptomatic phase, along with the travel rush during China's Spring Festival.

With these factors in mind, Dr. Zhong's team generated two versions of predictions regarding the spread of the disease, hoping that this would provide a more accurate assessment of the situation. The preliminary results were generated on February 6, after days of hard work.

In the first version, the data collected from January 11 to February 12 was input, and a prediction was generated using the SEIR model. According to the results, the spread in China would hit its peak in late February, with the curve flattening in April. A five-day delay in control measures would double the number of cases.

In early March, the paper detailing these prediction methods, entitled "Modified SEIR and AI Predictions for the Pandemic Trend of Covid-19 in China with Public Health Intervention," was published in the *Journal of Thoracic Disease*. The paper constructed a modified SEIR prediction model based on big data and proposed an AI LSTM prediction method that could be applied with limited data.

Joining forces with researchers from the First Affiliated Hospital of Guangzhou Medical University and the Guangzhou Institute of Respiratory Health, Dr. Zhong utilized all the data accumulated through practice. With this data in hand, the paper that resolved the critical problem of predicting the spread of the virus was put together.

Being the man of science and facts that he was, Dr. Zhong did not speak merely based on his own experience. Instead, he supported his arguments with facts and evidence. "Our team added two more influencing factors to the original model," he reported, "the intervention of the nation and the peak travel season of the Spring Festival. According to our predictions, the peak in cases will come around mid or late February."

In line with his predictions, the number of cases started to decrease on February 15. During a press briefing on Covid-19 prevention and control on February 27, Dr. Zhong announced, "We are confident that the situation will be under control by the end of April."

Dr. Zhong said, "When the virus first started to spread, using their well-established models, some foreign epidemiologists predicted that China's daily cases would reach 160,000 by the beginning of February. What they failed to take into account was the firm intervention of the Chinese government and the delayed resumption of work after the Chinese New Year. By contrast, our model suggested that the spread would peak in mid or late February at about 60,000 to 70,000 cases. Our findings were submitted to foreign journals, but the paper was rejected because it differed too greatly from their own studies. But as it turned out, our prediction was more accurate."

In order to develop a clearer understanding of the crucial points in the development of the virus's spread, Dr. Zhong's team immediately began working on a second version of the prediction. In this version, some changes were made to the earlier version, and machine learning was introduced, putting in place an artificial intelligence model. All data collected between January 11 and February 17 was input for this prediction.

Before February 9, data for new confirmed cases was used in AI training. From February 13 on, data for accumulated confirmed cases plus new suspected cases minus deaths and recovered cases was used to develop the prediction. The results indicated that the spread would reach a turning point around February 20, and the highest number of confirmed cases would be around 80,000.

In hindsight, it was not difficult to see that there would be a significant decrease of confirmed and suspected cases in Hubei and surrounding provinces around February 20, making that the real turning point. At ten in the morning of March 26, the number of confirmed cases nationwide was reported as 81,960, which was very close to the predictions made by Dr. Zhong's team.

Despite the use of different data-gathering methods, both versions introduced population flow into the SEIR model. As was later proven, the predictions made by Dr. Zhong's team were very accurate, providing a scientific reference for government action. It is safe to say that Dr. Zhong and his team made critical contributions to the prevention and control of the virus.

With the approval of President Xi, the Chairman of the Central Military Commission, the People's Liberation Army (PLA) dispatched 2,600 medical workers to Wuhan on February 13. Following the operating model of the Huoshenshan Hospital, they were assigned to assist the Wuhan Taikang Tongji Hospital and the Guanggu Branch of the Wuhan Medical Center for Women and Children.

Taikang Tongji Hospital planned to set aside 860 beds, while the Guanggu Branch of the Wuhan Medical Center for Women and Children planned to utilize 700 beds. Both hospitals established clinical wards with other supporting departments, such as infection control, testing, special care, diagnostic radiology, instruments and medicine, disinfection, information, and medical engineering.

The medical personnel provided by the PLA included medical workers from the Army, Navy, Air Force, Rocket Force, Strategic Support Force, and Joint Logistic Support Force, along with multiple medical departments from the Armed Police Forces. They were deployed in groups according to the capacity and progress of the hospitals. On February 13, the first group of 1,400 medical workers from the military arrived in Wuhan, and they were immediately deployed. By this time, a total of 4,000 medical workers had already been assigned to frontline work.

The entire nation came together and presented a united front. People all over the country went into voluntary self-quarantine. Commonly heard phrases at that time included, "Don't go out," or, "Let's not add to the government's burden," and, "the medical workers already have enough to deal with." Of these new common expressions, a specific type was particularly popular, usually including, "Dr. Zhong said," as in, "If Dr. Zhong said it, I believe it." Public participation reached an extraordinary level. What should one do when sneezing? Many preferred to cover their mouths with a hand, but a more hygienic method was to cover the mouth with a tissue, a sleeve, or an elbow. Later, the tissue was to be disposed in a rubbish bin and the hands washed with soap and running water. Public education on such issues became widespread.

During this time, Dr. Zhong paid special attention to the situation on the *Diamond Princess* cruise ship and similar information from around the world. According to CCTV, Japan's Ministry of Health, Labor, and Welfare confirmed on the morning of February 6 another ten coronavirus infections aboard the *Diamond Princess*, which was then harbored in the Yokohama port. With the ten confirmed cases from the previous day, the total number of infections on the cruise ship was now twenty. Over 3,700 tourists on the ship were placed on a 14-day quarantine in their own quarters. By the end of the day, the total confirmed coronavirus cases in Japan reached 45.

This led to Dr. Zhong to a horrible realization: a global outbreak might be coming. Humankind was a united community with a shared future. The virus had its own area of origin, of high risk, and of outbreak. No individual or nation could avoid its influence. A safe, healthy future for humankind could only come about if everyone joined together to face this common enemy. The virus did not care about borders, and science should not either. There was no room for politics in this situation.

On February 14, Dr. Zhong's team launched the rapid test kit they had developed. When the battle against the virus had first begun, issues with the rapid test kits constantly plagued frontline medical workers. Initially, the tests were not accurate enough, requiring patients to undergo multiple tests and causing problems in both containment and treatment of the disease. Further, supplies were constantly in shortage. Dr. Zhong involved his research team at the State Key Laboratory of Respiratory Diseases, of which he was a part, in a collaboration with multiple facilities. With this combined effort, the assessment of the newest IgM antibody rapid rest kit was soon completed, both clinically and in the lab. With just a single drop of blood, a result observable to the naked eye could be obtained within fifteen minutes. In addition, the test kit could detect traces of the virus even if the sample was diluted by a factor of 500 to 1,000.

Compared to the RT-PCR tests that were employed at the time, the new test kits had several advantages, such as simplicity of use, greater efficiency, greater sensitivity, and greater specificity. They could eliminate the more troublesome requirements of venue and personnel while also shortening the time required for obtaining results, allowing for a quicker, even on-the-spot, diagnosis of suspected cases and their close contacts. This led to an earlier, more local diagnostic screening threshold.

The test kit underwent a trial in a hospital setting in Hubei. By repeating the test on blood samples from patients who had already been diagnosed as Covid-19 positive (though PCR tests still appeared negative), the test kit detected a large portion of IgM positivity, suggesting that it would suitably complement the PCR test. At the same time, based on tests conducted on more than six hundred samples collected clinically in Hubei and Guangzhou, the IgM positivity detection rate of the test kits was proven to be highly accordant to clinical diagnostic results.

Before long, samples of this rapid test kit intended for scientific research were delivered in large numbers to local medical facilities in Wuhan, Huanggang, and Daye, and they were used alongside PCR tests to detect Covid-19 infections.

∾ 4 ∾

CHINA'S FORTUNE

He stepped forward and instantly strengthened China's international reputation in his role as a scientist.

China had made every effort to build a line of defense to control the spread of the novel coronavirus that was first identified in Wuhan. Since the initial outbreak, the Chinese government had taken unprecedented prevention, control, and treatment measures, with a highly responsible mindset regarding the lives and health of the public. Many of the measures taken even exceeded the baseline requirements of the International Health Regulation (IHR), including the complete virus isolation and sharing of its gene sequencing at record speed and the sharing of measures with the World Health Organization.

China had established a complete set of public health emergency response systems after the SARS epidemic nearly two decades earlier. With the outbreak of the novel coronavirus in Wuhan in late 2019, in only ten days, construction was completed on two specialized hospitals, Huoshenshan Hospital and Leishenshan Hospital, more than 40,000 medical workers from all over the country were mobilized to assist on the front line, and a national task force was organized to conduct research and development of drugs and vaccines.

Robert Kuhn, Chair of the Kuhn Foundation, stated that these initiatives demonstrated China's ability to mobilize its people to prevent the spread of the virus. The entire nation had taken action to fight the coronavirus, and this was a huge contribution China was making to the global community.

WHO Director-General Tedros spoke highly of the significance of China's race against time in the urgent battle against the spread of the virus. "China's epidemic prevention control measures have safeguarded the world's public health," he said, pointing to the window for global action that had been bought by China's quick action. The transmission of the virus was very fast, and only rapid mobilization orders would prevent a global pandemic at this point. "If the virus spreads in countries with a weak health system, we don't know what kind of damage it will cause," he added.

China's actions set a new benchmark for global epidemic prevention. From the earliest days of the spread of the virus, China adopted an open, transparent, responsible attitude, strengthened communication and close cooperation with the WHO and other countries, promptly distributed information, and made every effort to prevent the virus from spreading around the world. Chinese officials and ambassadors took the initiative to introduce the latest information on China's fight against the virus and candidly answered questions that were of concern to the international media. China also invited the WHO and other experts to Wuhan for an onsite inspection, actively cooperating with the WHO team as they ventured further into Beijing, Guangdong, Sichuan, and other parts of China. The WHO repeatedly expressed its appreciation for China's responsible approach and fully affirmed the decisive measures China had taken. Throughout the process, the organization demonstrated its full confidence in China's eventual victory over the virus, and many countries around the world echoed this sentiment as they lent their support to China.

China's courage in taking responsibility was an embodiment of the concept of a community with a shared future. In the face of a growing epidemic, it was not only human wisdom that was tested, but also humankind's spirit of solidarity and responsibility. In such times of diversity, the preciousness of a shared destiny is made all the clearer.

This mindset has been passed down in the Chinese saying, *Fear not the want of armor, for mine is yours to wear.* Boxes of supplies for use in fighting the epidemic arrived from Japan, with this and other similar sayings on cards tucked inside. These words and the timeliness of the assistance from Japan were such warm encouragement to the Chinese people. The people of China were grateful for the support and assistance from Japan, who dispatched planes to deliver supplies several times during the most difficult days of uncertainty and fear early in the pandemic. The aid came from both the official avenues set up by the Japanese government and from private bodies within Japan. Before long, Japan too was stricken by the virus, and the situation there became increasingly severe. The Ministry of Health, Labor, and Welfare (MHLW) in Japan issued a notification on February 27, stating that with the 705 confirmed cases on the *Diamond Princess,* there were now 912 confirmed cases in Japan.

Wanting to return the kindness Japan had extended in China's time of need, China now moved quickly to provide Japan with the supplies needed to fight the virus on their shores. There was a strong feeling in both countries that they were in the same boat, fighting against the same virus. Upon learning that Japan did not have enough Covid-19 test kits, China immediately expressed its willingness to help and shipped new test kits to Japan's National Institute of Infectious Diseases (NIID). Subsequently, WHO Director-General Tedros pointed out that "the WHO has always called on leaders of all countries to demonstrate their leadership and political will in the face of public health challenges, and China's performance in this area is a worthy example."

At the State Council's Joint Prevention and Control press conference on February 17, Director of the Department of Medical Administration, National Administration of Traditional Chinese Medicine (NATCM) released the latest data, which indicated that TCM had been used in the treatment of 60,107 confirmed cases nationwide, accounting for 85.2% of those infected with the novel coronavirus in China. The percentage of patients who had recovered or improved through the use of TCM was 87% in areas outside of Hubei. As of midnight on February 16, there were 58,182 confirmed cases warded in 225 designated hospitals in Hubei, and the rate of usage of traditional Chinese medicine was 83.3% (80% in Wuhan). Of these hospitals, 42 designated TCM hospitals had admitted 4,978 confirmed cases, and the rate of usage of traditional Chinese medicine in these facilities was 96.4%. At the time, 11 isolation hospitals were also distributing traditional Chinese decoctions and five types of Chinese patented medications. Undoubtedly, TCM made its own great contributions to the prevention and control of the epidemic. The quintessential idea of TCM was, *it is better to have medicine on the shelf collecting dust than to have people getting sick.* Among TCM practitioners, this sentiment carried over into a widespread readiness to act.

Many TCM practitioners were eager to see traditional medicines put to use on the front line. On January 29, 2020, as a doctor of Western medicine, Dr. Zhong Nanshan made clear in an interview that "Chinese medicine should be used from the beginning. It is too late to bring it in only when the patient is already severely ill." He said that not to try to keep the balance between TCM and Western medicine, and not in an attempt to appease anyone, but because he truly understood Chinese medicine. Dr. Zhong's team conducted in-depth research into Chinese medicines and discovered through evidence-based studies that traditional medicines were effective in treating Covid-19.

How did Chinese medicines treat Covid? And how could they best be combined with Western medicine? When interviewed by CCTV's *News 1+1* host Bai Yansong, a Central Pandemic Prevention and Control Steering Group member and academician at the Chinese Academy of Engineering Zhang Boli offered an answer to these questions that fully demonstrated the dignity and demeanor of TCM practitioners. He said, "I think it's meaningless and senseless to argue about this. The only thing that matters is the curing of the illness. Each sort of medicine has its own strengths and weaknesses. The methods Western medicine uses to rescue acute or serious illnesses are irreplaceable. However, for some chronic diseases and for improving the health of those with functional diseases, the advantages of TCM are very evident. The Chinese people should be happy that they have the protection of both types of medicine. What's wrong with that? Why should we determine which is better? Even our ten fingers are not the same length. I think ignorance lies behind such arguments, or perhaps they are manipulated by some groups with their own interests. Of course, it could just arise from some confusion."

Dr. Zhong had always advocated using existing cost-effective drugs to cure new diseases. In this instance, his approach once again benefited patients. Chloroquine, an existing, cost-effective drug, was found through clinical application to be an effective treatment for Covid-19. Chloroquine was an anti-malaria medication that, due to its low cost, convenient application, and minimal side effects, had played an important role in eradicating diseases in Southern Europe and the Southern US. Of course, there were potential adverse reactions to it as well, particularly gastrointestinal reactions such as nausea, vomiting, loss of appetite, abdominal distention, and diarrhea.

While debates over Chinese versus Western medicine were ongoing at home, Dr. Zhong also faces ludicrous claims and criticism from overseas sources. For instance, on February 2, Fox News Network host Jesse Watters demanded a "formal apology" from China for the Covid-19 pandemic. He stated that the pandemic originated in China because "Chinese people don't have sufficient food to eat, so they eat raw bats and snakes." His racist remarks were interrupted and challenged by his co-host during the program.

At 10:00 am on February 19, the second videoconference of the research team jointly established by the Guangzhou Institute of Respiratory Health, Harvard University, and the Evergrande Group was held in Guangzhou. The research team had a two-hour exchange and discussion on the rapid detection and diagnosis of Covid-19, its clinical treatment, drug screening, and vaccine research.

A Special Press Briefing on Covid-19 Prevention and Control was held at 10:00 am on February 27 at Guangzhou Medical University, hosted by the Office of Public

Press of the General Affairs Office of the Guangzhou Municipal People's Government. Journalists from all major domestic media outlets were present. At the time, the epidemic situation in Guangdong had improved and the public emergency response level in Guangzhou was reduced from Level 1 to Level 2, but mask-wearing was still required when people gathered indoors.

When Dr. Zhong took his seat, he removed his mask. Nine days earlier, on February 18, he had reached the one-month mark since his departure for Wuhan. It had been a very difficult month, but the epidemic was finally contained, and with China's great effort, the spread of the virus had begun to decline in China. He smiled that day, and the collective anxiety the people had relaxed a little.

Dr. Zhong said, "China is not afraid of criticism from the outside world, because we have confidence in ourselves." Led by the US, international opinion of China had taken an unfavorable turn, even reaching the point of crisis. When Dr. Zhong said these words, the journalists who had gathered applauded him. It was one of the most difficult moments in the battle against the virus.

Though Dr. Zhong looked tired, he was much more relaxed than he had been nine days earlier. He was an expert and a team leader. With the needs created by the epidemic, he took the lead in wearing a mask, not least out of solidarity and sympathy for the frontline medical workers who had been infected due to lack of protective equipment in the earliest days of the outbreak. Dr. Zhong naturally pulled the mask aside at times, which showed that he was not afraid of the virus. During the SARS epidemic seventeen years earlier, Dr. Zhong had checked the oral cavity of every patient to obtain first-hand information about the patient.

"Ah–" he had opened his mouth as he faced each patient.

"Ah–" the patient mimicked.

With his demonstration, the patient would open their mouth wide. He personally faced each patient.

He had been exhausted during the SARS outbreak, but he had never been infected with the virus. It was like magic, inexplicable. It seemed it was not because his immunity was strong, but because it was balanced, which was ideal for preventing infection.

As the leader of the high-level NHC expert team and the Director of the National Clinical Research Center for Respiratory Diseases, Dr. Zhong reviewed his experiences during the SARS epidemic in Guangzhou and introduced the characteristics and experiences of the SARS prevention and control efforts in Guangdong as he answered the journalists' questions. These were hot issues which had been on the minds of the people for some time.

Dr. Zhong noted that the origin of Covid-19 might have been in another country before it was then brought into China. "Covid-19 first appeared in China, but it may not have originated here," he said. After the briefing, he emphasized again that "discovered" could not be equated with "originated," thus it was impossible to say with certainty where the virus had come from. It was important to trace to the source and explain based on facts, rather than speculating.

The question of how to resume work and production loomed large. Before the outbreak in other countries, foreign observers had predicted that China could end the epidemic by the end of May. China had intervened with unprecedented intensity as it fought the spread of the virus, building stringent lines of defense across its entire society in a joint control and prevention mechanism, which was not only a shift in approach, but was in fact an emphasis on being strategic. Though it was possible to resume work and production at this time, a distance of 1.5 meters was to be maintained at all times, and both ART and PCR tests were to be carried out regularly. Dr. Zhong said, "Today is February 27, and I do not see this as the peak, because testing still must be done for those arriving by train or plane. Once an infected person is found, they must be quarantined immediately so that the natural transmission path for the virus is cut off."

He encouraged that work resume only with these restrictions in place, with workers undergoing dual tests, especially those who worked in large companies where more people were clustered together. Office spaces of large companies were to be partitioned, maintaining distances of at least 1.5 meters between workers. Other recommendations included ensuring that taps and drains remain unblocked in all factories to avoid aerosol transmission from the blockage of human waste in the sewage. "If we implement these measures, we are confident that there will not be a rise in cases," Dr. Zhong said.

Two journalists whispered between them. "Is this a briefing session or a pep talk?" one asked.

The other replied, "It's a courage-boosting session."

At that time, the virus was spreading in many countries. Dr. Zhong noted this, adding, "These countries that are now facing a rapid spread can refer to China's experience."

"China's experience!" The journalists noted the proud smile on Dr. Zhong's face.

After the press briefing, Dr. Zhong was asked to introduce China's experience to the European Respiratory Society in hopes that China's approach might prove useful for them too.

"This is a human disease, not a Chinese disease," Dr. Zhong said. The number of cases was increasing more slowly in China than in other countries. Iran and Italy were seeing particularly rapid rises in their numbers at that time. It was important for the world to unite in its fight against the pandemic. From the perspective of the international community, the cases in Japan were mainly those from the *Diamond Princess* cruise ship. Prevention and control had failed there. The ship's cabins were a confined space, which made it easy for the virus to spread among passengers and crew. The longer they were quarantined, the more infections there were.

There had been many unhappy rumors about recovered patients testing positive again. A journalist asked about the preliminary data from Guangdong. It was reported that 14% of discharged patients tested positive again. How were these repeat infections to be dealt with? Dr. Zhong replied that there could be many factors involved in the re-infections. Virus detection kits had only recently been developed, so there may have been problems with the testing. At the same time, the detection and sampling methods had a great impact on the positive rate, so it was possible that those who were being "re-infected" had not actually been negative in the first place.

Regarding the presence of nucleic acid fragments in the feces and whether that created any possibility of infection, Dr. Zhong said that further observation was needed before the question could be answered accurately. However, what was certain was that after a patient recovered and did an antibody test that showed a strong positive result, if the antibody level was more than four times, then the possibility of a repeat infection was very low. This was reassuring.

According to Dr. Zhong, during the SARS outbreak in Guangdong seventeen years earlier, the Chinese government had formulated many detection and prevention methods, some of which had been implemented very well with the current outbreak of the new disease. For instance, in the current outbreak, the pathogen was quickly discovered to be a novel coronavirus. This was a great improvement over previous experiences.

Dr. Zhong summed up four valuable lessons China had learned from its experience and which it now hoped to share with the rest of the world. The first was that, as with any infectious disease, the priority was to gain control as far upstream as possible. Early detection and swift quarantine would aid in the prevention work, as these measures would decrease the likelihood of cluster outbreaks. The second was to ward infected patients in dedicated hospitals, which were more experienced in acute infectious diseases and could thus offer patients better treatment. The third takeaway was that critical patients needed joint multidisciplinary treatment. Each discipline had its own strengths. What critical patients suffering from Covid-19 needed most was life support, supportive therapies needed to be developed, and investment in critical subjects needed to be strengthened. The final takeaway was that international coop-eration was of paramount importance for the best application of treatment methods and prevention and control measures. Through cooperation, countries could learn from each others' strengths and experiences.

At the briefing, Dr. Zhong warned that new cases might be imported into China. It was important to strengthen international exchanges, cooperation, and shared experience. More than 85% of early diagnosed patients would recover, as long as they had healthy immune systems. Researchers had found that there was a significantly higher mortality rate among patients suffering from hypertension, heart disease, chronic obstructive pulmonary disease, and kidney disease. There was also a significant regional difference in mortality rate, which was not seen during outbreaks of similar viruses in the past.

Dr. Zhong believed that international cooperation and joint prevention and control were very important. When crisis came, Japan and South Korea extended a helping hand to China. When the epidemic spread in South Korea and Japan, China could not forget their earlier assistance, but should instead repay it in kind.

Dr. Zhong emphasized that eating wild animals was an inherently harmful habit for humankind. On February 24, 2020, the Standing Committee of the National People's Congress passed a resolution banning the trade of wild animals in hopes of eliminating the consumption of such animals and protecting public health and safety. When asked whether this resolution would have a fundamental impact on the prevention and control of major infectious diseases in China, Dr. Zhong replied that nearly 80% of epidemics in recent years could be traced back to wild animals, so it was necessary to prohibit the trade in and consumption of such creatures. Unfor-tunately, though, prohibition was not effective in the current market. For instance, civet cats had been confirmed as a key intermediate host for the SARS virus. And many other wild animals that could be found in local markets carried coronaviruses as well. The animals would not get sick themselves, but these viruses often proved detrimental to the health of humans who consumed those animals.

It had been just twenty years since the world had entered the 21st century, and there had already been three outbreaks of coronavirus epidemics, in SARS, MERS, and Covid-19. Dr. Zhong suggested that with all coronaviruses, prevention of their spread must be implemented as soon as there was a cluster of infections. He estimated that if measures had been taken five days later than they were, the number of Covid-19 infections in China would have reached the hundreds of thousands. China was very fortunate to avoid this fate.

A GREAT OATH

He offered his heart with both hands, witnessed by the Party flag, and melting all the ice in the world.

In March, the Pearl River flowed outside Dr. Zhong's office, the sunlight shining on its face, as if trying to warm the entire world. It was a critical period in the fight against the virus, a time that threatened to crush all those engaged in the battle. Frontline medical workers put their all into the fight, and they needed more encouragement from the public than ever before.

On March 2, 2020, Xu Yonghao, an ICU doctor from the First Affiliated Hospital of Guangzhou Medical University, along with a nurse who had volunteered to assist the work in Wuhan joined the Communist Party of China (CPC). Dr. Zhong led them in their oath.

A Party flag hung over the meeting room. A breeze blew, and the room was covered in a red tint. The scene spurred Dr. Zhong's memory. Years earlier, his father had been the Director of the Central Hospital of the Kuomintang (KMT). Driven by patriotism and a hatred for the corruption he saw in the KMT, Dr. Zhong's father had chosen to remain in Mainland China and become a member of the CPC. Dr. Zhong had always followed in his father's footsteps. Though he had been given many opportunities to pursue a life in other countries, he could not – would not – leave his motherland.

As a CPC member for more than 55 years, Dr. Zhong had never forgotten the oath he had taken during his admission ceremony. "I affirm that I will join the

Communist Party of China, uphold the Party's program, observe the provisions of the Party Constitution, fulfill the obligations of a Party member, carry out the Party's decisions, strictly observe Party discipline, protect Party secrets, be loyal to the Party, work hard, fight for communism for the rest of my life, always be prepared to sacrifice my all for the Party and the people, and never betray the Party." He had taken this oath 55 years earlier, and he had continued to follow it to the letter ever since.

Just like his father before him, Dr. Zhong had decided to devote his entire life and passion to the development of medicine, in hopes of eradicating illness and fathering the welfare of the people. This was his greatest pursuit and his greatest joy in life.

As he faced the Party flag on that day in early March, leading two frontline medical workers in the oath-taking ceremony, a great sense of duty filled Dr. Zhong's voice as he said, "This is the exact moment that Party members must step up and rise to the occasion." In the video chat window, he saw the two medical workers in their protective suits standing before the Party flag, they raised their fists and took the oath.

Looking back on this period later, admission into the CPC during such a momentous historical moment would be a priceless memory. To achieve what had been accomplished thus far in the fight against the virus, frontline medical workers had made such great sacrifices, and great contributions too. Li Yingxian had signed up to be a part of the first group of nurses sent to Wuhan, and Dr. Xu Yonghao had returned to work in Guangzhou as soon as he heard about the virus. In Dr. Zhong's view, they showed great courage, putting their own interests aside for the sake of the people. To him, this was the defining quality of a Party member. It was often said that "true gold must be forged in fire, and true heroes are formed through peril." It was in this perilous moment that Party members most needed to unite and lead the charge in the face of great trouble.

Since its establishment, the Principle State Laboratory of Respiratory Disease, in which Dr. Zhong worked, had never stopped its research into and application of TCM. In recent years, in his work as a doctor and scientific worker, Dr. Zhong had put great effort into promoting Chinese medicines, especially *lianhuaqingwen* and *yupingfeng*. Since the beginning of the outbreak, his team had filtered out the effective constituents from Chinese medicines. By March 10, they had tested more than a hundred types of traditional medicines and found that twelve were effective treatments for the novel coronavirus, and there were another three hundred still to be tested. The team concluded that some Chinese medicines, such as *lianhuaqingwen* and *liushenwan,* possessed certain curative effects for patients suffering from symptoms of Covid-19. Based on these findings, these medicines saw widespread clinical use on the front line.

During a meeting of the European Respiratory Society in which the experiences of fighting the novel coronavirus were discussed, Dr. Zhong specially advocated Chinese medications. Even as a doctor of Western medicine, he had contributed to the use of TCM in China. During the pandemic, he promoted the efficacy of traditional medicines among his colleagues all over the world, and in so doing, he opened the door for TCM to go global.

Rising at dawn every day, Dr. Zhong had only three concerns: the pandemic, human lives, and scientific research. Even if he was not completely immune to the noise around him, he did not let it interfere with his work. He had always been as straightforward and courageous as he showed himself to be at this time. He would stop at nothing to do the right thing.

Using the evidence-based methods of Western medicine to conduct research on Chinese medicines, Dr. Zhong and his team worked tirelessly behind the scenes to protect public health. Some Internet media outlets falsely claimed that Dr. Zhong had engaged in a tug-of-war with TCM doctors, attempting to block the use of traditional medicines. Good-naturedly, Dr. Zhong shrugged off these rumors, unconcerned about trivial matters, especially with his busy schedule.

On February 8, the list for the Expert Panel for the Covid-19 Response of the China National Health Commission was announced. Dr. Zhong was not appointed to head the panel. Public backlash was swift and vociferous. A common refrain was, "Unacceptable! I hope Dr. Zhong will not overwork or feel upset about this development." Most citizens knew that the appointment did not mean that Dr. Zhong had lost his team, but they couldn't help themselves; they were enraged on the doctor's behalf.

On March 8, a friend called Dr. Zhong, hoping to console him during this trying time. "Dr. Zhong," he said, "I hope you aren't too upset about not being named head of the panel. Anyway, you've always fought for the people, not some meaningless title."

Hearing this, Dr. Zhong was confused. "Sorry, but what did you say? 'Head'? I'm very sorry, but I don't have any idea what you're referring to." He added a little guiltily, "I've lost track of so many things. I've just been so busy lately."

When word of this conversation circulated, people in Beijing pulled for Dr. Zhong all the more. Mrs. Zhao, a resident of Haidian District in Beijing, made a habit of watching for Dr. Zhong on TV. Near the end of February. When the situation was at its grimmest, she always said to his image on the television screen, "Brother Zhong, you're a shining example to us all. Don't forget to take care of yourself."

In Beijing, those who were self-quarantining at home sat wide-eyed when Dr. Zhong appeared on TV. Each time Chaoyang District resident Mr. Wang saw Dr. Zhong, he exclaimed excitedly, "Look! It's Dr. Zhong. Come quickly!" His family would then gather round to watch the latest report.

How could one man, or even a team, stand the test of such a plight? Every time Dr. Zhong gave an update or offered advice, the people of the entire nation felt a sense of relief. Dr. Zhong figured it was the stringent control measures that hindered the speed of the virus. It was often said in China that "the last ten percent of the journey is only halfway there," indicating that the closer one got to victory, the more important it was to keep the guard up. In the fight against the virus, medical workers were hit especially hard, with more than three thousand being infected by the virus.

On the afternoon of March 13, Dr. Zhong sat in front of a screen, taking part in a remote joint consultation from Guangzhou. His patient was Ms. Peng, who had just spent 42 days in Zhongshan Xiaolan People's Hospital and Zhongshan Second People's Hospital. She was scheduled to be transferred to a normal ward that day. After a few days of treatment and rehab, Ms. Peng was again able to eat and walk on her own. Seeing Dr. Zhong's face on the screen, she was suddenly tongue tied, finding it difficult to express her gratitude toward him. She could only break out into a huge grin, and Dr. Zhong smiled in response. With the help of Dr. Zhong and the medical staff, this once critical patient had endured a potentially deadly trial and survived it.

"With Dr. Zhong's help during three joint consultations, the efforts by the Zhongshan People's Hospital finally saved the life of this expecting mother!" Such news was exhilarating, and it always brought Dr. Zhong great joy and comfort. What he had always most loved doing was saving the lives of patients.

On February 1, Ms. Peng had been diagnosed with an infection of the novel coronavirus, and she was admitted to the Zhongshan Xiaolan People's Hospital in Guangdong. She was 31 years old, and it was her 35th week of pregnancy. She began to show symptoms of the infection when she returned from Wuhan to Zhongshan. Not long after she was admitted, she experienced shock and respiratory distress. A long list of near-deadly red flags kept popping up. *Day 1: White shadows seen on one lung. Day 4: White shadows seen on both lungs, multiple organ failure of the heart, lungs, kidneys, and digestive system.* For this patient, every second lost meant a slimmer chance of survival.

Ms. Peng was quickly transferred to Zhongshan Second People's Hospital. Pre-occupied with his work at the First Affiliated Hospital of Guangzhou Medical University, Dr. Zhong only participated remotely in the joint consultations. He gave an order to the medical workers at the former hospital, saying, "She still has a long life ahead of her. You must save her life." He added, "It is my personal request that you don't give up on her."

As a tracheal cannula and a ventilator were applied, the rescue effort went into full swing. In the end, with the help of the Zhongshan Second People's Hospital's most advanced life support system, the ECMO, Ms. Peng survived. After 21 days, she was finally able to breathe without the assistance of the ventilator.

"During the treatment of these novel coronavirus patients, it is critical that our medical workers are effective in handling the details. This is a very noteworthy experience, and we should make sure it is known by other hospitals nationwide."

Guided by Dr. Zhong's words, his team braved countless difficulties in its research, hitting one goal after another. The most frequently used phrase by Dr. Zhong during clinical treatments and joint consultation was, "I suggest." There was no trace of an alpha dog mentality about him. Everyone in the team had an opportunity to speak, and a cordial, democratic atmosphere was the driving force in their research. With such great encouragement and guidance, the team was bursting with vitality. It functioned like a well-oiled machine. Dr. Zhong led by example, and he was not the least bit domineering. The individual growth of each of the team members gave him all the sense of achievement he needed.

Dr. Zhong walked up to the screen and checked Ms. Peng's various health indicators. In her case, he had suggested the application of the Hydrogen-Oxygen-Hybrid-Inhalation method. It was suggested that two inhalation machines be used in parallel, should the need arise, to increase the airflow. Inhaling a hybrid of hydrogen and oxygen helped reduce airway resistance, making it easier for the patient to breathe and allowing for better nutrition and facilitating a more rapid recovery.

CHINESE-STYLE BRIEFING

He is on the international stage, fighting against a global pandemic and connecting the world with China's experience. With his motherland's backing, he puts his full strength into promoting a worldwide unified fight against the virus.

Since the outbreak of the Covid-19 epidemic, Dr. Zhong had again become the focus of media attention, and he was overwhelmed by interviews with journalists every day. Immersed in the fight against the spread of the virus, Dr. Zhong was anxious, often saying, "I don't have time for interviews." But most of the questions journalists asked were related to the confidence of the entire nation in the fight against the epidemic or to the international impact of China's fight. In other words, Dr. Zhong knew that doing interviews was a part of the larger fight against the virus, and he must thus give it his best effort.

But the interviews took a toll on him. They came in one after another, so that he often could not even sleep.

On the afternoon of March 18, the 46th Special Press Briefing on Covid-19 Prevention and Control by the Office of the Public Press of the General Affairs Office of the Guangzhou Municipal People's Government was held in the First Affiliated Hospital of Guangzhou Medical University. The briefing began at 2:00 pm. Dozens of news media and journalists from all over China and the rest of the world, including those from the US, Japan, and Poland, entered the venue one after another. A long row of cameras was set up behind the conference room, taking up the entire passageway leading into the room.

At 3:30 pm, Dr. Zhong walked into the conference room with Party Secretary of the First Affiliated Hospital of Guangzhou Medical University Li Yimin, Dean of the First Affiliated Hospital of Guangzhou Medical University Huang Jinkun, Dean of the Guangzhou Institute of Respiratory Health He Jianxing, Deputy Director of the Principle State Laboratory of Respiratory Disease Zhao Jincun, and Deputy Director of the Publicity Department of the Guangzhou Municipal Party Committee Zhu Xiaoyi. They were dressed neatly in suits and ties, and they were ready to answer the concerns of the Chinese and foreign media. Zhu Xiaoyi presided over the meeting.

Dr. Zhong was open and honest as he presented information on a series of sensitive issues and offered sound scientific judgments, frankly, offering his own opinions. For instance, some members of the media pointed out that in response to the pandemic, some countries planned to reach herd immunity by allowing 60% of their population to become infected with the virus, so that the spread of the virus would reach a peak and increase immunity in the population. Dr. Zhong replied, "The fight against Covid-19 cannot rely on herd immunity." He answered the journalist's question directly, noting that herd immunity meant that 60% of the population had been infected, but with this virus, there was not yet sufficient evidence that re-infection could not occur. As he spoke, there was an endless sound of camera shutters clicking.

The panel's conclusion was that "high transmissibility and a high mortality rate" meant that Covid-19 had to be taken seriously. Dr. Zhong emphasized that the virus was highly infectious, even more so than SARS or MERS, and it had a much higher mortality rate than influenza. At the time, the mortality rate of Covid-19 patients worldwide ranged from a few tenths to 7%. Different countries had applied different measures in the fight against the virus, so the results had varied geographically. In other words, the spread of the virus would not depend on whether a country was developed, and an evasive approach would not stop the spread. The virus was not a respecter of international boundaries.

Dr. Zhong pointed to the route of transmission. Covid-19 mainly spreads through respiratory transmission of droplets and the aerosol formed from pollutants such as urine and feces. The aerosols entered the human body through the respiratory tract.

"So far, there are no therapeutic drugs," Dr. Zhong said plainly to the Chinese and foreign journalists who had gathered. There had been some effective drugs used in China, including several traditional Chinese medicines, and they had played a positive role in treatments, but according to Dr. Zhong, "We have undertaken many trials, and so far, no specific drugs have been found to treat the disease." For this reason, he added, "We must rely on international cooperation." Once Covid-19 developed to a critical condition, treatment was very challenging.

Dr. Zhong said frankly, "We have discovered some characteristics of the disease, but we have not yet found a good solution."

So what had China learned from the pandemic? Dr. Zhong said that China's experience had led to practice-based conclusions regarding prevention and control, especially noting that these required joint effort. It was important that further spread be controlled. A nationwide outbreak would bring many problems, such as insufficient medical resources, as had happened in Italy. Dr. Zhong said confidently, "China's joint prevention and control measures are very important. Empirical evidence has proven that controlling any infectious disease from the source is the oldest, most effective method. Every country must do this." He then added, "This is my opinion." He made it a habit to emphasize when he was offering his opinion, rather than scientific fact, demonstrating a respect for both science and fairness.

When asked about immunization, he said he believed that developing safe, effective vaccines was an essential task, and that too required international cooperation.

"How can medical workers protect themselves while treating patients on the front line?" a journalist asked.

Dr. Zhong turned to an analogy to describe how the frontline medical workers had fought against the virus. Each time we take a plane, the flight attendant will remind everyone that in an emergency, each passenger would have an oxygen mask. The first step was to put on one's own mask, then turn to help others who needed assistance. Only by first protecting oneself could one hope to protect others. This was a principle known all over the world when it came to responding to emergencies. "It is the same for epidemic prevention and control," he said. "You must protect yourself before you protect others."

In the early stages of the pandemic, with the limited understanding of Covid-19, the weak awareness of the need for protection, and the lack of protective equipment, the public was largely in a passive sate. Medical workers were a critical line of defense in this stage, and a collapse of this line would have been catastrophic. Fortunately, the Chinese government's strong, rapid intervention prevented other cities and provinces from having a large number of infected medical workers, which enabled the country to organize more than 40,000 medical workers to assist Hubei.

"I went to Wuhan on January 18," Dr. Zhong said, "and I heard that there were many medical workers who had been infected. They were not from the ICU, but from other departments. A Neurosurgery Department in one hospital had thirteen infected members of their medical staff."

This was a huge lesson, based in solid fact. The protection of medical workers was of utmost importance. They had to protect themselves well if they were to protect others.

A Polish journalist asked Dr. Zhong why this virus was so fierce. Was it simply because it was new, or were there other reasons? He added, "And what advice do you have for European governments? What measures should be taken to prevent and control the spread of the virus?"

"It is recommended that the European quarantine strategy move forward," Dr. Zhong replied. He said that the virus was very new, and it had taught us a great lesson. Since the beginning of the century, there had been three coronavirus outbreaks: SARS in 2003, MERS in 2015, and now Covid-19. In addition to causing cell damage, Covid-19 also caused the destruction of the immune system and the development of inflammation. It had been seventeen years since the SARS outbreak. The world had paid great attention to the study of SARS in the early days, but it was later thought that it was a fluke event that did not require long-term observation. That led to a lack of preparation for the latest outbreak.

"What's the next step?" the Polish journalist continued.

"I notice that your country, Poland, is very concerned about the prevention and control of the spread of the virus, and it adopts the upstream prevention and control strategy, which includes timely detection and quarantine," Dr. Zhong said. "In my opinion, when there is a confirmed case in one place, the close contacts of that patient should be quarantined, even if they are asymptomatic, so that the virus won't spread to others. This is still the first wave of this virus, and it is highly contagious. Family members and close contacts of people with symptoms should be tested. Don't wait. It will be more difficult to control the spread once the scope of the epidemic expands."

Dr. Zhong repeated his "four early steps" to the Polish journalist, emphasizing again the need for early prevention, detection, diagnosis, and quarantine. It was easy to repeat the "four early steps," but difficult to implement. As is so often said, truth is simple, but living it is hard.

A journalist from NHK in Japan asked Dr. Zhong, "There are fewer patients in China, and more globally. Drawing on China's experience, what are your comments on Japan's current measures for prevention and control, and do you have any suggestions? The Tokyo Olympics are scheduled to be held in July this year. What suggestions do you have for that?"

"Nucleic acid tests must be done to prevent imported cases," Dr. Zhong suggested. "In fact, China has more imported cases than local. It may be because China has adopted the strongest intervention measures in the world. Joint prevention and control efforts were launched on January 23, and the number of confirmed cases reached a peak two weeks later. The measures prompted the peak and a natural drop off, so there are fewer cases now." Dr. Zhong reminded that "the earliest patients were very contagious, even when they were asymptomatic." For this reason, he suggested that Japan should pay attention to imported cases. He smiled and said, "Individual cleanliness and personal hygiene in Japan is excellent, but it is recommended that Japan be highly vigilant about imported cases and not relax any measures."

Dr. Zhong emphasized detection methods. At the time, IgM and other antibody detection methods were available, and these could be used as good supplementary detection methods, but they were not sufficient as the sole approach to screening. A nucleic acid test was required to detect imported cases. It had been found that in some asymptomatic patients with high nucleic acid readings, the antibodies had not yet appeared, as it took seven or eight days after infection before antibody rates increased. It was thus too early to rely solely on antibody tests.

A Europa Press journalist asked, "In your opinion, what experience and practices that China has employed in the fight against the virus can be shared with other countries? And for critical patients at this stage, what do you think is the most effective treatment?"

Dr. Zhong replied that Europe was currently developing in a positive, proactive direction. A hands-off approach was not acceptable, and the focus needed to be on upstream prevention and control. "As for the second question," he added, "there is no exact treatment method yet, but after all this time, we have found some methods. For instance, there is medication. We are currently experimenting with chloroquine. In 2004, an experiment in Belgium showed that chloroquine could effectively kill a coronavirus. Further, it is a safe, old drug. Later, we will publish a summary of our use of chloroquine. From the current point of view, it is quicker in turning confirmed cases to negative test results, when compared with other drugs. However, further observation needs to be made and more conclusions drawn, because there have not yet been controlled experiments. At the same time, we also have a team experimenting with Remdesivir.

"Traditional Chinese medicine has a certain effect on alleviating symptoms and speeding up recovery. Laboratory results have been published, and the clinical effect is currently being summarized.

"In general, although there is no specific treatment method, some methods have been found which speed up recovery and prevent infected patients from developing critical conditions."

Dr. Zhong added, "What matters is that these exchanges can help other countries avoid wrong turns."

Noting that Dr. Zhong had recently held several remote video conferences with experts from Harvard University and the European Respiratory Society, the journalist asked what issues had been most frequently discussed in these meetings and whether remote meetings of this sort would become the norm, and if so, whether they would involve more countries in the future. Dr. Zhong replied that the earliest such meeting was with the European Respiratory Society, and the slides and video recordings of those meetings were available online for everyone. He added, "We have held five meetings with participants from Japan, Singapore, Italy, Hong Kong, and other countries and regions. In addition, we have held three video conference discussions with Harvard Medical School, and we will have another discussion on pathology tomorrow evening. Because the rules of Covid-19 and other general respiratory diseases are not the same, we hope to conduct more joint research with more medical experts."

China had been the first to join the fight against this virus, and it had picked up great experience and learned many lessons in the process. The response through its exchanges with various countries and regions had been positive. "For instance," Dr. Zhong noted, "we found that once Covid-19 develops into a critical condition, treatment will become much more difficult. Critical patients have a great deal of mucus in the small airways, and other countries have provided good information on successful treatment in such situations."

Exchanges represented a good attempt to address the challenges presented by the virus, and they were done with little inconvenience, due to the technological advancement in communications in recent decades. In the future, China would continue in this sort of exchanges with other countries. So far, the number of confirmed cases in other parts of the world was growing rapidly, while that in China remained at about 80,000.

In this briefing, Dr. Zhong made his evaluations public. "In the first wave, the number of cases will grow very fast. I expect the same to happen in other countries. However, I have noticed that some countries have actively undertaken prevention and control strategies."

Dr. Zhong advocated international sharing of vaccines and testing technologies so that the whole world could combat Covid-19 together. The contemporary world had become a global village, and humankind was a community with a shared future. All nations would share joys and sorrows together.

A journalist asked, "How can countries strengthen cooperation, observation, and mutual assistance in dealing with public health emergencies in the future? And what kind of assistance can China provide to other countries?"

"There is no country in the world that can run away from infectious diseases. If a country does not implement strong intervention measures, the Covid-19 epidemic will not just disappear on its own. Every country must take action." Dr. Zhong's words were not harsh, but his tone was resolute. He went on, "We need to communicate and learn from one another. China's experience lies in controlling the source of the infection, confining areas with high numbers of cases, and implementing joint prevention and control in other areas."

Dr. Zhong noted that these measures had already proven effective. The heart of joint prevention and control was the "four early steps." Examples of the implementation of these steps included fewer gatherings, staying at home, and wearing masks when going out. Japan and South Korea had done well in this respect. Early detection included seeing a doctor as soon as one felt unwell. As an example of early diagnosis, Dr. Zhong said that soon after he returned from Wuhan, the Chinese Center for Disease Control and Prevention (China CDC) distributed nucleic acid test kits to his hospital, which had proven very useful in detecting cases quickly. Early quarantine was the final item in the "four early steps."

"In some countries," Dr. Zhong repeatedly said, "the reaction time is relatively long, as long as three or four weeks. But time waits for no one!"

He also often said, "We need to cooperate." He recalled that when China was struggling in the face of the growing epidemic, the President of South Korea said that China had helped his nation during the MERS epidemic, and it was now South Korea's turn to assist China. China was doing the same thing now, opening its arm not to some countries, but to all. "Because we have gone through difficulties ourselves," he said, "we need to support others when we can. This includes providing masks, nucleic acid test kits, and other such supplies. If any single country does not control the spread of this virus, there will be no peace for anyone on earth."

He added that by working together, "we can stop the spread of Covid-19 more quickly."

Dr. Zhong offered a detailed report on China's experience, but at the same time, he emphasized that China's experience was not the only way to fight the virus. It was essential to formulate plans for prevention and control according to the conditions of each country.

Dr. Zhong was pleased to note that, even though China's way was not the only way, many countries were in fact applying the "four early steps" to various degrees. He frequently reiterated that areas with a high number of cases must be contained.

China began to contain the epidemic in Wuhan, and it expanded the contained area to all of Hubei on January 23. Joint prevention and control were implemented in other regions as well, and the numbers peaked on February 4–5, then began to drop. The problem was managed within two weeks. After a month, the number of confirmed cases dropped to what it had been initially.

This was a valuable experience that China could share with the world. Since the first outbreak, Guangzhou, an "international window," had been very successful in prevention and control. There had been 354 confirmed cases at one point, but at this time, the number had dropped to just 22, and those who remained in the hospital were all critical cases. The overall situation was a huge relief to Dr. Zhong, but there were also seven imported cases in Guangzhou, which was not a small number. Why was this so?

Dr. Zhong stressed that Covid-19 was different from SARS because asymptomatic patients and virus carriers could be contagious, which meant that national prevention and control measures needed to be quite stringent. He thus proposed that close contacts of confirmed cases should be tested as well. "I don't agree with the practice in some countries, which is to only test symptomatic cases," he said. "This will result in many missed virus carriers during the incubation period. To overcome an infectious disease, all infected patients must be quarantined, regardless of whether they are symptomatic or not."

Dr. Zhong expressed great concern. "I think the problem Guangzhou is now facing is still very serious, so passengers traveling to Guangzhou by plane or ship must be tested. We have considered using IgM and IgG for testing, but it seems too early to do so. During the process, we have found that the results of nucleic acid tests of people from countries with a high number of cases are testing positive or even strong positive, but there are still no antibodies, so antibody testing is not a reliable indicator."

He went on, "Hospitals must also provide effective daily medical care. If attention is not given to the diagnosis and treatment of acute and chronic patients, the problems will snowball." Taking Guangzhou as an example, he pointed out that at that time, the outpatient volume of more than 160 hospitals in Guangzhou had reached 60%, making it necessary for patients to make an appointment rather than accepting walk in patients, in an effort to prevent hospitals from becoming sites where the virus spread. Hospitals needed to implement "dual channels," in which doctors and nurses working in the hospital and every patient needed to be tested to confirm whether or not they were infected before they could undergo routine treatments. Though this increased the trouble involved in consultations for patients with acute or chronic illnesses, it was an effective prevention and control measure.

Vaccines could likewise guarantee the safety of most people. Regarding the research and development of vaccines, Dr. Zhong said, "Vaccines are the most fundamental solution." Children were generally vaccinated against several illnesses, as with the pertussis vaccine. This was an example of a vaccine solution for a disease. Dr. Zhong observed, "When I was a child, the streets were full of measles patients, and the mortality rate was very high. The basis for the prevention and treatment of that disease was the vaccine."

There were five main directions for vaccine research and development in China. One was a whole virus vaccine, similar to the one used in the fight against the H1N1 epidemic in 2009. The second was an mRNA vaccine. The US had safely conducted preliminary tests of such vaccines on humans, and China was making rapid progress in this area, having already carried out the first phase of clinical trials. The others included a vaccine using an adenovirus as a carrier, a protein vaccine involving genetic engineering, and a vaccine using influenza as the carrier. Dr. Zhong said that all five types were under rapid development in China, and that there was tight monitoring of the development, similar to that seen in the US. "It has been reported that the US vaccines will be available by September," Dr. Zhong observed. "China is racing against time, so we don't expect our vaccines to take much longer than that." This prediction spread quickly, becoming a headline in all major media outlets almost instantaneously.

It was spring, and flowers were blooming all over the south. In this season of hope, Dr. Zhong further emphasized that the world needed great unity. He said, "Guangdong is currently conducting animal experiments for our mRNA vaccines and vaccines using an adenovirus as the carrier. The experiments are going on day and night, and we hope to see great progress within the next two or three months. No matter which country gets there first, there is no doubt that they will not be able to produce enough vaccines for the whole world. It is important to learn from each other and to have many manufacturers producing vaccines, so that there will be enough supply for the entire world."

Dr. Zhong noted that "unlike SARS, Covid-19 is highly contagious." According to the internationally accepted standard of the basic reproductive rate (R_0), the R_0 of Covid-19 was now 3 to 3.5 (each patient infected 3 to 3.5 people), making it more contagious than SARS.

Two noteworthy points arose in the debriefing. One was that studies had discovered that Covid-19 patients were highly contagious in the early stage, and the other was that virus carriers were already contagious during the incubation period.

In Europe, besides testing those who had developed symptoms, their close contacts were also tested as soon as possible so that positive cases could be quarantined and the spread minimized.

In response to the issue of the source virus, Dr. Zhong noted sternly that "the source and the place where the virus first appeared are two different things." He observed, "H1N1 first occurred in Mexico in 2009. Can you call it a Mexican virus? Similarly, MERS was prevalent in the Middle East. Does that make it a Middle Eastern virus? The outbreak of Covid-19 first occurred in Wuhan, but that does not mean that Wuhan was the source of the virus. This is a scientific issue, and it is irresponsible to casually draw conclusions before we have unraveled the data."

The sound of camera shutters clicking was like a series of thumbs ups in response to his statement. He was truly a hero of China.

"The epidemic occurred in China, but its source was not necessarily in China. China has made a good deal of progress, especially in determining the genealogy and evolution of the virus. In the future, more evidence will emerge through research."

At the press briefing, Zhu Xiaoyi displayed the high speed rail tickets Dr. Zhong and Secretary Su had used on their journey to Wuhan. The tickets and the information on them were instantly hot news. The *People's Daily* reported, "Standing room only for Dr. Zhong." The article read,

> Over the past two days, Dr. Zhong's standing room ticket has become a hot topic in the media. The ticket shows that this 84-year-old passenger traveled from Guangzhou to Wuhan without a seat, and the ticket was improvised. According to the report, Dr. Zhong returned to Guangzhou from Shenzhen after consultations the day before, and during a meeting that morning, he was told to rush to Wuhan. There were no air tickets available, and high speed rail tickets were selling out quickly. He was placed in the corner of a dining car when he boarded, and he immediately took out a stack of documents and began studying them.

Though he had been running to and fro to help manage the fight against the virus, Dr. Zhong looked good. The journalists who had gathered did not miss the chance to ask about his health tips for remaining young. He smiled and said, "Exercise, a positive mindset, and avoid overeating."

A journalist asked, "With immunity being an umbrella to protect our health, improving the immunity should aid in preventing Covid-19. As a respiratory expert, do you have any suggestions for how we can improve the health of people nationwide?"

Dr. Zhong replied that he had long ago realized the importance of investing in one's health. He liked competitive sports when he was young, and once he started working, he continued to pay attention to maintaining a healthy life. "Even today," he said, "I can do something for society. I'm not muddled yet. The key to this is maintaining a healthy body."

The solemn atmosphere in the briefing room relaxed. "I have learned some valuable lessons," Dr. Zhong said. "The first is that no amount of work can replace physical exercise. The second is to maintain a positive mindset. Half of health is mental health, and half of all illness is mental illness. I have much experience in life, and I have fought to maintain a healthy attitude. As I faced so many things, I faced them with a smile, then put them aside and carried on. And the third key for me was to avoid overeating. I never overeat, and I make breakfast a priority in my diet."

The organizers of the press briefing arranged for an especially warm segment of the session. A child named Cao Xinwen painted the nine health tips that Dr. Zhong had given to the people of China, and she presented it to Dr. Zhong during the briefing.

Immediately after the briefing, Dr. Zhong held a remote exchange with US experts on epidemic prevention and control. This was followed by an exchange with European experts on the same topic. Once these exchanges were completed, he could finally go home.

Since the outbreak of Covid-19, Dr. Zhong had lost 5 kg, but his driver's weight increased. Before the pandemic, the driver might not have dinner until 7:00 or 8:00 pm because he needed to transport Dr. Zhong to various events, but he was at least able to maintain a regular eating schedule. After the outbreak, he invariably got home after midnight, and his three meals a day became four, causing him to put on weight.

Always waiting at home for Dr. Zhong was his wife, Li Shaofen, who was a month older than him. The public liked to call her Auntie Li. No matter how late Dr. Zhong got home, she always went to the door when she heard his voice, knowing how exhausted he was and pleased that he was finally home.

During the SARS epidemic in 2003, Dr. Zhong had stayed with the critical patients, and he was in and out of the ICU all day long. But each time he returned home, Auntie Li waited by the door without any fear, never worrying that he would bring the virus home. Each time he walked in, she stood beside him and took his coat from him. Regardless of what storms raged outside, throughout her life, his wife offered him unparalleled consideration and care.

Auntie Li said that this was Dr. Zhong's pursuit and his ideal. "I must understand him and support him. In fact, our whole family understands and supports him."

At such an advanced age, in China as in other parts of the world, many elderly people wanted to enjoy these precious golden years, clasping their spouse's hand as they walked in the garden. But being such an extraordinary woman, Auntie Li was willing to dedicate herself to the support of her husband's career, and in everything he pursued.

At 11:00 pm, Dr. Zhong finally returned after a long day of consultations, briefings, and exchanges. After washing his hands, he went straight to the dining table. Auntie Li and her domestic helper hurried to put the food on the table. Dr. Zhong did not speak. His dog, Lucky, was also very clever, not making a sound as he stood staring wide-eyed at the doctor. Dr. Zhong held a bowl in his hand, but his eyes closed. It took all his energy just to chew his food. Auntie Li sat across from him, watching him eat.

Li Shaofen was selected for the national basketball team at the age of fifteen. She was the inspiration for the film *Women's Basketball Team, Number 5*. She was herself a national treasure, and she met and fell in love with Zhong Nanshan in Beijing, where they were married. After she retired from the basketball team, Li Shaofen chose to return to Guangzhou to take care of her parents and parents-in-law. Having experienced the Cultural Revolution, being sent down, a period of poverty, raising children, and caring for elderly parents, she had faced many hardships in her lifetime. It was only when Dr. Zhong was 35 years old and Li Shaofen was injured in an accident while working as a coach that her husband felt he had a valid reason to return home.

EYE OF THE STORM

"The China Experience" was shared all over the world by Dr. Zhong and his team. The gaze of the world was on China. Dr. Zhong was quick to share China's successful experiences around the world. With his international prestige and credibility, Dr. Zhong immediately received invitations from scientists in Europe and America, asking him to present information on China's experiences.

In just eight days of fierce struggle, Dr. Zhong organized a team to gather as much information and data as possible. He took charge of the verification of all sources of information and personally compiled a set of slides explaining Covid-19. He knew very well that the slightest falsehood would come with unimaginable consequences. He could not afford any error. It was not just about his own reputation, but the entire fight against Covid-19 in China, and even the whole world. It was about the shared destiny of all humankind, and human lives were at stake.

On March 10, Dr. Zhong offered a comprehensive analysis to his fellow medical practitioners in Europe, at the invitation of the academic community there. The entire webinar was live streamed through various media platforms all over the world.

Dr. Zhong and the other scientists spoke fluently in English, and they communicated in a harmonious atmosphere. His high proficiency in English did not come through his school education, as he had learned Russian in university. In 1979, as China's first group of scientists went overseas to study, Dr. Zhong was sent to the Royal College of Physicians in London. He only had three months of English classes before his departure, but he passed his proficiency test with a high score.

Remote video conferencing was a huge project. A huge screen displayed multiple windows, each with the face of a participant from a different country. The participants raised various questions from their own unique perspectives.

Dr. Zhong said, "My topic is China's experience in Covid-19 infection control. As we all know, Covid-19 is currently spreading across the world. This has happened in the very short span of just two months. Now, I am going to share with you some of our control measures. In the 21st century, there have been three coronavirus outbreaks: SARS in 2003, MERS in 2015, and Covid-19 in 2020. We should all be quite familiar with the SARS-CoV-2 virus. Its host may have been bats, but its intermediate host remains uncertain. But that is not what I want to emphasize here."

He went on to say that it was now believed that the SARS-CoV-2 virus belonged to the ß-level B lineage, which was different from SARS and MERS. The SARS-CoV-2 genome had a 96% homology to Bat CoV RaTG13. Phylogeny tests also showed that it had just a 76% homology with SARS and 33.8% with MERS.

Dr. Zhong pointed out that infectious viruses could be detected in a patient's feces, urine, and blood. However, it was still unknown whether the virus in the feces and urine was as infectious as that in the respiratory tract. Dr. Zhong made his deductions on the channels of infection aboard the *Diamond Princess*, and he discussed these with panel participants. He then moved on to discuss what was meant by an asymptomatic carrier, saying, "We call an asymptomatic person a carrier, and they might spread the virus to others."

Dr. Zhong raised the issue of the internationally recognized "infection dynamic." He said, "R_0 is the basic reproduction number. Here, we see that the R_0 of the seasonal flu is 1.5, that of MERS is less than 1, and SARS, which appeared seventeen years ago, is 2 to 3 indicating how highly infectious it is. For Covid-19, multiple analyses show that its R_0 is close to 3. In other words, it is highly infectious."

The scientific data, experience, and virus control measures discussed by Dr. Zhong were greatly admired by his fellow scientists all around the world.

The evening of March 12 in Beijing was morning of the same day in New York. In the First Affiliated Hospital of Guangzhou Medical University, Dr. Zhong and the hospital's ICU team had a video conference with American experts in intensive care from the Harvard Medical School. It was the fourth such meeting. To begin the meeting, Dr. Zhong shared China's experience in treating Covid-19 patients, especially severe cases or critically ill patients, and he shared information on effective drugs and treatment methods.

During the conference, Dr. Zhong's team introduced their clinical findings and highlighted the difficulties faced in treating severe and critical cases. It was suggested that "we should use the drug hydroxychloroquine for mild or moderately symptomatic patients, instead of for critical ones."

When he was later asked about the American experts, Dr. Zhong said, "In comparison, we are more focused on treating critically ill patients, because we have a gap here. We have already gone through two months of Covid-19, while they have yet to encounter the problems we've faced. That being said, they are doing a great job in fundamental research, and there will be issues about which we can exchange ideas."

In response to the nearly 3% fatality rate in the US at the time, Dr. Zhong went back to his own experience, saying, "This high fatality rate is probably because many cases remain undetected." He suggested that the key was "early detection and early quarantine."

On the afternoon of March 19, the 46th epidemic prevention and control press briefing was held in Guangzhou. Dr. Zhong once again emphasized, "Not only do we need to give attention to those with symptoms, but also to their close contacts." He again reminded that all countries in the world should give attention to the "four early steps" he had proposed and learn from China's experience in joint prevention and control. The pandemic could only be stopped when all nations across the globe joined hands together.

Regarding the term "China virus" being used in some countries, Dr. Zhong said that not a single scientist of any nationality said or asked about that in their conferences. Everyone in these meetings knew that their business was science and common sense, not politics.

In Guangzhou on March 25, a short massage managed to show how much a huge nation cared. It said, "Dr. Zhong attended a video conference today, raising four critical points."

At the time, Covid-19 was raging across the globe at alarming speed. Many Chinese experts, including Dr. Zhong, attended a media conference along with experts from Germany, Italy, the UK, Romania, and other countries to discuss the current situation and response strategies and to share treatment plans and experiences in the protection of medical workers. Dr. Zhong raised four critical points during the meeting:

1. Covid-19 is highly infectious and very lethal
2. Covid-19 carriers, even those who are asymptomatic, are infectious
3. Symptomatic cases in the early stage are the most infectious, so greater attention should be given to imported cases

4. Maintaining a well-functioning sewage system is crucial to containing the virus

Seeing the wisdom Dr. Zhong shared with the international community, the people of China swelled with pride.

On March 24, nominations for the 2020 National Award for Science and Technology were announced. Dr. Zhong's Team's Respiratory Disease Prevention and Control Innovations was among the nominees.

Such awards were certainly not won without years of hard work, blood, sweat, and tears. For forty years, the Fourth People's Hospital of Guangzhou had been a small, backward facility with barely enough resources to form even a treatment team for chronic bronchitis. At the beginning of his career, Dr. Zhong became one of the founders of the Respiratory Department in this hospital. Under his guidance, the team had gained a foothold on the world stage, making contributions that were previously unimaginable. For this, he received no grand accolades or wealth, but an eternal monument was constructed for him in the hearts of the people.

At exactly 8:30 every morning, Dr. Zhong walked across the hall to his office, clutching a bag of files. For him, it was just another day at the office.

✧ 8 ✧

THE YEAR OF SARS

SARS appeared in Guangdong in December 2002. In January 2003, doctors realized that the disease was spreading aggressively, and the use of high dose antibiotics did not help. During this period, frontline experts and medical workers endured not only a test of their persistence, but also the torment of uncertainty.

As Director of the Guangzhou Institute of Respiratory Diseases (today's Guangzhou Institute of Respiratory Health, or Guangzhou IRH) and a medical researcher, Dr. Zhong felt a deep sense of responsibility and a great deal of worry. What could be done to save these patients? And what sort of disease were they suffering from? There were no easy answers to such questions.

With a wealth of frontline clinical experience, Dr. Zhong's most direct assessment was that this was not a common bacterial lung infection. He therefore disagreed with the high dose antibiotic treatment, especially because the cause of the illness was unknown. He advocated the use of medication according to specific conditions. This became a focal point of the controversy over the treatment of SARS patients in 2003. This unprecedented academic dispute affected the treatment of many patients, and with the rapid spread of SARS, the dispute had risen to the level of the entire medical community, and it even affected politicians. Being on the front line with SARS, Dr. Zhong was pushed to the forefront of both academic and political affairs.

The first SARS patient reported in China, which was also the first reported in the world, was Huang Xingchu, from Guangdong. On the afternoon of December 15, 2002, Huang was sent to the Internal Medicine ward of the People's Hospital in

Heyuan City in Guangdong. Ye Junqiang was the doctor on duty in the ward, and he diagnosed the symptoms as high fever, cough, and difficulty breathing.

Two days later, the hospital admitted another patient, Guo Shicheng, with the same symptoms. Dr. Ye laughed and said it was "fate" that brought him two such patients. Both patients had returned to their hometown in Heyuan, after having fallen ill in other cities. After they had been treated with many fever-reducing methods and antibiotics, the conditions of these patients showed no improvement.

The situation was urgent. Dr. Ye personally accompanied Huang to Guangzhou General Hospital of the Guangzhou Military Region, and he sent Guo to Guangzhou IRH on December 22. Soon, Dr. Ye and six other medical workers at the hospital showed symptoms similar to those of the two patients.

By the time Guo was transferred to IRH, he had a persistent high fever and dry cough, and X-rays showed "white lungs." The inflammation in both lungs was diffusing and spreading, and the shadows covered all of both lungs. Treatment with various antibiotics had proven ineffective. It was a very unusual situation.

Dr. Zhong and his assistants, including Xiao Zhenglun and Chen Rongchang, determined that the toxicity in his lungs was something not seen or heard of before. Worse, it not only spread with ferocious speed, but was also very difficult to treat. As an expert in the diagnosis and treatment of respiratory diseases, Dr. Zhong intuitively believed that the toxicity of this lung ailment was particularly high. The disease struck quickly as well, catching people off guard.

Fortunately, Guo Shicheng pulled through. But while doctors were still looking into a treatment plan for this extraordinary case, similar cases appeared one after another in Guangdong. The same symptoms appeared in patients in Shunde, and as of January 20, 2003, 28 patients with these symptoms had been found in Zhongshan.

On the evening of January 21, Dr. Zhong rushed to Zhongshan, and with the expert team sent by the Guangdong Provincial Bureau of Health, he held consultations and sought to save the lives of the patients in Zhongshan. The following day, the team of experts drafted the Investigation Report on the Unexplained Cases of Pneumonia in Zhongshan City. In the report, the strange disease that had been wearing on the people's nerves for days was called for the first time "infectious atypical pneumonia."

By the end of February 2003, the WHO gave the infectious atypical pneumonia that had originated in China the name SARS, an acronym for Severe Acute Respiratory Syndrome. It was a severe, acute, highly infectious respiratory disease.

A large variety and large doses of antibiotics had been used in the emergency treatment of SARS patients. Unfortunately, these treatments had been ineffective.

There were outbreaks in various parts of Guangdong, and patients with the same symptoms were sent to IRH and to major hospitals in Guangzhou. The condition developed rapidly, and the public had started to panic. After Chinese New Year, the message, *A strange disease has appeared in Guangdong,* spread rapidly by SMS.

Since late December 2002, hospitals had begun accepting many SARS patients. Due to the still unclear understanding of the disease and the insufficient protective gear, many doctors and nurses were infected. The treatment of critical patients became a problem. Within IRH, a dispute arose over whether to continue to treat critical patients with antibiotics or switch to corticosteroids, a class of steroid hormones. Because corticosteroids would destroy the body's natural immunity, many opposed this approach from an academic point of view. At the same time, if the hormones were not used in time, the patients' symptoms would be further aggravated, and the hypoxemia would be more severe. Corticosteroids were a double-edge sword. It was thus difficult to unify a treatment plan for SARS patients in the short term, given the continued debate over whether to use antibiotics or corticosteroids.

Later, the controversy expanded as quickly as the SARS epidemic spread, ultimately encompassing the entire medical research community. At that time, if any hospital received SARS patients, the same dispute would rise from the department level to the hospital level.

For doctors, the primary concern was saving the lives of patients. They urgently needed a mainstream voice to follow. At that time, as he fought on the front line every day, Dr. Zhong's prominence made him a major influence.

In the initial treatment process, both treatment plans were retained for the time being. Those who supported the use of corticosteroids would use them, while those who preferred to use antibiotics could do so. Even when SARS spread across the entire country, a unified treatment plan had not been established.

A chlamydia was a pathogenic microorganism smaller than a bacteria but larger than a virus. SARS was not caused by a chlamydia, but by a new type of coronavirus. The nemesis of any chlamydia was antibiotics, but what about a virus? And especially such a powerful one?

The debate over these two treatment plans lasted for a month. After this lengthy exploration by medical experts in Guangdong, in the First Affiliated Hospital of Guangzhou Medical University, and IRH, some understanding of the rules that SARS seemed to follow had been gained, giving experts a better handle on the question of treatment and prevention. However, it was still very unclear what had caused the outbreak in the first place.

SARS continued to spread. News of the outbreak of the epidemic in new locations continued to arise. The term "strange disease" appeared with increasing frequency among the people, carried on the cold wind in Guangdong in the early months of 2003.

The most widely circulated story was that a strange disease had spread to Guangzhou from Shunde and Zhongshan. The incubation period was very short, with onset of the disease coming within a day, at which point the patient would quickly develop respiratory failure. And, the story added, there was no cure for the disease. Many patients had died, and the disease was extremely contagious. If one were even on the same bus with an infected person or met face to face with someone with SARS, the possibility that he or she would also be infected was high. An even more terrifying version of these stories said that more than a dozen medical workers fell ill in the morning, then x-rays revealed that their lungs were covered with white spots in the afternoon, and they died in the evening after all rescue attempts failed. It was even rumored that the bird flu and anthrax were spreading at the same time. All of these sensationalized stories circulated quickly and broadly, and many sounded very convincing.

These stories began in Guangzhou and spread to other parts of the Pearl River Delta such as Shenzhen, Zhuhai, and Dongguan. From there, they continued to spread to neighboring provinces and regions, such as Hainan, Fujian, Jiangxi, Guangxi, and Hong Kong. There were also rumors in various parts of the north of "an outbreak of a life-threatening pneumonia in Guangzhou and the rest of the Pearl River Delta."

January 2003 was a month for celebrating the new year, beginning with the turn of the Gregorian calendar at the beginning of the month and the turn of the Chinese lunar calendar at the end of the month. The news of this "strange disease" was spread in outrageous terms by some, while others took it lightly, thinking there were always outbreaks of some illness in Guangdong in the springtime, especially influenza, so they had grown used to it.

With its proximity to Hong Kong, the Pearl River Delta enjoyed close business ties with the region. Each Chinese New Year, Hong Kongers who had set up factories in mainland cities such as Shunde, Zhongshan, or Dongguan or who had settled in Guangzhou returned home to celebrate the holiday. When news of this "strange disease" came out, many were forced to return to Hong Kong earlier than expected.

Newspapers published cryptic articles stating that special attention should be paid to the "flu" during the Chinese New Year holiday of 2003. Generally, the public was not aware of what was going on, but people in the industry realized that it was an epidemic. For a time, it was difficult to get people to understand how fierce and dangerous the disease was. Later evidence showed that it even went completely beyond the expectations of insiders.

After a few days, there were even more patients in the Pearl River Delta, and numbers were continuing to rise. The condition could not be controlled, and there were numerous family and hospital clusters of infections. The Second Affiliated Hospital of Sun Yat-sen University (or the Sun Yat-sen Second Hospital), the Guangzhou Eighth People's Hospital, the Guangzhou Thoracic Hospital, and other facilities admitted more and more patients.

The first group of Guangdong hospitals that admitted SARS patients, such as the Sun Yat-sen Second Hospital, were at first completely unaware of the necessary prevention measures. As a result, many medical workers were infected and collapsed. The Third Affiliated Hospital of Sun Yat-sen University (or, Sun Yat-sen Third Hospital) was dedicated to treating liver diseases, but it saw similar infections among its staff.

Dr. Deng Lianxian, Deputy Director and Chief Physician of the Department of Infectious Diseases at Sun Yat-sen Third Hospital received the hospital's first SARS patient, an 11-year-old with both respiratory and heart failure. The child's heart stopped beating three times, with successful resuscitation by Dr. Deng and the medical experts each time.

On February 1, 2003, the first day of Chinese New Year, Deng Lianxian and his colleagues undertook the thrilling rescue of a patient, which later proved to be a "super spreader event," infecting many members of the hospital staff. At the time, the patient had difficulty breathing, and his life was at stake. During the tracheal intubation procedure and ventilator-assisted breathing treatment, his violent cough-ing caused a large amount of sputum and blood to spray out of the intubation tube, spraying all the way to the ceiling and contaminating the medical workers from head to toe. At 7:00 pm on February 3, after days of rescuing patients, Dr. Deng Lianxian was sore all over, and he had a fever. On February 5, inflammatory shadows appeared on his lungs. He died on April 21, 2003.

Ye Xin, Head Nurse of the Emergency Department of the Guangdong Hospital of TCM, Ershadao Branch, did not leave her post or return home for more than two months because she too had fallen ill. She died on March 24, 2003, at the age of 46.

Chen Hongguang, Director of the ICU at the Guangzhou Thoracic Hospital, spent seventy days on the front line, resuscitating patients. He intubated more than a hundred critically ill patients, and his face and body were often sprayed with sputum and secretions. Over this long period, he fearlessly stuck to his post. His bravery spread to all the medical workers around him, motivating them. This included not only colleagues from his own department, but those throughout the hospital. His inspiration even spread to the family members of the hospital staff.

A professor of medicine who had been working in a hospital in Guangdong which had admitted SARS patients traveled to Hong Kong in January 2003, to attend the wedding of his friend's child. At the time, even he was not aware that he was carrying the virus and was then in the incubation stage. When he got to the hotel where the banquet was to be held, he greeted many of his fellow guests. When those who attended this wedding later returned to their homes in other countries, they spread the virus like bees pollinating flowers.

Under Dr. Zhong's guidance, the IRH gradually worked out an effective treatment plan, which increased the success rate for rescuing critically ill patients and lowered the mortality rate. In addition, the treatment time for patients was significantly shortened. This plan was later adopted by many hospitals, and it eventually became a universal treatment plan. The Clinical Diagnostic Criteria for SARS Cases in Guangdong Province was soon issued under Dr. Zhong's direction.

As an expert in the frontline fight against SARS and other respiratory diseases, Dr. Zhong clarified his views at this time. He believed that for patients whose condition developed rapidly, the first priority was to perform non-invasive mask ventilation to allow the patient to receive sufficient oxygen, and the next, to avoid alveolar atrophy and hardening in the early stage. At the same time, a small dose of corticosteroids was to be given to critically ill patients to avoid further deterioration of the condition, and then to rely on auxiliary treatment to get the patient through the dangerous period.

SARS was a highly contagious disease, and everyone needed to work together to prevent cross infection in hospitals. For this reason, a ventilator fan was installed in front of each bed in the ward, and it was always turned on, even when it was cold.

There was no central heating in Guangdong in January, and the wind created by the fan made it feel like a frigid Beijing winter to those in the hospital beds. But with SARS raging in Guangdong, the consensus was that ventilation was needed, especially air circulation in all public places.

On April 12, 2003, the joint research team chaired by Dr. Zhong announced that the two viruses that had been isolated from organ secretions of SARS patients in Guangdong were the same as the coronaviruses that had been identified in Hong Kong three days earlier, indicating that a variant of this coronavirus might be the main cause of SARS. Four days later, this result was officially confirmed by the WHO.

9

A 38 HOUR GAUNTLET

Driven by both science and conscience, Dr. Zhong maintained a firm stand in the dispute over the SARS pathogen. Under enormous pressure, he stood his ground as he found and presented evidence to support his "coronavirus theory." In the face of great difficulty, he never backed down, and he even innovated a design for a "non-invasive ventilation treatment for SARS patients." Earlier, he had taken a firm stand on corticosteroid treatment, even in the face of great personal risk, and now, he supported a methodology he termed the "three proper principles" for treating SARS. Premier of the State Council Wen Jiabao stated that Dr. Zhong's contributions to the cause of stopping SARS "simply cannot go unnoticed."

"It was quite a story," Dr. Zhong noted calmly, as if he were telling someone else's story. Listening to him, it would be hard for anyone to guess that the amount of stress this "story" brought to the doctor was anything more than typical work-related stress. Stress, whether mental or physical, often made one weak, even potentially leading to the buckling of the mind.

Dr. Zhong's physique was that of a young man. Working 38 hours straight, even in the wards, was not a challenge for him. During this 38-hour span, he was called back from Shanghai to Guangzhou, then rushed to another meeting, not even informing his family where he was or where he was going. Stress from an unknown source chipped like a chisel at Dr. Zhong's energy, finally knocking him down after this 38-hour stretch. But once it passed, it was, to him, just another story of days gone by. Even so, he hesitated before revealing the truth that lay behind it.

The first item he wanted to emphasize was control – control of the spread of the virus and control of the condition of those infected by it. To achieve this control, the pathogen had to be found. What could the pathogen be, and what was its pathway of transmission? And just as importantly, what could be done in the face of the invasion?

Dr. Zhong was eager to determine what was to be done in the face of such difficulties. Was it best to wait for a solution to present itself? As a responsible scientist, Dr. Zhong could not do that.

Dr. Zhong concluded, "We need coordination on two levels." The first was on the level of epidemiology. The collaboration between pathological and clinical forces was the key to identifying the pathogen. The second level was the national level. The disease was a lethal plight threatening the whole of humankind. Only through examining the collective research results of all nations could the problem be solved.

When the epidemic first broke out, Dr. Zhong immediately recognized that technological collaboration must be achieved on the international level if the spread of the disease was to be stopped. By that time, the world was already on the verge of achieving collaboration on both the epidemiological and the international level. No one imagined that the last step would require so much effort.

From late January to early February 2003, there was a shortage of the supplies that were essential to the fight against SARS – medicine, medical instruments, and protective equipment. This was the darkest hour in the fight against SARS.

In late January 2003, Dr. Zhong attended a meeting regarding the ways to stop the spread of SARS in Shanghai. As soon as he arrived, he received a message from the Health Department of Guangdong saying that there was an emergency, and his presence was urgently required. As a result, he turned around and rushed back to Guangzhou.

He reached Guangzhou at 10:00 that night, and a car was waiting for him at the airport. As soon as he set foot on the ground, he was rushed to attend yet another meeting. At this point, his family only knew that he had rushed back to Guangzhou by plane, and after that, it was as if he had disappeared.

The meeting seemed rather grim. Dr. Zhong knew some of the officials who were present. One of them said, "We have received word that Hong Kong will announce the SARS pathogen tomorrow, and we need more information on this. Did you collaborate with anyone on their side?"

Hearing this question, Dr. Zhong realized that he had been summoned back because these government officials were worried. If Hong Kong announced its information, or even its data, on the following day, Mainland China would be put in a very embarrassing spot.

The officials from Beijing assumed that Dr. Zhong had determined that this epidemic was another outbreak of the bird flu. A familiar face among the officials asked him discreetly, "What on earth have you done?"

Dr. Zhong told the truth.

He was working with two of his former students, Guan Yi and Zheng Bojian, who were professors in microbiology at Hong Kong University. They had come to an agreement regarding the pathogen of this disease that had originated in China. SARS was posing a huge threat to all of humankind, so it was critical that the source of the disease be found and its pathogen determined. With so many types of chlamydia and viruses, it was difficult to settle on which was the culprit behind SARS. Dr. Zhong's only concern was to find the exact pathogen so that more targeted action could be taken against it. After all, no battle plan could be put into place without first knowing who the enemy was.

At the end of January 2003, Dr. Zhong had grown restless. Being the sole respiratory expert to whom the entire nation looked was taking a toll on him. He had never felt so much stress. Everything he did was out of a sense of duty, not for the pursuit of fame.

With greatest urgency, Dr. Zhong had contacted Professor Guan and Professor Zheng. In an effort to identify the pathogen as quickly as possible, he had provided them with some samples collected from SARS patients in hopes that they would bring the specimens to Hong Kong for further study.

His rationale for doing this was simple. The two professors were not only his former students, but also distinguished scientists in their own rights. Further, Hong Kong had a more advanced pathology research sector and better testing labs than those found in Mainland China. In order to save precious time, Dr. Zhong decided to conduct tests on the secretions from SARS patients and study the results with his two former students.

Before doing so, Dr. Zhong signed an agreement with his two colleagues, which included the clause, *Should any party involved in the research discover the pathogen, they must consult with all remaining parties. The results shall only be released with the consent of the Ministry of Health.*

Once the terms of the agreement had been clarified and ensured, Dr. Zhong signed the agreement. At the meeting with the officials in Guangzhou, he presented the agreement to all who were in attendance. After the briefing, tensions eased dramatically, but the problem of how to respond to Hong Kong's announcement on the following day still remained.

It was already 1:30 am. Seeing the importance of this matter, Dr. Zhong suggested a solution. "Let's do this," he said. "I'll go to Hong Kong and meet with my two former students. Is that possible?"

At 3:30 am, after some preparation, Dr. Zhong and Professor Li Yimin, another expert from the Guangzhou IRH, set off by car from Guangzhou to Kowloon via Luohu in Shenzhen. By the time they arrived, it was 6:30 am.

As soon as they reached HKU, the entourage suggested that Dr. Zhong call his former students. Dr. Zhong replied, "Let's wait for a while. They might not be awake yet."

He decided to wait in the car and avoid waking them, but this was not the only reason for his course of action. He was also concerned that his former students might not have the courage to meet him if they knew the situation was grim enough to warrant a call so early in the morning. He instead chose to wait until 8:15 to call.

Professor Guan had always been one of Dr. Zhong's favorite students. Dr. Zhong said of him, "He is very smart, a well-established microbiologist and an expert on the bird flu. He pours his whole heart into his research."

At 8:30 am, Dr. Zhong finally picked up the phone and called Professor Guan. Hearing Dr. Zhong's voice, Professor Guan sounded concerned. "How are you, sir?" he asked. "Have the past few weeks been tough on you? You must take care of yourself."

When he learned that Dr. Zhong was in Hong Kong, he was thrilled. "Where are you now, sir? I'll come pick you up right away."

When Dr. Zhong said he had been waiting for over two hours, Professor Guan was both surprised and distressed. "Sir, you shouldn't have done that!" he objected.

Dr. Zhong went straight to the point then. "I need to see you."

"Of course. I'll come pick you up now."

"There's no need for that. I'm at the door of your house."

Following Dr. Zhong's instructions, Professor Guan quickly contacted Professor Zheng and arranged to meet up. When they arrived, the two former students invited Dr. Zhong to join them for breakfast.

Dr. Zhong refused, saying, "Breakfast can wait. What is of utmost urgency is the matter of the pathogen. Are you two planning to announce it today?"

The question took Professor Guan by surprise. "What? Where did you hear that? We have not even identified the pathogen yet, and if we had, we have our agreement to follow."

He added, "You're my teacher. How could I ever lie to you? I won't announce anything without permission from both you and the Ministry of Health."

Relieved, Dr. Zhong signed. "Great! Then let's go have that breakfast you mentioned."

But after a moment's thought, he gave up the idea. "The officials might not be so easily convinced," he said. "It would be better if both of you could come back to Guangzhou with me and clarify with them in person."

Both professors eagerly agreed. They applied for the day off from their respective departments, then accompanied Dr. Zhong back to Guangzhou.

At noon, Dr. Zhong and his two former students walked into the meeting room. "Professors, please brief everyone on the situation," Dr. Zhong said.

Dr. Zhong's goal had been very clear: conduct tests on the virus and identify the pathogen so that an appropriate treatment plan could be determined. None of them had ever imagined there could be this sort of misunderstanding.

As a person with great political awareness, Dr. Zhong knew the attitude of high-ranking officials in such matters. But at the same time, he was still a scientist, and in the face of the raging epidemic, his first thought was to see all of humankind collaborating technologically and uniting against the common enemy, the disease.

Professor Guan and Professor Zheng presented a detailed explanation to the attending officials. They reported, "We have not yet identified the pathogen. Further, when we do identify it, we will abide by our agreement and jointly announce the findings with the mainland. We promised that there would be no unilateral announcement, and we will keep our word. Furthermore, Dr. Zhong is our teacher. We respect him and would never betray his trust."

When the meeting concluded, Dr. Zhong attended another meeting in the afternoon regarding the prevention and control of the disease. He offered a full academic report at that meeting.

The 38 hour gauntlet finally came to an end, but it was not without cost, Dr. Zhong fell sick.

10

"I AM NOT THE GOD OF THE PLAGUE"

Dr. Zhong was both physically and mentally exhausted. He fell ill, and he could do nothing but go home and recuperate. He had saved countless patients, but when he was ill, the best solution was for him to go home and recover. He was not down over his illness. He was then 67 years old, and had played sports all his life, especially when he was an athlete in his youth. He was very fit, and he knew that no matter how tired he was, his strength would be renewed when he woke.

But this was the first time he had been this tired. The meeting in Shanghai had been on infections, focused on the special infectious disease that was currently spreading. He wanted to return to Guangzhou after the meeting and take a break. He had never expected things to unfold so quickly, giving him no time to rest at all. When he was in Shanghai, he had begun his day of work at 7:00 am, and by 9:00 pm, he was rushed to Guangzhou, and then on to Hong Kong overnight, where he had a 9:00 am meeting the next day. He returned to Guangzhou from Hong Kong the same day and continued working until 9:00 pm, for a total of 38 hours straight.

Before going to Shanghai, Dr. Zhong had spent more than a month fighting to save SARS patients. "This is a critical time. I must take the lead," he said.

He felt as if his feet were filled with lead, and he could hardly move them. He had never been so weary before. He could not even walk as fast as was his habit.

But he was not afraid of hardship, and he could not be overwhelmed. He was filled with a strong desire to find the pathogen as soon as possible.

After his 38 hour whirlwind tour, he finally returned home, where his wife and children were worried about him. Because he immediately fell ill, he did not have time to give much thought to all that had happened. The next morning, he had developed a high fever, followed by a cough. He immediately went for a chest X-ray, and he found that there was inflammation in his left lung.

At the time, every day, major media outlets in Guangdong and other parts of the country were scrambling to gather information related to the epidemic, especially that about it being "very contagious, but not as terrible as it was first thought." The release of information had reached a fever pitch, but then suddenly stopped.

Many people remember that there were whispers at the time that Dr. Zhong's updates were grandstanding and self-promotion. On January 28, 2003, Dr. Zhong had to stop working so that he could be hospitalized immediately. Ideally, he would have been warded in the hospital where he worked, as it was the leader in treating respiratory ailments, and many of his friends and subordinates would take good care of him. However, he did not want this to happen. At such a time of emergency, he did not want to be the center of attention at IRH, where he knew other patients needed the best care and attention of the medical staff. Were attention to shift to him, the impact on the entire fight against SARS and the patients suffering from it would be great, and it would weaken morale. "How come the expert has fallen ill?" people would ask, and patients might lose heart in their fight against the disease. Dr. Zhong also felt that everyone knowing he was ill, how serious his condition became, how long his treatment took, and so forth would only make the impact all the stronger, and this was not conducive to social stability.

"I should find a secluded place to recover," Dr. Zhong said, determined. He quietly convinced his friends and subordinates who knew the situation, and after discussion, it was decided that he would be warded in another hospital.

Before long, Dr. Zhong was admitted into the cadre ward of a different hospital. Soon after he was settled in, he received a letter stating that there was a patient in his ward who was scheduled to undergo a kidney transplant, and a Hong Kong journalist was coming to the ward to report on it. The ward was likely to become tightly packed with media workers. At the time, Dr. Zhong had just stepped down as Dean of the Guangzhou Medical College (now Guangzhou Medical University), a position he had held for ten years. In the heat of the sun, Dr. Zhong felt somewhat desolate. "Am I the God of the Plague?" he asked. But the hospital staff helped him calm down, and he reminded himself, "It's not easy for the hospital either. I should think of them."

So he dialed his son Zhong Weide's number. As soon as his son answered the phone, Dr. Zhong said, "I am going home to recuperate."

On January 29, 2003, Dr. Zhong went home, though he was still ill. The most direct response he got from his wife was that she put aside all fears that she would be infected herself, instead feeling great empathy for him. Knowing how frustrated he was, she did not dare to say too much to him, not wanting to add to his mental burden. Her gaze was warm and clear. She spoke to him as if nothing out of the ordinary were happening. Dr. Zhong suddenly felt much calmer as Auntie Li arranged for him to recuperate at home.

The Zhong family's domestic helper had worked for them for ten years, and she was very anxious over Dr. Zhong's condition. Each day, she wholeheartedly took care of the elderly couple, as she respected and care a great deal for both of them. She could not conceal her emotions. As soon as Dr. Zhong came home, she had him change all his clothes. Before he arrived, room had been arranged to make things more convenient for the nurse who came to give Dr. Zhong an IV each day.

Dr. Zhong's life had always been busier than most people can even imagine. Aside from sleeping, he rarely had a free moment for anything, and he seldom stopped and thought about himself. Now, he lay on his bed at home all day long. Depression rolled over him like a cloud and struck at his heart. He did not know how to deal with this feeling.

Despite his bad mood, Dr. Zhong was relieved that his illness did not seem to be SARS, because many SARS patients had difficulty breathing, but he did not. He simply felt abnormally weak. After five days of receiving an IV at home, he decided to have his condition re-examined.

After the exam, he looked at the X-rays and was surprised to find that the cloud of pneumonia was gone, and the medicines with which he had been treated were all ordinary antibiotics. This confirmed for Dr. Zhong that his illness was not SARS.

When Dr. Zhong had returned home, though he suspected he had SARS, Auntie Li had not avoided contact with him out of fear of infection. Dr. Zhong was a man with a broad heart and mind, though he was often neglectful of what seemed to be small domestic matters. But what his wife had done for him during those days would remain in his heart forever, the memory retaining all its detail and clarity. Not only had Auntie Li spoken softly when he came home, as if nothing out of the ordinary had happened, and not only had she changed his clothes and bathed him, but she had also spent the following days ensuring that he could recover peacefully at home. She did not even allow others to visit him, aside from the nurses and a few officials who had to see him. She had refused to let him take phone calls, to the point that when an official had called and asked where Dr. Zhong was, she said he was on a business trip. She made easily digestible foods for him too. Dr. Zhong saw it all, and he was touched. To him, it was only his wife who could share all his joys and sorrows, and she was the only one who could really take care of him and give him the love and support he needed.

The results of Dr. Zhong's second exam made Auntie Li's worries disappear. Even so, seeing that he was still weak and tended to drop things, she insisted that he rest for another three days, and even then, it was only reluctantly that she allowed him to go back to work.

Antibiotics had proven to be an ineffective treatment for SARS at that time. The shocking facts were obvious – SARS was no ordinary pneumonia. The savage fact was that traditional treatments for pneumonia were useless against it.

The serious illness left Dr. Zhong very weak. "I'm tired, like I've moved a mountain," he said. He had no choice but to drag his weak body to the IRH, where everyone was busy fighting SARS. He was concerned about the institute, the safety of the patients, and the aggressive development of the epidemic. He spent nearly every waking moment thinking of how to control the spread of the epidemic.

Walking into the corridor of the office area, he tried his best to make it seem he was fine and had not just recovered from a serious illness. He always combed his hair back, and he tried to walk at the quick pace he was used to, and to do all of it with a smile on his face. Those of his subordinates who knew his situation were both surprised and delighted to see him. They held back their tears as they greeted him and said, "The director is back!" It had been eight days that he was away from work, and he had lost a lot of weight. They had never seen him look so haggard, but the expression on his face was strong. Most of his colleagues did not know he'd had pneumonia. They only knew he had missed work because he was ill.

Dr. Zhong got busy right away, but the colleagues in his office were surprised to see that when he dropped an item he was holding, he did not even seem to notice. He was surprisingly weak. How could he work in this state? To make matters worse, he needed to go into the ward with the SARS patients.

Dr. Zhong's low pitched, amiable, emotionless tone was familiar to them, and they knew there was no chance of persuading him. Though he was little more than skin and bones, they helped him into his white lab coat, mask, and cap, putting each piece of gear on in turn. In his protective suit, he looked just like everyone else, but they could still tell exactly who he was, as could the patients who were waiting for him. One patient said, "I knew it was him, and even though I didn't feel good at all, my spirits were lifted, and my mind was more at ease when I saw him."

Before and after Dr. Zhong's illness, Chinese television audiences and the general public had all been used to hearing what "Dr. Zhong says" each day through the difficult times, but while he was ill, they did not see him on TV at all, or in any other media either. Many citizens in Beijing were following the SARS situation, listening to Dr. Zhong every day, because they knew the virus was raging in Guangzhou, where the expert Dr. Zhong lived. What he said was first-hand information on new patients and what was going on in the wards. However, even the media wondered why they had not seen Dr. Zhong for so many days, and they were eager to learn more about his current situation.

Dr. Zhong chuckled and said, "I wasn't feeling well, but I'm better now." On February 11, 2003, in order to reassure the people, Dr. Zhong updated the public on the occurrence of SARS and the patients' conditions at a press conference held by the Guangdong Provincial Bureau of Health. Taking this opportunity, Dr. Zhong said that he must be responsible for the sake of the nation. He swore on his professional reputation that SARS was not terrible, but rather, it was preventable and curable.

In early 2014, as Dr. Zhong's house underwent a major cleaning, the worker who was helping with the cleaning saw a rusty nail on the wooden doorframe and reached up to pull it out. Auntie Li quickly objected, saying, "This is the nail where we hung the bottle from which Dr. Zhong received the IV eleven years ago. Leave it there as a memento."

11

A LOVELY COUPLE

Auntie Li never met with journalists. She never claimed any cash awards, and she was never overly thrilled about her husbands' accolades. In her youth, she was a national athlete of the highest caliber. She shared her husband's burdens, and she poured her own heart into caring for her family. After so many years, she had become an elegant woman of great benevolence and true virtue.

On the Chinese New Year Eve in 2009, the Guangzhou IRH held its traditional Spring Festival gala. On the evening of January 26, over four hundred Guangzhou IRH employees gathered in the ballroom of the Guangzhou Hotel. Auntie Li was among the guests, and she was seated next to her husband at the table closest to the stage.

At the end of the program, Dr. Zhong walked onto the stage for his performance, singing the Austrian folk song *Edelweiss* in both Chinese and English.

Edelweiss, edelweiss
Every morning you greet me
Small and white, clean and bright
You look happy to meet me
Blossom of snow, may you bloom and grow
Bloom and grow forever
Edelweiss, edelweiss
Bless my homeland forever

His voice was commanding, and the audience was completely captivated. But besides the enjoyment on the musical level, the symbolic phrase "blossom of snow" carried an additional, very profound meaning.

Two special guests made an appearance during the program. One was Mr. Finley, Dr. Zhong's son-in-law, and the other was Zhong Jiabin, his 12-year-old grandson. Mr. Finley performed an amusing two-man comedy routine with another worker from the Guangzhou IRH. Dressed in a red school uniform, Jiabin looked very much like Dr. Zhong had as a boy, with the same calm, elegant feel of a scholar. His performance was a flute solo, which was quite enjoyable. He walk back to his seat amid thunderous applause. Dr. Zhong's family, including his daughter, Zhong Weiyue, Mr. Finley, and Mr. Finley's mother sat a little farther from the stage at another table loaded with Cantonese dishes.

Auntie Li turned in her seat and looked at Jiabin's table. She slowly stood up and walked over. She was now 70 years old, yet she was gentle, refined, and of great stature. The image of youth still lingered on her face. Married to a workaholic "machine" like Dr. Zhong, all she could do was calmly carry on and try to share his burden.

Each time her husband came back from work or from a trip that had taken him thousands of miles away, even if he was too exhausted to speak to her, she was still happy and very satisfied. To her, these were the only moments she was truly relieved of her worries. A simple, "I'm exhausted," from Dr. Zhong made her drop all her grievances, because she knew how true those words were.

The time her husband showed the most concern for her was when she received her regular health reports. It took him only a few seconds to look through the report, but it always made Auntie Li very happy to see him do so, because she knew that no matter where he was or how busy he was, she would always be in his heart. Their marital bliss came from their tacit understanding.

As the director of the hospital and an academician with numerous titles, Dr. Zhong was immensely busy during the earlier years of their marriage. Auntie Li was naturally upset by this arrangement, and many squabbles broke out between them, but no matter how furious he was, Dr. Zhong put it all away to soothe his loving wife. Heaping apologies and praise on him, Auntie Li always gave in at the end of the day.

It is easy to imagine the amount of guilt Dr. Zhong carried. When he faced his patients, he listened to them and respected their opinions – shouldn't he be all the more willing to do so for the loving wife who had stood by him all these years?

After spending most of her life with Dr. Zhong, Auntie Li had gained a basic understanding of medicine. As an athlete, she had developed a personality that was often described as "fierce," but she was also very gentle and loving, as was particularly evident when unexpected circumstances arose, such as Dr. Zhong's sudden illness. At such times, no matter how anxious she felt, there was always a calm smile on her face.

Auntie Li was one of six children in her family, though, sadly, one of her siblings had died at a very young age. She was the youngest of the five surviving children, with three brothers and one sister, but she did not grow up with them. She was instead given as a foster child to a woman who had never married. As a child, she loved playing the piano and playing basketball. At the age of 15, she was chosen by the Central Institute of Physical Education (now the Beijing Sport University) to join the National Women's Basketball Team. Her foster mother was hesitant at first, but eventually agreed, thinking it would better the child's prospects in the long run.

Auntie Li always tried not to meet with journalists. She did not have anything against them, but she did not like the idea of being interviewed as "the wife of Dr. Zhong." Overall, she found no gratification in any sort of superficial "pleasures," but only found enjoyment in living a warm, cozy life.

She was a gentle woman who had no interest in celebrity or public praise. When Dr. Zhong won an award, she would celebrate with him, because she knew he had earned it through his own hard work. However, she never asked him about any cash awards he was given, but was always willing to wade through hardship with him. In all his working years, Dr. Zhong never took the cash awards he won home, so Auntie Li never put any stock in such things. She was pleased to see these awards invested in medical research or the training of medical workers.

Auntie Li was a very good cook. Early on, she had tried to leave the cooking to the family's domestic helper, but when Dr. Zhong developed a mild heart condition in 2003, she made it a habit to personally cook healthy, delicious meals for him.

In the 1990s, Dr. Zhong discovered that his triglyceride and cholesterol levels were a little high. However, he did not pay much attention to it. Auntie Li greatly regretted this neglect, feeling that it was her inattention to the issue that led to Dr. Zhong's later heart problems.

Dr. Zhong could not afford to stop working. Years of a heavy workload, especially with the added weight of the SARS epidemic, had put a great strain on Dr. Zhong's heart. It was not a life-threatening condition, but it was serious enough to command the attention of the elderly couple.

As Dr. Zhong's partner in life, Auntie Li knew that to him, everything they had been through and all the hardships they had endured were history. It was all so fleeting, and it was past. It was a history that, if not for all the repeated questions and requests for elaboration, he would not have bothered to recall at all.

12

CORTICOSTEROIDS – A DOUBLE-EDGED SWORD

"You know Dr. Zhong? Well, maybe you can ask him whether he was the one who said during the SARS period that corticosteroids should be used. So many people have developed osteonecrosis of the femoral head (ONFH), but now he has become a hero. How can he bear it?" said a doctor from a large hospital in Beijing. A colleague of hers was severely infected when participating in the rescue of SARS patients, and the use of corticosteroids led to her colleague's ONFH, which meant that for her life, she would be in a wheelchair.

Among the SARS patients with ONFH, some people were unhappy when they mentioned Dr. Zhong. "He's the one advocates the use of corticosteroids," they often said. After so many years, it is worth asking whether people's accusations are correct.

The fact is, it is slander, false accusations leveled at Dr. Zhong. The facts need to be clarified. The hormones from the corticosteroids did indeed have side effects. Why, then, were these drugs still used? For the sake of both conscience and justice, this question should be settled.

When various antibiotics used in high doses were declared clinically ineffective in the treatment of SARS, Dr. Zhong and all the other experts in Guangdong faced unprecedented challenges. This was not a normal pneumonia or a normal infection, and the number of infected cases increased every day. Dr. Zhong and other experts proposed the use of corticosteroids to control the conditions and protect the patients.

The role of these hormones was to reduce lung damage. The damage caused by SARS was first an abnormal lung immune inflammation process, and the use of the hormones aimed to reduce this immune inflammation and reduce lung damage. However, excessive use of corticosteroids could easily cause a secondary infection and bone metabolism damage, so it required great skill to use them. In other words, it was important to choose the right patient, the right time, and the right dose if one hoped to receive good results when using corticosteroids.

During the SARS epidemic, many patients were already in a critical condition when they were diagnosed. Their lung tissue became hard, and they could not breathe spontaneously. Doctors needed to ventilate them immediately, but when the tracheal intubation was used for artificial ventilation, as the condition progressed, the lungs would continue to develop into fibrosis, and the hypoxemia would continue to worsen. After the use of the hormones, the damage to the patients' lungs was suppressed, and through the process of immune regulation and auxiliary treatment, the lungs could gradually return to normal.

SARS was first discovered in Guangdong, so it was there that corticosteroids were first used in clinical treatment. The people of Guangdong took the lead, paving the way for China and the world to finally conquer SARS. Although there was a period of intense debate over the use of antibiotics or corticosteroids, medical workers in Guangdong persisted in using corticosteroids in clinical practice.

The patients in Guangdong who were treated with corticosteroids received relatively good results. Among these patients, only 2.6% had ONFH, which was the lowest in the world.

Workers from the Beijing Municipal Bureau of Health went to the Guangdong Provincial Bureau of Health to learn from the experience just after the Spring Festival holiday of 2003 ended on February 8. At that time, the epidemic was serious, and everyone panicked. They traveled to the site at the risk of being infected, but in the end, there were still many SARS patients in Beijing that ended up with ONFH. Why was that so?

In late January 2003, Wu Hua, a doctor of the First Affiliated Hospital of Guangzhou Medical University and the Guangzhou IRH, and another key doctor, was infected by a SARS patient. Wu Hua, the big sister of the IRH, had been working at her post for days after the SARS outbreak, rescuing patients and guiding the nursing care. After recovering from a serious illness himself, when Dr. Zhong learned that they were infected at the beginning of the battle, he was saddened and anxious, even to the point of shedding tears for them. The IRH he had established was now facing unprecedented challenges. The most serious question was, how big and how long would the battle be?

As early as December 2002, Wu Hua wondered why there were so many patients having the same symptoms. At that time, she was too busy to think too deeply about it, but by December 20, when the news that a "strange disease" had been discovered spread, Wu Hua had already had close contact with several SARS patients. At that time, there were no isolation suits, wearing of masks, or other general protective measures.

The patients' conditions were serious. Secretions from patients who needed intubation were left on Wu Hua's hands, which she did not disinfect or clean in time. This might have been the cause of her infection, she later realized.

The family members of two patients soon began to develop symptoms as well. This shocked Wu Hua, who was unprepared for how contagious it was.

Inserting the oxygen tube slowly into the lungs of a critical patient was a routine clinical treatment method. The patient often coughed violently due to physiological reactions, and the bloody sputum that sprayed directly from the lungs was the most toxic. All medical workers were well aware of its danger, but their spirit of professional persistence made them not worry about their own safety.

At the time, when the patients treated in the First Affiliated Hospital of Guangzhou Medical University and the IRH experienced obvious hypoxemia, instead of intubation or incision of the trachea for ventilation, the doctors first used a noninvasive nasal mask for ventilation. This method proved to be very effective, and it helped many critical patients get through the difficult period.

At first, in order to overcome this problem, Dr. Zhong and other experts, including Xiao Zhenglun, Chen Rongchang, and Li Yimin, developed a "non-invasive ventilation" method to give patients respiratory support, increasing their oxygen intake to provide a better opportunity to save their lives. This was the first step. Second, when patients had a high fever and their lung inflammation was further developed, corticosteroids were given as needed, and when the patients had a secondary bacterial infection, antibiotics were used accordingly. These steps led to a rescue success rate of 87% among critical patients. These steps not only reduced the mortality rate, but also significantly shortened the patients' treatment time.

Throughout the battle against SARS, Guangdong was able to win the final victory because of two powerful weapons which had played a decisive role. One was that Dr. Zhong always highlighted to the medical workers that corticosteroids should be used with appropriate doses at the correct time, based on the patients' condition, which effectively prevented more casualties. The other was the creation of "non-invasive ventilation" on the front line, which reduced patients' suffering and mortality, and also avoided more serious secondary infections.

These measures were issued by the Guangdong Provincial Bureau of Health on March 9, 2003, in the Guidelines for the Admission and Treatment of SARS Patients in Guangdong Provincial Hospitals, sent to various municipalities and provincial and subordinate medical units in Guangdong. This was an important contribution made by Dr. Zhong and the Guangdong expert team in the battle against SARS.

SARS had been over for six years. In the quiet office of the IRH, the Office Director Wu Hua was sharing her experience of being infected, always with a smile on her face. She had no tears or sighs, as if it were some thrilling or exciting game that had ended peacefully at last. Although she was not as young or beautiful as she was 30 years earlier, her big eyes still shone with passion and wisdom, setting off her cheerful personality.

Wu Hua said that her current physical condition should be considered pretty good. "The 24-hour cardiopulmonary function is not bad. It's just that the lungs have more texture," she said. She added that she seemed to be getting old. When she was young, she could climb to the top of the mountain without resting, but now she had shortness of breath while going upstairs. She also developed osteoporosis, so she now had the habit of taking calcium tablets with vitamin D for supplement purposes. She felt a bit regretful that she didn't take more time to exercise before, but she found the most appropriate reason, saying, "I am too busy to exercise."

She had personally brought up one group after another of medical workers in the IRH. This was her heartfelt pride as an excellent chief physician.

She should be proud and gratified because she used her seriously infected body to test the effectiveness of corticosteroid treatment in controlling SARS, which provided strong evidence for the later control and treatment of SARS patients. She was also a good partner of the IRH Director Dr. Zhong. When it proved difficult to unify the national medical and health authority's treatment plans and opinions on SARS when Dr. Zhong insisted that SARS patients must use corticosteroids to control the condition instead of using antibiotics because it was clinically proven that the use of large doses of antibiotics was not effective at all, she was the one who provided the greatest support and proof for Dr. Zhong's insistence. In particular, she verified a point that Dr. Zhong insisted on and worried about, which was that the use of corticosteroids required strict control of the dosage.

Wu Hua's main symptom after being infected was a sudden high fever, but it had started in the morning and was suddenly gone in the afternoon. Feeling it very strange, she took an X-ray. According to the X-ray results, there were no abnormalities in her lungs, so she resumed working again. However, the next day, she again had a sudden high fever, with temperatures as high as 40°C. By the third day, she collapsed. "I can't hold on anymore. I feel extremely tired," she said to the nurse, adding that she might be infected.

At that time, SARS was still regarded as "pneumonia of unknown cause." On the fourth day, Wu Hua was hospitalized as a patient. She was immediately given a large dose of antibiotics, but to no avail, and the high fever continued. This once again proved that conventional antibiotic treatments were ineffective.

Wu Hua asked that corticosteroids be used, but she was rejected, and her attending doctor insisted that they keep using antibiotics. The mainstream voices at that time believed that antibiotics should be used, so out of respect for experts who insisted on this treatment plan, Wu Hua had to continue taking antibiotics.

When the doctor on duty did not give her corticosteroids, she asked the doctor in charge to prescribe them. The doctor in charge was very hesitant and wanted to get approval from the senior management first, and he wanted to further observe her condition. She begged, "If you don't give me corticosteroids, I will die. I don't have any appetite at all, and I'm extremely tired." The weakness was unbearable for her.

"At that time, I hardly ate anything for a week. I could only take one or two spoons of porridge. How could I regain my energy without eating? I had no strength at all. I had a high fever all the time, and I felt cold all over. If I wasn't cold, I became unbearably uncomfortable." Wu Hua's narration transported us back to that time. It was Chinese New Year's Eve on January 31, 2003.

Wu Hua's request was finally granted, and she was very happy. She used corticosteroids in the morning, and she was more comfortable and no longer was breathless by afternoon. She could even sing along with the CCTV Spring Festival Gala.

"The doctor saw the good effect after I took corticosteroids. His worries were gone, and he continued to use it for me. At that time, my lungs were not severely infected." By the afternoon of the first day of the Chinese New Year, she felt that she had recovered. On the morning of the next day, she took an X-ray, and the film showed that the shadows on her lungs were gone, so she was discharged and allowed to go home to celebrate the Chinese New Year, where all her family members were anxiously waiting for their reunion.

Underestimating SARS, she unknowingly brought the virus home and spent the entire Chinese New Year with her family. Her younger sister and her family were home from Hong Kong, and they stayed in Wu Hua's house. The two older sisters of Wu Hua's husband had come back from abroad for the Chinese New Year. On the second day of the New Year, as soon as Wu Hua arrived home, she went to the nursing home to bring her mother-in-law home for the reunion dinner.

Initially, Wu Hua was wearing a mask, but later when she felt it was a bit strange, and her family was not used to it, so she took it off. She ate with everyone, but she used separate chopsticks to pick up dishes for her family. After she returned home with her family and relatives, her mood was much better, and her illness seemed to be much better too. Finally, she had some appetite. After the reunion dinner, she sent her mother-in-law back to the nursing home and returned home herself.

Wu Hua was unknowingly a SARS virus carrier. Fortunately, none of her family members were infected. "All the windows in the house were open. Ventilation is very important," she said.

When it was close to the noon on the third day of the Chinese New Year, she was again tired, and she found it difficult to breathe. Her younger sister persuaded her to go back to the hospital as soon as possible. Wu Hua knew that the symptoms indicated that she was about to have a fever again. At around 9 pm, Wu Hua had a fever of 39.8°C, and she had difficulty breathing. Early next morning, her husband and younger sister sent her back to the hospital. It was then that Wu Hua began to realize that she must be isolated from her family. She said to her husband and younger sister, "Don't stay here. Go home!"

On the fourth day of the Chinese New Year, her condition began to escalate. Based on the X-rays, her lungs again had shadows. Her condition developed very quickly. At about 11 pm, her breathing became labored, and the doctor decided to put her on a ventilator, which made her more comfortable. Dr. Zhong, who had been worried about her, called to ask about her condition.

Before the Chinese New Year of 2003, Dr. Zhong had been busy formulating countermeasures for the SARS epidemic, participating in expert consultations and various meetings for epidemic control, making rounds, rescuing patients, and calling for the emergency allocation of materials to fight SARS. He had no restful sleep almost every day. "I saw that his eyes were red when he came to round the ward," Wu Hua said, imitating Dr. Zhong's bowed body. "He bent down and examined the patients very carefully, even the patients' mouths, and he faced each patient directly. The doctors who saw were so worried about him."

After being on a ventilator for three days, Wu Hua's condition improved. She later elaborated on the process of how the doctor used corticosteroids. She was a doctor herself and had decades of medical experience. She also had her own experience in the application of corticosteroids. She was well aware of the side effects of the drugs, knowing that excessive use could cause ONFH. She said, "At the beginning, I had a dose of 40 mg once a day. Later, it was increased to twice a day. This increased amount played a key role in effectively controlling my condition. However, I only used it for two and a half days, and then the dosage was gradually reduced over seven or eight days, and it was in the end only taken orally."

Wu Hua continued, "I wasn't an obedient patient. Although I knew the side effects of this medicine, I didn't look at my medical records. If I did, I should have known that the sugar in my urine had increased, and the excessive use of corticosteroids would cause drug-induced high glucose content in the urine. The doctor did not notice it at the time. In fact, it was caused by the hormones.

"Later, I didn't take medicine to control the sugar in my urine, but slowly reduced the dose of corticosteroids. As expected, the high sugar content was just a superficial phenomenon. When my dose of corticosteroids was reduced to a low level, the sugar level was not high anymore."

Wu Hua could not remember exactly how many hormones the doctor prescribed to her at that time. She said it seemed to be 30 mg, and there were many tablets. She secretly packed them up and took four tablets a day for a few days, and then changed to three tablets a day.

Other SARS patients became fat after taking corticosteroids, but Wu Hua lost weight. Dr. Zhong went through the ward on rounds, and he wondered if she had taken corticosteroids. She replied, "I wouldn't lie to you. I started taking four tablets a day, but after three days, I changed to three tablets a day. I'm feeling good. No problem at all."

Wu Hua later told Dr. Zhong that she was indeed recovering well, and she didn't have any shortness of breath at all. She could even walk swiftly.

In October 2002, Wu Hua had made plans to visit relatives in Sydney with her family. She eventually broke free from the hands of death and survived, and her desire to travel to Sydney became even stronger. Originally, Dr. Zhong worried that she had not fully recovered, so he did not agree to her travel plans. A few more days passed, and after confirming that she was not contagious at all, Wu Hua couldn't hold back anymore. She resolutely boarded the plane to Sydney, traveling as part of a tour group. It was midnight when they boarded the plane, but she was in good spirits. She waited until dawn, and then transferred flights. After reaching the Gold Coast, she felt a little tired, even though she had been waiting so long to be there. She said, "I walked some distance, then sat down and rested for a while, and then we stopped for a meal. I felt better after the meal. It was just once that I felt a little tired on the trip, and that was because I had just been discharged from the hospital, took an overnight plane, and then stayed up late. By the third day, I felt much better, back to normal.

The air in Australia was so good. I was very comfortable, and I ate a lot." She had been out of the hospital for less than half a month, and she traveled overseas.

After she returned from Australia, she felt that she had recovered very well, so she returned to work immediately. At work, other than her daily busy schedule, she also squeezed in time to train medical workers. The time when she first returned to work was the most difficult in her fight against SARS. It was the peak period of patient visits and hospitalizations, and there was a shortage of frontline medical workers. Wu Hua was at the forefront again, and there was a risk of being infected again. However, she was experienced, so she became a good example for the patients.

Six years later, in December 2008, the weather in Guangzhou was warm, like spring in the north. It was quiet outside the window, and a ray of golden afternoon sun shone in.

"Corticosteroids have side effects. When given to patients, they must be given according to each patient's physical conditions, and the dosage must be well controlled and constantly adjusted so that the side effects can be minimized," Wu Hua said. "Only when the amount is inappropriate will side effects occur." She was confident that her corticosteroid dosage was accurate, so she didn't develop ONFH. Her confidence was touching.

Wu Hua said that the reason SARS patients in Guangdong rarely developed ONFH was undoubtedly because of the strict control of hormones consumption, and she was thankful to Guangdong's major respiratory disease expert, Dr. Zhong. In addition, she was thankful to the specialized hospital, the IRH, which closely integrated theory and practice and provided deep technical and scientific research support. In earlier clinical treatments, it was common for doctors to use corticosteroids. This allowed Wu Hua to self-manage the use of corticosteroids according to her body's condition.

In contrast, after the SARS epidemic gradually spread to other places in the country, from April to May in 2003, the correct corticosteroid treatment plan (what patients to use it, when to use, and how much to use) was not well understood. In addition, the epidemic in Guangdong had not been completely controlled at that time, so it was difficult for experts and professionals in Guangdong to be transferred to other places to guide in the treatment plan. As a result, in some places, the dosage of corticosteroids in some patients exceeded the conventional dosage by five to ten times. Corticosteroids thus became a double-edged sword for SARS patients. It saved patients' lives, but overuse made some patients disabled, even spending the rest of their lives in wheelchairs. These patients were helpless because they faced such cruel choices.

Wu Hua said, "Dr. Zhong always asks me, 'How much of the hormones have you taken?' He cared about me. Actually, he always knew how much I had taken. He just needed to observe and summarize at any time, because so many patients were using it." Wu Hua cherished the memory of her old leader and partner Dr. Zhong during the SARS period for many years.

The pressure pushed Dr. Zhong to his limits, and he needed to respond with hope. People trusted him and relied on him. He needed to use all his energy, and teamwork was essential.

"Sometimes, I went to the office to look for him, and he put his hands on his waists like this—" Wu Hua imitated Dr. Zhong. Dr. Zhong put his hands on his waists, arching his body slightly as if the blood and nerves all over his body were condensed in the deepest voice of his mind as he tried to decipher a code. He sometimes took off his glasses and pinched his eyebrows with his thumb and index finger. This was his most common gesture when thinking about problems.

Wu Hua said, "I saw him so silent several times. Just like he was thinking about things." She recalled how Dr. Zhong concentrated. "When you called him, he sometimes couldn't react because he didn't know that anyone was calling him."

13

CHECKING EVERY PATIENT'S ORAL CAVITY

During the SARS epidemic, Dr. Zhong never wore a mask when conducting preliminary diagnoses. During that time, he needed to demonstrate the proper way for the patients to open their mouths, allowing him to get a better grasp on the situation. He only asked the patients to hold their breath while he checked. Taking this enormous risk, he managed to reach a shocking conclusion: SARS patients did not show any laryngeal symptoms.

Before he identified the pathogen of SARS as a coronavirus, Dr. Zhong never wore a mask when checking the oral cavities of the patients, yet he was never infected at any point during the epidemic. This miraculous fact led to much consideration, and Dr. Zhong once said, "I have checked the oral cavity of every SARS patient."

Among the experts who fought SARS, it was common sense that coming into close contact with the open mouth of patients infected with this airborne disease would be an almost surefire way to get infected. And if a SARS patient coughed on a medical worker, he or she was essentially doomed. Initially, most of the SARS patients consulted by Dr. Zhong were virus carriers, and he had no protection put on while checking on the patients. He was later much more cautious and started donning protection equipment.

Protective equipment was rarely seen on medical workers in the early days. They did not know the danger brought by the virus, and they lacked the vigilance to fend it off. Many patients were coughing at the time. During the first two to three weeks, after careful observation of the patients, Dr. Zhong reached two conclusions. The first was that the patients all lived or worked in highly crowded areas, and the second was that they were infected via airborne droplets spread by the cough.

When asked why he was not infected, Dr. Zhong said, "I always told my patients not to cough during consultations. I think that was the reason why I was not infected during these sessions."

His voice was deep, yet every word sounded crystal clear. "Some said that I did this because I was not afraid to die or get infected. I wouldn't say so myself," he added.

Aside from this coughing ban, he did not have much defense. When checking the oral cavities of his patients, he opened his own mouth to demonstrate how the patient should "open wide," often with an *ahhh* sound. The patients inevitably breathed onto him.

"Well, in that case, all I can say is that I probably have great health and I am resilient to diseases. Other than that, I guess I had enough antibodies from all the contact I had with the patients," he observed, laughing.

At first, Dr. Zhong indeed did not have a robust enough view of the infectiousness of this newly-emerged virus. According to his subordinates, by not wearing a mask, Dr. Zhong unwittingly conducted a test of the infectiousness of SARS on himself. It is said that great courage often comes with great skill, and that seemed to be the case here. He plunged into the most direct, most practical situation for the sake of gathering valuable first-hand data.

When years had passed since SARS, a question still lingered in the minds of many. "Why did he say, 'just send all the critical patients to me?' Why would he involve himself in such a grim matter? Has he no fear?"

Dr. Zhong responded, "There were many considerations that led me to only put on a mask at a later stage. I wasn't 'not afraid of infection,' but I thought I should be the one to lead in showing no fear at all. As for why I asked all the hospitals to divert their critical patients to me, it was because I gained some confidence based on our practice. If I did not have enough evidence or felt uncertain, I definitely would not make that call. It wouldn't take much observation for a clinical doctor to figure out that you need to summarize the conditions by yourself. I was trying to gather real data from the front line."

In the fight against the virus, Dr. Zhong was quite sure about his diagnosis of SARS patients. One of the major reasons for this was that he had a firm grasp on the symptoms of the disease. Armed It was with this grasp, he said, "I have checked the oral cavity of every SARS patient." He mentioned it repeatedly just to make it clear and raise awareness that SARS was a very special kind of infection, rather than a common pulmonary infection. For the medical community to realize this, direct, perceptive understanding needed to be formed and condensed into concepts and conclusions. In one of the simplest examples, Dr. Zhong said, "Common pneumonia or the pulmonary infection that we know starts with swelling or laryngeal symptoms. However, according to my observations, none of the SARS patients I received showed any signs of swelling. In other words, the general symptom of throat congestion was absent. However, this concept must be supported by evidence, which requires adequate observation of patients on an individual level. As a result, I needed to check every single patient, no matter whether the case was confirmed or not. As we confirmed many more cases, a counterintuitive point appeared: the patients showed no symptoms in their larynx. SARS patients also showed other symptoms that were different from common pneumonia patients. They had a fever and low leukocyte count, and while they technically had a pulmonary infection, they did not have lung rales. Most notably, they had much more difficulties in breathing. When explaining these highly technical issues to others, Dr. Zhong always made an effort to make it as simple and clear as possible.

On May 18, 2003, at the American Thoracic Society (ATS) International Conference, Dr. Zhong delivered a report on the specificity of SARS in China to over 2,000 experts and scholars from all over the world. During the conference, clinical doctors from the US paid close attention to his report. Dr. Zhong insisted that medical workers should try to identify SARS patients via simpler and more direct symptoms, instead of unanimously sending patients off for preliminary blood tests.

"This discovery," he said, referring to his experience on the frontline in the report, "was acquired via real experience and practice. It will take some time for it to be proven, but it will eventually be trustworthy."

14

STANDING TALL LIKE A MOUNTAIN

How many more patients would appear? When would the epidemic end? How much more risk would there be to take? Who could predict all this? Where were the answers?

The beginning of March 2003 was the peak period of the SARS epidemic, and it was the loneliest times. No one knew how long the epidemic would last, and no one knew how it would end. The six hospitals in Guangzhou dedicated to receiving SARS patients were overwhelmed, and many medical workers collapsed. For most medical workers, the methods used to treat and control SARS were decided on the spot.

According to the relevant records, on March 17, 2003, the total number of SARS cases reported in Guangdong Province exceeded 1,000 for the first time. The IRH was a solid, stubborn and proud battlefield. All the brave medical workers there had no fear as they faced the danger.

Wu Hua returned to the front line in March. In the IRH, on the one hand, some medical workers were infected and suffered, but they eventually got over it. On the other hand, there were always medical workers who were infected and fell ill. A total of fourteen medical workers in the IRH were infected. The shortage of personnel on hand to fight SARS had reached a critical juncture throughout Guangdong. The front line and provincial hospitals faced an emergency.

"Send all critical patients to me!" In this time of crisis, Dr. Zhong's decisive voice, opened the way for total victory. His bold words were quickly spread by countless media sources, especially mainstream and authoritative media, and they provided a deep social foundation.

In any era, whether of war or peace, heroism is a kind of fire stored in the people's hearts. Even in an average person, the fire will be hidden deep in his or her soul, and it is sensitive to the call of light. The truth is on the surface, but also in the depths. This was all the more true of someone like Dr. Zhong, who in the face of such a critical situation took on a heavy responsibility. His words were risky, but how could the degree of the risk be measured?

Why did Dr. Zhong come forward? Wu Hua knew best. She said, "Yes, of course, I know. It is his sense of responsibility."

All the staff of the IRH respect Dr. Zhong, but they did not agree with him blindly. The collective was filled with an atmosphere of science, democracy and harmony. When everyone in the IRH learned that Dr. Zhong had volunteered to accept all the critical patients, they knew that "me" meant all of them.

With the increase in the number of SARS patients in hospitals in Guangzhou, critical patients had occasionally been transferred to the IRH. However, the transferred patients were often at the end of their lives, with barely a breath left.

Early diagnosis, early quarantine, early treatment, and reasonable use of corticosteroids and ventilators, which were instructed by Dr. Zhong, had been committed to memory by all the staff.

"The patient transferred from Sun Yat-sen Second Hospital was very sick, but he finally woke up. The patient transferred from Sun Yat-sen Third Hospital was also very sick. They were both transferred from big hospitals and were in serious condition." There were more transferred patients, and all were in a severe condition. Faced with patients whose lives were in danger, Wu Hua said, "There's hardly any way to cure them!"

When the critical patients were brought over, their hands were stiff, they were unconscious, and their nerves had problems. It was impossible to tell whether their brains had been infected by the virus or whether the brain lesions were caused by SARS.

It was imperative that the patients' clothes be quickly removed, but the clothes could not be taken off because the patients' arms couldn't bend. In the end, the clothes were cut off.

Dr. Zhong said, "It's too late to send them here only when they are in such a condition!" After this opinion was accepted by his superiors, patients who were not very seriously ill were sent to the IRH.

"This is the Guangdong Institute of Respiratory Health. If the patients are not sent here, where else can they be sent to? I should be responsible." This was Dr. Zhong's only thought.

Whenever he thought back to this scene, Dr. Zhong, who was now more than 80 years old, was very grateful to the relevant leaders of Guangdong for agreeing to his request at that time. It was a major decision by the leading cadres. Even if Dr. Zhong needed great courage to volunteer, without the approval of the leaders of the Guangdong Provincial CPC Committee, he would not be able to do anything. At least, there would have been much resistance.

The IRH drew out doctors and nurses to pick up SARS patients from other hospitals. There was a shortage of manpower everywhere, especially medical workers. However, unlike the IRH's hands-on approach, the patients of some hospitals were separated from the doctors and nurses. "When a doctor in charge and an attending doctor went to a hospital to pick up patients, a nurse checked patients outside a door," Wu Hua recalled.

The medical staffs at Sun Yat-sen Second Hospital and Sun Yat-sen Third Hospital were the worst-hit, with many infections in their ranks. When a large number of medical workers collapsed, the survivors and uninfected medical workers persisted in working on the front line, which required the conquering of many fears and exceptional performance in general.

It was difficult for two female doctors to carry a stretcher on their own, so a male driver would usually help. But it was still tough, because they needed to not only carry the patient, but also carry the ambulance equipment and injections that moved with the patient.

Dr. Zhong recalled the scenes one after another. "At that time, I felt helpless when I saw colleagues collapsing one after another. There were not many effective treatment methods, but we still had to continue rescuing patients."

In the end, Dr. Zhong's team resolved the crisis and survived. Under the harsh conditions at the time, there were no problems with the treatment and prevention done by the whole team, but it was extremely difficult.

In March 2003, there were two sisters from Inner Mongolia who had fallen sick. They came to the IRH for medical treatment. In normal times, this was a usual thing, but this was the most difficult time for the IRH in its fight against SARS, and the arrival of the two sisters from thousands of miles away moved the hearts of the medical workers. For the IRH, it became a most vivid scene, and they would not forget it. Ordinary patients who were so far away had also come to them, and the IRH's exhausted medical workers were suddenly motivated, and their enthusiasm returned.

The two sisters evoked their sacred sense of value and responsibility as medical workers. Their patients needed them.

The two sisters had fever and pneumonia. They came to Guangzhou from Hohhot, and they were transferred directly to the IRH. At that time, the two sisters were already in a very serious condition, and one was intubated immediately and put on a respirator. Eventually, both recovered completely, and they were very happy.

At the end of March 2003, at the most difficult moment, there was a turning point. Due to the timely delivery of face masks and full-body protective suits arranged by the health department, medical workers were effectively isolated and protected, and SARS cases began to decline in Guangdong. The infected doctors and nurses of the IRH gradually recovered and started working again. There was a doctor from another hospital whose condition was the most serious, and even his bones were damaged. He nearly died, but he eventually recovered after a long time. Fortunately, he did not become disabled, and he even returned to work after recovering.

THE PATIENT LIANG HEDONG

"By that time, I had started to show symptoms of mania. I was struggling so violently that five or six men could not contain me. When he came into the room, I hadn't completely lost consciousness, and I immediately recognized him. He was Dr. Zhong Nanshan."

Eight years after his encounter with SARS, Liang Hedong, a patient from Guangdong, recalled his consultation with Dr. Zhong. "He did not apply too much force, yet somehow, he managed to pin me down. I suddenly became calm," he said. "Please tell Dr. Zhong that I have been working out since I was discharged from the SARS ward. I am doing multiple exercises, and mountain climbing is my favorite. I am in great health. I don't have any pulmonary shadows, and I do not have osteonecrosis in my femoral bones at all."

Mr. Liang was a maritime worker in Yuexiu District, Guangdong, and he was diagnosed with SARS on February 10, 2003. "I hope to let Dr. Zhong know that his work was not in vain," he said. "The patient he treated back then has returned to his post and is doing important work." Emotional, Mr. Liang lit up with joy.

Before he was diagnosed, Mr. Liang was rather paranoid about SARS. Even so, he did not expect to be hit by it so soon. Six years after SARS, he was already over the age of 60 but was still of great health. He was not especially tall, but his sturdy build made him appear quite athletic.

"I managed to escape death in my encounter with SARS, and that was how I came to know Dr. Zhong." Mr. Liang remembered the situation perfectly. He only heard about the disease over the phone, learning that it was some sort of severe lung infection. "But we never realized that we needed to prepare accordingly."

On February 10, 2003, Mr. Liang's father-in-law, a 90-year-old man, fell from the bed while sleeping. The fall did not wake him up, and he slept on the floor for the rest of the night, causing him to catch a cold. On the second day, the old man developed a fever. "As we arrived at the hospital, the doctors seemed very grim, and they demanded that we put him in the hospital." He just had a fever. Why must he be hospitalized? Mr. Liang was confused at the time.

His father-in-law was admitted to the hospital on February 13. By the 15th, the hospital saw a massive surge of patients with similar symptoms. By this time, the hospital immediately announced that all patients who had a fever must be gathered and put in the same in-patient ward.

As these plans were implemented, the father-in-law of Mr. Liang was soon transferred to the Guangzhou Eighth People's Hospital, which specialized in infectious diseases and hepatopathy. As it turned out, Mr. Liang had been infected by his father-in-law. When the old man was transferred, Mr. Liang and his family began visiting him in his ward. Mr. Liang was shocked by what he saw. "In hindsight, the disease was quite formidable. We were infected as soon as we stepped into that ward."

When visiting his father-in-law, Mr. Liang did not wear a mask or any other protective gear. His daughter was the first to be diagnosed, followed by him and his wife. The girl was admitted to Guangzhou Eighth People's Hospital as soon as she was diagnosed. After a day or two, Mr. Liang started to show symptoms as well. The fever hit him hard, spiking to 102°F from the start.

On February 18 and 19, 2003, the three members of Mr. Liang's family all started to show various symptoms, yet the in-patient ward in Guangzhou Eighth People's Hospital where they stayed was already at full capacity. The first three hospitals that took in SARS patients had no choice but to send incoming patients elsewhere.

According to Mr. Liang, the doctors told him that the medical community did not know much about SARS, and they could not come up with an effective treatment plan. When he first got sick and was admitted to Guangzhou Eighth People's Hospital, his lungs were already turning white. As the days progressed, he entered a critical condition. He was placed in a single ward. In his X-ray shots, his lungs were almost completely white and showed signs of serious infection. This was the fifth day after his admission.

On the day before, he had begun to have trouble breathing, and on the fifth day, he was on the verge of suffocation. He started to fear that he was not going to make it.

The hospital was placed under complete lockdown to prevent the spread of the virus, as SARS patients were admitted to its ground floor. Lying in his bed, Mr. Liang felt miserable. He was soon transferred to Guangzhou Ninth People's Hospital. While falling in and out of consciousness, he heard the doctors' comment that his lungs were becoming "hard." He couldn't eat, drink, or sleep. His wife, who was in much better condition, was given special permission to look after him in his ward.

Recalling this experience, his voice trembled with tension and fear as he said, "The Ninth People's Hospital realized that I was in critical condition. They told my wife that my respiratory system was failing, and there was nothing they could do about it. The Department of Health also acknowledged that this hospital could not save my life. They knew that I might survive in Dr. Zhong's special hospital, so, my wife urged that I be transferred there." By this point, Mr. Liang's superiors at work also pleaded to the hospital to transfer him to the best hospital with the best doctors.

Mr. Liang's eyes started to gleam. "I was so lucky. Why? Let me put it this way. Should I have spent another night in the Ninth People's Hospital, I might be dead, but because Dr. Zhong specialized in research regarding respiratory failure, he could treat patients who were deemed hopeless by other doctors."

Mr. Liang was hopeful. When SARS came, not many people knew about Dr. Zhong, and there wasn't any specific medicine to treat the illness. But Mr. Liang knew that Dr. Zhong's greatest work was in the field of treating patients with respiratory failure.

After much trouble, Mr. Liang finally found Dr. Zhong. He recalled, "This was my greatest stroke of luck." A bright smile lit his face as he spoke.

It was the young Vice Director Chen Rongchang of IRH who took over Mr. Liang's case from the Ninth People's Hospital.

"When they called Chen, it was already after 9 at night. By the time he picked me up, he had just finished a long day of critical treatment for patients, returned home, and taken a shower. I could only imagine how tired he was." Mr. Liang added, "The doctors trained by Dr. Zhong are just so great! All the Vice Directors under Dr. Zhong were prominent in Guangzhou. My wife told me later that all the nurses in the Ninth People's Hospital were quite impressed by me, saying, 'How did he manage to get Dr. Chen Rongchang here?' It was obvious that the medical workers had great respect for Dr. Chen. I think it was Dr. Zhong who sent him.

"If not for Dr. Chen, my transfer might not have been so smooth, or I might have died on the way. Dr. Chen constantly held the manual ventilator when treating me. Without his help, I would be dead. He gave me artificial respiration during the ambulance ride. That was a highly dangerous move. Looking back, I think we were both very scared." It was not hard to see that Mr. Liang was immensely grateful to Dr. Chen and the other medical workers that helped him during his transfer process.

Upon his arrival at IRH, Mr. Liang fell into a five-day coma. Later, his wife told him that the first expert who conducted a consultation on him was Dr. Xiao Zhenglun, another famous Vice Director of IRH. "When my wife saw the expert, she begged him to save my life. Dr. Xiao was very kind to my wife and reassured her."

Mr. Liang was also very grateful to his wife. Staying with him, she was also infected and admitted to the hospital, yet she visited him every day. Without her, Mr. Liang might not have survived.

"When I was in a coma and being rescued, my wife was not allowed to witness the emergency treatments I underwent. I woke up on the fifth day, thanks to the fact that my wife was tirelessly calling my name. For this reason, I always believe that people in a coma can be wakened by their family's calls.

"I remember watching this on a TV drama. The male protagonist was heavily injured in battle, and everyone in his unit thought he was dead. They called his wife, but she refused to believe it, and she finally woke him up in the hospital. Such things are real. On the fifth day, I regained consciousness when my wife woke me up."

Mr. Liang was quite shocked when he woke up by the many tubes going in and out of him, including a special oxygen tube strapped to his right arm. "This was a very important treatment invented by Dr. Zhong and his team. They pumped high-concentration oxygen for the patient and conducted protective ventilation. Combined with corticosteroids, it preserved the patient's life and stabilize the vital signs." Mr. Liang said, "Dr. Zhong and his team must be talented inventors!" Also among their inventions during SARS was the intravenous nutrition tube that was plugged into the patient's left arm. When the patient fell into a coma, there was no way to feed them, and intravenous nutrition was the only option. "By that time, there were all kinds of tubes plugged into my arms, my nose, and my mouth."

In his coma, Mr. Liang vaguely heard a voice in the distance declaring that he had just lost blood pressure and that he was fading away. What followed were the footsteps of every doctor in the ward, and the shout, "Quick, apply the agentia!" When he finally woke up, everyone in the ICU let out a sigh of relief. Pan Yao, the chief head nurse, said to him cordially, "Do you know how many times you almost passed from life to death?"

"I am so glad that I lived to see this day, and I am so grateful to all these people who helped me." Happiness was written all over his face. "It is quite the coincidence, as Dr. Zhong graduated from the same school as me, only earlier. I had always known he was a famous doctor, but I never knew he was working at the IRH that his research was so advanced. If I had not fallen sick, I wouldn't have known of his great contributions to the fight against SARS."

According to Mr. Liang, he had heard about Dr. Zhong long before SARS. He learned about his story from the media, and he knew that Dr. Zhong was an academician. As he woke up, the first thing he saw was Dr. Zhong's face. "In some sense, Dr. Zhong was the main support for my survival," he said.

Mr. Liang spent twenty days in ICU. Whether he woke up during the day or during the night, it seemed that Dr. Zhong was always by his side. *Dr. Zhong must have a way to save me.* This thought boosted his will to survive.

"They all wore huge masks. Later, I heard that a single layer of masks could not stop the virus, so they usually wore three. Later on, safety goggles and surgical hats were introduced." Mr. Liang recalled, "Even with all the masks and gear, I felt like I could recognize Dr. Zhong, like I had some sort of telepathy with him."

Brushing his giant hand across his chest, Mr. Liang added, "As soon as he approached, I always recognized him. I still recall that one time, I felt tortured and I became agitated, even going into a sort of mania. I hallucinated, raging and thinking there was someone trying to kill me. As a result, I pulled out all the tubes, including the ones used for transfusions and blood-pressure measurements. I yelled at the top of my lungs. After my recovery, the doctors told me what happened. As it turned out, I was in such a weak state that the hormone used in my treatment caused mania. As my wife told it, I raged so frantically that the entire ICU was shocked. "Nobody could contain me. In my rampage, five or six men tried to hold me down, and I managed to fling every one of them off of me. That was when Dr. Zhong showed up. I hadn't completely lost my consciousness, so I knew it was him. He appeared by my side and pinned me to the bed. He didn't really use much force, but somehow I calmed down.

"'Do you know who I am?'

"'Yes, you are Dr. Zhong.'

"He pinned my body, saying 'Good. Since you recognize me, please don't struggle.'"

Mr. Liang continued, "After this, I became compliant and accepted the injection."

Later, he regained his consciousness and felt better. Yet, he still suffered from severe physical weakness, but he was sane by this time. "It was like whenever I opened my eyes, Dr. Zhong was there. Alongside him was another familiar face, Dr. Xiao Zhenglun. I always recognized their faces. They were both dressed in their lab coats under layers of gear, yet I recognized them." Mr. Liang repeated this several times, as if trying to prove how real it was.

As Mr. Liang regained full consciousness, he was moved to a general ward. "According to Dr. Zhong, among all his SARS patients, I was the second most critical. I was lucky to survive and recover from it."

In 2008, the *Southern Metropolis Daily* presented awards to News Figures in the 30 Years of Reform and Opening Up. Mr. Liang was invited by the newspaper to present the award to Dr. Zhong. Imagine how honored Mr. Liang felt, again meeting his hero 5 years after his recovery from SARS, the ceremony was so short that Mr. Liang did not get a chance to tell Dr. Zhong what he wanted to say, but it was still the opportunity of a lifetime. He presented a symbolic gift to Dr. Zhong, a statue of a pioneering ox. Holding it with both hands, Mr. Liang passed it to Dr. Zhong and commended him for his willingness to serve everyone like a tireless ox. He really wanted to shake Dr. Zhong's hands again and tell him how grateful he was.

At the ceremony, Mr. Liang seemed to be in good health and spirited. His sickly look from five years earlier was nowhere to be found. Mr. Liang wished to tell Dr. Zhong that even though he was 60 years old, he had returned to work. With his talent and great health, he still played a critical role at work.

∞ *16* ∞

MEETING WITH MARGARET CHAN AGAIN

In March 2003, Chan Fung Fu-chun (Margaret Chan) was eager to meet Dr. Zhong so that she could better understand the SARS prevention and control measures. However, she had to deal with criticism and even accusations from Hong Kong citizens. She was also anxious because she couldn't get in touch with the Guangdong Provincial Department of Health.

Margaret Chan joined the Hong Kong Department of Health in 1978 and became its first female director in June 1994. In August 2003, she was selected as the Director-General of the WHO for the human-environmental protection agency, which was mainly responsible for the prevention and control of infectious diseases. From then on, she enjoyed international renown.

Speaking of Margaret Chan, Dr. Zhong remarked, "She is very enthusiastic about her work and very good at coordinating. She under-anticipated SARS at first, but one of her qualities is that she respects facts."

During the SARS period, Dr. Zhong met with her twice. Their first meeting was in March 2003. Chan asked Dr. Zhong about the occurrence and development of SARS, along with the countermeasures adopted in Guangdong.

The SARS outbreak began in Hong Kong in March 2003. At that time, Guangdong's fight against the disease had reached fever pitch, and Hong Kong was aware of the situation there. Hong Kong citizens blamed Margaret Chan and criticized the

Department of Health for delaying news releases about the epidemic. When Hong Kong citizens heard about the SARS outbreak, they began to call for advice on how to prevent it and get treated. As officials didn't know enough about the epidemic, their response was unsatisfactory, and the severity of the issue was not properly explained. Moreover, staff at Hong Kong health institutions didn't know about the ongoing epidemic in Guangzhou. At the time, Yang Weiqiang was the Director of the Hong Kong Hospital Authority. Hong Kong citizens criticized his work as ineffective, as he failed to post timely notifications.

Margaret Chan was eager to meet Dr. Zhong to understand the prevention and control measures for SARS. Finally, she received detailed, authentic first-hand information, including mature treatment knowledge. Grateful, she said to Dr. Zhong, "You have done much work for the prevention and control of SARS in Hong Kong. Thank you so much. Let's keep in touch."

On hearing about the SARS epidemic, Hong Kong had begun to pay attention to Dr. Zhong, who had always been truthful in what he explained about the epidemic in the media, particularly his explanation of the pathogen behind it, a coronavirus. As a result, some Hong Kong media outlets used various channels to collect information for reports about Dr. Zhong, especially his remarks, resulting in major reports with large photo spreads.

At that time, the Hong Kong journalists who interviewed Dr. Zhong reported from a variety of angles. Looking at some of the information and reports released by the Hong Kong media, Dr. Zhong found that most Hong Kong journalists respected the facts, so he was always sincere in what he explained with them about the development of SARS and the measures taken against it.

Hong Kong journalists were friendly toward Dr. Zhong, and they trusted him. Whenever there was a new question, they went to him to gain a better understanding. Since then, Dr. Zhong's thinking underwent a drastic change after that. He noticed that most of the reports on SARS released by the Hong Kong media were based on facts. The more honestly he spoke with them, the more truthfully they reported, which impressed him greatly and led to mutual trust. Because of this trust, which continues to this day, they got on very well. In particular, Dr. Zhong was gratified that Wen Jiabao, then Premier of the State Council, also advocated discussing facts with Hong Kong journalists.

Mutual trust was very important, but first, one had to be sincere. Dr. Zhong cited an example. At the beginning of 2004, four people in Guangzhou had symptoms of SARS, the second appearance of SARS after the spring of 2003. Immediately afterward, there was a fifth suspected SARS case.

All Hong Kong journalists gathered at the IRH, but they were later asked to leave because Dr. Zhong wouldn't see them. As a result, Dr. Zhong was in a bad mood. He pondered for a long time why the journalists were so concerned about this recurrence of SARS. Generally speaking, the standard recognized by the WHO was that if five cases re-occurred in the same place, it meant that the epidemic had returned, which was terrible. If SARS re-occurred in early 2004, it would put great pressure on the economy of Mainland China and Hong Kong. Thus, the journalists were particularly concerned about whether this fifth case was confirmed as SARS.

The fifth patient was a high school student. Dr. Zhong carefully examined him several times and made a preliminary judgment that he did not have SARS. So, he suggested to the IRH that if they kept it from the Hong Kong media for now, they might make a fuss when they went back.

The situation was urgent, and Dr. Zhong was decisive. "Please call all the journalists back. I will talk to them," he said.

When they returned, Dr. Zhong quickly explained the pathology of the fifth patient using PowerPoint slides, proving that he was not suffering from SARS. The next day, the journalists reported truthfully that the fifth suspected case in Guangzhou had now been ruled out. The tense atmosphere finally eased.

Dr. Zhong had given several lectures in Hong Kong. The first was in March 2003. The two Chairmen of the Hong Kong Biotechnology Organization asked him, "Could you please come to Hong Kong to share with us about SARS?" Dr. Zhong readily agreed. After attending an academic conference in Japan, he flew directly to Hong Kong.

Early that morning, more than 600 doctors arrived for the lecture, and they all enjoyed it very much. Dr. Zhong explained the history of SARS in detail, from discovery to outbreak, focusing on how the epidemic was controlled. It was early March, and the SARS outbreak had just occurred in Hong Kong. The doctors listened very carefully and asked many questions.

Dr. Zhong took time to explain the three rules of using corticosteroids to the doctors: it should be used only with the appropriate patients, at the right time, and with the correct dosage. If these three rules were followed, the effect would be positive. The Hong Kong doctors took down all of Dr. Zhong's suggestions. Later, they followed Dr. Zhong's thinking while treating SARS patients. However, some increased the dose of corticosteroids five to ten times.

Since the lecture was arranged on the fly, Dr. Zhong didn't have time to write down the content. He improvised, and he hadn't brought much material with him because he'd been in transit to Hong Kong. However, he was gratified that combining their experience of treating more than 120 SARS patients at the Prince of Wales Hospital, doctors from the Chinese University of Hong Kong wrote a detailed report of SARS cases, working overnight for several nights, and published the report in *The New England Journal of Medicine.*

The second meeting between Dr. Zhong and Margaret Chan was an intense and in-depth discussion on how to prevent SARS and treat patients in Hong Kong, along with specific measures that could be taken. Chan listened carefully to Dr. Zhong's suggestions.

When SARS reappeared in the spring of 2004, Dr. Zhong and the Guangdong SARS expert team were prepared. Much work had been done to deal with the possibility of a second outbreak. And in the two to three years after SARS, Dr. Zhong, experts in places like Guangdong, and the scientific researchers under his leadership had been conducting tracking experiments on the virus, including experiments in biology labs. All of the outcomes proved that their claim in 2003 that the pathogen was a coronavirus was correct.

At that time, someone said to Dr. Zhong that SARS was over, and facts had proved that he was doing the right thing. It was not necessary to do all these experiments with summaries, reflections, and even self-examination. However, Dr. Zhong insisted, "No, it's not true. The experiments are very necessary."

It was always necessary to speak with facts when addressing scientific issues. Dr. Zhong would never permit the slightest ambiguity.

⁓ 17 ⁓

THE PATHOGEN

The IRH's discovery was aligned with the conclusion of the WHO, published only five days earlier. *Practice is the sole criterion for testing the truth.* The Chinese people were very fond of this phrase. By 2020, it had accompanied China on its journey of Reform and Opening Up for over forty years. In 2003, the People's Republic of China had undergone a historical "trial by virus."

"Is the SARS pathogen a chlamydia or a mycoplasma? Is it a germ or a virus?" Surrounding this academic debate were the lives of thousands of patients. A plan was needed to fight the epidemic.

Dr. Zhong didn't care about the risk of "being objected to," nor the possibility of damaging his reputation. He simply suggested a different opinion. Under enormous pressure, he upheld his integrity as a scientist. His discovery that no flu symptoms were observed in the patients' throats escalated the debate.

Under Dr. Zhong's leadership, Guangdong experts worked tirelessly to identify the SARS pathogen. On the afternoon of April 11, 2003, the Guangzhou IRH planned to hold a media conference the next day, announcing that the pathogen had been confirmed in Guangdong as a new type of coronavirus.

On April 12, the Guangdong news media posted the message at significant locations, announcing it for the first time. On April 16, the WHO announced in Geneva that after joint efforts from scientific researchers worldwide, it had been discovered that the coronavirus could still cause the same disease when it was taken from SARS patients and given to macaques. The SARS pathogen was thus identified as a variant of a coronavirus. The establishment of an animal model was the "gold standard" of pathogen identification, just as a pathological section report was to a cancer diagnosis.

Since the outbreak of SARS, this was the most valuable progress made during this stage. The IRH had already tried treating the disease with antibiotics, but to no avail. If this treatment was used, many SARS patients would die. It was a matter of life and death, and Dr. Zhong simply could not back down. Who knew that holding one's ground could be so stressful?

The reason Dr. Zhong could insist on his view was that he had tested it in practice, and he was speaking based on facts. Should he choose to treat SARS using the nationally published treatment plan, no one could blame him or hold him responsible, even if the plan turned out to be wrong. After all, it was published by authoritative organizations and was meant to be practiced all over the nation. But should the wrong plan be announced and practiced; all exploration would cease. Even if dire consequences arose, none of the experts would take the blame – certainly not Dr. Zhong. However, he did not choose to play it safe.

One must wonder, what would have happened if he had been wrong? Wouldn't that be a huge blow to his reputation? People would surely have said, "Who are you to challenge the decision of the authoritative China CDC? And now that you got it wrong, how are you going to take responsibility?" If he had turned out to be wrong, Dr. Zhong would not only have been subjected to criminal accountability, he would also have been condemned by his own morality and conscience. At the time, Dr. Zhong did not speak for several days.

Because he voiced his concern and expressed his opinion that antibiotics should not be used against SARS, those who disagreed with him saw him as a loose cannon, and they chose to distance themselves from him. Those who thought that CCTV held the authority of the central government and dared not to question anything it announced saw Dr. Zhong as a rebel. He felt pressure creeping in from all directions. For decades, he had followed the Party's commands and acted by its volition. He trusted the CPC. But how could he just blindly follow its every word without questioning anything, and then write that off as loyalty?

Facing this challenge, he did not run away or concede. Instead, he chose to go down the most difficult path: he shouldered his responsibility as a scientist, even if it meant taking all of the pressure head on.

In 2009, to celebrate the 60th anniversary of the founding of People's Republic of China, eleven departments, including the Organization Department and the Publicity Department of the Central Committee of the CPC, held a "Double-100" selection event (100 Heroes of the Paragon that Made Key Contributions to the Founding of the People's Republic of China and 100 Inspirational Role Models after the Founding of the People's Republic of China). Dr. Zhong was elected as an Inspirational Role Model. He received high acclaim at the event. It was announced that "in the battle against SARS, he sought truth from facts and fought with unparalleled courage, volunteering to treat critical patients, formulating treatment plans, and saving lives. In doing so, he demonstrated a great sense of responsibility and scholarly professionalism as a scientist. During the debate regarding a critical issue when battling SARS, he ignored the controversy at the risk of tainting his own reputation, standing firm as a promoter of fact, upholding the conscience of a scientist."

No one would ever know the amount of stress hidden beneath this commendation. At the time, Dr. Zhong was faced with gargantuan pressure and misunderstandings.

In 2003, the WHO listed China as an "epidemic area" and issued a travel restriction, majorly hindering tourism, commerce, and political affairs. The annual China Import and Export Fair (Canton Fair) was held as usual that spring, but was met with minimal attendance. For fear of being infected, multiple regions across the nation applied complete lockdown measures, including Beijing and Shanghai. Roads were closed in villages and counties, practically cutting off all traffic. Without the flow of people and goods, how could anyone make a living? Social stability was put at risk. By that point, a simple cough was all it took to incite panic. During this period, there was a joke in Guangzhou: "An employee called his boss in the morning, saying that he might need the day off, as he had a fever. The boss said in a panic, 'Please do not come to the office! I will grant you a week's leave of absence.'" This actually happened in many instances. And worse, as soon as someone developed a fever, they would go to hospital without a second thought, which led to a huge waste of resources.

In early May, 2003, Dr. Zhong set off on a difficult journey. He was going to convince all relevant parties to reverse the incorrect decision by telling them the truth of what he was seeing on the front line.

On Chang'an Avenue in Beijing, at 9:00 in the morning, the situation was unusual. On normal days, the road was filled with a glut of slowly moving cars, but that was not the case that day. Five minutes passed, then ten minutes; fifty meters on the road, five hundred meters … Dr. Zhong only saw two cars passing by. He took out his camera and captured this eerie yet historical moment. The entire nation was in a state of panic. An authoritative voice was critical to stabilizing the situation, and that voice was telling people to use antibiotics against SARS. However, it had already been proven that this treatment was ineffective.

In early April 2003, Beijing was still besieged by SARS. Upon hearing that SARS was caused by a chlamydia and could be treated by antibiotics, people from all sectors of society breathed a sigh of relief. For them, the disease was not frightening anymore, and they could let down their guard. The restaurants that had once stood empty began to see more customers, as did malls, markets, and cinemas. People showed up once again. Both domestic and international flights saw a significant increase in passengers. People tried to return to their daily routine. Little did they know, a bigger wave of panic was approaching. If everyone returned to their norm and let down their guard, massive case numbers would be inevitable.

Experts soon realized that if the SARS pathogen was indeed a chlamydia, general medicines such as erythromycin would prove to be highly effective. Chlamydia pneumonia was usually sporadic, with little chance of causing death or achieving epidemic status. The first expert to promote the hypothesis that the SARS pathogen was chlamydia was Dr. Hong Tao, head virology researcher at China CDC and an academic at the Chinese Academy of Engineering. During an interview in late May 2003, he cordially told a journalist that he had many failures in his life. In his career as a scientist, he had seen much more failure than success. For this reason, he encouraged his fellow scholars to persevere when faced with difficulties and setbacks and to carry on their good work no matter what.

Dr. Hong disclosed that during multiple tests conducted on the corpses of SARS patients, he did not see any coronavirus under an electron microscope. Instead, he only managed to separate chlamydiae from the samples. "A lot of medical researchers were restless, including us," he admitted during the interview. The reason he managed to separate chlamydiae from the samples was that the SARS patients he processed suffered from secondary chlamydia infections. Obviously, Dr. Hong did not forge his results.

Born in July 1931, Dr. Hong Tao devoted over five decades to virology research. He presided over the foundation of the first Laboratory of Viral Pathogenesis and Biomedical Ultrastructure and achieved world-leading results in the study of Adult Diarrhea Rotavirus (ADRV) and Hemorrhagic Fever Virus. His research into SARS began on February 7, 2003. Dr. Hong observed via electron microscope that chlamydiae were present in the autopsy samples retrieved from SARS patients. He announced his results to the public on February 18.

Looking back on this event, Dr. Hong recalled that he asked the media to "leave a leeway of 20%" when publishing his findings. However, as it turned out, it was still not enough. The "leeway" was not granted. Given the urgent circumstances, Dr. Hong's words were considered definitive. CCTV and Xinhua News Agency quickly followed up with articles. "It has been basically confirmed that the SARS pathogen is a chlamydia." Soon after, the chlamydia theory was considered medical proof for the official conclusion that "SARS is not as great a threat as expected."

However, on April 16, 2003, the WHO announced in Geneva that after joint effort from scientific researchers worldwide, the SARS pathogen had been identified as a variant of a coronavirus. While Dr. Hong's conclusion was accepted by officials, he only analyzed samples from a few dead patients instead of living SARS patients. Even without firsthand evidence, he had decided to announce that a chlamydia was the SARS pathogen. However, Guangdong medical staff fighting on the front line against SARS did not agree with him, especially Dr. Zhong, who considered the conclusion to be baseless.

In May 2003, one of the biggest controversies in the field of medical research in China – the "battle" between the chlamydia theory and the coronavirus theory – came to a conclusion. Dr. Hong Tao's theory was proven to be false. Dr. Hong personally announced a correction to journalists: after genetic analysis, he was sure that the SARS pathogen was a coronavirus.

18

RECOGNITION FROM THE WHO

On returning to Guangdong from Hong Kong, Dr. Zhong was surprised to learn that when he was presenting about SARS to Hong Kong medical staff, a WHO officer had become interested in his presentation and was shocked by the content. This officer was Dr. Evans. He had not known that there was a doctor like Dr. Zhong in Guangdong. Dr. Zhong's research on SARS had reached a high level, drawing detailed conclusions on how to diagnose, treat, and prevent the disease, which was far beyond Dr. Evans' expectation. Evans returned to Beijing and praised Dr. Zhong's work. However, Dr. Zhong wasn't interested in this grandiose affirmation. "Anyway, I had finished my presentation. My work was done," he said.

At that time, there were no answers anywhere in the world regarding what kind of virus SARS was and how to prevent and control it. For a while, no one could identify it. At the end of March 2003, there were sporadic SARS cases in several countries and regions, and it quickly spread to Australia, Singapore, Canada, Taiwan, and Hong Kong.

Before his presentation, the WHO did not know Dr. Zhong very well, nor his scientific measures for the prevention and control of SARS. Some Hong Kong media outlets thought that the epidemic on the Mainland was a "pneumonic plague." Dr. Zhong corrected them, saying that there was no evidence of adenovirus in the outbreak, and that the claim was thus appalling. As a result, WHO officers were intrigued by Dr. Zhong's presentation, and they wanted to hear more. Dr. Evans was strongly urged to go to Mainland of China. In early April 2003, Evans and his team visited Guangdong. Huang Qingdao, then Director of the Guangdong Provincial Department of Health, received them. According to Evans' wishes, Huang Qingdao invited two experts for a discussion. One was Dr. Zhong, and the other was Xu Ruiheng, an authoritative expert from the Guangdong Provincial Center for Disease Control and Prevention.

Before getting to know Dr. Zhong, the WHO had major doubts about SARS prevention and treatment in Guangdong, which Evans and his team expressed directly. The first doubt was whether many SARS patients in Guangdong had been reported, and the second was whether many people had died from SARS there. Dr. Zhong had anticipated the sort of questions Evans might raise, so he was well prepared to deal with them. He made a set of informative, intuitive, and persuasive PowerPoint slides from a large amount of data on prevention and control since the emergence of SARS. The slides gave a detailed description of the characteristics of SARS, how to conduct medical prevention and control, and the effective measures used to achieve a low mortality rate.

Although it was the first time that Dr. Zhong had come into contact with Evans, he remarked, "He is very experienced. I know what the WHO wanted to hear, so when I gave my explanations, he must have thought, 'What you have done goes beyond all of our expectations.'"

Dr. Zhong's English was proficient and witty. Evans and his team found his explanations to be quite reasonable. Dr. Zhong provided many thorough, feasible, and reliable treatment plans. This was extremely rare literature, and that was why the WHO officers were so surprised. In addition, Dr. Evans also discovered that Guangdong had done an excellent job of prevention. This surprising, comprehensive information surprised the WHO team.

Evans was full of admiration. "Knowledge was exchanged for lives and blood," he observed.

When the WHO inspection in Guangdong was complete, Dr. Evans told journalists that what they had discovered was totally unexpected and somewhat shocking. He said, "Dr. Zhong has extensive experience, which is a valuable asset in the global fight against SARS. Guangdong has done a good deal of work in the prevention and treatment of the disease."

Evans and his team left Guangdong but stayed in China, traveling north to Beijing, where they spoke highly of Dr. Zhong's work to the Chinese officials who received them. They expressed surprise over the prevention and treatment of SARS in Guangdong.

Dr. Zhong was not interested in the commendation Evans gave him in person, because his mind was on the epidemic and his patients. He felt that his work was done once he had convinced the WHO that his theories and methods were effective, even though some people might not necessarily agree.

To this day, Dr. Zhong still does not know what Dr. Evans said about him when he arrived in Beijing. He didn't have time to consider Evans' subsequent actions. However, his first contact with the WHO convinced them of the credibility of the Chinese doctors. Dr. Zhong did all of this very naturally and confidently. He was affirmed, but he did not rest satisfied.

"I think other than letting them know what we are doing and telling them the truth." Dr. Zhong used a habitual gesture to help him emphasize the tone – a vertical index finger positioned very close to the bridge of his nose, "the most important thing is to solve problems."

SARS, a global medical challenge, originated in China. The Chinese found the answer to it themselves, proving their world-leading exploration in science and technology. Overcoming SARS was achieved by the Chinese themselves. Dr. Zhong was a Chinese expert who dared to speak out, and a Chinese icon in the eyes of the WHO. This was why Dr. Evans, and his colleagues were impressed.

Dr. Zhong was delighted that since the emergence of SARS, foreigners who had attended his presentation had been surprised by what he said. It gave him a feeling similar to the fusion and echo that he felt from his students. Throughout the entire SARS outbreak period, he felt it on several different occasions.

The format and style of the presentation Dr. Zhong had designed followed the Western way of thinking: scientific concepts, accurate data and examples, and clear description of methods, which he had picked up during his studies in the UK. In the eyes of Westerners, there was no doubt that the presentation was in line with international advanced academic standards. This was why foreign experts were surprised and excited when they heard it.

In addition to the acclaim from the WHO, the international media had also reported the emergence of SARS and Dr. Zhong's work in China with an air of surprise. The British newspaper *The Times* commented that Dr. Zhong not only dared to tell the truth, but had also searched tirelessly for the pathogen, studying the routes of infection, and querying why it was being transmitted to humans.

Through the very comprehensive and satisfactory inspection by Dr. Evans and his team, the WHO affirmed that the conclusion reached by Dr. Zhong and the Guangdong experts was sound and scientific. However, if either of two points had been lacking, the WHO wouldn't have been convinced. The first was respecting facts. How was SARS developing? In response, Dr. Zhong laid out the facts. As a first line expert, he had seen it with his own eyes. The second was to make timely summaries. It was from a summary that Guangdong experts discovered how SARS spread, meaning that they could convert the initial tentative treatment to effective control later on, and summarize their findings for broad distribution.

19

SPEAKING THE TRUTH

"The truth is that the disease is still spreading, our medical staff are still under-equipped, and the pathogen is yet to be found." A "loose cannon" had been set off at the welcoming press conference for the WHO experts in Beijing. The truth Dr. Zhong presented was terrifying.

On the Qingming Festival of 2003, Dr. Zhong was visiting his parents' graves with his family. "Dad, what should I do? I want to tell the truth, but I can't," he said, arms crossed over his chest as he stood in front of the tomb of his father, Zhong Shifan. He had never felt so hesitant. Usually, he remained silent at the resting place of his parents, who had dedicated their lives to medical research in China. During such hard times, with the epidemic wreaking havoc and the medical staff falling, Dr. Zhong found it hard to express his depression. At his side, his wife Li Shaofen watched in pained silence.

Dr. Zhong missed his parents. His father had always been his beacon of justice, conscience, and truth. However, at that moment, Dr. Zhong found himself shrouded in confusion, hesitation, struggle, and torment. "Dad, can you point me in the right direction from beyond the grave?" Dr. Zhong would have given anything to have his father's spirit guide him in such turbulent times.

In April 2003, SARS was yet to be contained, but rumors of the epidemic being controlled were circulating. This deviation from the truth was burning Dr. Zhong from the inside. In mid-April, tensions among Guangzhou citizens were dissipating, but unrest was rising to a boiling point in Beijing. Residents of the capital were panicking due to the lack of information, while government officials were worried about the instability caused by the spread of the disease.

The epidemic was affecting all of humanity, and containing it required a joint effort. The situation had to be tackled, or humanity would be doomed. For Dr. Zhong, this was the ultimate truth. Seeing the overall situation, he was worried sick. The burden of responsibility lay on his shoulder like a boulder.

When Dr. Evans and the other WHO experts went to Beijing after observing the situation in Guangzhou, journalists from all over the world met them there. With great excitement, Dr. Evans told everyone how he had discovered Dr. Zhong. Before the media conference, a grand meeting had been held in Beijing. During this meeting, Dr. Evans and his colleagues received information from the Chinese government indicating that the epidemic had been controlled, medical staff were now working with proper protection, and the pathogen had been identified. Dr. Evans was relieved.

Before the WHO representatives arrived in Beijing, this information had already spread across China. At that time, the medical team led by Dr. Zhong was still in Guangzhou, trying to contain SARS. Hearing this authoritative announcement, Dr. Zhong was taken aback. A notice arrived from Beijing, asking for his presence at the press conference for the WHO officers and journalists from China and elsewhere. It was set to take place over two days.

At 10:30 am, the conference began at the State Council Information Office (SCIO). The room was quiet, and the atmosphere was heavy. Cameras from all over China and the rest of the world pointed directly at Dr. Zhong. His voice was transmitted to every corner of the globe. He said, "As a doctor, I found our collaboration with the WHO to be very pleasant." With a certain solemnity, he went on, "We discussed three aspects of the problem. The first was the diagnosis and treatment of SARS, the second was epidemiological patterns, and the third addressed etiology. By now, over 50% of SARS patients are in Guangdong. The WHO is very interested in the diagnosis of the disease, the treatment of patients (especially in the early stage), and the methods of lowering the death rate."

Then, an expert from the WHO remarked that with Dr. Zhong's guidance, the Guangdong expert group had summarized a set of treatment plans, which would play an indicative role in the fight against SARS all over the world. Needless to say, this was conclusive praise for Dr. Zhong's and the Guangdong expert group's efforts.

Dr. Zhong informed the journalists that he had engaged in high-level communication with Dr. Evans' team. In a mere five days, they had already established a friendly relationship. Dr. Zhong also expressed his hope of building a closer relationship between China and the WHO. It was clear that they all had the same goal: to fight human disease.

As soon as Dr. Zhong finished his speech, a foreign journalist asked the big question about patient numbers. Dr. Zhong answered, "There are indeed some patients that were not diagnosed. This is because some of our doctors do not specialize in this aspect, and they could not recognize the disease." Upon hearing this, the confused journalists bombarded Dr. Zhong with more questions. Speaking from the government's standpoint, Dr. Zhong patiently and carefully answered all of them, providing much-needed explanations.

Furthermore, he said, "As an expert in medical science, I believe we can control this disease, as long as we carry out quarantine procedures. Now, you have all heard about this disease in China. It has spread to quite a few places. However, the reported numbers are still quite low. Why? You have to understand that some patients were transferred to other departments, and they could only be diagnosed after a certain amount of time." This explanation was given to address the question regarding the truthfulness of the reported numbers, while at the same time explaining why the numbers might be inaccurate.

The first day of the conference came to an end. On the second day, the second session went ahead as scheduled, but on a considerably smaller scale, with around seventy people attending. They were mainly journalists from Japan, Hong Kong, and Taiwan. Despite the smaller audience, the questions asked were much trickier to answer. From the beginning, some journalists asked the same questions as the day before, obviously not satisfied with the answers. By this point, the journalists were much more direct in their methods, resulting in questions like "In your opinion, has the epidemic been successfully contained?"

Dr. Zhong's skillful answers on the first day put many of the officials' minds at ease, and many of them did not attend the second day of the conference. However, as the questions became increasingly sharper, Dr. Zhong decided not to hold back anymore. "Contained? It has not been contained *at all*."

The audience erupted. The "loose cannon" that was Dr. Zhong had finally fired its shot. Also in the room was a friend of his, who could not help but quiver at the tension. As Dr. Zhong continued to speak, the audience quietened down. "It is critical that we define what can be counted as 'successfully contained.' At this point, we have no means of prevention, and we have no significant plans for treatment. Most importantly, we have no idea what the pathogen is. The disease is still on the loose, so how can we possibly say that it has been contained?" With an immense sense of gravity, he added, "I can only say that it has been hindered, but definitely not controlled."

With this viewpoint aired, the journalists continued with their questions. An overseas journalist asked, "Are the medical staff in China properly protected and equipped?"

Dr. Zhong immediately answered, "No." This question contained an issue of great importance. How could the epidemic be controlled when even the medical staff were not properly equipped and protected? Subsequently, Dr. Zhong shared more of his ideas. "We must put in more effort regarding research into the pathogen. We must protect our medical workers, and we must bolster our communication with other countries." Several local and Hong Kong media outlets published his words.

On the morning of April 14, 2003, then General Secretary of the CPC Central Committee Hu Jintao visited Guangdong and held a meeting with several medical experts. During the meeting, he made a speech that went down in history. "We are very concerned about the threat posed to the health of our people by SARS, but at the same time, we are relieved to see that our medical staff have done their best, facilitating the speedy recovery of many patients," he said.

Accompanied by then local officials Mr. Zhang Dejiang and Mr. Huang Huahua, Hu Jintao visited the Guangdong Provincial Center for Disease Control and Prevention. There, he held a meeting with representatives from 23 frontline SARS hospitals. The event was reported on Xinwen Lianbo on CCTV, and it became known around the country.

Dr. Ye Guangchun, then Director of the First Affiliated Hospital of Guangzhou Medical University, was one of the designated speakers at the meeting. He told Hu Jintao about the treatment of SARS patients at the First Affiliated Hospital of Guangzhou Medical University and the IRH, and he mentioned that many medical staff had voluntarily given up their vacation and family time, risking their lives to treat SARS patients. During his report, he said that in the early stages of the epidemic, for every intubation treatment given to a SARS patient, an average of three medical staff from the ICU were infected. However, the angels in white did not falter or cower. They returned to their duties as soon as they recovered, without a single word of complaint. This applied to all the medical staff in Guangdong.

The report was rather brief, yet Hu Jintao paid attention. After his report, Dr. Ye stood aside silently, waiting to hear the response. To his surprise, Mr. Hu pointed at him, saying, "It seems that there are still some things you wanted to say. Is there something you would like to add?"

This question blew Dr. Ye's silence to pieces. He pointed out the issue of international coordination, a problem to which he had given much thought. This had also been one of Dr. Zhong's major concerns since the first outbreak of SARS. Dr. Ye said that SARS was a threat to the health of humankind. Therefore, coordination among the provinces of China and among all the countries of the world was critical to its containment. After a brief moment of contemplation, Hu Jintao said, "If that's the case, then total coordination we shall have."

The moment the meeting concluded, Dr. Ye dialed Dr. Zhong's number on his phone, very excited. He had barely finished his sentence before an overjoyed Dr. Zhong exclaimed, "I am so happy!"

After much grief and anticipation, the day had finally arrived. International coordination – Dr. Zhong's primary goal – had finally been realized. Satisfied, he hung up the phone. Surrounded by nothing but utter silence, he could barely hold back his tears.

According to Dr. Zhong, the first step in the fight against SARS was the application of epidemiology, with collaboration between pathological and clinical parties being the most critical. This was the only way to identify its true pathogen. It would take international coordination and the combined scientific effort of all the countries in the world to overcome SARS.

When the SARS epidemic first started, Dr. Zhong had already voiced his opinions. However, he faced much pressure for his openness. This pressure came from multiple sources, with criticism against him being the most prevalent. He immersed himself in his work, but the stress was definitely there. And now, the instructions and decisions from the central government proved that he was correct.

He had begun to cooperate with Hong Kong University as preparation for international collaboration, but he was misunderstood for that. Even so, he still held to his belief that obtaining academic support to solve the problem as quickly as possible was the right thing to do.

On April 11, 2003, a joint announcement was made by Mainland China and the Hong Kong Department of Health in Guangdong, confirming that the SARS pathogen was a strain of a coronavirus. Three days earlier, on April 8, experts from Hong Kong and the USA had already announced this finding. Little did everyone know; the discovery was first made by Chinese researchers. On February 26, 2003, Dr. Zhu Qingyu, Dr. Yang Ruifu, and their colleagues had already found the virus in the Institute for Microbial Epidemiology at the Academy of Military Medical Sciences. Unfortunately, due to their attempts at repeating their observation results, they delayed the publication of this finding.

In the July 2003 issue of *Science*, an article was titled "China's Missed Chance." It explained that the Academy of Military Medical Sciences of China were the first to discover the SARS pathogen, yet they remained silent, which resulted in the USA announcing the findings. Despite this, reports on the Internet and other platforms showed that it was China that first made the discovery.

In late April 2003, while SARS was spreading from Beijing to the rest of China, the CPC Central Committee and the State Council made a series of decisions, emphasizing that the government must be responsible in its actions and be proactive in detecting and reporting SARS cases. They also announced that any attempts at concealing the true situation should not be tolerated. The State Council decided that SARS should be regarded as a notifiable infectious disease, to be managed under the appropriate laws. The central government also acknowledged that some regions were "lacking in working mechanisms such as data analysis, case monitoring, and situation tracking, leading to egregious errors in SARS statistics and failure to report correct figures." Corresponding punishments were issued. By decision of the State Council, the frequency of announcements regarding the SARS situation was updated from once every five days to once a day, in accordance with the requirements of the WHO.

20

THE FACE-TO-FACE INTERVIEW

The central government began to see the importance of real reports about SARS. China Central Television News Channel (CCTV) made a major move and played to powerful public opinion. The most influential show on CCTV at the time was "Face to Face," a feature-length interview program hosted by Wang Zhi as part of the *Oriental Horizon* series. Talking about his meeting with Wang Zhi, Dr. Zhong said, "To me, it didn't matter whether he and I were face to face. What counted was his pursuit of a career and his professionalism. Why do I say that? Before he entered the ward, he had come to me many times, and I never had time to talk to him. He still came every day. Later, I asked him if he came to see the patients. He replied 'Yes.'"

On April 15, 2003, Wang Zhi's "Face to Face" was shown to the Guangzhou IRH. The interview with Dr. Zhong was not Wang Zhi's original plan, because he didn't know much about Dr. Zhong at that time. The show used real people to interpret news and witness history, so who better to talk about fighting SARS than him? Wang Zhi had heard about Dr. Zhong from others, so he decided to interview him.

On April 26, the show was broadcast. In addition to understanding Dr. Zhong's heroic deeds in battling and challenging the disease, the audience also saw the many twists and turns in the fight against SARS—the pathogen, international cooperation, and the debate between control and containment.

In the early morning of April 16, 2003, Wang Zhi followed Dr. Zhong up the staircase from the first floor to the eighth floor. He wondered how this 66-year-old expert could go so fast. The strong, young television host was out of breath as he tried to keep up with Dr. Zhong.

As Wang Zhi had been following Dr. Zhong all the way, Dr. Zhong thought, "Will he dare to follow me into the SARS isolation ward?"

"Are you coming in?"

"Of course."

Their exchange was as simple as that.

"OK, then. Come in." Dr. Zhong's initial intention had been to test Wang Zhi to see if he was a coward, so this impressed him. "Good job!"

Wang Zhi entered the ward and quickly changed clothes based on a nurse's instructions. The sound recordist outside the ward hurriedly called the TV station to notify them. Wang Zhi had changed his clothes. His colleagues outside waited anxiously for the reply from the TV station. Wang Zhi was standing in front of the second door. One more door to go, just a step forward, there were beds of SARS patients, a world of despair where whiteness and fear seeped into their very marrow. Doctors and nurses were busy taking care of the patients.

Wang Zhi stepped inside, raised his camera, and recorded Dr. Zhong and his colleagues, the white-clad angels fighting on the front. These were touching historical scenes that shocked the Chinese nation. Wang later told the media that he and his colleagues spent more than an hour in the SARS ward that day. Right beside the SARS patients, they interviewed the medical staff who were caring for the patients, gathering every detail possible until the camera ran out of batteries. Everything around them – the protective suits covering the medical workers' bodies and the solemn expression on Dr. Zhong's face – told them that this was the real front line in the fight against SARS. This was the place where the patients came face to face with death, and where white-clad angels used all their energy to return their dying patients to the world. It was this experience of close filming and fighting together that allowed Dr. Zhong and Wang Zhi to initiate a dialogue of trust.

Dr. Zhong recalled that Wang Zhi came to the SARS ward every day after his initial visit. When he saw that Dr. Zhong had some free time, he would go to him. Dr. Zhong began to see how dedicated and passionate Wang Zhi was about his career, so he felt that he should support him. Dr. Zhong recalled, "Back then, I thought that when a person has such high expectations and intense pursuit of his career, I had a duty to support him. Later, he came to my house and tried his best to interview my wife, but she turned him down quite adamantly. He wanted to invite her out for meals and tea, trying to get to know her. Even though he had no success, he was still very persistent. What touched me was not the show itself, but his dedication to his career."

Dr. Zhong went on, "The spirit of perseverance and persistence is essential for a journalist. It's the same for people in other industries. With such a spirit, a person will surely succeed."

After the show, a journalist interviewed Wang Zhi and asked him to comment on the doctor. "Dr. Zhong is beyond reach for a person like me. I think he is perfect. He has both great courage and wisdom." Clearly, Wang Zhi's days in Guangzhou touched him deeply. He explained that he was moved by the daily stories of the front line medical staff. They were the loveliest and most respectable people in the battle against SARS. "If tears can explain, the Pearl River would rise for sure." When he conducted the interview at the IRH, he even said to the doctors there, "If we get infected, we want to be hospitalized here."

The synthesis of this episode of "Face to Face" took place in Beijing. In mid-April 2003, Dr. Zhong met Wang Zhi there. "He dragged me to a hotel, saying he had something to ask me." However, Wang Zhi didn't ask right away, which puzzled the busy Dr. Zhong. "I had no idea what he was going to ask me. I planned to go back to Guangzhou at 4:00 pm that day, but he took me to the TV station at about 1:00 pm and told me he would talk to me there." Dr. Zhong had no idea what "Face to Face" was. He was so busy all day that he had almost no knowledge of the show. However, he was willing to listen to Wang Zhi.

"He once told someone else that being able to interview me was like catching a big fish," Dr. Zhong said, amused. "I don't know if this is a common media saying. It's probably because I can answer the questions practically." By this time, Dr. Zhong had a good impression of Wang Zhi. And coming from the front line of treating SARS patients, he didn't care what others said about him, as he knew the reality of the situation. If there were still people pointing fingers when faced with facts, did they really understand what was happening on the front line?

Dr. Zhong's attitude was tough. For him, if there was pressure, it was from the professional responsibility of saving lives and helping the sick. "I believe the most important thing is the patients' lives," he said, "As long as I'm saving patients' lives, I'm fine with whatever you say about me. Everything else is secondary. As long as you recognize that I helped people recover, I don't care what you think of me." He even refused to put on makeup for the filming, even though he looked exhausted. When Wang Zhi was putting some on, Dr. Zhong just sat beside him saying, "Hurry up. I have to go after the show is done."

Dr. Zhong had always spoken from an objective, impartial point of view about problems in the medical industry, and he never tolerated a lack of principle. Once, at a conference, he said something related to infectious diseases, and he linked it to SARS. He mentioned that during the SARS period, none of the medical staff resigned or took time off work. Why? "Because we doctors have a conscience." The more than 400 people at the conference venue applauded loudly. Dr. Zhong had expressed exactly what was on their minds. He spoke of injustice with tears in his eyes, and he criticized false boasts in a cold tone. He said that the media's attitude toward medical staff often changed 180° and that publicity blindly followed trends. He cited a real life example. There was a young female doctor named Liu Xiaoqing at the IRH. When the SARS epidemic was at its worst, she had to go to a hospital where the medical staff were heavily infected to transfer six SARS patients to the IRH. Dr. Zhong said to her, "OK, you can transfer them all over." In the end, only five patients were brought in, and there was a seriously ill driver. Dr. Liu came to Dr. Zhong and said that she wanted to bring the driver in as well. Dr. Zhong agreed. "Just do what you think is best," he said. "You have my support."

Dr. Zhong later recalled that he had told this story in detail on the "Face to Face" show as he explained doctors' feelings about their patients. "I cried while I was telling the story. Wang Zhi listened with great emotion, because he wanted to talk more about the medical staff who were treating SARS patients. That was the moment when they needed to hold on the most. They were risking their lives to save SARS patients, and many of them collapsed on the front line."

Later on, Dr. Liu Xiaoqing went to fetch the driver, who was seriously ill, but there was not enough manpower. Many people were afraid to get close to SARS patients at that time, and they would only observe them from outside through windows. As a result, many SARS patients wanted to be hospitalized at the IRH. Over there, they were immediately put at ease, and they had no fear because nurses personally came to them, talking to them and comforting them, which was a completely different feeling.

The slender Dr. Liu Xiaoqing carried the heavy stretcher by herself. She couldn't remember a day when she had a good rest. The driver, whose life was at stake, was so tall and heavy that the stretcher seemed to be sinking and sagging. Everything was covered in the darkness of the night. When was such a huge hospital ever so deserted? The air of death threatened to overwhelm people's consciousness. Dr. Liu Xiaoqing gritted her teeth and stepped forward. Carrying the stretcher, she was holding the driver's life in her hands.

Dr. Liu's bravery touched Dr. Zhong deeply. He remembered everything about that day. Now, the light outside the window was no longer bright, but the movements of a person who had seen extraordinary things merged into the fiery sunset.

21

THE GREATEST POLITICS IS TO DO OUR JOBS

When the journalist Wang Zhi interviewed Dr. Zhong, he asked, "When you fell sick, were you frightened?"

Dr. Zhong responded with a rare show of frustration. With a wave of his hand, he answered, "If you're going to continue obsessing over this question, I will stop this interview right now. I never thought about it. I was too busy saving our patients."

As it happened, another question from Wang Zhi apparently hit a little too close to home. "Do you care about politics?"

With his usual frankness, Dr. Zhong answered without a second thought, "I think the greatest politics is to do our jobs and stop the disease in its tracks. We all have our own 'politics.' Let's take you as an example. For you, the greatest politics is to conduct good interviews that will be enjoyed by your audience. You give your best when doing your job. That's the greatest politics."

Wang Zhi followed up with another question. "It was mid-February 2003. Our government announced that a type of chlamydia might have caused this disease. Why did you disagree with that conclusion?"

Dr. Zhong answered with a fact. "At first, the announcement was that SARS *was* caused by a type of chlamydia, not *might have been*. They were decisive. They also said that with proper anti-chlamydia medicines and enough time, say two weeks, the problem would definitely be solved. I wondered if this conclusion was based on sufficient investigation and research and if it was drafted from clinical data. From our clinical observation, there were two main points that did not fit the symptoms of chlamydia pneumonia. First, chlamydia pneumonia cases of such severity were rarely seen, and second, we had used a decent amount of anti-chlamydia medicine to treat patients, yet they were not effective at all. For this reason, I concluded that SARS could not be attributed to a chlamydia infection, unless it was a rare variant of chlamydia."

Next, Wang Zhi raised a rather critical issue. "At that time, the chlamydia theory was confirmed by quite an authoritative source."

Without any hesitation, Dr. Zhong responded, "In the world of academics, we must voice the facts – the truth. However, there will be times when the most authoritative voice does not align with the truth. In such cases, we must first respect the truth, not the authoritative voice."

Wang Zhi followed up with another statement. "But from the viewpoint of interpersonal relationships, or some other considerations and concerns, you could have stayed silent. You could have stayed put."

What happened next was a brilliant display of Dr. Zhong's integrity, shocking many who were watching the interview. Again, without any hesitation, he answered. "Yes, I could have done that. Most definitely. But this was no ordinary academic discourse. There were lives depending on it. If we had adopted the wrong method of treatment, more people would have died. Under such circumstances, we didn't have any choice except to depend on the things we saw and the experience we gathered and to treat our patients accordingly."

Looking back on this session, Dr. Zhong remarked, "It was a while after the interview that I noticed that the specific episode of 'Face to Face' drew quite a lot of attention. Many TV stations aired it. *Yangcheng Evening News* even published some of my answers. Wang Zhi was really put under the spotlight."

This was all that he could recall about an interview that mattered so much. It was obvious that he didn't really pay much attention to the press he got, especially the compliments and acclaim. When he was criticized, as long as he believed that he had done the right thing, he simply brushed it off with a, "How come I have never heard of this?"

The media chased Dr. Zhong for his prestige and integrity. He always did and said the right thing. No matter how bad the situation, no matter how sharp the question, he remained professional and never took it personally. He didn't want to see anyone receive overly harsh punishment for something they said, no matter if it was advice or criticism. To ensure justice, to educate society, and to promote civil practices were his ultimate goals.

Recalling his milestone interview with Wang Zhi, Dr. Zhong was lost in thought. "Later on, I finally understood why he had asked those questions. It was because I was much 'sharper' than others." Even after so many years, upon hearing words like "stability," "truth," and "politics," it still seemed that he had something to say.

Stability was the final goal. But how should it be achieved? During the SARS epidemic, this question plagued him constantly. "By then, there was much controversy regarding this issue. Which is better for the stability of society? A hush-up? Or a full disclosure? From the very beginning, I was in favor of the full-disclosure."

It was precisely that interview on "Face to Face" that got Dr. Zhong elected as one of CCTV's Top 10 Inspiring Role Models of China of 2003. Inspiration was what the audience felt. That episode of the show confronted many issues head-on, such as democratic politics and the medical system. In other words, it was filled to the brim with politics.

Dr. Zhong's cellphone was ringing non-stop, like an impatient boss. He needed to return to his job. He answered calls quickly. "Yes, I'll be there very soon." Just before he left, he said, "Such matters need more discussion and contemplation. I did not know the issue would be this complex." This "issue" was most likely Wang Zhi's questions.

It was 2008, the thirtieth year of Reform and Opening Up. As one of the most prominent figures to experience those three decades first hand, Dr. Zhong had been receiving invitations for interviews from all over the place, ever since the year had begun. Among the invitations, many were from Guangdong. At the award ceremony held by Nanfang Daily Newspaper Group Co., Ltd. for 30 Figures of the 30 Years and 30 Influential Figures in the 30 Years of Reform and Opening Up, Dr. Zhong gave a speech as the Top Hero in the Fight against SARS. Again, he expressed the opinion that he had always held. "The reason people voted for me is because I dare to speak the truth. Although the truth is not always 'correct,' it is still my go-to way of handling things. Because the value of the truth lies not in its correctness, but in its honesty. I believe that in a group, a company, or a family, everyone must tell the truth. When we talk about truth, many will take it as 'fact.' For me, that's not the case, because many of the things I said were met with heavy criticism." Dr. Zhong also mentioned his speech during the 2009 Two Sessions as a representative of the National People's Congress of Guangdong, which had the same theme.

There was no going back when it comes to reform. It needed heroes who took it upon themselves to make it happen.

22

INTERNATIONAL ACCLAIM

In 2003, under pressure from international public opinion about China and out of a strong sense of responsibility to the country and as a medical expert and citizen, Dr. Zhong presented the work and efforts of the Chinese government to international peers in a factual manner. He took this responsibility voluntarily and consciously.

According to statistics, from March 31 to April 12, 2003, four major Western media outlets – *The Washington Post, The New York Times,* CNN, and BBC radio – released 202 reports on the SARS epidemic in China. Among them, 132 were negative, accounting for 65%; 46 were public accusations, accounting for 23%; 69 were neutral reports, accounting for 34%; and only one was positive. Some scholars considered this to be the largest wave of anti-China sentiment since the late 1980s.

During the SARS epidemic period, Dr. Zhong was engaged in frontline clinical treatment, and he was busy visiting many countries and regions, seeking every opportunity to promote China's prevention and treatment of the disease. With China's practical actions and his success in combating SARS in Guangdong, he won international acclaim.

He was invited to Australia, Denmark, the USA, Japan, Singapore, Malaysia, the Netherlands, Switzerland, and Sweden, as well as Hong Kong and Macau. His trips were all short, because he was always thinking about the epidemic in Guangdong and other regions in China. For example, he spent only one day in Geneva and the UK, and the rest of the time was spent in transit.

In normal life, many people would ask him how a certain place looked, as he had been to many countries. This was difficult for him to answer, because when he was in a place, he tended to rush among three locations, the airport, conference venue, and hotel. If it was a one-day trip, it was only from the airport and the conference venue. With such a tight schedule, how would he have the time and enthusiasm to stop for sightseeing? However, if you asked him how and what he had spoken about there and what the feedback was like, no matter how many years had passed, it remained fresh in his memory. People were always impressed by his excellent memory.

Dr. Zhong went to Japan first to speak about SARS, but the real academic discussion on the illness overseas was in the US. He recalled this as he reclined on a couch, one of the few times he could rest. He slowed his voice and fell into a long, lingering memory. It was the end of 2008, and he was 72 years old, but his memory was still crystal clear.

The International Conference of the American Thoracic Society was held in Seattle in May 2003. It was the conference that made the deepest impression on him – so deep that he would not forget it for as long as he lived. His provisional invitation from the US was so urgent that it arrived only twenty days before the conference. Dr. Zhong was not just a participant. It was a global-scale academic conference, and he had to write a speech to explain the SARS epidemic to the world. He felt underprepared.

"I can do it," he said, trying to cheer himself up with confidence.

However, Dr. Zhong was well prepared mentally. At that time, in the USA, there had been many stories about SARS in China. He wanted to go and tell the Americans that China's fight against the disease was successful. In the eyes of the Americans, there was no doubt that Dr. Zhong belonged to the "infected region" of China and that he would be subject to travel restrictions. He went directly to the US Consulate General in Guangzhou to explain that he had been invited to a conference in the US. May 2003 was the month when SARS had just appeared in the US. He said to a US consul, "China has some proven experience to present, so you should issue me a visa." And so, at the time when the world was on guard against SARS, the US Consulate General in Guangzhou made an exception and granted a visa to him, a Chinese expert who was on the front line of treatment and exposure to SARS patients.

However, Dr. Zhong was still worried that he would not be able to pass through US customs. When a customs officer asked him if he was from China, he replied frankly, "Yes."

The blue-eyed American immediately became interested. "How is the research into SARS going in your country?"

"We are working on it. That's what I've come here for. Don't worry. I have no health problems or fever."

The American smiled and waved him through.

Americans were friendly to Dr. Zhong and the friendliness was contagious. When he opened his mouth to speak, people were naturally disposed to like him.

Two things made a strong impression on him in Seattle. The first was that when he was waiting in the lobby with many other people before the conference started, he noticed a magazine called *US News & World Report*. He took it and flipped it through, and he saw an article titled "SARS is China's weapon to destroy the world." It was a long story about someone at the Chinese Academy of Military Medical Sciences who had discovered a biological virus, SARS. The article also claimed that the SARS virus was a biological weapon that China used to destroy the world.

He was furious, and he could not imagine why the American press would vilify China to such an extent for the sake of political propaganda. He put the false report down to the unpleasant diplomatic relations between China and the US in 2003.

At the conference, there were more than 2,000 thoracic medicine experts from various countries and regions worldwide. Dr. Zhong was added to the list of speakers on an ad hoc basis. The title of his speech was "SARS in China." The order and content of the conference speeches had been decided a year before. In order to insert Dr. Zhong's contribution, the organizer took time out at noon and arranged a large conference room accommodating 2,000 people.

As Dr. Zhong began to speak, the room soon filled up. They didn't stop coming, even sitting on the floor and standing in the aisles. More and more people gathered, and it became crowded. The staff had to set up a gate post to stop people from coming in.

The lobby outside the conference room was also full of people. The staff had to pull the line for live TV from the fourth floor, where the conference room was located, to the second floor, so that people on the first floor were also able to hear Dr. Zhong's speech. People were keen to hear what he had to say about the SARS situation in China.

Initially, Dr. Zhong planned to explain the facts about China's fight against SARS to the international community, hoping to win the world's respect and understanding. However, after reading the magazine article, unquenchable indignation made him determined to clarify that SARS in China was not as horrible as some people with ulterior motives made it out to be.

"We've done a lot of work, and the mortality rate of the disease is now very low." Dr. Zhong's fluent English rang out loud and clear. Many people stood up to ask him questions, which he found easy to answer.

"How did SARS emerge?"

"How is China dealing with the epidemic?"

Dr. Zhong's speech was highly acclaimed by medical authorities from the USA and many other countries and regions who attended the conference. An official from the US Centers for Disease Control and Prevention subsequently invited him to hold a press conference on SARS to answer questions from American journalists. His confident, humorous English expressions made the journalists warm to him. They felt a sense of affection for Dr. Zhong, an expert from the epidemic region, and they were impressed by him. Immediately afterwards, news agencies including Deutsche Presse-Agentur and the Associated Press conducted special interviews with Dr. Zhong, along with various American journalists.

"The feeling I got from the trip was that they were willing to listen to us, and it was totally different from before," Dr. Zhong recalled, sighing with emotion. In the past, at international academic conferences like this, Chinese experts usually only sat in and listened to the foreign experts. Now, finally, foreigners were listening to the Chinese.

More than eighty Chinese students from various US states had attended the conference knowing that Dr. Zhong was going to give a speech about SARS. After he had spoken, they didn't leave, but stayed with Dr. Zhong until late. They were proud that America was impressed by Chinese research.

Dr. Zhong used much data and facts, which he had accumulated during the fight against SARS. It gave his speech a strong persuasive power.

Talking about his powers of persuasion, Dr. Zhong remarked, "Generally, I don't use official language, so people don't find me unapproachable. Now, on some occasions, they want me to preside over meetings. But honestly, in 2003, I was appearing in the media a lot."

The media always asked him questions about the SARS epidemic. He had to answer appropriately without violating his principles, which gave him a great opportunity. Fortunately, he liked a challenge. "So, I slowly got used to it, and I came through."

This referred to the period of time when he had to deal with both domestic and foreign media frequently, especially in order to improve China's image in the world. It took a good deal of his energy.

23

DR. WANG ZHIQIONG
– THE NEXUS

"I have never seen anyone like Dr. Zhong," exclaimed Dr. Wang Zhiqiong, who was known as the "iron lady" among Guangdong medical workers. "I always say that it's easy for a person to excel at one thing, but nobody can reach Dr. Zhong's level. His professional knowledge is unmatched, and he always treats his patients kindly. Some doctors are kind, but they are not excellent at doctoring, while some doctors are very skillful, but they are not as kind as Dr. Zhong. So, I always say that Dr. Zhong is 'omnipotent,' a great person in general." Dr. Wang overflowed with praise for her fellow physician.

As the Deputy Director of Guangdong's Department of Health at the time, Dr. Wang Zhiqiong achieved major victories in the war against SARS, leading the provincial government as well as the expert group. When he looked back on the good old days, Dr. Zhong was filled with gratitude. He said that the Guangdong Department of Health gave full support to the fight against SARS. Among the multiple forces of effort, Dr. Wang Zhiqiong impressed him deeply.

Dr. Wang showed great respect for the Guangdong SARS expert group, agreeing to all of their suggestions. Dr. Zhong noted, "She was very practical. She recognized that we were experts on the subject. She respected us as long as we were right. She provided us with much help, and she always did so with a gentle attitude."

As Dr. Wang recalled, Dr. Zhong always took on the heaviest of burdens. Dr.

Wang remarked, "Even a young man in his 30s would not be able to handle the amount of work that Dr. Zhong currently has. Dr. Zhong has always been driven by one motivation, China's benefit. When he was studying overseas, he made the decision to use all that he had learned to contribute to his motherland. That was exactly what his father, Professor Zhong Shifan, had done back in his day."

Holding firm at the Guangdong Department of Health's 510 office established especially for SARS, Dr. Wang played a critical role in the province's fight against the virus. However, she was not willing to take much credit for it. "If anyone should take the credit, it was the Guangdong Government and the Guangdong Provincial Party Committee. They were the ones who made all the right decisions. Our Secretary of the Provincial Party Committee visited the Department of Health four times to deploy our defenses. *Four times.* That is an unprecedented number for a secretary of that level." She humbly proclaimed that she was merely one of the 70 million people in Guangdong who fought against SARS. However, in reality, she not only served as a nexus between the experts and the government, but also as a medical expert and a combatant on the front line against SARS. From the beginning, she worked alongside her colleagues on the wards. She was even infected and had to be hospitalized.

Practicality and cooperation were the defining features of the people of Guangdong, and Dr. Wang Zhiqiong was very typical of this. In 2008, she was over 60 years old. Even though she wore normal clothes, her professional temperament couldn't be concealed. It was easy to see that she was doctor. Dr. Wang's days as the Deputy Director of the Guangdong Department of Health were long past. As the fight against SARS concluded, her career as an administrator also came to an end. By 2008, she was appointed as the Director of the Guangdong Medical Doctor Association.

Dr. Wang came to her own conclusions about SARS. "We beat it rather quickly, even though we hadn't really figured out what it was, even to this day. It was gone as fast as it came, but we made it. We sought the truth, and we believed in our medical experts. There were many voices of disagreement, including those targeted at Dr. Zhong's plan for treatment."

Dr. Wang did not feel too much pressure when faced with all of the different voices, no matter how powerful or authoritative they were. This was because she held the firm belief that they would definitely come up with the best course of action.

Dr. Wang recalled a meeting regarding the treatment and control of SARS. There was some argument regarding the usage of antibiotics and corticosteroids, as it would depend on whether the SARS pathogen was a type of chlamydia or a coronavirus. Back then, many of the experts fell silent, disapproving of the coronavirus theory.

"This was mainly caused by pressure from above." After rounds of discussions, the experts finally gave their true opinions. Many were inclined to agree with the coronavirus theory, thinking that the SARS pathogen could not be a chlamydia. In the end, they came to the conclusion that their plans for treatment were correct.

At the same time, Dr. Zhong was treating patients. The truth was spoken under a dense atmosphere at the meeting, but he hadn't been able find the time to attend. In the afternoon of the meeting, Dr. Wang again called Dr. Zhong, urging him to attend. On hearing that he couldn't make it, Dr. Wang decided to brief him on the spot. "According to our discussion, judging from a clinical point of view, treatments for coronavirus are proving to be more effective. We can assume that the SARS pathogen is a coronavirus. To prevent SARS from spreading, we will need antiviral methods. Using corticosteroids will increase patients' ability to fight off the disease. But speaking from a broader view of the situation, it is assurance that we need most."

Her words filled Dr. Zhong with confidence. She said, "We must listen to the experts no matter what. They are the ones who truly know about the subject."

Merely hearing Dr. Wang's recollection of the discussion that happened in the special office, many would find no trace of the controversy surrounding the matter. On that day, the theory that the experts almost unanimously agreed upon went against the announcement by the government, which claimed that SARS was a type of chlamydia infection, and thus could be treated with antibiotics.

For Dr. Zhong, the result of this discussion brought immense encouragement. As the Deputy Director of the Guangdong Department of Health, Dr. Wang had always been strict in her standards of right and wrong. She was the cornerstone decision-maker at the CPC Guangdong Provincial Committee Control Center Against SARS. She worked alongside medical staff on the front line. Never giving up on her principles, she respected scientific facts and experts, and she served as a nexus connecting medical experts and government officials.

At that time, she needed to report to the group of superior officials from the Guangdong Department of Health. In other words, she needed their support. When the officials disapproved of the plans, she had to advise them to respect the opinion of medical experts. If she failed to convince the officials, it would be impossible to implement the plans drafted by the experts.

First, she needed the officials' approval, then the support of the experts, and lastly the confidence of the community. Whether Dr. Wang's narrative was due to her sincerity, humility, or something else, it was undeniable that for the decision-makers to do well, they would have to command a group of competent decision-realizers. In other words, the decision-realizers were one of the most critical links in the chain of command. Dr. Wang's efforts could not be underestimated.

According to Dr. Wang, the truth was always reported to the government. That was how Guangdong had always functioned. She remembered calling the then Director of the Guangdong Department of Health, Dr. Huang Qingdao, on Chinese New Year in 2003. Dr. Huang was in his hometown. In the many years before 2003, he had never returned to his hometown for the holiday. Coincidentally, this was the year he chose to go back.

"Director, we have a problem here."

"What is it?"

"It seems that an infectious disease has entered Guangzhou. Patients are piling up in our hospitals, and many of our doctors have fallen sick."

"Oh my. That is quite serious."

"Are we going to report this to our superiors?"

"Certainly. I will report it now."

It was obvious from this conversation that Dr. Wang maintained an amicable relationship with her superiors, facilitating smooth communication. Although Dr. Huang was not in his office, he was still capable of handling the situation in a contained, calm, clear-headed fashion.

For officials like Dr. Wang, the matter of whether to report or not had always been a huge challenge. Dr. Wang explained, "Why should we report the situation? Because if we don't, it would create a risk, and there is no way of telling the consequences. However, if we do report a situation and it does not develop into anything significant, we would be accused of interfering with the affairs of the government. The provincial government would probably blame us for not being able to handle the situation ourselves. This is the dilemma we find ourselves in." In such situations, officials like Dr. Wang were put between a rock and a hard place.

"When the Director confirmed that we should report the situation, it made our jobs so much easier. Our experts began writing a report about how many SARS cases there were, how many doctors were infected, and our plans for the next step. Later, all relevant files were submitted along with our report."

Looking back on the situation, she still believed that was the right thing to do. She felt that the frontline doctors were correct to report the situation. Whether the information should have been announced or escalated and whether it ought to have been made known to the central government were decisions for superiors. The officials from the Guangdong Department of Health did their job when they seized their earliest chance to report everything to the CPC Provincial Committee.

Regarding Dr. Zhong's collaboration with Hong Kong University on the analysis of the SARS virus, Dr. Wang said, "Back then, I heard that Dr. Guan Yi from Hong Kong was going to publish a paper claiming that SARS was initially a type of bird flu, and expressing that our government was trying to cover it up. At first, I thought it was nonsense. But later on, the rumor became a claim that Dr. Guan had already identified SARS as bird flu and had leaked the information. I was outraged. There were people claiming that Dr. Zhong analyzed the serum of SARS patients and collaborated with Dr. Guan. If that really had been the case, then what we had on our hands would have been a ground-breaking scandal. I couldn't believe it."

According to Dr. Wang, things were quite heated between Dr. Guan and the Chinese Ministry of Agriculture regarding the bird flu. However, it later turned out to be a misunderstanding, and the incident was soon forgotten.

On February 8, 2003, some officials from the Beijing Bureau of Health visited Guangzhou. Dr. Wang recalled telling them, "It is very brave of all of you to come to Guangzhou, considering that we have an epidemic going on here." They responded that it was their duty to come, as they had to learn how to control the disease.

Dr. Wang greeted them in the 510 office. With the utmost sincerity, she told them, "First and foremost, if you find something worthy of reporting, just do it. Whether these issues should be announced to the public is for our superiors to decide, not us." Her explanation was clear: as subordinates, their duty was to report new situations without any hindrance or hesitation. Whether the information was worthy of escalation was to be decided by their superiors. Even if they decided not to, when the central government was trying to find the person responsible, they could be excused from such responsibilities. "If you choose not to report, how are our superiors going to know the situation? If things go wrong, it will be your fault. If you choose to report it, and our superiors decide not to escalate it afterwards, it would be their fault, not yours, because you told the truth. Whether our higher ups announce it and how they are going to announce it is for them to decide."

Along with the officials from the Beijing Bureau of Health, another thing planted itself deep into Dr. Wang's memory. By the end of the SARS crisis, some official from the Bureau of Health called her, asking how much Guangdong was going to pay in compensation. At first, she was confused by the question. As it turned out, the official was asking about the compensation budget Guangdong had to pay SARS patients for their pain and necrosis of the femoral head caused by the use of corticosteroids.

"We didn't really have this problem with most of the patients. Some of them experienced some pain in the femoral head, but it was nothing serious. Based on Dr. Zhong's advice, we did not simply use corticosteroids whenever the patients developed a fever. We were always cautious, only using them when needed. However, our Beijing colleagues told us that after prolonged periods of heavy usage of corticosteroids, sometimes as long as a few months, many SARS patients experienced major problems with their femoral heads."

Corticosteroids could indeed fight off SARS and protect the lungs. However, it was critical to keep a short leash on the dosage and duration of usage. "We cannot just use corticosteroids at first sight of fever. That is simply not the way," Dr. Wang said multiple times during the interview.

In Guangdong, some SARS patients fell into critical conditions. Most of them were elderly, with some underlying chronic diseases. As a result, some suffered a less than ideal recovery. "We tried our best to reduce the problem with their femoral heads. However, their lives must always come first."

24

MEETING WU YI

In 2003, Dr. Zhong was received by Wu Yi, then the Vice Premier of the State Council. It was like a glimpse of light in the darkness to him. In the end, he did not disappoint Wu Yi.

Dr. Zhong said, "The central government has never criticized me to my face."

Anyone who knew Dr. Zhong's nature would confirm that he was not afraid of anything except telling lies and going against his conscience. Since the beginning of the SARS epidemic, he could not help but feel that he was going against someone, and that no matter where he went, he was not a popular person. He knew how much trouble he had caused the government and the Guangdong Provincial Committee of the CPC, from "privately" allowing Hong Kong experts to test the SARS virus, to the dispute over the pathogen, to telling the truth to WHO officers, to embarrassing Chinese officials at press conference. At the same time, he had always understood people who were timid and reluctant to cause trouble. So when these people chose to stay away from him, he was fine with it, as he didn't think it was a big deal to be excluded. However, he also wondered, for a doctor like him, treating patients on the front line, why would the leadership criticize him?

"It could be that I am an academic, and they didn't want an academic to look bad, so they didn't criticize me to my face. Anyway, what I said was the truth, and I'm just a doctor."

The truth had to be told, and the disease had to be treated. Depression and grievances didn't affect him too much. He was not seeking money, nor an official position. It was enough for him that he could treat patients and be liked by them.

At the end of April 2003, Beijing citizens who believed that the epidemic was far away were suddenly faced with the appearance of SARS patients in the capital. On March 31, a bold media outlet in Beijing had reported that gauze masks had been out of stock there for days, meaning that citizens had already taken preventative action. The general attitude toward SARS in Beijing was one of terror. Citizens had been on guard for a long time, even though they felt that the epidemic was far away. They just hadn't expected it to reach them.

On April 3, the same day that WHO officers praised Guangdong's efforts, the Beijing media told people not to panic. The person in charge of the Beijing Municipal Department of Health announced, "The city's health administration and disease prevention and control agency have established a comprehensive monitoring system and an effective emergency response mechanism throughout the city."

Only two days later, on April 5, a SARS patient showed up at Peking University People's Hospital. Soon, 93 medical staff at the hospital were infected. On April 23, the entire hospital was put into isolation, a measure that wasn't lifted until May 17.

Lü Houshan, then President of Peking University People's Hospital, said helplessly that it was because the hospital did not have an infectious disease department, and the patient could not be transferred or rejected. He was straightforward, saying, "I believe that I would have been well prepared if I had known earlier what SARS was and if I'd learned lessons from Guangzhou." He continued, "We were aware that SARS was spreading, but we had no idea how it was being transmitted, and how powerful it was. We lacked knowledge about such a severe infectious disease of the upper respiratory tract."

It had been nearly two months since the Beijing Municipal Department of Health officials risked their lives to go to Guangzhou to learn from the city's experience. Beijing citizens wouldn't forget the TV News they had watched earlier, which had made them feel secure. *We are backed up by our government*, they thought. *Beijing, such a big city, the heart of our motherland – how could SARS get the better of us?* Although they were afraid, the citizens, who still went out for a walk in the morning and evening, never lost their faith in the Beijing municipal government.

It had been two months. What had the Beijing Municipal Department of Health learned? Other than the invaluable experience exchanged for lives and blood in the fight against SARS in Guangzhou, the number of fallen medical staff was already a serious warning to them. It was a very high price, but how much was it worth to them?

Later, the people of Beijing started wondering why Dr. Zhong from Guangzhou always told a different story from what they had seen on television. The media was saying that SARS was not so severe, which made them feel safe, but what Dr. Zhong said was completely different.

In April 2003, the CPC Committee decided to remove the Party Secretary of the Department of Health for concealing the SARS epidemic, and on April 26, the Second Meeting of the Standing Committee of the Tenth National People's Congress voted to remove the Minister of Health.

In fact, the first SARS case in Beijing had appeared on March 7, 2003. Unfortunately, the uninformed Beijing citizens still believed that they were safe.

Jiang Suchun, a native of Ningxiang in Hunan Province, born in February 1929, was the former Vice President of the 302 Military Hospital of China and the former Director of the Department of Infectious Diseases at the hospital. He was a leading expert in infectious diseases, and he had participated in saving the life of the first SARS patient in Beijing and performed the autopsy on the capital's first SARS death. He was also the first SARS patient in the world to use his own body for a successful serum injection test.

At about 8:00 pm on March 7, 2003, the retired Jiang Suchun received a call from a leader of the 302 Military Hospital of China at home, asking him to come to the hospital ward immediately to help save the life of a SARS patient. Jiang Suchun was old, and had been suffering from nasopharyngeal cancer. His respiratory system was his most vulnerable part in terms of his immune system. When he arrived at the ward, he immediately noticed the seriousness of the problem, but he didn't hesitate. At that time, he only knew that SARS was a highly contagious disease, and that this patient was the first imported case in Beijing. According to the director of the hospital, the patient from Shanxi was showing symptoms of pneumonia and had developed the disease after leaving Guangdong. Jiang Suchun knew that this was not good. Previously, he had only heard of SARS in Guangdong; this was the first SARS case in Beijing.

That day, Jiang Suchun, a lifelong practitioner of infectious disease medicine, inserted two extra layers of gauze into the mask he was wearing. The SARS patient was not saved in the end. Dr. Jiang thought, "I have seen many infectious diseases in my life, but one so fatal as this is very rare. The patient was eating half an hour ago, and now he's dead. What on the earth caused this?" He suggested performing an autopsy on the patient right away. There was a large amount of the virus remaining in the body, which would spread upon opening the chest. The danger was greater than ever. Despite his old age and history of nasopharyngeal cancer, Dr. Jiang performed the autopsy on the first SARS death in Beijing as quickly as possible, accumulating valuable first-hand information for research into the disease.

On the night of March 14, Dr. Jiang suddenly felt a chill, and he realized that he might have been infected with SARS. Despite his high fever, he kept asking himself whether he should use his own body for a test. This idea had no precedent at that time. On March 22, his body was injected with the serum collected from a recovering SARS patient in Guangzhou. The result was miraculous. After being injected with the serum and treated with medication, the 74-year-old Jiang, who had been hospitalized for 23 days, recovered and was discharged after being examined and passing all physical indices.

By April 6, 2003, Beijing citizens had begun to lose their trust in the media. On April 12, the WHO announced that Beijing had been listed as a SARS epidemic area. Opinions about China in the international media were already extremely unfavorable. By the end of the month, the whole of China was gripped by a deep-seated fear of the epidemic.

On April 16, SARS broke out at the Central University of Finance and Economics in Beijing's Haidian District. The university immediately announced the suspension of classes. The densely packed neighborhoods around the university suddenly exploded in panic. The wider city panicked as well. SARS was right on their doorstep.

Many were puzzled. "I thought it wasn't that bad?"

On the campus of the Central University of Finance and Economics, students dragged their luggage as they rushed toward the campus gates in terror. They couldn't wait to get out. As far as the eye could see, the avenues were full of fleeing students wearing masks. An hour later, the once noisy campus lay silent and empty.

On April 3, the 309 Military Hospital of China in Beijing admitted sixty SARS patients in a day. The media announced on the same day that there were twelve SARS patients and three deaths. At the age 72, Jiang Yanyong had been the Director of the Surgery Department at the 301 Hospital before retiring, and knew what Beijing hospitals were like. He was angry about the false announcement, and he wrote a signed letter the next day and sent it online to two Beijing media agencies. On April 8, an article titled "Beijing hit by SARS" was published by *Time* magazine in America, quoting his letter. On April 20, the CPC Central Committee removed the main leaders of the Ministry of Health and the Beijing Municipal Government. China's battle against SARS finally opened up a new dimension.

The State Council Press Office held a press conference on the afternoon of April 20. Gao Qiang, then Deputy Minister of the Ministry of Health, discussed the prevention and treatment of SARS in Mainland China and answered questions from Chinese and foreign journalists. He confessed that the work of the Ministry of Health was flawed and that the epidemic reporting system needed to be improved. He said, "The MOH is not adequately prepared to respond to public health emergencies, and the epidemic prevention system is weak. The requirements of the regional reporting system are unclear, and the guidance is insufficient. The mechanisms of the relevant departments in Beijing, including information and statistics, monitoring and reporting, and tracking and investigation, are not sound. There are large omissions in the statistics, and the number of confirmed cases is not reported accurately."

The people of Beijing and other parts of China gazed at their TV screens, seeing the sweat on Gao Qiang's forehead. Finally, the deceit was swept away and the light came back on.

On April 23, Wen Jiabao, then Premier of the State Council, presided over a State Council executive meeting and decided to set up a State Council command center for SARS prevention and control, with Vice Premier Wu Yi as the Commander-in-Chief. The central government would grant a fund of 2 billion yuan for SARS prevention and control. After the meeting, Wu Yi twice met with Dr. Zhong to discuss SARS prevention and control in Beijing.

"At that point, I felt that she was humbly asking me for advice rather than encouraging me," Dr. Zhong said, with sincere respect for Wu Yi.

The first time Wu Yi met Dr. Zhong was to learn about SARS and its prevention and control. The second time was after Wen Jiabao took Dr. Zhong abroad to attend an international conference. At that time, SARS was already severe in Beijing. She asked him what exactly Beijing should do, and she was eager to hear his opinions.

Dr. Zhong replied without hesitation that Beijing's standard of medical care, academic standards, and medical forces were much better than Guangdong's, but speaking of SARS prevention and control, the work in Beijing was much worse. Why? He heard that even the ICU doctors had not yet been mobilized to play their role, and many capable doctors remained idle because no one had assigned tasks to them. If the situation continued, there was no way that critical patients could be saved.

Solemnly, Wu Yi asked Dr. Zhong, "What do you think Beijing should do?"

Dr. Zhong said, "First of all, we should consider gathering critical patients in one or two places. Then, we employ high-level medical staff to treat them."

Although the later establishment of the Xiaotangshan Hospital for SARS was not proposed by Dr. Zhong, Wu Yi adopted all of his suggestions. It was the right time to meet the right person. Dr. Zhong could exercise his talent freely, since he now had the ear of the central leadership.

On October 15, 2007, a report from the 17th National Congress of the CPC proposed a new scientific outlook for development. The reason the people-oriented scientific outlook for development continued to be so familiar even to ordinary people was that it represented their fundamental interests and realized their long-cherished wishes. The recognition and commendation of the merits of a practical person like Dr. Zhong, who was outspoken and pragmatic, became a testimony of the Party and government to the people.

What pleased Dr. Zhong was that the universities he and Wu Yi had attended in their early years were so close. Wu Yi graduated from the Beijing Institute of Petrochemical Technology in 1962, which was next door to Dr. Zhong's alma mater, Peking University Health Science Center. On the other side was Wen Jiabao's alma mater, the Beijing branch of China University of Geosciences. Wen Jiabao graduated from the university five years after Dr. Zhong, while Wu Yi graduated one year after him. Dr. Zhong was received by the central leadership thanks both to his talent and his connection with his contemporaries. With this recognition, he was given an important duty.

Wu Yi was in charge of the Ministry of Health at that time. She suggested that the Chinese Medical Association should not be like an administrative agency. A scholar should be the President. The first candidate she considered for the position was Dr. Zhong, who understood why.

Later, the media reported Dr. Zhong's remark, "Wu Yi, I didn't fail you."

CCTV had invited Dr. Zhong to participate in four special programs on carrying out SARS prevention and control. There were many more medical experts in Beijing than in Guangdong, and the standard of medical care in the capital was much higher, so why did Beijing still have such a high SARS mortality rate? The main reason was that the ICU wards in Beijing were not being used to their full potential, and some specialized treatment techniques were not being put in place.

After Wu Yi had solicited expert opinions, including Dr. Zhong's, the critical SARS patients in Beijing were temporarily gathered in two hospitals. At the same time, medical teams were dispatched to provinces and cities where the SARS epidemic was severe. A few days later, Wu Yi met with Dr. Zhong again. Based on the likelihood that SARS might become more severe in Beijing, she asked him to send a medical team to Beijing for support. Dr. Zhong headed straight to the capital to guide the frontline work. However, he had to leave Beijing because the situation in Guangdong still worried him. He left Professor Xiao Zhenglun, the Deputy Director of the IRH, in Beijing.

In 2004, Wu Yi formally spoke to Dr. Zhong about making him President of the Chinese Medical Association. In 2003, following the removal of the Minister of Health on April 26, Dr. Zhong accompanied Wen Jiabao to Thailand to attend the special China-ASEAN leaders' conference on SARS on April 29. The Chinese government's fight against SARS began to draw the world's attention.

25

THE SEARCH FOR ZHONG NANSHAN

On April 30, 2003, Premier of the State Council Wen Jiabao said, "Dr. Zhong Nanshan is a valuable expert of ours. His contribution to the containment of a national public health emergency is invaluable."

When he returned from a trip abroad, Premier Wen wanted to visit the school that Dr. Zhong had attended, the Affiliated High School of South China Normal University (SCNU). Premier Wen sent for Dr. Zhong and waited for him and his convoy for over half an hour.

Dr. Zhong had achieved great success in the fight against SARS, and this attracted the attention of the Party and the nation's leaders. On the morning of April 29, 2003, Premier Wen arrived in Bangkok via Kunming to attend a specially conducted conference regarding SARS among the leaders of China and other ASEAN countries. Dr. Zhong also attended as part of his entourage.

On April 22, 2003, Dr. Zhong returned to Guangzhou after attending a meeting held by the Chinese Medical Doctor Association in Beijing. As soon as he arrived, he was informed that Premier Wen was about to join the special summit in Thailand, and he needed three medical experts to attend alongside him. And the Premier specifically asked for Dr. Zhong to be one of the three. Dr. Wang Longde, then Vice-Minister of the Ministry of Health, gave Dr. Zhong the news. The trip was scheduled a few days later, and Dr. Zhong worried that he might not have enough time to apply for a visa.

Dr. Wang put his mind at ease. "There will be no problem. I have already obtained your visa for you," he said.

On April 27, 2003, Dr. Zhong arrived in Beijing yet again. For this trip, he would join the rest of the entourage on Premier Wen's designated jet as they traveled to Thailand. Premier Wen sat in the front of the plane, with Dr. Zhong, Dr. Wang, Dr. Li Liming, and a few other ministers in the middle part. Other assistants and journalists were seated in the rear. Within 30 minutes of takeoff, Premier Wen summoned the three doctors to his room. Flying with the leader of the country, Dr. Zhong couldn't help but feel the trust bestowed upon him by the Party and the nation. He also saw first hand how the Party and the leaders were trying their best to serve the people.

At 8:30 am local time on April 29, 2003, the jet landed in Thailand. That afternoon, a press conference was held after the conclusion of the special conference of China-ASEAN leaders. Four national leaders hosted the press conference, namely the Prime Minister of Thailand (the host country) Thaksin Chinnawat, the Premier of China Wen Jiabao, the Prime Minister of Cambodia, the rotating chair of ASEAN Hun Sen, and the Prime Minister of Singapore Goh Chok Tong. The room was small, and it was filled with journalists from all over the world. Over 400 journalists who could not fit were forced to watch the livestream of the conference outside.

No matter where the journalists were from, their questions always focused on China. Premier Wen remarked that he knew the journalists were highly concerned with the situation in China and that he would take this opportunity to answer their questions as best he could. He said that the conference was not only timely, but also necessary. As it turned out, it was also successful. He said that the government of China was a responsible one. It would take up the responsibility of protecting the 1.3 billion people in China, and also people from the rest of the world. The reason he attended this conference was to show that China was not afraid of the truth.

When questioned by Western journalists, Premier Wen answered with utmost sincerity, "When the epidemic hit us, we did not know how to control or prevent it. Our response was not ideal. However, we have learned lessons and gained much experience. In the fight against SARS, the people and leaders of China learned a lot, which might serve as an invaluable asset when dealing with similar situations in the future."

Premier Wen spoke confidently about the next steps in controlling the disease. "Now, if any of you were to go to China, you would see that the people and the government have already started to take action." He claimed that hope lay in action. No amount of talks, meetings, or policies could match the effect of action. The true test of the final result resided in the lowering of the incidence rate, the reduction of death, and the increment of the recovery rate. These were what truly mattered. In the end, Premier Wen urged the journalists to continue to follow the situation in China. He said, "We will prove the determination of our government and the perseverance of our people with our actions."

In Premier Wen's 24 hours in Thailand, he attended a total of nine meetings. To announce information regarding China's fight against SARS, he attended nine Q&A sessions, barely resting in between. He was in no way condescending, arriving early at every meeting and greeting the other leaders with a warm smile.

As part of Wen's entourage, Dr. Zhong also attended the meetings and was interviewed by Chinese journalists. Again, he expressed his opinion that SARS was a threat to the whole world. It was not a regional or national disease, but a global epidemic. It had already spread to 30 nations and regions, and it would take a joint international effort to eliminate it. Southeast Asia was practically a neighbor to China, with a high level of interaction. It did not matter which nation became the first target of SARS, as it would eventually spread to all the neighboring countries, affecting not only health but also the economic and social situations in these nations. China's attendance at the meeting showed that it was willing to cooperate with Southeast Asian countries.

By then, the SARS pathogen was yet to be identified, as well as its ways of spreading and methods of prevention and treatment. Dr. Zhong noted that the sharing of information could help all the nations in their understanding of SARS and subsequently increase the chance of fighting it off. When questioned about the effect this conference would have on China's fight against SARS, he answered that many ASEAN countries such as Singapore had formed their own health systems to prevent and treat infectious diseases, and China needed to learn from them in this aspect. He added that he knew ASEAN countries had a solid foundation in virological research. He believed that collaboration among China and ASEAN countries would accelerate the research, helping scientists to study it and identify its pathogen. His answer was met with acclaim around the globe.

When the special conference concluded, Premier Wen Jiabao left Bangkok on April 30, 2003, and arrived in Guangzhou the same day. He was scheduled to visit the school that Dr. Zhong had attended, the Affiliated High School of SCNU. However, Dr. Zhong was not part of the Premier's convoy at that point. Thinking that the Premier must have other matters to attend to in Guangzhou after they arrived, Dr. Zhong stayed in his hotel room.

On the coach, the Premier looked around him and asked, "Is Dr. Zhong here?" He received a negative answer.

"But I want him to come with me to the Affiliated High School of SCNU."

The convoy stopped to wait. The Security Office of the CPC Guangdong Provincial Committee immediately dispatched its officers to look for Dr. Zhong, who eventually found him in his room. The officers urged him, "Dr. Zhong, please come quickly. The Premier is waiting for you."

As soon as Dr. Zhong heard this, he rushed over. By then, the convoy had already been waiting for thirty minutes. He apologized profusely.

Knowing that Dr. Zhong had graduated from the school, Premier Wen kept him by his side as he posed for photos with the students, saying "Our friend Dr. Zhong here is your alumnus. Study hard, and you might become great like him one day."

A meeting was held that evening, and Premier Wen praised Dr. Zhong again to the Governor of Guangdong, Huang Huahua. Looking back on this experience, Dr. Zhong said, "My memory of what Premier Wen said is vague. I think he said that I had made great contributions to our fight against SARS, and that as an expert, my involvement in the containment of a national public health emergency was invaluable."

26

REORGANIZING THE WILD ANIMAL MARKET

In five days, more than 10,000 civet cats disappeared in Guangdong. In January 2004, the appearance of four SARS cases in Guangzhou worried Dr. Zhong. A second outbreak had to be strictly prevented. The time of onset of the four patients was the same as those in 2003. Was the epidemic coming back?

The situation was becoming tense again. The first SARS patient, a freelance photographer living in Huadu District in Guangzhou, contracted the illness from eating wild animals. The second case was a waiter at a restaurant, and the third was a farmer living in the Guangzhou suburbs.

The re-emergence of SARS was a very serious situation, and it was only contained by good measures. Speaking of this, Dr. Zhong voiced his acclaim for Zhang Dejiang, Secretary of the Guangdong Provincial Committee of the CPC. "He is a leader with true Party spirit. Governor Huang Huahua chaired the meeting, and it was the first time I had asked to meet with him. The heads of various departments came to listen to our presentation, and they finally made a decision. The decision made by Guangdong Provincial Committee of the CPC and the Provincial Government effectively put an end to the second outbreak of SARS. It was a contribution, because it was a decision made at a very critical moment."

Dr. Zhong and other Guangdong experts had never given up on tracking SARS. In September 2003, along with Shenzhen Center for Disease Control and

Prevention and Professor Guan Yi, their joint research initially identified that the carnivorous cats in the wild animal markets, including civets, badgers, and raccoons, were connected to SARS. A paper titled "The Civet is the Main Intermediate Host of SARS Coronavirus" by Professor Guan was published in the American magazine *Science*.

During the publication of this academic paper, Dr. Zhong went through an unimaginably difficult process, seeking truth and pragmatism. At that time, although civets had been identified as the origin of the SARS virus, there were still disagreements. Some authoritative research institutions in the north had performed analytical studies on civets and had not found the SARS coronavirus.

Dr. Zhong was convinced of Professor Guan's findings, but civets in northern feedlots were not found to carry the SARS coronavirus, so the experts in the north did not recognize the finding. However, as civets were part of Guangdong cuisine, specifically in winter as a tonic for the season, experts in the south believed that they were connected to SARS.

Dr. Zhong said, "I remember that the American magazine *Science* behaved very responsibly. It asked the Guangdong side to provide two pieces of information: one was whether the coronavirus was carried by civets, and the other was about the virus from SARS patients. The reasoning behind this was to compare and analyze whether the two viruses were highly homologous from the perspective of the gene sequence. If they were homologous, SARS was highly likely to be transmitted from civets to humans."

The publication of the paper was delayed because the US side heard that there were disputes on the issue. The samples of the virus collected from SARS patients and civets were sent to a lab in the US. It was only after their homology was verified that the paper was published in *Science*. Before that, the National Forestry Administration had issued a document stating that the civet was one of the 54 species of carnivores that could be raised for food. At the time, carnivorous wild civets were legally allowed to be traded and eaten, so the claim that the SARS coronavirus came from them was no longer groundless.

Since the paper was published, there had been two different views in the academic community, because the results of the examination of civets in the feedlots in the south and north were different. The Institute of Zoology at Jilin Agricultural University in Changchun conducted a nationwide study of civets. A total of 103 experiments on antibodies against the SARS virus in civets were conducted. The results showed that civets from the feedlots in Hubei, Hunan, and Hebei were free from the SARS coronavirus, while many civets from Shanwei in Guangdong were found to be positive, accounting for 40%. As for civets from the Zengcha Market, a well-known wholesale wild animal market in Guangzhou, 78% were found to be positive for the SARS coronavirus. Although the institute's experiment had confirmed that civets were highly susceptible to the SARS coronavirus, it was still unclear what infected them with it.

Why did civets in Guangdong carry the SARS coronavirus? Experts detected it in the cages used to ship civets. It emerged that the wild animal markets used the same cages for shipping civets as all the other wild animals. Also, civets were often stored and shipped with other wild animals in the same space. There was a wide variety of wild animals, and many markets were selling them. Most critically, civets were easy recipients for the SARS coronavirus.

Thus, experts speculated that mixed transport and housing of wild animals had led to the spread of the SARS coronavirus. It was also speculated that the appearance of SARS in Guangdong in winter was due to the popularity of civet as a delicacy in that season. Dr. Zhong said, "Back then, we already had some information, and the September 2003 issue of *Science* magazine had endorsed our view that the human coronavirus was likely transmitted from wild mammals. We did a genetic analysis in collaboration with the Guangdong Center for Disease Control and Prevention."

The coronavirus was isolated from all four SARS patients identified in January 2004. It was also found in the civets from the restaurant where some of the patients had dined. After being compared and analyzed, the two coronaviruses were found to be highly homologous.

Dr. Zhong believed that it was time to advise the government to ban or close the wild animal markets. However, some experts had different views. After Dr. Zhong had collected sufficient information, he discussed it with Professor Guan. Professor Guan was a Hong Kong resident, making it inconvenient for him to come forward, so Dr. Zhong asked Xu Ruiheng from the Guangdong Center for Disease Control and Prevention, a warm-hearted man, and a highly authoritative expert, to help.

They got together one Sunday. Dr. Zhong called the Guangdong Provincial Vice Governor Lei Yulan, and then Governor Huang Huahua's secretary, requesting a meeting. There were four new SARS cases, and people were on edge.

In the spring of 2004, the China Import and Export Fair (Canton Fair) was approaching, but the number of international exhibitors was significantly lower than in previous years. When Japanese exhibitors heard that SARS was re-emerging, they decided not to attend.

At this critical moment, Dr. Zhong had to see Governor Huang. He told the governor's secretary that he wanted to explain the current situation and discuss what to do next, and also to share his and other experts' opinions. The secretary agreed to pass this on. Unexpectedly, the secretary got back to Dr. Zhong in the afternoon, telling him that Governor Huang would meet them that evening at the Guangzhou Yingbin Hotel.

Dr. Zhong immediately began to prepare detailed information. When he arrived at the hotel that evening, he saw many other people. Governor Huang attached great importance to this matter, so he had summoned people in charge of departments in Guangdong Province, including the Department of Health, the Department of Forestry, the Department of Civil Affairs, the Department of Public Security, the Department of Culture, the Department of Commerce, and the Department of Agriculture, as well as the head of the Guangdong Center for Disease Control and Prevention.

Dr. Zhong spoke on behalf of all the experts. He analyzed the four SARS cases in detail. First, two of the patients had a history of contact with civets and a habit of consuming wild animals. In addition, the coronaviruses isolated from civets and the four patients were highly homologous. Further, the experts believed that wild animal markets were important vectors of infection.

Dr. Zhong then raised the question of what to do next. He pointed out that the mutual agreement among them was to immediately cut off the routes of infection, so that a second outbreak of SARS could be avoided. "Once there is a second outbreak and it spreads from Guangzhou to Hong Kong, the situation will become very dangerous."

Hearing Dr. Zhong's report, Governor Huang sought advice from the others. The head of the Department of Health said that if the situation was real, they had to take measures, and the key was prevention. The head of the Department of Agriculture added that it was right to do so, but there were seventeen civet feedlots in Guangdong Province. If all of the civets were eliminated, should the farmers be compensated appropriately? Once the seventeen civet feedlots were closed down, how would the farmers make a living, and how should their employment problem be addressed? The head of the Department of Public Security suggested that in the future, civets from other provinces should not be allowed to be shipped to Guangdong for sale. The head of the Department of Commerce suggested bringing the wild animal markets under tighter control. In general, they all agreed with the experts' suggestions.

After Governor Huang listened to everyone's views, he decided that what Dr. Zhong had reported was reasonable. Wild animal markets must be reorganized immediately, and all civet feedlots must be closed down within five days. It was also agreed that each affected farmer would receive monetary compensation. After the meeting, the attendees sprang into action.

The word "wild" was removed from the signages of restaurants selling wild animals in Guangdong. The owners were aware that the provincial government was about to take action.

On January 11, 2004, 1,500 Guangzhou citizens signed a petition titled "Don't Eat Wild Animals," and all of the civets in Shaoguan were eliminated. Five days later, more than 10,000 civets were eliminated in Guangdong. From then on, civets returned to their natural home and were no longer consumed by humans. After that, there were no more SARS patients in Guangdong.

According to Dr. Zhong, several pieces of evidence proved that the province's measures were correct. The first was an article published in *Science* magazine in 2004, written by Zhao Guoping of the Shanghai Institute for Biological Sciences of the Chinese Academy of Sciences. The article noted a total of 63 strains of coronavirus found in China, and revealed that they began to mutate after they had infected humans. At first, the viruses were not infectious to humans, but they became so after some time. With the mutation of the viruses, the person-to-person infection began, which meant that civets were not the only transmission route. People could infect each other even without civet transmission. It was hazardous when the situation developed to an extent that the viruses were completely separated from their original host, civets. Once the transmission path became person-to-person, the virus would be more virulent, and the difficulty of controlling the outbreak would be increased. By promptly cutting off animal-to-human transmission, the virus could be stopped from escalating and spreading. That was why, after the SARS epidemic in 2003, Dr. Zhong had been on the alert for a second outbreak. It was also why he suggested that the government should improve the management of wild animal markets.

The reality was so cruel that there was no other way out, and this was the only choice. Civets were easily infected by other animals, and people could easily be infected while killing, cooking, and eating them.

Another piece of evidence was found by the Guangzhou Center for Disease Control and Prevention. Initially, about 25% of personnel who sold and transported wild animals tested positive for coronavirus antibodies. After the elimination of civets, the percentage dropped from 25% to 5% by July 2004, which showed that the measures taken against civets were effective.

Dr. Zhong was pleased. "Governor Huang often used this matter as an example, claiming that the second SARS outbreak was avoided because the Guangdong Provincial Committee of the CPC and the Provincial Government accepted the advice of the experts. This was a very important event at the time."

In the battle against SARS, the final action against civets was a major crucial initiative. The collaboration between experts and the government avoided another major spread of the SARS virus. But why had the SARS virus not appeared before? Dr. Zhong was still pursuing the answer to this mystery. Civets might not be the only source. Later studies found that bats – specifically Chinese rufous horseshoe bats, which were found in both Wuhan and Hong Kong – had the same virus as civets. They were eaten in Guangdong too.

Dr. Zhong said, "Earlier, the Department of Forestry had not prepared a document based on our opinions, and the document issued was somewhat one-sided. However, in 2004, the Minister of Health issued an official document banning the sale of civets. We were glad that they accepted our opinions."

This harsh lesson was a reminder that humans would not be spared the consequences of slaughtering and selling wild animals.

When the SARS epidemic of 2003 began to calm down, relieved Guangzhou citizens were confused one quiet morning by a media report regarding an "investigation on Dr. Zhong." Since the SARS outbreak, except for a period of silence, the media had been positive about Dr. Zhong. Why was there to be an investigation?

According to Dr. Zhong, the report contained many things, such as how he had used any means possible to pursue fame and acclaim, and how he tried to push himself into the limelight. The report was centered on the fact that he had identified the pathogen and wanted to treat all of the patients himself, being reluctant to share the glory with other doctors. To this day, Dr. Zhong still has no idea what went on at that time. The journalist behind the report never interviewed him properly, despite claiming that he had.

Dr. Zhong recalled that the publication was called *The Bund*, and it was based in Shanghai. In fact, the journalist had only asked him a few questions, taking less than three minutes. He didn't answer them, and he even asked the journalist a few questions of his own. Unexpectedly, the journalist ended up writing a report of more than 20,000 words.

"I really didn't understand. Maybe the journalist was trying to publish breaking news. Whatever it was, it didn't have much of an impact on me." Dr. Zhong added that the incident taught him that he needed to collaborate and cooperate more. His current domestic and international collaborations were not enough.

This report involved several other people, including Zheng Bojian from the University of Hong Kong, and Wen Yumei, a scholar of Chinese Engineering. They called the journalist to clarify the facts. Zheng Bojian was irritated that the journalist had made something out of nothing and completely reversed the facts, because Dr. Zhong had never done anything like that.

27

THE "NANSHAN SPIRIT"

With the grim situation that China found itself in during the late spring of 2003, it was somewhat risky to speak the truth. But the way that Dr. Zhong told the truth triumphed over the practice of lying, ending a bad habit.

Employees at the IRH didn't think that SARS made Dr. Zhong the man he was. Rather, it was justice that bestowed duty on the hero who heeded its call. It was just that the gauntlet of SARS that placed him on the scale of history.

The sudden outbreak of SARS made Zhong Nanshan a household name throughout China. As the old Chinese saying goes, in probability lies inevitability. Dr. Zhong rose to the occasion due to his constant hard work and unstinting diligence.

Talking about Dr. Zhong, Cheng Donghai, then Secretary of the CPC Branch at IRH, had much to say. A secretary appointed in a time of crisis, Dr. Cheng had a deeper than usual understanding of the term "Nanshan Spirit." He said, "Way before SARS hit, Dr. Zhong was already regarded as a great doctor by his patients. It is the times that create heroes, and SARS engendered a situation that he could rise to." He added, warmly, "To really understand Dr. Zhong, you must look deep within him to his humanistic soul. It is only then that you can truly appreciate his charm. Dr. Zhong is a man of many merits."

As Secretary of a CPC Branch, Dr. Cheng was well-versed in both politics and leadership. In just a few words, he highlighted some of Dr. Zhong's best qualities. He thought that one of Dr. Zhong's best qualities was his firm belief in serving the country and society. When he studied in the UK in 1979, his mentor and peers suggested that he stay, as China was then struggling with poverty and other adversities. However, without a second thought, he chose to return to his homeland. In the many years after his return, he had many chances to leave and work in other countries, but he rejected each one.

When SARS was at its worst, many international media agencies, including in the US, tried to depict China in a bad light with news reports that demonized it and its efforts against the epidemic. Meanwhile, Dr. Zhong was busy writing papers on the treatment and prevention of SARS and treating critical patients at the IRH. He was busy and tired, but he took every chance he got to make speeches abroad. Everyone knew that he was the one voice in China to listen to when it came to respiratory diseases, and many foreign academics approved of his approach.

Cheng Donghai believed that Dr. Zhong's efforts and speeches around the world took an enormous amount of pressure off the government. As a scholar of science, he explained what he saw how SARS happened in China, how the government handled it, how the response efforts took effect, and how he treated patients. Foreign journalists were in the dark, and foreign governments were confused. They thought China was concealing the truth and facts about the situation and that it was lying to its people. Many took this opportunity to launch a smear campaign against the Chinese government. In this critical situation, Dr. Zhong chose to go overseas, serving as a voice of reason. Full of pride, Cheng Donghai explained, "And this is why our Party and our government showered him with awards and honors. The situation was bad. It was as if all the other countries put up a blockade against China. When the Canton Fair was held, many merchants simply decided not to show up. Many countries marked China as an 'epidemic area' and tried to ostracize it on the political and diplomatic levels. It was a time of darkness. One of Dr. Zhong's many contributions was his way of telling the truth."

In 2003, under enormous pressure, Dr. Zhong chose to do the right thing. In the face of defamation and misunderstanding, he stood behind his coronavirus theory and held firmly to his plans for treatment using corticosteroids. At the most critical stage, he stepped up and told the truth. In addition, he tried his best to protect China's position on the global political stage, as a scientist with a great sense of responsibility and duty. During the later stages of the epidemic, he went on a herculean journey to search for its virus host, conducting much research and verification that led to a perfect end to the fight against SARS. In 2004, when there were signs that SARS was making a comeback, he rose to the occasion again, speaking the truth in front of Hong Kong journalists.

As a medical expert who fought the virus on the front line, his words carried great weight and proved to be highly credible. With his rigorous pursuit of science and his rational approach to talking to the West, Dr. Zhong naturally became the face of China and its government during the epidemic. It was not something he was ordered to do, but was his own choice.

Cheng said, "Had the Chinese government tried to explain how China was responding to the epidemic, it would have been highly unlikely that foreigners would have believed us. Since we approached the situation in a less than ideal manner during the earliest stages, we had lost the trust of the world by that point. However, Dr. Zhong won back a good deal of trust with his tireless pursuit of science. Aa a man of science, he proactively reached out to the outside world, talking about a range of matters from the first SARS case to China's effort in fighting the epidemic. He always told the truth, and the world believed him."

As Cheng Donghai saw it, the emergence of Dr. Zhong, his scientific spirit, and his public speeches during the epidemic had a great impact on the bad habit of selective reporting when it came to major affairs. In an era of information globalization, even a minor event could cause massive ripples and attract global attention. Attempts at hush ups only made things worse. This was proven in later incidents as well, such as the milk scandal in China in 2008.

Additionally, SARS resulted in the creation of an emergency management system in China. After the epidemic, China's central government, along with local governing bodies on the provincial, municipal, and district levels, established a full set of emergency management systems. From then on, most calamities and disasters could be handled with minimal loss.

SARS also promoted better hygiene standards among the Chinese people. For example, hand-washing, a minor detail that has a great impact on the prevention of diseases, was put under the spotlight and treated with an unprecedented level of seriousness. Furthermore, SARS greatly reduced the capturing and eating of wild animals.

After the epidemic, the nation started to treat healthcare on a completely new level, resulting in a boom of investment in the healthcare industry. What's more, the government, medical institutions, and the people learned to treat prevention as one of the top priorities for health issues. People became more willing to adopt a healthier lifestyle.

In his battle with SARS, Dr. Zhong demonstrated a strong scientific spirit that won people's respect and promoted social progress. This spirit, in its essence, included the habit of telling the truth based on material and factual evidence. Dr. Zhong always spoke with truth and evidence. As a scientist, his words were always based on science. During the SARS epidemic, these qualities were especially valuable.

It had been many years since the SARS epidemic ended, but Cheng Donghai still recalled Dr. Zhong's contributions, and he does so to this day. In his opinion, it was precisely the rivalry between truths and lies that manifested during the epidemic which proved Dr. Zhong's rationality and scientific knowledge. In the "chlamydia vs. coronavirus" controversy, Dr. Zhong stood behind his observations and research. Even under great pressure, he stood his ground until his theory was accepted by the CPC Guangdong Provincial Committee. It was precisely due to his persistence that these theories played such a critical role in China's war against SARS.

28

THE PEOPLE THANK YOU

On July 20, 2004, at the 10th All-China Federation of Returned Overseas Chinese, General Secretary of the CPC Central Committee and President of the People's Republic of China Hu Jintao personally honored Dr. Zhong as one of Ten Outstanding Overseas Chinese, saying to him, "You have made outstanding contributions to the prevention and control of SARS. The people thank you."

At the opening of the Touching China, People of the Year 2003 award ceremony on CCTV, host Jing Yidan said, "Some people rarely shed tears, but at a certain moment, tears will start streaming down their cheeks. Some people are rarely affected by emotions, but at a certain moment, they will be greatly touched. On those days full of doubt and expectations, there is a person who grounds us and moves us."

The dazzling ceremony saw the nation overwhelmed with excitement. On stage, the much-awaited hero appeared and gave a deep bow. The stage was only ten meters long, but each of Dr. Zhong's steps was reminiscent of hardships, difficulties, and delight. He raised one arm to the cheering audience in his customary calm, kind manner.

Amid all the flowers and applause offered, the heroes' place in people's hearts was cemented. A member of election committee said, "When SARS struck, Dr. Zhong Nanshan put his personal safety aside to save patients, and also fruitfully explored methods of preventing and controlling SARS. He is a hero who has made great contributions to people's health."

The spring of 2003 was a season that Chinese people would remember, not least because they came to understand the importance of self-reflection. A virus called SARS broke out, bringing a horror that spread more rapidly than the omen of death it carried. It was a war without smoke and mirrors – a real victory, and a baptism of unprecedented pomp. Faced with this unfamiliar virus, both the mainstay of medical professionals and ordinary medical workers bravely stood at the forefront and did not retreat from their positions for fear of infection.

In February 2004, on behalf of the country, society, and people, CCTV commented in a solemn tone that this was a disease not known to human society, an epidemic whose cause was still unknown to the medical community. However, in the south of China, where the spread of SARS originated, an accomplished 67-year-old expert, with the scientific, rational mind of a medical practitioner, requested to transfer critical patients to the IRH where he was in charge for isolation and treatment.

In a statement that is now legendary, Dr. Zhong said, "This is our line of work and our responsibility." He had been appointed in time of a crisis to serve as the leader of the SARS medical rescue expert team of Guangdong Province. He also said, "The greatest politics is to do our jobs well."

Faced with danger and the threat of death, he stepped forward and never retreated. "This is the real Zhong Nanshan. Despite the honor and academic status he has achieved, he never blindly followed authority, but only spoke fact-based judgments to his SARS patients." After enduring so much difficulty, the words of acclaim were precious.

At that moment, Dr. Zhong repeated an idea he had shared many times: "Pursuing the unknown is my greatest motivation." He respected facts and did whatever it took to fight for his country and people. "When seeing that facts are different from what the authorities say, of course we first respect facts, not the authorities."

He told ceremony host Bai Yansong that when facing such a new disease with a high mortality rate in 2003, he felt as if he was participating in a war. Was there ever a battlefield field without trumpets? Dr. Zhong was touched by his colleagues, who gave their lives like heroes. The sudden arrival of the deadly disease was a test for every medical worker. As soon as they rose from their sickbeds after contracting SARS, they stepped right back to the front line.

Finally, after much pain and suffering, China safely passed through the spring of 2004.

Although the epidemic was a dark shadow that would not be forgotten, the clear sky offered hope.

Dr. Zhong gave a speech at the ceremony. Faced with the sudden outbreak of the SARS epidemic, he was calm and fearless. He saved lives with the kindness of a doctor and responded to the crisis with the practical, scientific attitude of a scientist. He said, "The greatest politics is to do a good job of preventing and controlling the disease." These resounding words demonstrated his life motto and professional ethics. His admirable academic courage, noble medical ethics, and in-depth scientific exploration gave people the power to conquer the epidemic.

PART 2

THE DOCTORS

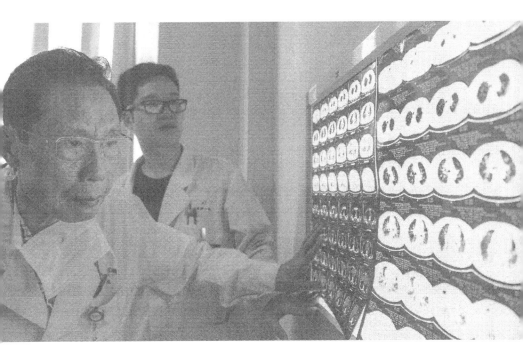

DEDICATED TO PATIENTS

A journalist who had had doubts about Dr. Zhong found that his attitude towards his patients could be measured at any time and anywhere.

"What's wrong with you? Why haven't you finished your work yet?" Dr. Zhong growled, pointing at the doctor who was standing in front of him with his head bowed. This happened during the SARS outbreak in April 2003, when Dr. Zhong had just started work in the morning, and he had come across this doctor in the hallway. Even before the epidemic, he could not afford to slack off, let alone in such severe, extraordinary times. He was furious, and he grilled the doctor about when his work would be done. A patient's family member ran over with trepidation and begged him for help. Dr. Zhong's angry gaze softened instantly. "Hi," he said. "It's an emergency, isn't it? I'm Zhong Nanshan. How may I help you?"

The concern in his voice surprised the family member. "Oh, you're quite kind. My relative is very sick. Can you help her?"

"Don't worry. I'll be over in a short while. I promise. What is your relative's name? Which bed is she in? What's her condition? Who is her attending doctor?" Dr. Zhong spoke quickly but amiably.

Cheng Donghai, Party branch secretary of the IRH, made an appointment with a journalist from Shanghai who was supposed to arrive before noon. However, the journalist arrived early in the morning and coincidentally came across this scene in the hallway. When he noticed the family member approaching Dr. Zhong with trepidation, he kept quiet and carried on observing.

The journalist was amazed at how a person so furious could instantly turn his anger into peace and be so humble, calm, and compassionate while facing a person who was not related to him and had come to ask for his help. Later, the journalist recorded this incident in detail. He was very impressed and stated in his article, "It seems that Zhong Nanshan's reputation for treating his patients as family is true. His attitude toward them can be measured at anytime and anywhere." The use of the word "measured" was notable.

Cheng Donghai snatched some time from his busy schedule to write an article on Zhong Nanshan's dedication to serving his patients. "Doctors all want to do their best for patients. But Dr. Zhong goes above and beyond, anytime and anywhere."

After being transferred to the IRH in April 2003, Cheng Donghai witnessed Dr. Zhong's wholehearted dedication to patients over and over again. Cheng remarked, "People who work around him know very well that he is a highly efficient person, and he expects others to be efficient too. He is strict and stern with people in the workplace. This is why the IRH has been a notable platform and how its rigorous and efficient working style has been developed. Without his strictness and high standards, the IRH wouldn't be what it is today, and he wouldn't have trained so many medical practitioners."

Dr. Zhong was extremely busy with work during the SARS outbreak. Due to his short fuse, he had failed to control his temper and got angry at that doctor. Subsequently, when the Shanghai journalist interviewed Cheng Donghai, he admitted to being skeptical about the Guangdong media reporting that in winter, Dr. Zhong would warm up his stethoscope with his hands before using it on a patient, but now, he was convinced beyond doubt.

Dr. Zhong bent down to patients to check them, held them up to test their blood sugar palpate them, and then helped them lie down and straightened their quilt. Regardless of the age and condition of the patient, Dr. Zhong treated them all equally, even if they were severely contagious.

There were many other stories about Dr. Zhong caring for patients. In the 1980s, the *Guangzhou Daily* newspaper reported that he had been taking care of Qu Jieqiong, who worked at a small coal store in Guangzhou. He treated her through an illness and then through her daily life for more than a decade until her death in 1996. Before she died, Qu said that Dr. Zhong was her great benefactor. She had been suffering from myasthenia gravis, and Dr. Zhong had organized several expert consultations for her, which was common practice for him.

He never lost sight of his role, no matter how his work changed or how famous he became. He never forgot that he was a doctor, and his faith did not waver since the 1970s.

Many people underwent radical changes to their views after SARS. Dr. Zhong did too. The only thing that had remained was his dedication to his patients. To relieve their pain and suffering, he maintained a devoted, enthusiastic service mindset for the best part of forty years.

Many people made their mark and became famous in the 1980s and '90s, but most of them changed with the passage of time and faded into obscurity again. By contrast, Dr. Zhong was well known for decades, and he still had a reputation. Those who lived through the 1950s and '60s remembered what Chairman Mao said about the revolutionary hero Lei Feng: "It is not difficult for a person to do a good deed, but it is difficult to do only good deeds and not bad deeds in a lifetime. This requires a broad mind."

Over the decades, Dr. Zhong formed a habit of putting patients first, and it was now almost an instinct. He could not stay away from them. This may have seemed vain or boastful to the general public, but for him, it was an instinctive revelation of his true feelings.

If Dr. Zhong was considered a practiced paradigm, then it was unchangeable, because it had been cultivated for decades. He once said, "What exactly is a doctor for? I always advocate that doctors should have good medical ethics, and more importantly, should be able to solve problems. A good attitude gains patients' trust and cooperation to cure diseases together. Patients will cooperate only when they trust you. They will provide a very true picture of their condition, and they will follow your instructions about taking medicine. They will not doubt it because they trust you."

Dr. Zhong gave an example of a miner's daughter in Xi'an. The girl was 14 years. He checked her and diagnosed her with severe asthma, a very frightening disease. Dr. Zhong told her not to worry too much. While she was being treated in Guangzhou, she had an attack, and it caused the doctors to wonder, "Why is this happening when she is taking medication?" Dr. Zhong asked the doctors to focus on observing her condition. Less than a week later, she had another attack, and all the doctors were immediately on alert. They filmed her on a cell phone and showed it to Dr. Zhong. He found that it was not an asthma attack at all, but a panic attack. When panic struck, she desperately fought for breath and got cramps. The situation finally became clear. It was caused by psychological factors.

Once a patient trusted a doctor, it made treatment much easier. Many patients were uncertain about their doctors' diagnosis or medication, so they didn't fully comply. After a while, when they found that the medicine didn't work very well on them, they stopped taking it. The fact was that some medications only took effect when they were taken consistently. Why did the patients stop taking them, then? It was because they didn't trust their doctors. Therefore, a crucial issue was to build patients' trust in doctors. This required doctors to put themselves in their patients' shoes.

It was essential for doctors to gain patients' genuine trust, even the terminally ill. For instance, in the case of a patient with an advanced tumor, Dr. Zhong said, "I talked to him and tried to bring him some good news, such as that his breathing was getting better after a period of treatment. This was to encourage him by conveying a message that his condition could still be improved. Once he became hopeful, he was no longer in a completely desperate state of mind."

Dr. Zhong believed that doctors' attitudes could determine patients' conditions. That wasn't to say that doctors had to smile all the time, but as long as they had a positive attitude, it would naturally be reflected in their words and actions. There was no way to fake it. A doctor who only learned techniques like a student and didn't have a positive attitude would find that this dealings with patients would stay at a superficial level, a fake smile showing a few teeth.

Sometimes, patients came to Guangzhou from other places, like Xi'an, to see a doctor. Dr. Zhong told them that they didn't have to travel so far, and he gave them the names of doctors local to them. While this may have lost income for his hospital, it was more important to think about the patients. When patients were in financial difficulty, doctors needed to try to provide simple treatment and show them how to take their medicine.

The cordial atmosphere between Dr. Zhong and his patients was like that of friends and family. He found the patient-doctor disputes that had intensified over the years, often involving violence towards medical staff, to be painful and regrettable.

One afternoon in October 2013, Dr. Zhong was at a clinic when his assistant handed him an urgent letter saying that a doctor at the Second Affiliated Hospital of Guangzhou Medical University had been beaten and injured by the family of a dead patient. The injured doctor was a department head and a former student of Dr. Zhong. He was beaten because the family wanted to take the patient's body home, but the hospital refused because it was illegal. The doctor was injured very badly by seven or eight attackers, even suffering loss of vision, a mild concussion, cracked ribs, a subperitoneal hemorrhage of the spleen, and blood in his urine. That afternoon, Dr. Zhong faced a number of media outlets and expressed his indignation. "This is violence. The rights and wrongs of the incident are obvious." He called on government functionaries to protect the lives of medical staff by enforcing the law. Shortly after the incident, in December 2013, another violent attack on a doctor occurred in the city of Wenling in Zhejiang Province. A town health center was smashed up, and many members of the medical staff were injured. The incident happened late at night on December 15 at about 10:00 pm. A man surnamed Chen from Hengchen village in the town of Ruoheng felt unwell after drinking alcohol. He went with some friends to the Ruoheng Town Health Center for medical treatment. After being infused for about ten minutes, Chen's condition became critical, and he died despite attempts at resuscitation.

Faced with the constant threat of violence, medical staff began to call for zero tolerance. On May 28, 2014, another violent incident against a doctor occurred at the Gansu Hospital of Traditional Chinese Medicine. This was the third attack on medical staff in Gansu since May 14. The medical and health industry demanded that medical-related crimes be punished according to the law and order be maintained.

On the morning of May 28, 2014, a receiving doctor in the outpatient room at the Department of Trauma and Orthopedics at Gansu Hospital of Traditional Chinese Medicine was beaten. At around 11:00 am that day, a patient left the outpatient room after an examination to collect her medicine. Her family suddenly rushed into the room, picked up a stool, and flung it at the doctor, who was treating another patient, causing multiple injuries to his arms and head, including a six-centimeter-long head wound and a severe concussion.

In a violent assault on a medical professional in Hunan on June 13, 2014, a pregnant nurse was beaten so badly she suffered a miscarriage.

During the Two Sessions of the National People's Congress in March 2014, Dr. Zhong pointed out that there had been no significant breakthrough in medical reform in the past five years and that violence against medical staff was a problem of the hospital system.

Problems such as violence against medical staff, high medical costs, and difficulty seeing a doctor were common in large hospitals. Dr. Zhong pointed out that in bigger hospitals, more examinations and prescriptions led to expensive medical costs. It was difficult to improve the patient-doctor relationship because of long waits, short consultations, and less communication. Data from the Chinese Hospital Association showed that 73.3% of hospitals above tertiary level had experienced violence against their medical staff. The keywords "violence against medical staff" in Baidu brought up more than 7.4 million web links, and it was the second most searched health event after "smog."

In response to the frequent violence against medical staff, Dr. Zhong indicated that although conflict between patients and doctors was a global problem, a Chinese doctor has to see fifty patients in half a day. How much time did they have to communicate with patients? Waiting for three hours and seeing a doctor for only three minutes inevitably led to frustration, as a lack of communication often leads to conflict. Instead of saying that this was a problem of doctors' morals, it needed to be seen as a problem within the hospital system. Of course, the issue of medical staff's attitudes toward patients and their families, as well as medical standards, could not be ignored.

Before the Two Sessions, Dr. Zhong researched all the tertiary hospitals in Guangzhou and concluded that the majority of the doctors' income came from the hospitals' operating income, not from government input. He remarked, "This is a typical operation mode: the state-owned, privately operated system, where the government simply establishes some policies, and hospitals have to expand their income sources to ensure operation." He explained that these income sources included medicine price differences, treating more common diseases, and even increasing the number of examinations and prescriptions, thus making it difficult and expensive to see a doctor and causing conflicts between medical staff and patients.

The hospital system was one of the factors in this problem. Another was that the government's investment in the healthcare industry was too low. Dr. Zhong said, "In early February 2013, I told Minister of Health Chen Zhu that China's annual medical expenditure only accounts for 5.5% of the GDP, which is far lower than all other developing countries. Even Afghanistan and Cuba are higher than us."

In 2014, Dr. Zhong, now nearly 78 years old, spoke fondly of his heartfelt wish to reform the healthcare system, choking up a little as he spoke. He said that he was looking forward to the day when medical staff were able to work in an environment where they can be fully committed to serving patients, and where patients could admire the medical staff as "angels in white" who were saving people's lives.

THE HERITAGE OF
MEDICAL ETHICS

Dr. Zhong's noble medical ethics nurtured one group of medical students after another, His ideas centered on asking "why" more, and thinking carefully about each case. He taught his students to study medicine and to help patients get better by any means. When it came to teaching medical skills, he always prioritized mindsets.

Once, one of Dr. Zhong's students made a mistake about a patient's condition, thinking that it was not tuberculosis. Despite later pathology proving that it was, they had used some other medications on the patient and invited experts from Beijing for a consultation. However, the result still showed that it was not tuberculosis. Dr. Zhong refused to give up. He asked the student to keep track of the patient and make observations. The patient, a 30-year-old woman, understood and was willing to cooperate, as she had been to many hospitals and still had not been diagnosed. When she spoke to Dr. Zhong, she said that she was no longer worried, because she trusted him no matter what the outcome was. Her condition was extremely rare and difficult to diagnose.

After four months of treatment, her health improved so much that she hoped to have a baby when she recovered. Even though her CT scan and chest X-ray showed improvement, Dr. Zhong still doubted his diagnosis, because the patient's condition was not obvious. His students were confident that their mentor would not be wrong.

Again, Dr. Zhong took the patient's lung biopsies and all the other information and spoke with experts, finally proving that it was in fact tuberculosis. The patient's treatment continued, and Dr. Zhong's assistant followed up with observations. After a year and a half of follow-up treatment, the patient finally recovered and gave birth to a child as she had hoped.

Dr. Zhong readily accepted cases like this, seeing them as challenges for his academic research. He knew that some patients came to him because they had already been to many hospitals without a diagnosis. For example, one patient had been seeing a doctor from the Department of Ophthalmology and Otorhinolaryngology for some time when he came to Dr. Zhong to see if there were any problems with his digestive tract and trachea.

Dr. Zhong said, "If you cannot diagnose a patient, then why should they come to consult you?"

He had one key characteristic when it comes to consulting with patients. He always said that it was not solely his responsibility to solve the problem. He invited doctors from different disciplines to joint consultations.

Under his leadership, his students developed a habit of putting themselves in their patients' shoes. Each year, Dr. Zhong mentored a new group of students, and he always told them, "You won't be able to see a lot of patients in a year here. There are only four patients a week, so it doesn't add up to a lot in fifty weeks. However, you have to learn the ways of thinking, and more importantly, learn to consider your patients. Don't ever say that you can't handle a case and then escalate it to a higher level. You need to think and explore solutions. This is something very basic." He added, "Consulting with a patient cannot be like the railway police, with each person in charge of a section of railway." Sometimes, when he noticed that a patient had a problem other than respiratory disease, he would not hesitate to ask a doctor from that discipline to take a look.

Dr. Zhong was strict in judging himself. "Actually, my capability is very limited. I know a bit about my discipline, but in other areas like the heart, gastrointestinal tract, liver, rheumatism, and kidneys, I am a layman."

During the most severe period of the SARS crisis in 2003, many doctors and nurses were extremely worried about what they should do if patients started dying in large numbers. Dr. Zhong told them, "If that happens, and even if only one out of ten patients survives, you will still learn a lot from the experience of curing that patient. In the future, you will be able to save more lives. The first SARS patient we received had white lungs. Various indications showed there was no hope, but I didn't agree. We still had to try. I tried hormones on the patient. Unexpectedly, their condition improved the next day." He continued, "As doctors, we often have to turn chances into inevitabilities."

After the ward rounds, Dr. Zhong pulled at his mask and the strap broke with a gentle tug. He removed the mask and went straight to the conference room on the eighth floor. Behind him, his students, the head nurse, attending doctor, and chief physician followed him at pace.

They took off their white coats before they sat down, folding them and putting them aside just as Dr. Zhong did. The movements flowed smoothly, without delay. Going upstairs, the septuagenarian Dr. Zhong took two steps at a time. The others had to trot to catch up with him, even though they were much younger.

In the conference room, every patient's pathological data and diagnosis were available, presented in the form of PowerPoint slides. There was no hierarchy; everyone was free to elaborate, argue, and express their views. The only goal was to find the best solution to cure the patients.

Dr. Zhong told everyone that the patients who came to the IRH for a doctor's consultation or hospitalization had already been passed around among several hospitals. They were critically ill and suffering from severe illnesses. They had to think from different angles and be very careful.

In his work, Dr. Zhong never slacked off. He treated patients with great clinical skills. Returning to the office, he focused on his scientific research. He operated with a system that paired the strong with the weak and the senior with the junior. A vibrant chain was formed over the years, cultivating a backbone of scientific research in each new cohort.

The overall office environment at the IRH was cramped and simple, but there was a conference room that could accommodate two to three hundred people for pathological analysis. It was spacious and well designed. The group sat looking at the PowerPoint slides, which showed a variety of images and diagnoses of patients. The conference room was filled with a scholarly atmosphere. Dr. Zhong guided their thinking, encouraging them to use logical and divergent ideas to analyze problems. This academic perspective brought out the best in the gathered medical staff.

Practical medicine involved practicing and studying concurrently, and the results were quickly apparent. In this way, after clinically treating a patient for a period of time, the result could be transformed into the fruits of scientific research through induction, analysis, and conclusion.

Dr. Zhong said to the team, "We carry out research frequently, but mere research is not enough. The main purpose is still to solve patients' problems. It's true that you are under a lot of pressure and are very tired now, but keep it up, and you will make great progress in just a few years."

In such an environment, there was no right or wrong, only facts. When he encountered a problem, Dr. Zhong behaved like a student, saying that he didn't understand. Sometimes, he even claimed he had never heard of such an issue before. This was a psychological tactic that offered invisible encouragement to others, causing them to unconsciously offload their inferiority complex. Some of Dr. Zhong's students were initially timid and did not dare to say a word, but spoke so eloquently once he created this space, as if they were different people.

Dr. Zhong cultivated talent in two main areas. One involved emphasizing basic skills. No matter how bad the IRH's financial condition was, it would still spare some funds for cultivating backbone staff. These staff members were given one or two years of study opportunities, either in China or overseas, then they took on good roles when they return. Dr. Zhong always adopted the philosophy of learning advanced things.

The other area involved encouraging active thinking. This reflected the fact that Dr. Zhong was a person who would only appoint virtuous, talented people, regardless of their relationship to him. He believed that it didn't matter where a hero came from. There were some very young doctors, but as long as what they said made sense, he would recognize them. Young people felt very comfortable with Dr. Zhong, even though he was a respected elder.

The students were very different from each other, each having their own characteristics. Some lacked confidence, while some were very conceited. When Dr. Zhong commented on a matter, he only focused on the matter itself and did not involve personal feelings. As for people who had strong personalities and seemed unacceptable to others, Dr. Zhong accepted them with generosity, including their strong opinions. He said, "As long as it's right, I will adopt it. If it's wrong, I will still encourage the person."

He paid special attention to cultivating young people's basic skills, such as self-expression, which was connected to thinking. The IRH's elite graduates made excellent lecturers. Dr. Zhong believed that they may have been influenced by him. They often listened to his lectures and tried to imitate him, so they improved quickly. He always encouraged them to think and guide them on how to express themselves clearly.

His view on basic skills was that language was the most important. Language was not about how brilliant one's self-expression or powers of description might be, or how many beautiful words were used. It was about being able to analyze problems accurately with a clear, logical hierarchy. It was also a fundamental skill for people in all industries. If a person had this ability, they could do anything well, so Dr. Zhong often consciously gave his students the opportunity to express themselves. And being highly conscientious and responsible toward patients, maintaining the passion to pursue his career, and insisting on constant scientific innovation, Dr. Zhong not only taught his students with his words and actions, but also deeply influenced his colleagues, subconsciously nurturing a dynamic team that was brave, dedicated, and willing to take responsibility.

At the end of April 2012, Vice President of Guangzhou University of Chinese Medicine Wang Xinhua received a transfer order to serve as the Director of Guangzhou Medical College (now Guangzhou Medical University). The day after the Department of Organization of the CPC Committee of Guangdong Provincial announced the transfer order, Wang rushed to Dr. Zhong's office at the First Affiliated Hospital of Guangzhou Medical University early in the morning. He wanted to ask this highly respected senior figure for some guidance and advice.

The weather in Guangzhou in May was as hot as the summer in Beijing. The golden morning sunlight was like dancing children, playing and chasing the slight ripples of the Pearl River. Waiting outside Dr. Zhong's office, Wang Xinhua felt calmer as he took in the view from the window.

Wang had met with Zhong several times and was familiar with him. However, he was still anxious about speaking to him after all this time. Would Dr. Zhong be impressed with his plans? Would he accept and recognize a person with a TCM background being put in charge of Guangzhou Medical University?

The door opened, and Dr. Zhong appeared with a smile on his face and a warm greeting. He welcomed Wang into his office, offered him a seat, and handed him a bottle of water. Being treated like a long-time friend, Wang Xinhua completely relaxed. Taking a seat, he looked at Dr. Zhong and could not believe that this man – physically fit, talkative, and quick-thinking – was 76 years old. Wang was warmed by Dr. Zhong's kind words, which also carried an invisible encouragement: as a younger person, he should be more energetic.

Dr. Zhong listened intently to Wang's report on the future development of the hospital, followed by an earnest, sincere talk.

"Even now, I am still touched by Dr. Zhong's warmth to me that day. He is not a person who will put on airs. Most importantly, his trust in me was full of his expectations and hopes for the medical industry." Wang felt that although Dr. Zhong was no longer part of the hospital leadership team, his mind was still on some major events in the development of the hospital, which he considered his responsibility. The first was the renaming of Guangzhou Medical College to Guangzhou Medical University. The second was the establishment of a project in Datansha by the hospital's Respiratory Center. The third was the construction of the new campus in Panyu.

"That day, Dr. Zhong urged me to speed up these events," Wang said. Today, all these things have become or are becoming realities.

"He also urged me to ask the CPC Committee of the university to remove him as Director of the State Key Laboratory of Respiratory Diseases and put a young person in charge. This is what I saw with my own eyes: a senior leader and a visionary scholar, whom I admired, saw it as the greatest joy to be a ladder for young people to climb up to higher positions. He was so earnest, like a teenager. His words were refreshing to me, and they were the motivation for the rest of my life. As one of Dr. Zhong's students, how could I not keep exploring and moving forward? I have to shoulder my responsibilities."

3

REFORM OF THE CHINESE MEDICAL ASSOCIATION

Since Dr. Zhong became President of the Chinese Medical Association, he had avidly promoted democracy and a sense of service, reforming the "officialist" work style of the association. It was Wu Yi, then Vice Premier of the State Council, who had encouraged him to be the President. So, after the reform, he said with emotion, "I didn't let her down after all."

At the first full board meeting of the 23rd Council of the Chinese Medical Association in the afternoon of April 13, 2005, Dr. Zhong Nanshan, Chairman of the Respiratory Medicine Branch of the Chinese Medical Association, was elected as the new President of the Chinese Medical Association, and Wu Mingjiang was elected as the Secretary-General. Fourteen vice presidential candidates were put forward, including Ba Denian, Wang Haiyan, and Wu Mingjiang.

Standing adjacent to the Huaqiao Building to the west, the traditional gray, sloping-roofed office building of the Chinese Medical Association was located in the heart of the bustling city, at 42 Dongsi West Street, Dongcheng District, Beijing. Traffic there was always smooth, which was indeed an exception for Beijing, where the roads were jammed day and night.

The year Dr. Zhong took office, 2005, was also the 90th anniversary of the founding of the association. At that time, its official and civil status and influence were equivalent to the MOH.

It was 6:00 pm, and Dr. Zhong was still in the midst of a special meeting at the Chinese Medical Association, a place he frequently visited from Guangzhou. When the meeting concluded, he walked slowly and quietly out of the meeting room into the courtyard, as if the day's hard work was fading as he went. The soft sunset brought an orange-red haze to the sky.

Dr. Zhong was the first academic to hold the position of President of the association as a non-government official. Since then, the role has been concurrently served by the ministers of the MOH. Hu Yamei, a pediatrician who participated in the vote, said that the Chinese Medical Association was an academic community, and the election of an academic was good for facilitating academic exchange and communication.

After coming on board, Dr. Zhong carried out a thorough reform of the management of the association. During his tenure as President, he focused on two themes for the association to work on: democracy and service. He saw the association as more like a government office than an academic community. He proposed that it should practice democracy and service, and all staff, both from the specialized branches or the main office, must comply.

Originally, the work style of the association was somewhat bureaucratic. Dr. Zhong was not happy with this, leading him to instigate a new mindset. By democracy, he meant that all staff should have the right to express personal opinions and have equal opportunities. By service, he meant that the staff would serve members.

Once, the chairman of a specialized branch wanted to be re-elected, but some didn't agree. Many conflicts ensued. Dr. Zhong believed that appointment would not have been necessary if there had been full democracy and a vote to decide who would take over the position. Everyone would respect and recognize the leader they elected, as this was how democracy worked. Since Dr. Zhong had been President, a significant number of branches were no longer as compliant with the previous standing committee's decision on the appointment of the next post. The situation had changed: people were free to express their opinions and even put themselves forward. Many of the branch leaders democratically elected through competitive recruitment were approved by everyone.

Under Dr. Zhong's leadership, the Chinese Medical Association made several major reforms. The first was that, in principle, the tenure of the chairs of all branches was three years, after which they must step down. They could be re-elected, but not without stepping down first. This was to enable younger people to have the opportunity to be promoted. It was a very significant reform, and it was supported almost unanimously. The second reform was to deal with any leaders who were elected through improper means.

Once, during an election at the association, a booklet was prepared as a gift to each attendee, including the association members and the association secretary. The secretary opened his booklet and noticed there was one more thing inside, a small envelope. Inside the envelope was a shopping voucher worth 9,999 RMB. The voucher had been slipped to him by someone he did not know, in an attempt to bribe him to vote for him. The secretary immediately handed the voucher to Dr. Zhong.

Dr. Zhong did not compromise, "We will not allow such behavior." It was inevitable that conflict would ensue.

Later, the person sent some people to the association to "reason" with Dr. Zhong and wrote a letter to claim that the association did not have the right to interfere in this way. They even threatened to escalate the issue and leak it to the press. Dr. Zhong responded, "Great. Please go ahead. I will even go along with you." He made himself very clear, saying, "No matter who you are or where you come from, it's absolutely wrong to bribe people to be elected. It won't work."

Despite well-meaning mediators and attractive exchange conditions, Zhong Nanshan would not give in. From that time on, the association completely changed its image, reversed its work style, and played its proper role.

Dr. Zhong explained his guiding principle: the only way to be the branch chair was by a democratic election, and the tenure must not be too long so that everyone had an equal opportunity. Also, it was completely acceptable to be re-elected. Now, the atmosphere of most branches was much better, and only a few still had problems. He took the approach of letting people nominate themselves and agreed that the person with the most votes would be the winner. In this way, the staff were able to work in a relaxed environment. Before, it had been one man's decision. Even if there were opposing voices, they held no weight, so capable staff were never elected. If only the leader had a say, and the subordinates had no choice but to obey. However, when their obedience was not sincere, rumors swirled.

Alongside instituting democracy, Dr. Zhong aimed to establish the image of service. During Dr. Zhong's tenure as President of the Chinese Medical Association, he mainly addressed these two aspects. He also made considerable efforts to establish a brand of academic conferences and improve the specifications of the association's academic journal.

He said, "Most importantly, I didn't fail Wu Yi. However, I offended a lot of people."

Dr. Zhong spoke about the numerous tasks of the association with great familiarity, and he mentioned some of his regrets as well. He felt he hadn't fulfilled Wu Yi's requirement, which was to let the administrative departments actively undertake normative, technical, and self-regulatory functions. This was what Dr. Zhong strongly supported and what he had been working to reform for several years. He completely understood the influence of the association on the regional branches and the considerable appeal to the medical and healthcare community and all related industries and institutions.

"Because of their influence and appeal, the branch chairs should not be viewed as symbols of power and money. Rather, they should be representatives of high academic standards and a passion for service," he said.

When someone was chosen as a branch chair, it proved that the medical authorities considered them to have a positive image and be good in all aspects. Because of this, the election had to be very careful and thorough. Dr. Zhong said, "We have to be very strict in this regard, unlike the undemocratic elections of the past."

Dr. Zhong felt that the Chinese Medical Association could not be a second MOH. Holding a position at the association or serving as a member of the main committee or standing committee of the academic community could not be seen as a symbol of status and power.

The Chinese Medical Association was an academic, public-welfare, non-profit organization registered under the law and established by Chinese medical science and technology professionals. It was the bridge to unite the CPC and the government with these professionals and an important social force for the development of medical science, technology, and public health in China. The association was founded in 1915, and by this time, it had 88 specialized branches with 670,000 members. It had published 183 medical and scientific journals, and it hosted and organized nearly 200 domestic and international medical conferences every year. The main business scope of the association consisted of carrying out academic medical exchanges; editing and publishing medical academic and scientific journals, books, and electronic audio and video products; conducting continuing medical education; performing medical exchanges and cooperations with the international community, including Hong Kong, Macao, and Taiwan; making evaluations and argumentation of medical science and technology projects; selecting and awarding excellent medical science and technology achievements (including academic papers and works of popular science); participating in post-graduation medical education and training and assessment of specialist physicians and discovering, recommending, and cultivating outstanding medical science and technology personnel; promoting and rewarding medical staff with high medical ethics and excellent practice; implementing a technical identification of medical accidents; and promoting the transformation and application of medical scientific research results. The most critical of these to reflect the opinions of medical science and technology professionals to the Party and the government.

During his tenure, Dr. Zhong had led the association's staff to loosen the "officialist" work style. For example, whoever became chair would only serve three years, after which the position would be open for a democratic election. Just because a person had served as chair did not mean that the person was the best for the job. The bad habits of the past were quietly changing and even coming to an end. Dr. Zhong smiled and said, with emotion, "It's not easy."

China's "officialist" mentality was deeply rooted. People were accustomed to matching each position to a certain national hierarchy, such as a position equivalent to a department, bureau, or ministry level. Dr. Zhong thought that it was necessary to change this. It was one of his most important guiding principles.

He didn't ask to be made President of the Chinese Medical Association. He took the position because he wanted to implement reform and do something for the medical staff. He explained that in 1983, when he had just returned from his studies abroad, he was appointed as President of Guangzhou Medical College (renamed Guangzhou Medical University in 2013), but he refused. He knew what he needed most, and he had decided to focus all his energy on building his discipline.

In 1992, again, the Organization Department of the CPC Guangzhou Municipal Committee asked him to be President of Guangzhou Medical College. He declined. However, the organization said that as a member of the CPC, he must take the role, so he had to choose.

Dr. Zhong recalled, "Wu Yi asked me to be President at the Seventh All-China Federation of Returned Overseas Chinese in July 2004."

Wu Yi had called him backstage to make the request. She said that in the future, it should not always be people from MOH being President. Dr. Zhong replied that he was too old and did not live in Beijing, so he was not suitable for the position. Wu Yi did not say anything more, so Dr. Zhong thought the matter was over.

Unexpectedly, then Minister of Health, Gao Qiang, stepped in and asked Dr. Zhong to accept the position. Gao had gone to Beijing, Shanghai, and Tianjin to seek the opinions of medical staff, and an overwhelming majority wanted Dr. Zhong to be President of the association.

Dr. Zhong hesitated for a long time. It happened that he wasn't in the best of health, so he had a check-up. Initially, he thought that if he had any health problems, he would simply refuse the offer. It turned out that he was perfectly well, so he became the President.

"These things are not secrets. I didn't fight for these positions, but since I have taken them on, I must do it well."

Dr. Zhong said his main interest and energy was to treat patients and conduct medical research. He was helpless because he had limited time to conduct research directly on the front line. Even when he went to consult, treat, and cure patients, he thought there was too little time. He was now in his 80s, and after experiencing so many things and meeting so many people, he was still doing the same old business. He didn't care what others thought of him because he had never left his fundamental role of serving patients as a doctor. Having said that, he seemed very pleased.

This was the real Zhong Nanshan. If he were not allowed to be a doctor, he would lose his fundamental purpose. Even with all of the honors bestowed upon him, he could not be happy without his work.

4

MAKING THE WORLD BELIEVE IN TRADITIONAL CHINESE MEDICINE

Zhong Nanshan had long noted that the essence of Traditional Chinese Medicine (TCM), its long history and millennia of knowledge, were only one step away from evidence-based medicine. So why could TCM not break through the bottleneck?

His hands touched patients' shoulders, jaw, arms, and neck, pinching the muscles in their arms, legs, and feet. Then he examined the patients' fingertips and tongue. Most importantly, he auscultated patients with his stethoscope both in the outpatient clinic and ward rounds. Each of these steps was essential for him to diagnose a patient's condition. These diagnostic methods reminded many of his patients of TCM.

A Western-trained doctor with high medical ethics and superb skills, Dr. Zhong had studied TCM intensely, so he understood it. Many patients had been ill for a long time, and by pinching their shoulders and arms, checking the elasticity of their subcutaneous fat and muscles, he could judge whether they had been malnourished for a while or whether they had recently lost weight. He could tell the difference because the loose feeling of subcutaneous fat and skin was completely different, which was related to a patient's condition.

His method of touching his patients was known as palpation. For example, some malignant diseases had a sudden onset, and patients would lose weight quickly. There was a similar method in the West, known as percussion. In the past, in Western medicine clinics, some doctors performed percussion on their patients. This method had long been obsolete, but was still sometimes used because it had a psychological benefit: patients felt that their doctor was checking on them. But how useful could percussion be? It had an auxiliary diagnostic role and often provided a strong reference for the final diagnosis, even though an X-ray was sufficient to confirm the extent of a patient's condition. Thus, other than detecting some obvious onsets, percussion was mainly used for comfort. From the perspective of psychotherapy at least, it was meaningful. This was how Dr. Zhong viewed palpation.

He said, "Why do patients sometimes ask me to check on them personally? It is because when I'm palpating them, they get the feeling that I'm examining them and caring for them."

Dr. Zhong had always valued palpation, particularly when examining a patient's chest for spider angioma, a central red dot with small red lines radiating out from the center. The redness of the lines disappeared with direct finger pressure, but rapidly returned when the pressure was released. If there were a lot of spider angiomas on the skin, the patient probably had liver problems. Dr. Zhong also explained that palpation was a traditional Chinese method of diagnosing medical conditions. There was no X-ray in ancient times. His palpation was a blend of TCM and was inspired by it.

Dr. Zhong was an expert in Western medicine in China, but how he diagnosed his patients made people think of TCM treatments such as Observation, Olfaction, Inquiry, and Palpation. The great virtue of TCM was also reflected in his practice. He said, "I don't always wear a mask, because I feel it brings me closer to my patients. There is no barrier to communicating with them. It's not the same with a mask on."

When Dr. Zhong asked a patient to open their mouth, he would subconsciously demonstrate first. Observation of the tongue was a part of TCM practice, so he also observed the color and coating of patients' tongues to check if there were problems with their digestive systems or hypoxia. He indicated that doctors today seemed to rely too much on instrumental examinations, which is not good, as it weakened communication with patients.

Unlike with sudden illnesses, elderly people preferred to see TCM doctors for chronic diseases because they were suspicious and even resentful of Western diagnostic methods, which were based solely on slides and lab test reports. Dr. Zhong pointed out that this approach would make doctors lose their leading role.

In addition, Dr. Zhong was always a great lover of Chinese herbs, particularly those that had curative effects. Once, there were arguments in the media about Chinese herbs' effectiveness against H1N1. Some said the herbs were effective, while others said they were cold in nature, so they should be taken cautiously. Dr. Zhong saw such arguments as unfounded rumors. "One day, someone asked me if Chinese herbs were effective for H1N1. I replied that I wasn't sure. TCM treatment is effective for general fever and reducing symptoms, but I can't confirm if it also works for H1N1 because I haven't seen the evidence."

With the emergence of H1N1, Chinese herbs began receiving unprecedented attention across the country. Every province and region launched its own prescriptions of Chinese herbs to fight H1N1. It was a great opportunity for TCM to flourish. Dr. Zhong was excited, as he had always hoped that TCM, a national treasure dating back thousands of years, would make its voice heard around the world.

In May in Guangzhou, gloomy clouds were restless outside the windows, lightning struck like a flying dragon in the sky, and heavy rain poured down. Dr. Zhong felt helpless. TCM had been ridiculed by foreigners due to the lack of experimental data. He said, "Some people just don't like me. Actually, I'm very supportive of TCM, but in the past few decades, it has been going the same way with no changes. That's not going to work."

He believed that as an accumulation of empirical medicine, TCM must follow the path of evidence-based medicine to really convince people of its curative effect in the clinical setting, and then delve into the mechanisms. Research on TCM could come from different perspectives.

"Some veteran TCM practitioners disagree. If you go further, some will say that you are politically opposed to TCM. This makes me sad," Dr. Zhong said.

He loved TCM. People who were familiar with him would agree with this statement.

On multiple occasions over the years, Dr. Zhong appealed for more effort to be put into TCM. It had many high-quality treatments which were simple, convenient, and inexpensive, meeting the medical needs of China's grassroots level. Besides, many of the philosophical ideas of TCM were suitable for modern medicine, such as the concept of holism (treating diseases by first improving the condition of the whole body), the concept of prevention of diseases to stop progression, and the concept of personalized medicine (diagnosis and treatment based on an overall analysis of the illness and the patient's condition).

The TCM treatment strategy for tumors, particularly the theory of survival with a tumor, which had received attention from the international medical community, was similar to TCM's holism concept. For the treatment of tumors, the TCM theory was to strengthen healthy *qi* (life force) to improve physical fitness and the ability to resist diseases, in order to cure diseases and restore health, and finally figure out how patients could live peacefully with tumors. Dr. Zhong greatly appreciated the theory that after strengthening healthy *qi*, even if the tumor were still there, it would no longer be a threat to the patient. He added that this medical idea of co-existence with tumors was developed by TCM. Today, the world proposed a new concept of progression-free survival, and it shared the TCM view of co-existence with cancer. "It means that you don't desperately attack the tumor, but improve the body's resistance and immunity so that it can fight the tumor itself. This is a major new concept in the current international medical community." Dr. Zhong stressed, "This actually has something to do with TCM."

In the past, there was not so much observation and dissection. Instead, the idea was to adjust and improve patients' whole bodies based on their response. Resisting diseases by strengthening healthy *qi* and regulating the *yin* and *yang* was one of TCM's grounding concepts.

Dr. Zhong often compared TCM to Western medicine in his medical work and teaching, particularly when encountering specific problems. In this comparison, he clearly saw the problems of Western medicine and the advantages of TCM.

He felt that Western medicine was too specialized, and that specializations were extremely one-sided. For example, a patient had been seeing doctors in more than a dozen hospitals. All of the specialists said that it was a cough, but couldn't diagnose what was causing it. They kept asking the patient to have their trachea and lungs examined. Eventually, it turned out that the cough was caused by the patient's heart problems. Every time there was an irregular heartbeat, the patient started coughing. In other words, specialists only looked at one organ and did not investigate the others, so they could not analyze patients' conditions comprehensively. Such an approach frequently led to wrong diagnoses.

Dr. Zhong's greatest concern was whether (and how) TCM could break through the bottleneck of empirical medicine. Translational medicine, a current global advocation, brought the basic research theories and techniques into clinical and preventive practices as quickly as possible. Whenever he attended international medical conferences and had the opportunity to support TCM, Dr. Zhong always tried his best to do so. In May 2009, he articulated his views on the concept of translational medicine at an academic conference on influenza prevention and control in Washington, DC. He stated that in addition to promoting the translation of basic research to the clinic, China had another direction, which was to translate the empirical medicine of millennia-old TCM to evidence-based medicine. This meant taking individual cases of TCM that were effective in treating patients and translating them through the modern research model of evidence-based medicine into a protocol that was effective and common to all groups suffering from the disease.

Dr. Zhong sighed, "To be honest, in order to prepare to support TCM at this conference, I searched all the TCM-related information and literature published from 1982 to 2009. Still, I didn't manage to find a decent paper. Only two barely qualified, but they were too rough. Today, Chinese herbs like andrographis and *banlangen* are commonly used, and they are very popular, but data proving their effectiveness is just not available. This is something we cannot avoid."

Time was running out. He could not find a decent paper to prepare for the conference, so he specifically consulted some TCM experts. Their response was that no one had ever written such a paper.

Both his desktop phone and cell phone rang incessantly. His secretary knocked gently on his door with various urgent matters, but he didn't bother, continuing his conversation instead. "For instance, we randomly divide influenza patients into two groups. One group takes our experimental drug, and the other takes a placebo. The experimental process should be dual-blinded, meaning that neither the doctor nor the patients know which is the experimental drug and which is the placebo. We then compare the difference in curative effect between the two groups. Unfortunately, there is not even a report like this that can be used as evidence."

Data and evidence to prove that TCM works was needed. Chinese herbs had been in use for thousands of years, and there was no need to worry about their side effects. They do not need to be tested on animals, because knowledge had been accumulated for thousands of years. This could all be turned into evidence-based medicine.

5

HEALTH PRESSURES

Long years of heavy work required Dr. Zhong to have exceptional physical fitness. If his health declined, he became anxious about his lack of efficiency, and when his health was good, he worked day and night. Day after day, year after year, he often had no choice but to attend numerous academic conferences and presentations. He laughed at himself, saying, "It seems that I'm specialized in meetings." However, his presence was essential. "I really want to calm down and focus on medical research. In fact, if only I had a little more time to do my research, I would be able to produce some results," he observed.

He was not only busy with various meetings, but also with his official duties. His schedule was often out of his control.

At the end of 2008, Dr. Zhong had to attend an academic conference in Greece. He expressed helplessly that he didn't have enough time. Giving two presentations in Greece wasn't the biggest problem; it was that when he returned, he had to prepare another speech for a conference at the Guangzhou Institutes of Biomedicine and Health (GIBH). The great pressure he felt came from having so many meetings back to back. Speeches needed to be drafted in advance, and most importantly, Power-Point slides had to be made, and lots of them. It took quite a bit of time to illustrate a problem this way. Good slides required fewer words and numerous graphics, and they needed to be concise, intuitive, and clear at a glance. To make his slides, Dr. Zhong usually spent at least a week conceptualizing and preparing, noting, "I have to take it seriously." He said that he was afraid of being given more work, fearing he would be overloaded.

As soon as he sat down to rest, he was immediately called to other urgent matters. Several things went on at the same time, and his presence was required at each. It took courage to say no. People knocked on his door and requested his help, all claiming that he was indispensable. He was like a spinning top, forced to spin constantly between different matters.

Two days before his interview with me, Dr. Zhong hurriedly asked his assistant to help him prepare the slides based on his design and plan. Finally, he was able to take a break from his busy schedule. He smiled gently. "If I continue working this way, my blood pressure will go up." His smile was vivid, revealing vibrant energy. "Now I have a couple of minutes to talk about topics not related to work. Being able to take a break like this is the greatest enjoyment for me."

He settled down quickly, and his focused demeanor showed his ability to tackle complicated problems in an easy manner. Dr. Zhong said that during the SARS outbreak, he was very reasonable, and the officials of the Department of Health of Guangdong Province were willing to listen to him. He felt that he was on the front line to save patients' lives, and it was all he could think about. Therefore, "I didn't think about what the officials said about me."

No matter what the occasion or situation was, his thinking and context always reflected the fact that he was a doctor. He respected facts and didn't compromise. Instead, he put extraordinary courage and action into turning the facts into ideal results. He sought neither officialdom nor wealth, wanting only to clarify the unknowns and save patients' lives. Even though he knew he was justified in the case of SARS, he still had to find a way to convince all the parties involved.

Dr. Zhong said he would never confront a particular person or group. To help the world, one had to adapt to it first. Integrating into society and then influencing others with his own behavior was his life philosophy, and also a challenge. After integrating into society, his moral bottom line was not to use improper means, flattery, or bribery to advance his career. He believed this was a crucial reason people trusted and recognized him. When bombarded with unscheduled conferences and meetings, he always managed to start with a helpless, passive acceptance and end with a cohesive academic atmosphere and unanimous applause.

Dr. Zhong flew to many places every year, so he has friends all over the world. He didn't need much leisure and freedom, although he was romantic and a man of passion. He was happiest when he could have some time to make an academic breakthrough. Leisurely ease was not as important to him as delving into clinical research, curing problematic diseases, and freeing more patients from suffering.

Dr. Lu Dongxiao, who often accompanied Dr. Zhong on business trips and took care of him, knew his health condition best, and he has expressed concern on many occasions. "Honestly speaking, we hope that he will always be healthy, because once he is sick, his efficiency drops. He gets particularly anxious and loses his temper easily. However, if he's healthy, he will keep on working around the clock, and we will be worried about his health again," Dr. Lu said.

Since 2005, Dr. Zhong experienced several episodes of cardiac atrial fibrillation, as happened in early 2007. His overburdened heart protested by beating irregularly. Would it suddenly stop? "I made my peace with death a long time ago." Dr. Zhong's hand swung to the side, his arm muscles bulging. "I have stopped playing basketball, but I still swim, run on the treadmill, and do some pulling ups. The amount of exercise I do has decreased." This was in June 2007, a few months before his 71st birthday. Was it a problem that he stopped playing basketball at such an age?

He felt tired all the time because he was overworked. Sometimes he didn't even have time to read a newspaper. When Dr. Zhong talked about his health, he couldn't help discussing work.

He was in very poor health when he was at the Two Sessions in Beijing in 2008. When he went home, he deteriorated even further. He was a little scared by the fact that he lost six kilograms in two months, making his ribs protrude. He feared that he had a malignant disease – perhaps esophageal cancer – because he often had difficulty swallowing. He told his doctor to just give him the necessary treatment. He was very rational, and he would not take any chances where diseases were concerned. He would accept whatever befell him, so he was able to face all kinds of medical examinations calmly and peacefully.

He had a gastroscopy, and a large scar was found on his esophagus, the result of a medical treatment he had undergone in 2007, to eliminate his atrial fibrillation by performing radiofrequency ablation. It was this goiter that was making it difficult for him to swallow. Fortunately, it turned out that it was not cancer, but thyroiditis.

The year that Dr. Zhong had his heart defibrillated, none of the famous cardiologists would agree to do it. Back then, defibrillation technology in China was immature, and there was only a 60% success rate internationally. He listened to detailed analysis from several experts in China, including President Yang Yanzong of the First Affiliated Hospital of Dalian Medical University, and he took their advice. After that, he invited Ouyang Feifan, a specialist from Germany, to do the surgery for him. Before the operation, Dr. Zhong calmly wrote a will and carefully revised it.

At 8:30 am on April 29, 2007, Dr. Ouyang began to prepare his fellow physician for the surgery. At nearly 71 years old, Dr. Zhong laughed and chatted with the doctor about family matters to relieve his psychological stress. At 11:00 am, his surgery was successfully completed, and he was cared for in the observation room.

A fine rain had begun to fall during the night, and it did not stop until close to noon. When Dr. Zhong woke up from the anesthesia, it was a brilliant spring day.

"I'm fine. I'm alive. But I still have tubes all over my body," he said the day after the surgery. Hearing his voice over the phone early in the morning was a pleasant surprise.

Dr. Zhong risked defibrillation surgery at such an age for the purpose of work. He told his doctor that without it, the disease would always affect his efficiency. "I don't have time to maintain my health." He said that his age was not commensurate with the function of his body. In fact, his body was functioning very well. However, no matter how good one's physical fitness was, it was still not enough to avoid becoming ill from overwork.

Often, people who had always been in good health had trouble accepting it when they suddenly fell ill. Sometimes the psychological shock was too much for them to bear, and they deteriorated quickly. However, weak people usually paid more attention to taking care of themselves because they have long accepted the fact that they were not in good health.

TCM focused on mind-body medicine, and it could not be ignored. Dr. Zhong cited a good friend of his as an example. This friend was head of a stomatology department, and he was found to have a tumor during a tracheoscopy. Unexpectedly, he had a mental breakdown, and he lay in bed all day in the ward, staring at the ceiling. He died three weeks after his surgery.

Dr. Zhong said that he had experienced the same feeling. In 2004, he had a myocardial infarction (MI). After a stent was installed, he didn't feel like anything was wrong, so he didn't take it seriously, and he went for a meeting in Shenyang three days later. "It's just a minor issue. I don't need to take leave." Later, he developed atrial fibrillation. He had misjudged his own stress, and he became depressed at the outcome. People who fell sick frequently would be mentally prepared for it, while healthy people often struggled to accept the sudden change, as Dr. Zhong did.

When asked how some people who had tuberculosis or other diseases could still live into their 90s, offered an apt analogy, saying that weak and sick people knew that the bowl was cracked, so they held it carefully when they used it. By contrast, healthy people were more careless, so they ended up dropping and breaking many bowls. Minor diseases were not necessarily bad things, because they served as reminders.

This idea was derived from Dr. Zhong's own experience.

Despite his busy day-to-day schedule, Dr. Zhong looked much younger than his actual age, thanks to his athletic physique. Once, when he was in a long line at customs in Hong Kong, there was a window for senior citizens over the age of 65. It had fewer people in it, so Dr. Zhong joined it. The customs officer told him to go to another counter. Confused, he asked, "Isn't this counter for people over 65 years old?" The officer gave him the once over, and said, "Yes. Please go ahead." This happened from time to time when he was entering or exiting customs, because he didn't look like he'd been born in 1936. However, he always used the line for those over 65, as he was usually in a hurry.

The fact that customs officers doubted his age because of his youthful looks made him happy, but it made him even happier to be able to treat more patients thanks to his high energy levels. But now, out of concern for him, the Guangzhou IRH reduced the number of consultations considerably, with only about ten patients on a weekday afternoon. This had not been the case before.

Before 2003, Dr. Zhong had consulted with patients from 1:00 pm to 9:00 pm, a full eight hours. Many of the graduate students studying by his side could not take it. He came back from the UK in 1981 and worked at this pace from 1982 until 2002.

Dr. Zhong said, "As long as I'm around, I can usually consult with 50 patients." Seeing this number of patients in eight hours meant that each patient got ten minutes, which was much longer than doctors in many large hospitals, who only spent three to five minutes on a consultation, including asking questions and prescribing medication.

Usually, his consultations started at 1:00 pm, with patients waiting beforehand. His workday ended at 9:00 pm, which was exhausting for both Dr. Zhong and the nurses. Snacks would be delivered around 7:00 pm. Other than that, Dr. Zhong only drank a bottle of milk between patients.

This was how his clinic had previously been arranged. Dr. Zhong decided to change things partly because he felt it unnecessary to see patients with common conditions. He wanted to consult and diagnose those with intractable diseases. The other reason was his gradual realization that he was no longer young, and was thus unable to take on as much work as before. Now, Dr. Zhong was mindful of his health. He arrived at the clinic at 2:30 pm and finished consultations at 6:30 pm.

Dr. Zhong talked about the fact that because of the length of time it took to book a specialist appointment with him, some patients either got better or passed away. He blamed himself for this.

When people remind him to take care of his health, whether the words were to his liking or not, he would listen. "What you just said, that I look young when I'm well rested and old when I'm not. Is that true?" He asked.

He wanted more rest, but most of the time, it was out of his control, and his presence was urgently required, both for academic and ceremonial purposes. He simply could not take on so much work.

Being badly rested generally made a person look older than their years, and Dr. Zhong was an aesthete, so he kept these words in mind. However, it was not always possible for him to rest.

6

WORLD-RENOWNED ACADEMIC ACHIEVEMENTS

Thanks to his contributions to the international community during the SARS period, many of Dr. Zhong's global peers saw him as a "Chinese hero." The chairman of the WHO, who was responsible for developing the guidelines for *The Global Initiative for Asthma*, spoke enthusiastically about him on many occasions. "This gentleman has done great things in asthma research, but his greatest contribution was in the control of SARS."

"I've read your articles."

"I heard about you a long time ago."

Dr. Zhong was very touched by these generous compliments. In Hong Kong, he was even more warmly embraced.

He attended the World Conference on Chronic Obstructive Pulmonary Disease (COPD) in Rome in June 2009, along with representatives from more than forty countries. He made three speeches about the prevention, control, and treatment of COPD in China. He elaborated on the Chinese concept of early intervention by using facts and data, using PowerPoint slides to illustrate that China was at the forefront and among the most advanced in the world.

He gave examples of China's attitude toward COPD. It was not right to start treatment only when patients developed dyspnea after activity or sat and wheezed.

Early intervention was preferable. When a physical examination revealed a faster than normal decline in lung function, intervention should be immediate, even if there were no symptoms. As with hypertension, patients needed to be reminded to treat the problem when their blood pressure was found to be high during a physical examination, rather than being reminded only when they suffered a stroke. Another example was coronary heart disease. It was too late for patients to be treated when they had a myocardial infarction. Early intervention needed to be put in place when high blood lipids appeared. This was even truer for diabetes. Chinese medical institutions monitored patients' blood glucose at all times, not waiting until they showed symptoms such as excessive drinking, eating, and urination, weight loss, or ketoacidosis. Addressing medical experts from around the world, Dr. Zhong proudly concluded, "This practice is the embodiment of modern medicine."

In the case of COPD, Dr. Zhong explained that China had been working on a systematic project for early intervention and early treatment at the community level for five years. It had been proven that the rate of decline in lung function could be reversed, and that a cure was possible for COPD patients. Early intervention and early treatment at the community level had proven very effective in monitoring the disease.

In 2000, the WHO estimated that 210 million people worldwide had mild to severe COPD. In 2005, more than three million people died from it, accounting for 5% of global deaths. Nearly 90% of the deaths occurred in low- and middle-income countries. COPD used to be more common in males. However, as females in high-income countries began to consume more tobacco and the risk for people in low-income countries exposed to indoor air pollution became higher (e.g., fuels used for cooking and heating), the number of males and females suffering from this disease was almost the same. Unless urgent action was taken to reduce high-risk factors, particularly tobacco consumption, the total number of deaths from COPD was expected to increase by more than 30% over the next ten years. In 2005, tobacco consumption was responsible for 5.4 million deaths. By 2030, tobacco-related deaths were expected to increase by 8.3 million per year.

When COPD reached an advanced stage, treatment was ineffective, similar to advanced hypertension. The reason the death rate for COPD was so high was that many patients only sought treatment when they reached the advanced stage and could no longer bear the pain. In the early stage, the symptoms were not very obvious and could not always be perceived. Some patients did not pay enough attention to their condition even when they discovered it. Once the lung function started to decline, failure to treat it in a timely manner would inevitably lead to serious consequences. Thus, early intervention and early treatment were the best protection for COPD patients.

Dr. Zhong was very vocal about his view that every country's medical institutions should establish a system of early intervention for COPD. His view was appreciated by many representatives. After he finished his speech, an expert from the UK asked, "Other than China, are there any other countries that have early treatment for COPD?" No one raised their hand.

In Dr. Zhong's speeches, he expressed two points of view. The first was about the modern medical concept of early intervention and early treatment. He noted that the current international guidelines involving COPD treatment were all at a relatively late stage.

The second point of view was very clear. Dr. Zhong proposed that developing countries must cultivate their own effective, safe, simple, inexpensive medicines and medical treatments, so that the majority of people could afford to be treated. As soon as Dr. Zhong's words were out of his mouth, the conference venue erupted in applause. Representatives from India, Bangladesh, and Kyrgyzstan were so excited that they stood up and expressed their agreement loudly. "Our country also has many people who are very poor and cannot afford to buy expensive imported medicine. They spend a lot of money on medication every month. Developing our own inexpensive medicines can help them save a lot."

7

THE PROUD CARBOCISTEINE

Dr. Zhong published two papers in *The Lancet*, and both received a great international response. In the 6,000-word article "The Emergence of Atypical Pathogens in Guangdong" submitted in July 2003, he and his partners verified that SARS did originate in China based on their knowledge of the development of the epidemic and the process of effective control.

This classic paper, destined to go down in the history of human medicine, became an invaluable document in the fight against SARS. It condensed the efforts of Dr. Zhong and his comrades and recorded the historical facts of China's victory over the illness.

The other paper, considered to be "truly creative" by Dr. Zhong, was titled "A Study on Carbocisteine in the Treatment of Chronic Obstructive Pulmonary Disease." Also at about 6,000 words, it consisted of research into carbocisteine, an expectorant medicine for the prevention of COPD.

The Lancet was one of the leading international journals for clinical medicine, recommending the most influential research papers and experimental projects of the year to scholars worldwide. On January 24, 2009, *The Lancet* announced three of the top papers of 2008. In addition to one from China, the other two were from Germany and Bangladesh. The paper from China received the highest number of votes. This paper was the result of the joint effort of a team of researchers from 13 cities and 22 medical units led by Dr. Zhong, discussing a commonly used, inexpensive, domestically produced expectorant medicine, carbocisteine. The results showed that it could reduce the acute onset rate of COPD by 24.5%, and also cut the cost of its conventional treatment by 85%.

During the Two Sessions in 2009, a joint group meeting by the medical and health sector of the National Committee of the Chinese People's Political Consultative Conference (CPPCC) was held in the Jilin Building in Beijing on March 7. Toward the end of the meeting, Chen Zhu, then Minister of Health, made a concluding speech from the center of the rostrum. He said, "Recently, I received a letter from the editor-in-chief of *The Lancet,* the world's most authoritative medical journal. He said that the highest award had been given to Chinese scholars, that is, Dr. Zhong and his team. The paper is about the use of a common, inexpensive, domestically produced expectorant medicine, carbocisteine. It is a new use of old medicine, and it can significantly lower the acute onset rate of COPD, as well as greatly reducing the burden of medical costs for ordinary Chinese patients." Chen Zhu added, "I have to say that our medical staff should learn from Dr. Zhong, both in terms of being a good person and performing academic research."

At the end of January 2009, a post from a netizen spread rapidly online. "Recently, Professor Zhong and his team found that the long-term oral medication carbocisteine is highly effective for COPD and can improve some lung functions. The price of the medicine is low."

Every year in China, around 1.28 million people died from COPD, and about 1 million died from cardiovascular disease. However, much less attention had been paid to the former than to the latter. The data published in the press was alarming: the incidence rate of COPD – "the third killer" – had tripled in 10 years. Moreover, there was enough data to show that young people were increasingly suffering from COPD in recent years.

Carbocisteine reduced mucus secretion in the bronchus, resulting in a decrease in the viscosity of sputum and making it easier to cough it up. It could be effective in the treatment of chronic bronchitis and diseases caused by bronchial asthma, such as thick sputum, difficult expectoration, and insufficient pulmonary ventilation. In addition, the side effects of carbocisteine were minimal.

The paper published in *The Lancet* by Dr. Zhong and his team clarified that carbocisteine had a more important role to play: preventing the acute onset of COPD. With its low price and good curative effect, carbocisteine was very suitable for China's national conditions, and it should be promoted nationwide. Dr. Zhong, carbocisteine, and low-cost medicines became a hot topic in the media, yet the social response was not desirable. The deeper reason for this was that a large number of old low-cost medicines were facing extinction. Despite the fact that so many COPD patients across the country needed effective, low-cost medicines like carbocisteine to ease the burden of their years-long medical bills, pharmaceutical manufacturers either went out of business by producing low-cost medicines with meager profits or revamped those medicines. The same problem existed in developing nations worldwide.

In June 2009, Dr. Zhong spoke at the World COPD Conference in Rome about China's strategy for the prevention and treatment of COPD. After his speech, Professor Lyoner gave his views as a reviewer of the paper. He pointed out that in addition to its significance, the paper's most important feature was its "rigorous design." He said, "We reviewed the paper carefully." He told the rest of the representatives from all over the world, "You should study this design, because it is a very good example. It was created cooperatively by 22 hospitals in China after careful observation."

Dr. Zhong explained that he and his team had conducted many animal experiments with antioxidants. COPD was mainly caused by smoking or smoke, mainly because smoking produced peroxides, which damaged the alveoli and stimulated the cells to release free radicals. Could antioxidants be used to treat or prevent COPD?

The warm afternoon sunlight was a perfect backdrop for Dr. Zhong. He spoke calmly but quickly, stating that there had been some controversy on this point. Expectorants had been used in antioxidant experiments on animals suffering from COPD in foreign countries, and the results were positive. However, when applied to clinical experiments, the results were too confusing to be conclusive. Therefore, he and his team switched to a medicine called carbocisteine, which had been seen more clinical use in China and had proven to be effective over the years. They used it to perform a dual-blind clinical observation with a large number of samples.

Dr. Zhong described the entire process of clinical observation. "The dual-blind process was strictly implemented, with two groups of patients for comparison. Doctors gave one group carbocisteine and the other group a placebo with the same appearance. Only the researchers knew who was taking carbocisteine, while neither the doctors nor the patients knew."

Dr. Zhong and his team experienced the thrilling final moment in 2007. It was an extensive experiment, involving 700 patients and 22 hospitals over the course of a year, with an investment of over $4 million. The findings were scheduled to be presented at the Annual Congress of the Asian Pacific Society of Respirology. However, time was passing quickly, and the results had not yet been released. Twelve days passed. The team waited quietly and nervously. If the experiment proved to be ineffective, the researchers would then have to tell the world that carbocisteine was ineffective in the treatment of COPD.

The results finally came in. Compared to the group taking the placebo, the group taking carbocisteine had a 24% reduction in the acute onset rate of COPD. Compared to some of the internationally recommended medicines, inhaling corticosteroids combined with long-acting receptor bronchodilators, carbocisteine was not only much cheaper, but also had a similar curative effect. Most importantly, patients taking carbocisteine had fewer COPD symptoms, and they were able to have a better quality of life.

The research team was overjoyed by the results. Dr. Zhong was both relieved and glad.

The experiment was awarded the Asia Pacific Award and was exhibited in large print at the Annual Congress of the European Respiratory Society (ERS) in 2008, where Professor Zheng Jinping presented it to the delegates. It was ultimately named the best large print paper at the congress.

All of the papers approved for the ERS annual congress were posted on the wall in eye-catching large print. "There were so many," said Dr. Zhong, "Hundreds of them were posted throughout the conference hall."

After the publication of this paper, two top experts were present at a press conference held by *The Lancet*. One of them gave the paper high marks. He said, "This is a very typical novel use of an old medicine, and it is very useful for developing countries."

In January 2009, Dr. Zhong was notified that the editorial board of *The Lancet* had arranged for several dozen experts to select the world's best academic papers, not only those published in *The Lancet* but also those published in New England and elsewhere. *The Lancet* editorial board selected six of the best papers of 2008, and published them for readers around the world to vote for the best. More than 25,000 people voted.

"We have the highest number of votes. We are number one." This was a true, fair result, but it surprised Dr. Zhong and his team. It was the first time that a Chinese paper had been selected for first place in *The Lancet,* a century-old authoritative medical journal. Dr. Zhong was awestruck. His global peers were impressed. Foreign experts in China and experts in the field of respiratory medicine in other parts of the world expressed their respect for him. The fact that *The Lancet* invited him to be a reviewer for the journal was proof of the publication's respect for Chinese scholars.

8

MOTIVATED BY PATIENTS' NEEDS

Having experienced so much in his life, Dr. Zhong's practice reached a level where he was able to bypass almost everything, except one thing, the needs of his patients. This is also the root of his medical research and the source of his motivation. He regarded it as the value and meaning of his life.

He told secretary of the CPC Committee of Guangdong Province Zhang Dejiang that his only hope was to expand the hospital. He explained that his guiding principle was that when there were fewer patients in large hospitals, the reform of the medical and healthcare system had been successful.

On May 5, 2009, the 11th World Asthma Day, instead of providing free consultations to patients, Dr. Zhong and specialists at the IRH gave lectures to community doctors. These doctors listened intently and learned a lot. Some of the knowledge was very common to Dr. Zhong and the IRH, but new to many of the community doctors.

Dr. Zhong said that passing on knowledge to community doctors to allow them to treat more patients was much more efficient than treating patients directly. He participated in charity clinics twice a year, once in May and once in October. He never missed them, and he always felt an upsurge of emotion, with security guards standing in a row to maintain order and the aisles and courtyard filled with patients.

From 2004 to 2005, early in the morning on the day of the charity clinic, more than 400 people lined up outside the clinic, and several hundred people waited inside. In total, there were nearly 800 people. Dr. Zhong was touched, because his motivation didn't come from himself but from his patients. When a doctor put himself or herself in a patient's shoes, the sense of responsibility was about more than simply curing them. The patients' hope gave Dr. Zhong great motivation, both for his clinical work and his academic research. When faced with a special condition, he was always keen to study it, and he was very happy when he was able to figure it out, because he gained new knowledge from the entire process. These two aspects gave him endless motivation.

The charity clinic was tiring, but Dr. Zhong took strength from being able to treat a few more patients. He always told them to prioritize opening their hearts and being cheerful. His own happiness and joy come from their treatment and recovery.

When patients were cured by his diagnosis and targeted treatment, Dr. Zhong was delighted. The motivation he got from patients was very important to him, which was why he participated in the charity clinic no matter how busy he was and always spared time for rounds in the ward whenever possible. He felt that he could not gain motivation without visiting the ward or consulting with patients. Some said that he didn't have to, because there were already so many consultants in Beijing, and many others for provincial and municipal leaders. However, Dr. Zhong believed that constant contact with ordinary patients gave him motivation to focus on patients. Their health improved and their families were relieved, and this was the happiest thing for him. "That's why doctors are respected," he noted.

His other source of motivation was academic research. He was satisfied when he was able to identify an unknown disease. Speaking of this, he always emphasized, "What do you teach intern doctors? I think the most important is to help them develop a sense of responsibility toward patients." No doctor was omnipotent, but it was important that they have a sense of responsibility.

Dr. Zhong mentioned that the impact of the Cultural Revolution on him was not entirely negative, but also has some positive aspects, making him understand the ups and downs of life. He observed, "I've been through so much in my life, and now my practice is enough for me."

He was able to concentrate all his effort and try all means to cure patients even under so much pressure during the SARS crisis because he believed there was no reason for leaders to criticize him for trying to save lives. "You don't think this is right? Well, you come and do it." When he was no longer the president of Guangzhou Medical College but just an expert facing the SARS epidemic, his righteousness and boldness were enough to make him proud. At the time, he had just stepped down from his post as the president of Guangzhou Medical College. He said that the battle against SARS gave him many tests. If SARS was like laying mines in people's path, he and his colleagues were the demining team. "If we don't step forward, who will?" It was an essential task. If they won the battle, the image of the Guangzhou IRH would be greatly enhanced. Of course, it could also fail, which meant that the IRH would be unable to treat SARS, and also that other patients would not come to see a doctor because it was an infectious disease area. However, after careful consideration, the leaders of the IRH agreed. "They had faith that I could handle it because I was confident. We had to win the battle. If it was left to me, the chances of winning would be greater."

Dr. Zhong said that five of the six critical SARS patients he jointly consulted with at Sun Yat-sen Second Hospital were transferred to the IRH, and the sixth died before the transfer. When he had another joint consultation at Sun Yat-sen Third Hospital, he requested that SARS patients be transferred to the IRH. All the patients were transferred except one – a department head at the hospital – because he insisted on staying in his post. Unfortunately, he ended up losing his life.

The new Guangzhou IRH building would welcome medical staff with a wide range of experience and technological knowhow, as well as medical equipment. Dr. Zhong said, "The situations now are quite similar. For example, if a puerpera has an amniotic fluid embolism, and if the hospital can't handle it, they will send her to the IRH. The same goes for other patients, such as those with poor circulation and septicemia."

He explained that in the future, the Guangzhou IRH would be a comprehensive hospital that would be able to treat all kinds of diseases. Their ICU was far-reaching, not only treating respiratory diseases but also able to perform dialysis, aortic balloon counterpulsation, and extracorporeal membrane oxygenation. An entire floor was devoted to the ICUs, adding up to a total of forty beds. At the time, 60% of the patients were transferred from other hospitals, and there would be more patients after the move into the new building. Some of the patients were in poor health when they were transferred there. "They should have been sent over earlier, when there was still hope of a cure." Transfers like this showed that the IRH's image had been established.

There were too many unknowns with diseases. Human beings were living organisms that had gone through several millions of years of evolution to reach their current complex form. Therefore, the study of the human body would always be challenging, and the possibilities for exploration were endless.

Dr. Zhong pointed to the IRH's new building in the rain and mist through the window. He said, "It's very spacious, so the conditions will be much better. During

SARS, Zhang Dejiang, Secretary of the CPC Committee of Guangdong Provincial, set his sights on our hospital. When he received me, I told him that my only request was to expand it. He was very supportive."

Dr. Zhong took trust from leaders and the safety of the people very seriously. He saw what he had personally endured as inevitable. He spoke a very standard form of Mandarin and had an accurate intuition for language. When he talked of his regrets, his voice took on the low tone of a cello.

"The patient was from Sun Yat-sen Second Hospital," he said. "His condition was at the advanced stage. Resuscitation was not successful, and the patient died. Another patient's brain was full of fungus, which spread all over his body. He was in a coma. He didn't receive effective treatment, and too many hormones were used on him. Sadly, he died at just 39 years old. There was another patient. If he had been sent here a little earlier, he could have cured. What a pity."

9

H1N1 AND TRUTH-TELLING

It was said that with Dr. Zhong in China, the atmosphere of telling lies would be broken. Dr. Zhong admitted that his truth-telling behavior sometimes embarrassed leadership. "But, I still have to tell the truth," he said.

In May 2009, when a woman in Beijing was checking her stock quotes, a report on the influenza virus, H1N1, jumped to the forefront. *Beijing news – The MOH announced that on May 29, Guangzhou City in Guangdong reported a suspected case of imported influenza A (H1N1) was confirmed, and a close contact of the case was diagnosed as a suspected case.*

Influenza A (H1N1), originated in Mexico, spread to the US, and was imported from the US to China. On May 29, 2009, the Chinese Center for Disease Control and Prevention did a laboratory testing of a throat swab specimen for the first suspected case, and the result was positive for the nucleic acid for the H1N1 virus. The Department of Health in Guangdong organized a consultation with a group of experts. In accordance with the influenza A (H1N1) diagnosis and treatment plan, and based on the patient's clinical presentation, epidemiological data, and laboratory test results, the suspected case was determined to be a confirmed case of H1N1.

In the morning of May 29, MOH held a video conference to study the situation with the Guangdong Department of Health, conducting prevention and control work. That afternoon, MOH held another video conference with the national health system to further deploy prevention and control work across the country.

Beijing and some areas of the country found imported suspected cases of H1N1. MOH urged the Guangdong Department of Health to strengthen the clinical treatment of patients, conduct further epidemiological investigation and tracing of close contacts, and send the patient's specimen to CCDC for laboratory review and testing.

The CPC Guangdong Provincial Committee appointed Dr. Zhong to lead the Guangdong expert team for the prevention and control of H1N1.

Combining the patient's epidemiological history, clinical presentation, and reviewed test results, the experts needed to clarify the diagnosis as soon as possible. MOH continued to closely monitor the progress of the patient's treatment, further epidemiological investigation, prevention and control, and the reviewed lab results. China promptly informed the WHO and relevant countries and regions about the situation.

A new term was born in China, "carpet search." It referred to the search for any close contacts of H1N1 patients.

The streets of Guangzhou's old town, particularly along West Yanjiang Road, were lined with small stores. One of the store owners, Mr. Wang, a typical Cantonese man, shouted and sold his cheap clothes to the hustle and bustle of people on the street. "No one knows how bad the flu is going to be. How come there are still so many people traveling here? Are they all like us Cantonese, unafraid of the flu?" he opined.

Mr. Zhang, who sold cigarettes next door to Mr. Wang's shop, came over for a chat after dinner. He asked, "How many people are wearing masks in Beijing?" It seemed that wearing a mask was a ridiculous idea to him.

"At the time of the SARS outbreak, none of us wore masks. We were not scared."

"So you're not afraid, even if you are infected?"

"You're not infected yet. How do you know you'll be infected?"

Calm, or perhaps indifferent, this was Guangzhou.

Mr. Wang criticized Mr. Zhang, saying that he shouldn't be so absolute. When SARS was raging in Guangzhou, everyone rushed to buy vinegar, and it was soon out of stock. But Mr. Zhang said crossly, "My family didn't go and grab the vinegar at that time!"

Shengji Restaurant, on Guangzhou's Changdi Road, was the same age as the People's Republic of China, and it was famous for its Cantonese dishes made from pork, such as braised pork and big bone soup. The dishes were very popular during the H1N1 epidemic. In Guangzhou, pork dishes were not as expensive as roast goose, but they were a must-have for the local people's daily meals.

"I know the price of pork has dropped all over the country. It's especially dropped a lot in Beijing. But that won't happen here." The fresh faced restaurant owner complimented the braised pork on her tray as she discussed pork prices.

The diners sitting around the largest table were all locals. They devoured various delicacies and discussed where to get snake and rat meat, and even authentic pufferfish. Of course, civets were no longer included in their quest for meat.

An imported case, a patient with H1N1 in Guangzhou, had a cough for two to three days after he returned from abroad, and he developed a fever after arriving in Guangzhou by train. He took the initiative to contact the health department and was then quickly sent to Guangzhou No. 8 People's Hospital for isolation and treatment. Soon after, another case in Beijing was handled the same way. "It speaks volumes that our nation has become more resistant to diseases and has a national sense of responsibility," Dr. Zhong commented. "The whole country has a sense of responsibility, which is reflected not only in the government and the health sectors, but also in the people."

In his view, honesty was equivalent to responsibility. He cited the example of the re-emergence of SARS patients in 2004, first discovered by three primary care doctors who immediately reported it to senior management. This demonstrated the fact that grassroots doctors had a strong sense of vigilance and national responsibility. "A very important principle we can demonstrate is honesty," Dr. Zhong noted.

At that time, China was honest. There was even a law which made concealment a crime.

Compared to some other countries, Dr. Zhong appreciated China's pragmatic attitude in the face of influenza A (H1N1). "Pragmatism is reflected in the fact that both professionals and general masses will consider what they should do based on the actual situation," he noted.

In speaking of being pragmatic, he compared the momentous past during the SARS crisis. At that time, it was announced that anti-chlamydial medicine, antibiotics, were found to be very effective against SARS, and everyone started using it. Controlled experiments were done. If some leaders had stepped forward to support the finding because they believed that the academic authority really thought so, wouldn't that create a wrong result? In exchange for openness, transparency, and science, the whole society faced the plague disaster with unprecedented rationality.

"Now, I think people can be quite rational about virus transmission," Dr. Zhong said. In June 2009, he was pleased with the level of rationality seen in Chinese society and the public. He even felt that it was slightly ahead of the US.

It didn't matter how much the US thought China was making a big deal out of it. China didn't yet know how contagious the influenza was, but if it was highly contagious, it would rapidly spread in China, and all aspects of Chinese society would be greatly affected. China's rapid response was because of the lesson learned from its previous experience with SARS.

Thanks to the policy of "blocking the imported cases and preventing the internal spread," China managed the first peak of the spread of H1N1 very well. The peak was kept low, and the time was expanded, which not only maintained social stability, but also bought time for vaccine preparation.

Once H1N1 landed in China, how long would it last? Such a bewildering question, like a dark cloud, had haunted Chinese society and the common people. Everyone was looking forward to an authoritative voice.

As the first wave of H1N1 raged in June 2009, Dr. Zhong shared his true opinion with the media, who had been pursuing him for a while. He said that there were three possibilities. The first was that the epidemic would get significantly worse, the second was that the virus would disappear silently, and the third was somewhere between the first and the second, that is, it could be a moderate situation. He said that based on past experience, there would not be just one wave of such a vicious flu. What did it mean to go waves? Basically, it meant that after summer was over, the flu would come back in winter and perhaps reappear the following spring.

In 1957, 1968, and 1978, there was not just one wave of influenza, but two or three, so it was essential to be very vigilant about influenza. Dr. Zhong painstakingly reiterated the need for vigilance. At the end of 2009, though influenza was already at a low ebb, it made a sudden and aggressive comeback. Objective, rational, fair treatment of people, viruses, and everything was paramount. Telling the truth over and over again, whether the result was winning praise, being accused or being attacked, would not affect Dr. Zhong's insistence to speak the truth in the face of this challenge.

In November 2009, the H1N1 epidemic became increasingly serious, but it was reassuring that the number of confirmed H1N1 cases announced by the official was 69,160, with 53 deaths. This figure was widely quoted in the media and the Internet. Some experts said that the H1N1 mortality rate in China was only 1/20 of the world average. But when he heard this figure, Dr. Zhong insisted, "I don't believe it at all!"

In response to the media reports that Zhong Nanshan was questioning the reporting of H1N1 deaths in individual regions, on November 2009, MOH spokesman Deng Haihua reiterated that all levels of health administrative departments must shoulder the responsibility to accurately report and publish information of prevention and control, and he strictly prohibited concealed reporting, underreporting, and delayed reporting of H1N1 deaths.

Dr. Zhong's disbelief was based on the fact that "in some areas of China, H1N1-related deaths were concealed or not reported." As his students were located in ICU of hospitals across the country, he learned from them that many patients had died from H1N1, but the deaths were not reported due to various reasons.

The relatively few cases and deaths from H1N1 at that time were due to the effective overall prevention and control for a period of time. However, the statistics were also affected by the large size of the population, the wide range of susceptible people, and the abolishment of free H1N1 testing. After the SARS outbreak in 2003, health agencies again prioritized performance, so they covered up the facts and misreported or underreported the number of H1N1 cases.

Underreporting caused panic, which was already a lesson from the experience with SARS in 2003, so why again did this phenomenon arise again? It was clear that some administrative departments had a tendency to avoid harm to their own reputations. Many experts privately questioned the statistics at the time, but it was Dr. Zhong who openly questioned them, alerting the relevant departments once again.

Dr. Zhong was positive, optimistic, and full of hope about the country and the nation. He once said, "It takes time for things to be made ready. I am also making progress. After 2003, I slowly learned how to have better interpersonal relationships, and I am still learning, which includes learning how to tell the truth in a better way."

At Two Sessions, held in 2008, Dr. Zhong first attended the National People's Congress (NPC). Premier of the State Council Wen Jiabao attended the discussion of the Guangdong delegation. Dr. Zhong made a speech on medical reform and put forward some suggestions, which Wen affirmed.

The next year, at the Two Sessions group discussion, Dr. Zhong noticed that the majority of NPC deputies were leaders from different levels, and some spoke "official language." At the group discussion on March 10, 2009, as one of the NPC deputies, Dr. Zhong could not restrain himself from criticizing the speech of these deputies, saying, "When some people speak, their remarks are complimentary and full of praises, but in private, they are full of complaints."

Some NPC deputies, especially representatives of enterprises and the masses, did not dare to speak much when members of the leadership were present, but when the leadership was not there, they spoke incessantly. Dr. Zhong said, "This practice is not desirable." He bombarded the phenomenon, saying, "We each have ten minutes to speak. The first eight minutes are for singing praises to the leaders, another minute is for self-praise and then we say a few irrelevant words in the remaining time. How can we improve our work?" These words were quickly reported by journalists in charge of the Two Sessions.

Although the media did not fully publish his original words, many excerpts were published in the press and online. A speech entitled "NPC Deputies should learn from Zhong Nanshan," published by the *Guangzhou Daily*, was reprinted in the *People's Daily Online* on March 12, 2009. It read:

> Zhong Nanshan highlighted his view that on one hand, the people's governments, supreme people's courts, and supreme people's procuratorates (have performed well and are extremely popular. It's fine that NPC deputies praise them, but after all, the main purpose of the NPC and the obligations of NPC deputies are not to praise others or themselves, Instead, the main purpose and obligations of NPC deputies are determined by the function and obligations of the NPC organization. On the other hand, it is their duty for the governments, courts, and procuratorates to do a good job, so there shouldn't be too much praise, and if they fail their duty, they should be held accountable.
>
> The obligations of NPC deputies are to exercise political rights on behalf of the people and supervise the governments, courts, and procuratorates. Supervision is certainly not meant for making things difficult or being against them, and of course, it is also not to overpraise them, spending eight minutes of a ten minute speech simply for that purpose. Flattering, bragging, and praising creates a happy atmosphere, but do they help with the work of the governments, courts, and procuratorates? Or will they improve people's livelihood? What is the point of such a "harmonious" congress? Supervising bodies should not be subservient, not cover up, and not exaggerate, but should instead truthfully lay out the facts for reasoning, so that those supervised will be persuaded to improve.
>
> People expect the NPC deputies they elected to speak for them, supervise the government, actively contribute ideas and suggestions, and introduce policies to benefit society and the public, not to sing praises. Justice is in people's hearts, and they have their own judgment on how the government is performing, so it is not necessary for the NPC deputies to use such precious time and opportunities to express this.
>
> It is a sign of incompetency for NPC deputies to only sing praises. At

this moment, those Goethe deputies should bear in mind their identity and responsibilities, understand what to say and what not to say, and do not take the NPC congress as a workplace commendation ceremony or celebration. In this regard, these NPC deputies may wish to learn from Zhong Nanshan. In his eyes, when the NPC deputies are not speaking the truth, but are speaking in a roundabout way, how will they properly perform their duties? Only when they perform their duties properly is there a real exercise of the power given by the people. This is the real embodiment of political democracy, and it is responsible to the Party and the people.

Dr. Zhong served as a member of the 8th, 9th, and 10th National Committee of the Chinese People's Political Consultative Conference (CPPCC) in 1993, 1998, and 2003. He was elected as a deputy of the 11th National People's Congress in 2009.

10

MORALITY AND JUSTICE

His name was applied to the style. His influence formed a driving force, creating harmony and bringing order. His every initiative and his voice pushed the process of civilization. What he said did for society caused different levels of response. He was benevolent and loving, but acted with an iron face when defending justice. After SARS, serving the community became more of a conscious, voluntary act for him. Such things happened every day and every second.

Mr. Li was a state organ cadre, and his hometown was Shunde, Guangdong. During the 2003 SARS outbreak, he went back hometown to visit his family, and when he was talking about SARS with one of his friends, the friend told him, "Roxithromycin has been snapped up, and even the pharmaceutical manufacturers cannot produce it. It is a big mistake to treat SARS as a chlamydia! The problem caused may become an international disaster." At the time, SARS deaths had appeared at the Sun Yat-sen Second Hospital in Guangzhou.

Regardless of the fact that it was wrong to treat SARS with roxithromycin, the confusing price of roxithromycin frustrated Dr. Zhong. He used roxithromycin as the basis to confront the National Medical Products Administration while media coverage was in full swing during the national Two Sessions in 2006. Before implementing a medicine tender procurement, the antibiotic, roxithromycin, was a joke between patients and hospitals.

In the years following the battle against SARS, the market performance of roxithromycin grew. There were more than 30 varieties, and prices ranged from 2 to

30 yuan. Roxithromycin, a medicine with many brands, allowed manufacturers to make more money, but only through trickery.

At the CPPCC National Committee breakout session, Dr. Zhong spoke forcefully, even though the director of the National Medical Products Administration was sitting next to him. But this did not ease Dr. Zhong's righteous indignation. China had such a chaotic, disorderly situation with just roxithromycin. How could the quality of medicines be guaranteed?

The National Medical Products Administration approved more than 10,000 new medicines a year, causing an increase in the price of medicines. The price of a medicine could be increased by simply changing the name of the product. Putting the same medicine in a new package made the price go up if the relevant materials were submitted to the Department of Price of National Development and Reform Commission.

However, the medicine tender procurement did not bring a standardized order to the chaotic medical market. Instead, another tendency emerged. Originally, the tender system was meant to find medicines with higher quality and reasonable prices. As a result, the only tender criterion seemed to be, the cheaper the better. Thus, the original intent of the tender system was distorted.

With sadness, Dr. Zhong expressed that the costs of many of China's real, outstanding national pharmaceutical enterprises couldn't be further reduced, and this gave various speculative or informal enterprises a loophole to exploit. Many medicines recruited through the tender were unqualified, while the good medicines were unable to pass through the tender. It was indeed a strike for the national pharmaceutical enterprises, and as a result, some good quality medicines had to be imported from abroad, and their high price increased the burden on the Chinese people. Moreover, many of the tender committee members were not even experts. They did not know medicine, and they had no clinical experience.

In May 2009, there was an event that delighted Dr. Zhong. The MOH and the Ministry of Ecology and Environment (MEE) jointly developed a standard that included hazy days in the category of air pollution. This was something he had strongly advocated, and now it had finally come to fruition.

In recent years, the MEE had always broadcasted that the sources of pollution were decreasing, and the air quality had improved, but the people did not feel it, because the sky overhead was still grey and gloomy. What exactly was the problem?

Previously, air quality was measured by the measurement of dustfall, PPM, including the assessment of sulfur dioxide and carbon dioxide. But haze had a different composition. Its main components were nitrogen oxides, carbon monoxide, and ozone. When these substances encountered ultraviolet light, they formed tiny particles and generated ozone. It had been proven that inhaling haze could cause health problems in humans. However, in the past, this was not considered pollution. Times were changing, though, and China's air pollution had shifted from soot-type to vehicle exhaust type.

In 2008, prior to the Olympic Games in Beijing, the President of the World Allergy Organization (WAO) invited Dr. Zhong to write an article on air quality in China. At that time, athletes from various countries participating in the Beijing Olympics, including the team leaders, expressed their dissatisfaction with China's air quality. Dr. Zhong wanted to prove through facts that China's air quality met the standards of the Olympic Games. He was tied up with work, but he asked his secretary to gather relevant data from the Beijing Olympic Organizing Committee, and he personally consulted the journalists who had interviewed him for valuable information.

The report read, "We've done quite a bit of research, read through a lot of information, and did a good deal of work. Dustfall and hydroxide have greatly improved, but haze and ozone are still substandard." Dr. Zhong did his best to help the Beijing Organizing Committee to combat air pollution in Beijing.

"Many people in Guangzhou over the age of 40 have black lungs," said Dr. Zhong in 2008. On this point, in addition to his clinical experience, he had sought advice from many surgeons. Later, some people questioned the statement. In fact, there was no need to question it, because surgeons knew best. They opened the patients' chests, especially patients with lung diseases and those above 40 years old, they knew well that the patients' lungs were indeed black.

In 2008, Dr. Zhong called for daily exercise for college, high school, and elementary school students because he had learned that the physical fitness of teenagers was significantly declining. On October 26, 2008, the Ministry of Education (MOE), the General Administration of Sports of China, and the Central Committee of the Communist Youth League jointly organized the second National Sunshine Sports Winter Distance Running for students, which was the result of Dr. Zhong's participation in the vigorous appeal for more exercise among students. He had seen an MOE fact sheet showing that both male and female students' average height had increased in 2004 to 2005, but their physical fitness was much worse than before. What was meant by physical fitness? It included speed, strength, sensitivity, and endurance. The students were weak at these aspects, especially lung capacity. For example, the normal lung capacity of a student should be 3,000 ml, but was only 2,700 ml, in the statistics from MOE. Dr. Zhong found that the problem of declining physical fitness of Chinese youth was serious, and he was concerned.

MOE's findings also showed that within the previous twenty years, although Chinese youths' height had generally increased, the indicators of endurance, strength, speed, and sensitivity had decreased, particularly endurance and strength. Jogging was one of the best ways to exercise the heart and lung function, enhance endurance, and improve lung capacity. The effect was significant, as compared with other activities. Jogging and brisk walking were the basic items included in Dr. Zhong's own regular exercise. Sports taught children not to concede defeat, to have the spirit of striving for excellence, to attach importance to collaboration and cultivate team spirit, and to be more efficient.

In Dr. Zhong's home, documents and materials occupied a lot of space, and there was nothing his wife could do about it. Even so, he had arranged a small room for exercise equipment, including a treadmill, rowing machine, and dumbbell set. There was even a pull-up bar installed on the wall. It was a happy space for the family to share.

In his view, space restrictions and other reasons were excuses people used to avoid physical exercise. "Running is most unrestricted by time and venue. It can be done any time and anywhere, whether in the classroom, in the neighborhood, or anywhere else." He usually ran on the treadmill at home, and sometimes ran in place at his office.

The key to students being able to stick to long-distance running lay in educational guidance. Whenever he talked about this issue, Dr. Zhong couldn't help but look solemn. "At present, the main criterion we use to measure students is the scores and the examination results, which have nothing to do with physical fitness," he observed. "On the surface, sports is said to be a part of education, but in fact, it is just exam-oriented. Good performance in sports in an exam-oriented educational system is not equivalent to good physical fitness, which is really ironic." Only with good physical fitness and an early foundation can China adapt to more challenges of the future society. Dr. Zhong always said, "Some people with poor physical fitness do not feel anything at all when they are young. They will only slowly notice their poor health in their 30s or 40s."

In 1958, the goal of Peking University Health Science Center (PKUHSC) was to train students who were "red, specialized, and healthy." Red meat good ideology, specialized meant good academic performance, and healthy meant good physical fitness. The slogan aimed to call on students to serve the motherland with healthy bodies for fifty years. By 2020, Dr. Zhong, who graduated from university in 1960, had been serving his country with a healthy body for exactly sixty years. He achieved the PKUHSC goal, always serving his country with a healthy body.

By contrast, many other doctors who had retired much earlier were plagued with diseases because they had too little "health savings" in their lives. "In those days, the awareness was not that high, and it was only enhanced later," Dr. Zhong said. He shared that he was used to engaging in competitive sports, which was not the same as daily exercise. But gradually, he stopped participating in sports competitions and discontinued competitive sports, though he still liked sports very much.

Dr. Zhong felt that exercise was very useful to him, as it improved his efficiency and clarity of mind. Gradually, he turned sports into a habit and developed it to a certain extent, viewing it as of equal importance with eating. Eating was a way to add nutrition to the body, but many people didn't realize that the same was true for exercise. With the oxygen going to the brain, one would be less likely to be drowsy, and the internal organs of the human body, blood, and bones all needed oxygen too. Physical exercise was part of mental activity. The main tissue of the body was muscle, and aside from the water content, it accounted for 80% of all organs. If the muscles were not exercised, the person's metabolic level would not improve.

The purity of the Party, the country's prosperity and development, and all the big and small things always touched Dr. Zhong's heart. This was all out of love.

"I care very little if others are happy or offended by what I say or what I do," he said.

The roof of the new building of the Guangzhou IRH was a helipad. Critically ill patients brought from Baiyun Airport and those brought by helicopter could be immediately resuscitated. "This is a wish that has been fulfilled in my life," said Dr. Zhong when he had been working for more than sixty years. There was no noise, no wind and no rain. Everything seemed so peaceful.

On a night cruise on the Pearl River, the guide pointed her finger at this new building standing on the river and said, "You know, Dr. Zhong Nanshan, who fought against SARS, has moved into this new building. He works and treats patients there. He is now working hard to fight H1N1 for us."

Dr. Zhong had devoted more than forty years of his life to the IRH. He had formerly been the dean of Guangzhou Medical College, now Guangzhou Medical University, and he was once the dean of the First Affiliated Hospital of Guangzhou Medical University. His students were now all over the world, but he was still training postgraduates and nurturing students of each new Nanshan Class.

The north gate of Guangzhou Medical University was located on North Renmin Road, and its library could be seen on the right side of the courtyard from the entrance. Situated west to east, the library was connected by a simple platform and reading rooms. The entire building had reading rooms on both sides and a spacious balcony in the middle of the first and second floors. On the first floor, the statue of the old dean was in the center. On the second floor, there was a statue of Zhong Nanshan. This vivid image of Zhong Nanshan had firm, fearless, trustworthy eyes. The black and dark metallic texture expressed strength. Where the outline of the eyes reflected the sunlight was the familiar and clear gaze, looking beyond the balcony to the clear blue sky. The corners of Dr. Zhong's mouth conveyed his inner fortitude. In the face of difficulties, his tightly closed lips reflected resilience. In the face of danger, he would open his mouth to cry out, but faced with patients, he smiled to warm them, and faced with the Party and the country, he silently expressed his endless loyalty.

"I've become ancient. They made this statue and wanted to put it in the new hospital building at first." Dr. Zhong smiled. "I did not agree. I am still working here. It would be weird if I saw it every day as I walked around. They eventually agreed to put it in the library instead, as part of the cultural construction of the university campus."

China was a country full of hope and a nation that had gone through thousands of years of ups and downs. It was characterized by a strong resilience, and even the colonial rule of foreign powers had not brought it down.

The Chinese people loved their country so much. Many overseas Chinese family members were persecuted during the Cultural Revolution, yet they still had a deep love for their motherland, ensuring that the Chinese nation would never collapse. Dr. Zhong too had been through a lot of hardships, but he had never changed.

The sunlight after the rain, shimmering on the dense leaves of the tree canopy downstairs, was like golden butterflies. The breeze blew, and the flowers and trees rustled in response, creating a scene of vigor and vitality.

On the streets of Guangzhou, the people were in a hurry, but they were peaceful. The inseparable old couples held each other's hands as they filled the streets. In the sky overhead, a plane took off from Guangzhou Baiyun Airport, like an eagle soaring in the sky.

11

RESPONSIBILITY AND PERSEVERANCE

At the beginning of 2010, the First Affiliated Hospital of Guangzhou Medical University and Guangzhou IRH finally moved into a new building. The old hallways, tables, and chairs all seemed difficult to part with. Scientific research had been conducted here, and SARS had been conquered here. So many tears and joy were going to be left behind in the old facility.

Dr. Zhong's office in the new building faced the Pearl River, and it was arranged with great care. But he was too busy to stop and enjoy the beautiful view of the river. He chose the red pattern of the carpet in his office because it seemed full of enthusiasm and vitality. He did not like dullness, and he needed to keep himself in an energetic state to cope with his daily work.

A new blueprint had been brewing in his mind: he hoped to establish an international IRH. A building of considerable size would be needed, and a world-class research team. This was his greatest wish in life.

The IRH had been trying to address the difficulty of "early detection" of respiratory disease. By 2012, the IRH reached the scientific research level of "early detection" and achieved satisfactory clinical results, which made Dr. Zhong feel great relief. The older he got, the more he thought about how he should contribute to society and leave more wealth for future generations. He had always taken to heart the teaching of his father, Dr. Zhong Shifan, asking himself, *What should I do in life to contribute to society?*

Due to his considerable social influence, there were too many unanticipated social responsibilities that he needed to take up at any given time. There were too many unanticipated rights and wrongs that required his voice and participation, his actions for promoting the good, and his attitude to help others persevere.

Based on his determination of the basic facts, Dr. Zhong did not flinch or compromise when a national sensation occurred in 2011, an event that became known as the tobacco academician controversy.

For Zhong Nanshan, the title of academician was sacred, and no bureaucracy was allowed during the election of academicians. It had to be scientific, democratic, fair, and open. An academician as him, couldn't bear having single speck in his eye. He saw it as his duty to let those who were qualified and had both virtues and talent be elected as academicians. On this point, he could not go against his conscience and take into account or yield to anyone's ego. On the contrary, he would argue with an unjust ruling and not back down.

On December 8, 2011, an expert in tobacco research was elected to be an academician of the Chinese Academy of Engineering for achieving a research result in "reduction in tar to reduce harm." It was technology that aimed to improve the safety of smoking by reducing tar, a health hazard, in the cigarette. Based on the common sense that smoking is harmful to health, questions from all walks of life continued.

Tobacco research did not have a good reputation in China, but it was never short of funding. Although some research had made "breakthroughs," it was still difficult to get praise because of a basic scientific fact rooted in common sense: smoking is bad for health. The WHO Framework Convention on Tobacco Control, of which China was a signatory, clearly stated, "Tobacco products using terms such as 'low tar' are false, misleading, and deceptive. Smoking extreme low-tar or low-tar cigarettes have the same risk of death from lung cancer as smoking medium-tar cigarettes."

Chen Junshi, an academician of the Chinese Academy of Engineering, published a blog post stating that research on "reduction in tar to reduce harm" was misdirected. He said, "I really can't imagine that it will become a high-level scientific, technological achievement. Obviously, it is the wrong direction. The government's project support and incentives in science and technology departments and institutions need to learn from this."

Yang Gonghuan, former deputy director of the Chinese Center for Disease Control and Prevention, was the first to get involved in tobacco control. He told the media bluntly that the reduction in tar to reduce harm research was a false proposition. Over the decades, thousands of studies in many countries had long proven that no tar reduction measures or additives, including traditional Chinese medicines, could make cigarettes less harmful.

Undoubtedly, Dr. Zhong was firmly opposed to the election of the tobacco academician. His opposition pointed to the so-called reduction in tar to reduce harm research results. Zhong Nanshan, Qin Boyi, Ba Denian, and other academicians of the Chinese Academy of Engineering who expressed strong opposition believed that the tobacco academician had no credible results, and there was no evidence to ensure the health of smokers. At best, only some tar reduction research had been done, but no harm reduction effect had been seen.

The controversy had not yet come to an end when the tobacco academician was elected. But, this national debate involving academic ethics and the title of academician gave the public a deeper understanding of the dangers of tobacco and the deceptive nature of reduction in tar to reduce harm.

12

SCIENTIFIC PREVENTION AND CONTROL OF AVIAN INFLUENZA

In 2013, patients with avian influenza A, H7N9, were identified and some deaths occurred. The live poultry farming industry was hit again. The responsibility to stop H7N9 and the blame from the live poultry farming industry was added to the National Health and Family Planning Commission (NHFPC) and related experts.

Dr. Zhong had two points of view. First, most patients were infected with H7N9 in live poultry markets, so strict controls should be imposed on live poultry markets. Second, once signs of human-to-human transmission of H7N9 were detected, live poultry markets needed to be closed immediately. However, either control or closure would cause losses and panic in the poultry industry.

Even so, Dr. Zhong believed that it was important to only respect facts.

When the clock struck the New Year in 2014, Dr. Zhong still had not left the ICU where patients dying of H7N9 were staying. The patients' families called over and over again asking about their conditions. Dr. Zhong replied, "I will do my best."

At the turn of the 21st century, Dr. Zhong's students, as well as some other experts, had begun research on avian influenza viruses. The viruses had formerly been found only among poultry, but at the end of the 20th century, there had been cases of human transmission of avian influenza, H5N1, though the transmission was limited. H7N9 was a new type of avian influenza. According to the diagnosis and treatment protocols researched in 2013, the incubation period after human infection was generally within seven days. Patients usually presented flu-like symptoms, such as fever, cough, and some sputum, which might be accompanied by headaches, muscle aches, and general malaise. In severe cases, the disease developed rapidly and manifested as severe pneumonia, with body temperatures mostly persisting above 39°C and respiratory distress, with coughing of bloody sputum. Once the disease developed further, acute respiratory distress syndrome, mediastinal emphysema, sepsis, shock, disturbance of consciousness, and acute kidney injury, among other symptoms, would appear. Most critically, people infected with severe avian influenza could die in a relatively short time.

The novel avian influenza, H7N9, was first identified in Shanghai and Anhui in late March 2013. It was the first new subtype of influenza virus discovered in the world, and it was not yet included in China's statutory infectious disease surveillance and reporting system. By early April 2013, there was no vaccine introduced in China. All H7N9 patients developed fever and other symptoms in the early stage. Later in Apr 2013, human-to-human transmission of the virus was not yet proven, and it was found that the genes of the virus came from the genetic reassortment of wild birds in East Asia and chicken flocks in Shanghai, Zhejiang, and Jiangsu.

Avian influenza in humans was a human disease caused by the avian influenza virus. Avian influenza was a variant of the influenza A virus, which was divided into three levels: high, medium, or low non-pathogenic, according to the different pathogenicity of avian influenza virus to chickens and turkeys. The highly pathogenic H5N1 subtype and the novel avian influenza H7N9 subtype first identified in humans in March 2013 were of particular concern because they had caused human casualties while hitting the live poultry farming industry hard.

Because of the seriousness of the situation, Dr. Zhong called for the control and even closure of live poultry markets, and this was where the dispute arose. Once the authorities issued this order, it meant that many poultry farming enterprises and live poultry marks would be closed down, so the owners of live poultry markets came forward to challenge Dr. Zhong.

Chinanews.com reported on April 13, 2013, that Chinese officials clarified that exposure to live poultry markets was a risk factor for the development of H7N9 avian influenza. The report said that the number of people infected with H7N9 in Mainland China was continuing to rise. Notably, this new subtype of the influenza virus had moved north and infiltrated into Beijing. The report also noted that officials were warning against buying live poultry and slaughtering of poultry by the people themselves and advising the public not to buy fresh, live, or frozen poultry or related products without quarantine certificates. If one had fever or respiratory symptoms, they should see a doctor and report their history of poultry contact.

Media agencies such as the *Yangtse Evening Post* and *Xiamen Daily* continued to publish reports about contact with live poultry before the onset or death of avian influenza patients in various parts of China. A report on January 24, 2014, noted that a human case of H7N9 avian influenza was found in Beijing, and the patient had bought and eaten pigeons before the onset of the disease. A report on January 28, 2014, stated that the first case of human infection of avian influenza was confirmed in Xiamen, and the patient had bought live chickens before the onset of the disease. A report on February 5, 2014, noted that Jiangsu had its first case of H7N9 avian influenza death, and the deceased had bought live chickens before the onset of the disease.

By the time of the national congress Two Sessions held in 2014, there was still no conclusive evidence of human-to-human transmission of avian influenza in China. During the Two Sessions on March 10, 2014, Dr. Zhong highlighted his distinctive view in the face of journalists, stating that live poultry markets were one of the main factors in the spread of avian influenza.

On March 10, 2014, at 9:00 am, the Press Center of the second session of the 12th National People's Congress held a press conference in the multi-function hall of Beijing's Media Center. NPC deputies were invited to the press conference, including Dr. Zhong.

A journalist from Kyodo News asked, "I would like to ask Dr. Zhong a few questions about avian influenza. A city has partially closed its live poultry markets but not fully closed down. What do you think about this? And what do you think about the Chinese government's response? Another issue that the public is most concerned about is genetic change. Is there a possibility that the virus will become a new type of influenza infection? If this happens, do you think the government can deal with such a problem?"

Dr. Zhong replied, "I'd like to thank our Japanese friend for raising questions of common concern. Let me answer your first question about the situation of avian influenza. Let's not discuss the name first because I think the key issue now is not the name but the current situation. Now, H7N9 is occurring across the country. The not-so-accurate statistics are that more than 340 people have been infected nationwide, and the death rate is close to 30%. In Guangdong, where I come from, we have more infected cases, with 82 people in the past, and now 84 people. Among these 84, 23 died, a death rate of 28%. The statistics show that avian influenza is still occurring, and it is characterized by dissemination."

What was meant by dissemination? It had two meanings. First, it meant that they were not connected, and cases happened individually, which implied that there was no passing of the virus between humans. If there were, it was no longer individual, but interconnected. Second, it meant that avian influenza was still occurring because there were sources of infection out there. However, where the sources of infection came from was still a question. At the time, there did not seem to be an accurate assessment of the transmission route, but from the perspective of epidemiology, more than 80% came from poultry markets. Dr. Zhong was emphasizing the markets, not poultries, because infection appeared in markets.

Dr. Zhong continued, saying that at the time, in most places where poultries and birds were farmed intensively, even in those farming households, the H7N9 virus could not be detected. However, once the poultry and birds were taken to the market to be sold and there was human contact, infection could occur, and the infection rate of the local environment was significantly increased. He pointed out that in poultry farming areas in Guangdong, the detection rate of the H7N9 virus was almost negligible, while it was 2.6% at the markets, an increase of more than 100 times, indicating that the markets were the main factor in avian influenza infection.

Dr. Zhong continued answering the Japanese journalist, addressing what was currently being done. Unlike H5N1, which was a disease in poultry and humans, when people were willing to kill all the chickens to prevent humans from the disease, the problem now was that the chickens were not sick, but humans were. People who were involved in agriculture production and poultry farming often asked, "Why should we kill our chickens?" There were always contradictions and views on this issue, and it involved the careers of millions of poultry farmers in China.

During this press conference, Dr. Zhong distinctly put forward his view, stating that more than 80% of patients with avian influenza were infected in live poultry markets. Therefore, he proposed that the live poultry markets be controlled first, and as soon as there was human-to-human transmission, the markets must be closed down.

Dr. Zhong indicated that there were two ways to control live poultry markets. The first approach was to close the markets down, which was a large move. What was the meaning of the closure? It meant that the markets would never re-open. This had to be considered carefully, because it would impact a large number of poultry businesses. The second approach was currently being implemented in many places, and it included cleaning once a week, disinfecting once a month, and shutting down once a month. Shutting down was not the same as closing down. Shutting down meant that markets would re-open after being cleaned and disinfected. Guangdong had implemented this approach, which proved to be effective to a certain extent. Now, it was crucial to have live poultry markets under control, and this was what China was doing now.

Once the genes mutated, he said, there would be human-to-human transmission, just like with SARS, and that was a different situation. Human-to-human transmission indicated a massive outbreak. The markets had to be closed down and thoroughly disposed of in this case. At the same time, people found to be infected must be isolated, while now, such people were isolated and treated in designated hospitals. But so far, no medical worker or other close contacts had been infected. Once human-to-human transmission happened, it was necessary to implement early detection, early isolation, and early treatment.

In addition, a vaccine needed to be developed to address the problem. When it came to human-to-human transmission, a vaccine was essential. Of course, the virus strains used to produce the vaccine were now ready, and once there was a massive outbreak, the vaccine could be produced immediately. Just like the H1N1 epidemic in 2009, China had effectively produced the vaccine in just five months and immunized nearly 100 million people. The vaccine played a part in this epidemic. Later, it was learned that the natural progression of avian influenza was to slowly decline after the peak, which was the trend of the disease.

Dr. Zhong added that China was now doing the right thing. If the gene mutation caused human-to-human transmission, a vaccine would play a prominent role.

WORRIES ABOUT AIR QUALITY

The primary reason Dr. Zhong spoke out about air pollution was that it caused a steep rise in the incidence of lung cancer. Air pollution had a serious impact on people's livelihood as well. During the Two Sessions of the National People's Congress in 2014, Dr. Zhong again spoke on the issue of people's livelihood, addressing questions such as medical reform, medicine prices and doctor-patient disputes. For these important issues, Dr. Zhong always conducted meticulous investigations and research before the Two Sessions. In 2012, in order to submit a motion on the issue of rural doctors, he went to poor rural areas in Guangdong before the annual Two Sessions. At the age of 76, he endured the cold, damp weather so that he could personally experience how rural doctors worked.

Dr. Zhong traveled to many regions and mountain villages, and he fully investigated the local shortage of medical care and medicines and the difficult working and living conditions of rural doctors. He wrote an informative call for rural doctors to stop being given no social status, protection, or treatment. He voiced that the situation of rural doctors was worrying. More than six million village doctors nationwide faced many problems, including work, treatment, retirement, and succession.

A basic national policy was introduced in 2012. In Dr. Zhong's words, the policy was "very encouraging," as it made resource conservation and environment protection a basic national policy and monitored fine particulate matter PM2.5 in key regions, such as Beijing, Tianjin, Hebei, the Yangtze River Delta, as well as municipalities and provincial capitals. It aimed to cover all cities above the prefecture-level by 2015. Atmospheric environmental monitoring and prevention and control were put on the agenda.

After the beginning of winter in 2011, the severe haze in Beijing made people breathless, and the grey sky looked gloomy. Beijing residents did not know whether the situation would get worse and when it would get better. Some of the topics they discussed were always inseparable from relocation, at least to the distant suburbs of Beijing.

On the afternoon of March 5, 2012, the Guangdong delegation to the Fifth Session of NPC held a delegation meeting, which was open to the media. As an NPC deputy, Dr. Zhong spoke in accordance with the requirements of the meeting. He said solemnly, "The title of my speech today is 'Concern About Atmospheric Pollution is Vital for People's Livelihood.'"

As a scientist in respiratory medicine, he said pointedly, "The government's performance should not be judged by the GDP alone, but also by whether there is pollution in the environment and air."

He said that after the SARS outbreak in 2003, the central government took SARS prevention and control as an opportunity to put forward the concept of being people-oriented and building a harmonious society. A harmonious society was first and foremost a healthy society, and the priority of people's livelihood was people's health. However, in the previous five years, many people often asked questions like, "I don't smoke or drink, and I pay attention to diet and hygiene, so why do I still get lung cancer, stomach cancer, or bowel cancer? My house is clean, so why does my child have leukemia?"

There were different kinds of pollutants in the living environment, including pollution of the water, food, and air. Of these, the most critical was air pollution, especially small particles of PM2.5 and ozone. In the past, many people questioned China's environmental authorities' claim that air quality had "greatly improved," because people felt that the air quality was actually getting worse. The core of this problem was that the environmental authorities did not monitor PM2.5 and ozone, the small particles that could directly enter human alveoli and cause irritation and disease to the airways and lungs. This was what happened on hazy days.

Dr. Zhong pointed out that many countries and regions had researched PM2.5. In 2006, the US observed 204 towns and cities and found that for every 10 $\mu g/m^3$ increase in PM2.5, the hospitalization rate of heart failure patients increased by 1.28%. Research data from 2000 to 2005 in Hong Kong also showed that for every 10 $\mu g/$

m^3 increase in PM2.5, there was a 1.94% increase in hospitalization for patients with acute respiratory disease and a 3.1% increase for patients with chronic obstructive pulmonary disease. "Our research has found that whenever there is hazy weather, the number of patient visits increases by 10% to 15%. We are studying why the incidence of lung cancer in our major cities has skyrocketed, and whether it is related to PM2.5," said the report.

PM2.5 was closely related to visibility. Data from the Chinese Academy of Environmental Sciences in 2010 found that visibility started to deteriorate with PM2.5 levels greater than 75 μg/m^3, and when PM2.5 levels were less than 50 μg/m^3, visibility was inversely proportional to it.

The air quality in China's large cities was very poor compared to the rest of the world. In 2011, WHO counted the PM10 concentration in 1,085 cities around the world, with a total of 33 cities in China being included in the statistics. Among them, the worst was Lanzhou, ranking 24th from the bottom, and the best was Haikou, ranking 273rd from the bottom. Among the five major central cities in China, Beijing ranked 46th from the bottom, Chongqing ranked 63rd from the bottom, Tianjin ranked 72nd from the bottom, Shanghai ranked 103rd from the bottom, and Guangzhou ranked 119th from the bottom. Guangzhou was considered to have a relatively better air quality, but compared with large cities across the world, it was among the worst.

The above shows that China's air quality was in the lower reaches of the world. Dr. Zhong commented that the economy had gone up, but the air quality went down. Vice minister of the Ministry of Ecology and Environment (MEE) Wu Xiaoqing said that even by Class II standards, more than two-thirds of China's cities were substandard. Appealed to and urged by people, public opinion, NPC deputies, and CPPCC members, the Government's Work Report formally proposed monitoring PM2.5 as an important item.

As an NPC deputy, Dr. Zhong also made suggestions and contributions to the government while performing his sacred duties. He noticed the specific operations of China's MEE: starting from 2012, the Yangtze River Delta, the Pearl River Delta, Beijing-Tianjin-Hebei and municipalities and provincial capitals had all carried out PM2.5 monitoring. The Government's Work Report mentioned that only by 2015 would PM2.5 monitoring be carried out in all parts of China, and it would preliminarily be conducted for the regional pollution in these key areas.

Dr. Zhong said, "Without national monitoring and multi-sectoral collaboration on specific measures to save energy and reduce emissions and improve ecology, I think that control of serious air pollution in some key areas will be empty words."

"First of all, we need to have multi-location integrated management, as it is not enough to only manage it locally. Secondly, we need to strengthen monitoring and prevention and control. Vice Minister Wu Xiaoqing has said that fifty cities in China are now able to monitor PM2.5 and ozone concurrently. Since the whole country is now able to measure these, why was the practice only fully implemented in 2015? Is it because the pollution is so serious that it will affect investment? Or is it because of some other reasons that are not so nice to mention? In particular, for some less developed areas, there is no monitoring, and there is industrial transfer. With the growth of regional GDP, the pollution will aggravate. Shall we only address the issue when the pollution is even worse?"

Based on the above, Dr. Zhong put forward his proposal. First, the construction of the environmental monitoring point should be fully launched right away, rather than waiting until 2015. Second, comprehensive measures for energy conservation, emission reduction, and ecological improvement should be developed, such as optimization of industrial structure and energy structure, control of industrial pollution and automobile emissions, protection of natural ecology, return of farmland to forest, and planting of trees.

He said, "Guangdong should take the lead. The leadership must realize that although improving air quality temporarily cannot improve regional GDP, it can make Guangdong residents healthier, and future generations will certainly benefit from it. People will thank us. I hope that when people come to Guangdong, they can breathe fresh air."

At the Two Sessions in 2012, Dr. Zhong was overwhelmed by a sea of journalists. The Guangdong delegation decided to hold a special press conference for him.

The main topic was air pollution, and the conference lasted for one hour. He had no script, and he sat on the sofa, speaking incessantly in a hurried tone. More than a hundred statistics were involved in his remarks. Some journalists marveled, wondering how he could remember so much data.

At the Two Sessions held in March 2013, Dr. Zhong again brought a motion on combating haze and solving the air pollution problem as quickly as possible. When a journalist asked him about the relationship between air pollution control and GDP, he said, "If we don't even have the opportunity to breathe fresh air, what is the point of having a high GDP? The measurement of the government's performance should not be a single item. Like merely looking at Liu Xiang's victory of the 110-meter high hurdles is far from enough, as it should include looking at all five victories. Overall development is essential. If there is one item we fail to pass, especially the environment quality or air quality, then that is poor performance."

For five full years, from 2008 to 2013, Dr. Zhong spoke out on behalf of the fight against air pollution. He did much work, advising and urging the government to develop policies as soon as possible and put in more effort to govern with an iron fist. As a result of Dr. Zhong's focused "fire" on the governance of air pollution at the Two Sessions in 2013, he attracted questions and criticism from various quarters. Some accused him of making a big deal out of it, saying he was clamoring for attention. They asked him to come up with evidence that air pollution causes cancer.

His critics felt that his evidence was not convincing enough. On October 18, 2013, in Guangzhou, Dr. Zhong received a letter in English from the International Agency for Research in Cancer (IARC), of the WHO. The subject of the letter was outdoor air pollution as the leading environmental contributor to cancer and death. On October 17, 2013, a press conference was held, where it was suggested that air pollution was the cause of lung cancer and that this statement had Category I evidence (i.e., solid evidence), and it was also clear that outdoor air pollution was an important factor in increasing the risk of bladder cancer. The IARC was relieved to note that the theme of the press conference had brought an unprecedented level of awareness to the issue of air pollution.

Even looking back on the months of questions about his claim that haze caused cancer, and even the accusations and personal attacks, Dr. Zhong had no complaints. He sat at his desk and reviewed his elaborated point of view against the information confirmed in this letter from the IRAC. The IRAC further emphasized the importance of controlling air pollution at a press conference. Dr. Zhong said, "Now I believe that people will take my word for it, because it's what the WHO says as well."

According to the director of the IRAC, the air Chinese residents were breathing was contaminated with a mixture of particulate matter that could cause tumors. Outdoor air pollution was not only a major health hazard, but also a major environmental contributor that caused cancer and death, and this environmental contributor included indoor air pollution as well.

There were more than a hundred papers published internationally on five continents, all of which specifically addressed the impact of outdoor air pollution, especially that caused by traffic. The results of these studies were drawn from some epidemiological studies in Europe, North America, and Asia.

What were the major sources of outdoor air pollution? One was traffic, and another was energy generation, such as thermal power generation and electricity, as well as emissions from industrial and agricultural production. Next was air pollution caused by cooking. Of course, there were also some natural forms of pollution, but they were not critical. Defining outdoor air pollution as a key risk factor for human carcinogenesis was a meaningful step.

Dr. Zhong stated that there were many ways to effectively reduce air pollution. The studies sent a very strong signal that the international agencies involved recommended countries to resolutely intervene in the protection of the environment and health without any delay.

The WHO's conclusion reinforced Dr. Zhong's suggestion from a few years earlier. Dr. Zhong clearly remembered that when he pointed out the serious consequences of air pollution, he was accused of not having conducted any experimental studies and it was suggested that he could thus only raise the issue after passing the research evaluation, so he should not take advantage of the Two Sessions, a political platform, to discuss nonsense. Dr. Zhong continued to insist and reminded them, "If the prevention and control of air pollution is not taken seriously, it will pose a greater danger than SARS."

Dr. Zhong's tone had been calm as he said these things. Now, there was conclusive evidence from the WHO to back him up. After all, SARS affected a group of infected people in the relatively short period of half a year. So, what about air pollution? It would affect the entire Chinese population, and its effect was both chronic and long-lasting. In a few years, what if the prevalence of cardiovascular disease and tumors, especially lung cancer, increased steeply? At that time, people would complain about the government and the MEE. It was hard to think about the potential trouble.

"Ten years ago, I said that most people in Guangzhou in their 40s and 50s had black lungs. Some thought I was talking nonsense. Why will you only reflect on yourself when something happens, or when a doctor tells you that you have lung cancer? What can you do at that point?"

Before the 2008 Beijing Olympics, Dr. Zhong had called for attention to the problem of air pollution. At that time, many foreign scholars invited Dr. Zhong to advise their countries' athletes on the air quality issue.

Following the appearance of American athletes wearing masks at the 2008 Beijing Olympic Games, foreign athletes wearing masks appeared against the 2013 Beijing International Marathon, which was quite ironic. In the same year, Beijing's poor air quality urged the government to step up its efforts to manage the problem.

Dr. Zhong reiterated, "To solve the air pollution problem in Beijing, it is necessary to solve the related problems in Hebei and Shanxi. The whole country must act together to solve the air pollution problem in the Beijing-Tianjin-Hebei, Yangtze River Delta, and Pearl River Delta regions." He went on, "The worsening air quality in Hong Kong over the past decade is closely related to the air pollution in the Pearl River Delta region. Pollution has no boundaries. One country, two systems can be done, but it is not possible to have one country, two airs."

On March 1, 2014, the annual national Two Sessions was held. On March 2, the sky in Beijing was surprisingly clear. On March 3, an NPC deputy from the Guangdong delegation joked, "People of ability are all coming to Beijing. A breath from each of them drives away Beijing's haze."

The appearance of blue skies in Beijing had become increasingly common since March 2014. Beijingers, who cared about the air quality, went to Linfen, a region in Shanxi once regarded as toxic, and they were surprised to find the haze there was almost gone. Locals said that the air quality had improved dramatically. The government of Shanxi sacrificed the production of coal mining to bring back a blue sky. Dr. Zhong was very pleased to hear this news.

At 4:30 pm on March 6, he was interviewed at the Guangdong media's Two Sessions Live Room, and the topic of the interview was tobacco control. He said, "Tobacco control has been ongoing for many years. Why is it difficult to control tobacco? There are objective reasons for this. The deep-seated reason is that tobacco is a pillar industry in many provinces. It's not possible to reduce their revenue income, which would cause lots of employment problems. This is a significant reason. I participated in several meetings of the Academy of Engineering, and we are very determined to pull down the tobacco academician."

He publicly broke the news with the media, and he commented on the central decisive decision. He said, "At least we can ban smoking in public places. I think that the no smoking at this Two Sessions is a huge step forward."

One NPC deputy, an old smoker, just happened to pass by the interview room at this moment. He couldn't help but tremble slightly. "Hey, Zhong, you've got guts," he said. He shook his head, but he raised his thumbs as he walked away.

The media published Dr. Zhong's comments. "I advocate that three kinds of people should not smoke. One is the leadership at all levels, the second is teachers, and the third is doctors. If these groups of people control smoking well, the effect of tobacco control will be greater, and the tobacco control work will go more smoothly." This effective interview made Dr. Zhong feel that time spent on it was not in vain.

On May 21, 2014, CCTV's news program Xinwen Lianbo, a newscaster with a sweet voice broadcasted that the air pollution prevention and control law enforcement inspection team under the Standing Committee of the National People's Congress had held the first plenary meeting on May 21. The law of enforcement inspection of air pollution prevention and control was officially launched, aiming at promoting the implementation of the air pollution prevention and control action plan. Dr. Zhong had been working hard all day, and he was yet to finish his dinner. He saw the news and could not help but breathe a sigh of relief.

∞ 14 ∞

SACRED DUTY

During the Two Sessions in 2015, Dr. Zhong was too exhausted, and he eventually collapsed. He had once been a member of the CPPCC, and now he was an NPC deputy, but others might not know that he was also the leader of the Guangdong NPC delegation. The leader had many responsibilities, such as managing group discussions, including but not limited to organizing and managing the discussion, making concluding remarks, summarizing discussion, and submitting the results in the form of a report. He was also required to report on the work to the chief officer on behalf of the whole delegation and attend various high-level meetings that were required for team leaders. Moreover, as a doctor, he needed to receive important consultations that could come at any time, and also meet the journalists who always seemed to chase after him.

Not every CPPCC member or NPC deputy performed their duty wholeheartedly like him. Every motion he made, just as he done as a member of the CPPCC in the past, was always made after a full investigation and research of the facts and data on the issues, and after he personally visited and collected evidence. In other words, every year before the Two Sessions in March, he was busy with the content of his motions for over a month.

Many people said that Dr. Zhong was a pedant, focusing on medical research in an ivory tower, and it was thus not possible for him to think about politics. Some even inferred that his attendance at the Two Sessions was done entirely to please his superiors. Even the former CCTV host Wang Zhi had asked him, "Are you interested in politics?" Dr. Zhong replied, "Doing my job well is politics." But what about participating in the Two Sessions?

Every year, Dr. Zhong enthusiastically regards the Two Sessions as a concrete manifestation of the Party's governance on behalf of the people. It was the mission that the Party entrusted to every representative and deputy to participate in and discuss government affairs. He cherished the opportunity to perform such duties, so he was fully committed.

It was only after he spoke many truths that he looked back and thought to himself, "Oh, I've hurt someone again." But he also thought, "Actually, I wasn't making it personal." To make it worse, the person he offended was often a friend of many years.

In the early morning of March 10, he suddenly started developed a high fever. "I have to go to the congress," he thought. He tried to get up, but couldn't even stand up.

The congress service staff knocked on the door and came in, saying nervously, "Oh, no! Dr. Zhong is sick!" He was immediately taken to the emergency room. He was given fluids and lay unconscious for a whole day. The next day, he had minor abrasions under his nose and above his lips from repeatedly wiping his nose due to a cold.

After the Two Sessions of 2014, the passionate media summed up Dr. Zhong's "classic quotes"

About H7N9:
1. 30% death rate of human H7N9 infection
2. H7N9 vaccine seeds are already available.
3. Concerned about promoting centralized slaughter rather than re-naming H7N9
4. Be alert to limited human-to-human transmission of H7N9 avian influenza

About haze:
1. Evidence of haze causing disease is clear
2. Haze is more frightening than SARS, and national action is required
3. With every 100 micrograms / cubic meter of haze increase, life expectancy is shortened by three years
4. Use air purifiers to against haze, as dust fall affects the respiratory system

About the doctor-patient relationship:
1. Medical reform fails to grasp the most central issue
2. 3/4 of the real income of doctors comes from patients
3. How to improve the doctor-patient relationships when a patient spends three hours in line for a three-minute consultation?
4. When will medical reform solve the problem of expensive medical care and difficult medical consultation?

About medical reform:
1. The medical reform has not been successful.
2. The medical reform has reached a critical stage, and the situation has not been accurately estimated
3. Medical insurance is getting better, but the actual progress of medical reform has not been significant.
4. Suggest using the medical insurance balance to improve the public welfare of hospitals

As a deputy of the Two Sessions in 2015, Dr. Zhong confidently promised journalists, "I have confidence in managing haze." He also said with certainty, "If the entire nation is determined to manage haze, we can see the effect in ten years." By the time of the Two Sessions in 2016, Dr. Zhong expressed his satisfaction directly with journalists, saying, "I will give last year's haze control work a score of 70." But such kind words still made the back of the relevant functionaries chill.

Hard-working and responsible, Zhong Nanshan was scary to some people because at any time he might take aim at wrong things. At the Two Sessions in 2015, Dr. Zhong fired hard at one thing.

On March 6, 2015, at the group discussion of the Guangdong delegation at the Two Sessions, one of the topics was scientific research papers. One delegate spoke with confidence and self-assurance, and the overall gist of his speech was that the number of published papers indicated the innovative achievements of a scientific research unit.

"Publishing a paper is not an innovation," Dr. Zhong said, firing directly at the matter itself, but he inadvertently embarrassed a speaker once again. The speaker looked at him with his mouth half open and thought to himself that Dr. Zhong was simply being difficult. Dr. Zhong continued to explain his point of view. "It is a misunderstanding of innovation for scientific research units to measure the goodness of technological innovation by publishing papers." To put it plainly, he meant that if the quantity of published papers alone was pursued, then practical technological innovation would definitely deviate. Back when he was president of the Chinese Medical Association, he had resolutely rectified this bad habit of academic "deviation" and corrected the academic atmosphere.

His words, whether eloquent or straightforward, were well-reasoned and based on facts. He noted, "China has 3.2 million R&D personnel in science and technology, the highest in the world. The number of scientific and technological papers is the second in the world, as well as the number of patent applications and authorizations. However, our scientific and technological innovation ability is only the 19th in the world, and the amount of scientific and technological research that has become reality, according to preliminary statistics, it only accounts for 10%." Statistics revealed that 90% of China's medicine were generic, and from 1949 to 2008, the profits obtained from the generic medicines in the previous fifty years were not as high as that of a new foreign medicine.

The most crucial thing for a science and technology powerhouse was to make concrete things real and seek truths from facts. Medical science and technology innovation was Dr. Zhong's long-cherished wish, and he would not stop because of hardships. He said that Premier Li Keqiang's work report had mentioned the issue of innovation-driven strategy several times. In terms of innovation-driven strategy, the country had taken a relatively positive step forward, but the pace was slow, especially in medical science and technology, and there were two major bottlenecks, one of which was the problem of cognition.

He said unflinchingly, "Some scientific research institutes, academies of science, and prestigious universities measure scientific and technological innovation by the number of published papers, thinking that publishing papers is innovation. This view is absolutely wrong." He believed that the publication of a high-level papers was at most a creative idea, and only after the idea was successfully implemented was it actually an innovation.

In his opinion, innovation should be a discovery or an invention that was finally transformed into a result through hard work. It also depended on whether the result produced economic or social benefits. Only after this process was completed could it be called an innovation.

"I don't know about other fields, but the majority of Nobel Prize winners in medicine were not high-level paper writers initially, but after more than a decade or even longer of practical practice, the ideas they proposed achieved economic or social benefits, and that's why they are the winner of the prize." He added, "Ranking by papers will only hinder innovation."

In addition, Dr. Zhong also pointed out on different occasions that the medicine review system was a major bottleneck for medical innovation. He hoped that the National Medical Products Administration would increase the number of reviewers and improve their treatment.

He said with great concern, "Even if the slogans are loud and the projects are many, failing to pass the review in time will stop innovation, and there will be no hope for innovation then."

He believed that the publication of papers was not the only criterion to measure the standard of doctors. If medical research only remained on papers and was not put into clinical trials, it was just empty talk. Therefore, only when the results of high-level papers were applied to clinical diagnosis, truly solving intractable diseases and being turned into concrete productivity, could they be considered innovations and represent the highest level of the medical profession.

The other bottleneck that affected innovation was the review mechanism for science and technology innovation. Dr. Zhong had a complicated feeling about it, because this mechanism constrained innovation. Taking stem cell transplantation as an example, China started very early, but it got stuck when it came to clinical use due to the lack of review criteria, and even now, the clinical review criteria were not available.

Dr. Zhong understood the central government's advocacy of requiring scientific research results to come out of the laboratory and be transformed into productivity to serve society. This was a policy that aimed to make a country strong.

As a doctor, Dr. Zhong had dealt with patients all his life. He noted that the success of medical reform lay in allowing people to benefit from it. He knew the needs of patients, hospitals' ways of doing things, and the stories behind doctors. He expressed that mainstream medical care needed to be for the public's benefit. But at the time, 80% of the income of medical workers depended on themselves. This approach made him unable to see the public benefit that public hospitals should reflect.

Who paid for doctors' salaries? In the current system, it was the hospitals, which caused many issues that the public thought inappropriate. He said, "One of my students came to see me and told me that he received 70 outpatient visits in one morning, and he was so exhausted that his mind was unclear."

He went on, "We can do the math. Doctors go to work at 8:00 am and leave at 11:30 am. Within that three and a half hours, they do not go to the restroom, or answer phone calls, and their full attention is on seeing patients at a rate of one every three minutes, which is yet to include the time it takes the patients to go in and out, filling in case reports, and prescribing medicines. There is very little time to truly interact with patients with adequate inquiries."

The Two Sessions in 2016 was one of the last two years for Dr. Zhong to perform his duty as an NPC deputy. He treasured the opportunity, and he decided to make good use of the last two years to speak the truth.

He decided to throw a heavy punch to medical reform, an old, stubborn problem, and highlight the core of the issue. He decided to point out that the seemingly promising network medical care, in fact, was unable to replace traditional medical care. He decided to continue to appeal for the low treatment of medical workers and to underline the danger of linking medical workers' salaries to income generation. He also decided to continue to promote haze control, and to call attention to the massive loss of pediatricians.

On the evening of March 12, he finally managed to squeeze in a little time to be interviewed by the journalist he knew best. He hoped that the issue of true public ownership of public hospitals could be brought to light through the media as he intended. When the journalist entered the door, she saw the admired Dr. Zhong holding a few sheets of A4 paper covered in neat handwriting. She thought to herself, "He has never been interviewed like this before because he always speaks eloquently without a script." Dr. Zhong asked the journalist to take a seat, and he sat next to her, reading out his script word for word for the journalist, pointing to each word. The script was his speech of the Two Sessions. He was afraid that the journalist could not fully understand the original meaning of his text, so he said, "The departure of public hospitals from the market-oriented guidance and market-oriented mechanism is the key to solving all the problems, but so far it has still not been solved."

Around 2017, first-time visitors to Guangzhou were no longer attacked by mosquitoes, because the authorities had strengthened mosquito control work to preempt a Zika outbreak. Dr. Zhong expressed that in the face of the epidemic, the whole country had done a good job of blocking the external import and preventing the internal spread. Now there were about eight suspected cases in the country, and all the patients were discovered early and had been properly quarantined. The mosquito control work had been strengthened, so a large-scale outbreak like was seen in Brazil was unlikely to happen in China. He told journalists this reassuring information at the Two Sessions.

In March 2017, at the Two Sessions, the Fifth Session of the 12th National People's Congress of the People's Republic of China marked Dr. Zhong's tenth year as an NPC deputy, and also his last year to perform this sacred duty at the Two Sessions. Worrying about the country and the people, he had many words on his mind.

A journalist sat on the floor in front of Dr. Zhong's room from morning until afternoon. When the busy doctor saw the journalist, he bent down and took the young man's arm to pull him up. "Oh! Academician Zhong, you are so strong!" The journalist was surprised.

That year, Dr. Zhong had called for "public hospitals to serve the public benefit." He said in the group discussion that the problem of the market-oriented operation of public hospitals was still not solved, and medical reform was still facing many problems. To ease the doctor-patient relationship and fully implement the medical reform, first of all, the treatment of medical workers needed to be improved so that the public benefit of public hospitals could be realized. It was important to truly implement the public benefit of public hospitals instead of the current state, which was neither public nor private.

He clearly stated that increasing the public benefit and equity of public hospitals would allow the people to receive cheap, safe, effective treatment, so that medical workers could get social respect and reasonable treatment. "This is medical reform, where both medical workers and patients benefit together. But now, public hospitals' market-orientated operation is still spreading." Dr. Zhong said.

There was also supply and demand in the medical field. On the demand side, in 2017, Premier Li Keqiang pointed out in the report that the funding for basic medical care should be increased and the subsidy for serious diseases should be increased, and it was hoped that more than 70% of regions would achieve graded medical care. On the supply side, the report proposed to motivate medical workers by increasing their salaries based on the nature of their work.

What Dr. Zhong pointed to was actually an obvious and unpleasant phenomenon, but no one was willing to talk about it. The problem was not a simple topic that could be discussed carelessly. Much investigation and research needed to be done in advance. Otherwise, people would think it was just nonsense.

Dr. Zhong hit the bullseye. The main contradiction of medical reform was a supply problem. A reasonable increase in medical workers' salaries had great significance in mobilizing them. But where would the pay come from? In fact, there was still no certainty whether public hospitals should take the road of public benefit or continue to take the market-oriented road.

"Eight years ago, it was said that medical reform had entered a critical stage, but in my opinion, it has entered a dangerous stage. In my 56 years of medical practice, I have rarely seen medical workers in such a state," Dr. Zhong observed. His tone was mild, but his words had completely entered the "cannon" state. "Medical workers should have been the main force of medical reform, but now they are forced to become the resistance army," he concluded.

He sincerely made suggestions, and he believed that the root cause of the problem, as well as the difficulty and the high cost of seeing a doctor, was the unsolved positioning of public hospitals. Graded medical care, reform of medicine prices, and other issues were the downstream problems of medical reform, while the positioning of public hospitals for the public benefit was the upstream problem. "Only when the upstream problem is solved can the downstream problems be solved," he noted.

If the public benefit of public hospitals was not addressed, it would not be surprising if more excellent doctors left and organized their own medical groups. The treatment of doctors was so low that the current drain of pediatricians in China was likely to have a domino effect, with the loss of doctors of obstetrics departments, emergency departments, and other departments. "In addition to low social status and lack of respect from society, another very important reason is that doctors' work is highly risky and but low paid," Dr. Zhong added.

How much increase would be needed to constitute a reasonable salary? At that time, the average annual income of medical workers in public hospitals in urban areas nationwide was about 63,000 yuan, roughly equivalent to 1.12 times the average social wage. He said, "Along with colleagues from several research institutes, we did an in-depth survey in which it was found that the income of medical workers in UK was three to five times the local average social wage, five to eight times for Hong Kong medical workers, and for doctors, more than nine times."

Not only was there a tremendous loss of doctors, but the number of students willing to study medicine was falling too. He cited an individual survey which found that medical specialty scores at institutes such as Fudan were dropping, and most notably, Hebei's college entrance examination medical major had the lowest enrollment score, which was 125 points less than veterinary major.

15

GLOBAL PREVENTION

"Internationally, research on the prevention of hypertension and diabetes took twenty years, while our research on Chronic Obstructive Pulmonary Disease (COPD) prevention was less than a decade." On September 27, 2017, Dr. Zhong hit a landmark success as a personal achievement over SARS when his scientific research paper on Chronic Obstructive Pulmonary Disease (COPD) entitled "Tiotropium Bromide in the Treatment of Early-stage COPD" was published in *The New England Journal of Medicine*. The paper represented a proud, solid scientific result, and it provided a strategic direction for early prevention and treatment of COPD.

What was the significance of this feat? In part, it meant that from that day on, Western medicine around the world would finally recognize that COPD could be prevented. Finally, there was evidence that the incidence of the disease could be reduced through prevention, and there was a specific implementation method for preventing and intervening in the early stage of the disease. Once the method was applied worldwide, the number of COPD deaths will be greatly reduced every year. "More than 70% of people with COPD in China have no symptoms or only mild symptoms, and most of them have not been examined or seen by a doctor," Dr. Zhong announced on September 15, 2017, at the First Annual Review of Progress in COPD.

In China, 100 million people suffered from COPD. The disease had become the third-largest killer nationwide, and globally, it was a disease with a high death rate. The prevalence of the disease among people over 40 years old in China had reached

13.7%, which was second only to stroke, and followed by ischemic heart disease, with lung cancer being the fourth deadliest.

Dr. Zhong called for a reshaping of the concept of diagnosis and treatment of COPD, which sought to reduce the incidence rate through early diagnosis and early treatment. "With unremitting effort, we have finally obtained the valuable first-hand information, and it has been confirmed for the first time in the international arena that early diagnosis and early treatment are very effective for COPD and may lead to the reversal of the disease," he stated. When COPD developed to the middle and late stages, on top of the issue of patients' sickness and ineffective treatment, each hospitalization cost about 20,000 to 30,000 yuan in medical expenses. If the disease could be treated early like hypertension, diabetes, and other similar ailments, the cost could be greatly reduced, while the treatment effect could be twice as effective with half the effort.

As early as 2009, Dr. Zhong was so determined to publish worldwide the fact that COPD could be prevented and cured. At the International Conference on COPD held in Rome, Dr. Zhong put forward his view that diagnosing and treating COPD early like hypertension and diabetes was the correct approach. The president of the conference supported this idea, but when the president asked if anyone was prepared to do so, no one raised their hand.

"That scene pushed me." Dr. Zhong would never forget it. These international experts all thought that it was an unworkable project, but Dr. Zhong, then 73 years old, raised his hand as a pledge.

He was always up for a challenge and was not afraid of any difficulty. He has always been glad that back then, he approached the German pharmaceutical giant Boehringer Ingelheim and requested that they produced the medicine for the treatment of COPD. He managed to reassure and convince the company to provide medication and financial support for the exploration of early intervention into COPD.

Boehringer Ingelheim eventually provided Dr. Zhong's team with the medication and $4 million for the research. From then on, Dr. Zhong, his partner Professor Ran Pixin, and their team went to the grassroots and started a huge project, spending several years searching for potential COPD patients. He squeezed out the time and fully devoted himself to this project.

The patients had no symptoms or very few symptoms. How could they be convinced to accept that they had the symptoms of the disease, or that the disease had already started, and they needed medical attention or early prevention? After completing a dual-blind controlled trial on 841 patients, the result was produced:

lung function of the patients in the medication group (oral tiotropium bromide) had significantly improved. The result of the medication use demonstrated for the first time that early medication could alter the natural course of annual lung function decline in COPD patients. Dr. Zhong noted, "My team and I have been working for almost a decade to discover for the first time that if intervention is involved in COPD's early stage, where there are no symptoms or very few symptoms, lung function can be significantly improved, and the quality of life is then enhanced. It is also proven for the first time that anticholinergic medicine can reduce the annual rate of lung function decay to slow down the deterioration of the disease."

Dr. Zhong spoke in a calm tone as he poured out the many emotions in his heart. Once again, his words appeared in the *People's Daily*.

The research result embodied in the paper was a relief to scientists like Dr. Zhong who had been diligently pursuing scientific research in their field. For ten years, he and his team were immersed in the front line of investigation, and the number of people tested rose from dozens to thousands, and then from thousands to tens of thousands.

He presented PowerPoint slides, conducted free medical consultation for the public, and went to urban and rural areas across the country to give lectures, using metaphors and humorous language that the public could understand, so that the public would enjoy the message and be willing to accept his theory of COPD prevention. His hard work and dedication were not in vain, and the public accepted his preventive measures.

It was not easy to be diligent, putting great efforts into his career to reap its fruits. Dr. Zhong had gone through untold hardships, but he was content. He said, "Compared to Europe and the US, China has the advantage of a united people. As long as a government sector comes forward, the neighborhood committees and village officials will gather the masses together." He said that this was not doable in foreign countries, because the governments did not have the same authoritarian relationship with their people. He said, "If they want to achieve the same goal, their battle line is bound to be a long one, because this is not an easy job for them."

He also thanked the government, saying, "Under the strong leadership of our government and health authorities, we have actively intervened in the causes of COPD by reducing air pollution, promoting the use of non-polluting natural gas for cooking instead of indoor biofuels such as firewood, and increasing education on the dangers of smoking tobacco, along with other similar initiatives. These are the primary means of preventing COPD, and early detection, early diagnosis, and early treatment are the secondary means."

He said, "This secondary prevention has not been practiced internationally before, but I believe that through our in-depth research, we will be able to advance the strategy of prevention and treatment of COPD. I'm confident that with a few more years of hard work, we will lead the world in the early diagnosis and early treatment of COPD."

Dr. Zhong remembered that when he was in his third year of college, his teacher taught him that the symptoms of diabetes were "three more and one less," which referred to eating more, drinking more, urinating more, and weighing less, accompanied by diabetic foot, glaucoma, and kidney disease. In fact, these were the advanced complications of diabetes, which were more difficult to be treated and the effect was very poor. After twenty years of practice, people realized that when blood glucose was repeatedly elevated and glucose tolerance was reduced, even without other symptoms, diabetes could be diagnosed, and if intervention and early treatment were carried out at this stage, the more severe complications could be completely avoided. Why couldn't COPD be addressed in the same way?

"Faced with this reality, we did not retreat, but relied on the local governments and the general masses. First, we screened outpatients with lung function meters, and then educated them and convinced them to accept medication," Dr. Zhong reported.

The team delved into two aspects. The first was to prove that early treatment could lead to greater reversibility of the disease by studying the possibility of medication intervention reversing small airway abnormalities in patients with early-stage COPD. The other was to further demonstrate that interventions for early-stage COPD could effectively stop the progression of the disease to its moderate and severe stages by conducting a real-world study of a large community-based sample of people with early-stage COPD. Patients' suffering and healthcare cost would thus be greatly reduced.

The medical cost of treating COPD with inhalation therapy recommended abroad was quite high. Simple, inexpensive, safe, and effective medicines and devices that are suitable for China's national conditions were needed instead. After years of research and practice, it was found that regular administration of oral medications containing sulfhydryl could reduce the acute onset rate of moderate to severe COPD by 24 to 29%, and its medical cost was only about a fifth to a sixth of the cost of the internationally recommended therapy.

They also observed the effect of the prescription of the Chinese patent medicine, *yupingfengsan,* on the acute onset of COPD and found that the medicine could reduce the acute onset rate by 28%, and the medical cost would be greatly reduced. It was also observed that Tai Chi, a unique physical exercise and rehabilitation tool that had been used in China for thousands of years, had some benefits in the treatment of COPD. The team's study of diaphragmatic electromyogram and respiratory central excitability found that Tai Chi had greater advantages than the international practice of walking in that it could regulate breathing and increase respiratory muscle strength. This suggested that Tai Chi could be an important tool in the rehabilitation of COPD.

Before, intervention had not been carried out until symptoms became apparent, but with their study, Dr. Zhong and his team finally rewrote this history.

16

A PIONEER OF REFORM

The 40th anniversary of China's Reform and Opening Up and the 70th anniversary of the founding of the People's Republic of China both fell in 2019. Taking this opportunity, many journalists requested an appointment with Dr. Zhong. He couldn't help but look back on his past as the questions kept coming in. In early 2003, when SARS broke out, and the situation was at its worst, he led a team to work on the epidemic with the unknown cause, adhering to the truth, respecting the facts, and carefully developing treatment plans that saved the lives of many patients throughout his work and leading Guangdong to become one of the regions with the highest recovery rate and lowest mortality rate in the world. The things that happened during the raging epidemic seemed like they had occurred just yesterday.

Dr. Zhong had advised and promoted the construction of the public health emergency response system and advocated cooperation with international health organizations. He led the development of guidelines for diagnosing and treating acute infectious diseases such as SARS in China, and he was the first to formulate the Clinical Diagnostic Criteria for Atypical Pneumonia, explore the "three early and three reasonable" treatment protocols, (i.e., early diagnosis, early quarantine, early treatment), and promote "reasonable use of corticosteroids, reasonable use of ventilators, and reasonable treatment of complications." He was the first in the world to develop a set of prevention and treatment protocols with significant efficacy, and the WHO believed that the protocols were instructive in the fight against atypical pneumonia worldwide. He felt gratified that, as a medical worker, he and his team had made their due contribution to the motherland.

Looking back to 1971, the country called on the national medical system to research the prevention and treatment of respiratory diseases such as chronic bronchitis. That year, at the age of 35, Dr. Zhong returned to Guangzhou from Beijing and chose the Guangzhou Fourth People's Hospital (now known as the IRH of The First Affiliated Hospital of Guangzhou Medical University), which was nearest to his home. At that time, he and his team were just a chronic bronchitis group, the prototype of the IRH. Apart from doing his job well, in order to quickly grow into a skilled clinician, he spent most of his rest time in places such as X-ray room, cardiac EKG room, and library.

He always recalled how he used to ride his bicycle to inspect one hospital after another, even squatting on the ground to analyze a disease from the sputum spit out by respiratory patients.

The group eventually stood out for their diligence. They were the first in Guangzhou to use the broncho fiberscope for the treatment of respiratory diseases. They established several laboratories and conducted animal experiments to provide supplements and controls for clinical research. At the same time, they wrote a number of high quality papers, which were first published in the *Chinese Medical Journal* and *Chinese Journal of Internal Medicine*, and then in authoritative journals at the forefront of international medicine. They put in great amounts of hard work, but none of them cared about personal gain.

In 1978, China ushered in the spring of science. The National Science Conference was held in Beijing. Dr. Zhong participated in this historical event as a representative of Guangdong, and he was awarded the first prize of the National Science Conference Achievement for the research results of his collaboration with Hou Shu, entitled, "Integration of Traditional Chinese Medicine and Western Medicine in Categorized Diagnosis and Treatment of Chronic Bronchitis." The conference brought together almost all of China's living scientific and technical workers of that time. It was a thrilling scene for all of them.

The past was not far away, but the years had gone by. Dr. Zhong recalled, "After decades of medical practice, my greatest happiness is always being on the front line of treating and saving patients, and my greatest comfort is being able to fully devote myself to patients as a doctor. My greatest wish is to make more contributions to my motherland so that more scientific research results can come out of our laboratories and become productivity for the benefit of the people. This is my repayment to the country and the people, and my primary intention as a medical worker."

He went on, "I expect that I can do more work in multiple areas. The first is to make early diagnosis and treatment of COPD a national treatment strategy, the second is to have success in developing new anti-cancer medicine after more than twenty years of effort, and the third is to have a new understanding and new treatment plans for chronic airway diseases such as asthma and COPD."

In 2016, Dr. Zhong was honored with the 11th Guanghua Engineering Science and Technology Award, the highest award in China's engineering industry, and in November 2018, he was selected as one of the 100 outstanding contributors to Reform and Opening Up. On December 18, 2018, he was awarded the title of Reform Pioneer, an honorary title awarded by the People's Republic of China at the conference celebrating the 40th anniversary of Reform and Opening Up. The CPC Central Committee and the State Council decided to award the title to 100 individuals who had made outstanding contributions to Reform and Opening Up and present them with medals. Dr. Zhong was awarded this honor and was honored as "the key promoter of the construction of the public health emergency response system." The theme of the award was, *a nation with hope cannot be without heroes, and a country with a future cannot be without pioneers*

Dr. Zhong said, "Science can only be sought through facts, not avoiding issues of principle to protect oneself." On February 13, 2019, Bai Jianfeng, a journalist from the *People's Daily*, wrote an article, praising the style of this Reform Pioneer. The article was entitled "The Word Stop is Not in Zhong Nanshan's Dictionary."

Among his academic works, he led the formulation of guidelines for the treatment of various diseases, such as influenza A, chronic cough, and COPD. He described himself as a "post-80s" academician, and he was leading a team to develop an anti-cancer medicine, research he had been conducting for 26 years.

As he engaged in scientific research, education, weekly consultation, and remote grand rounds, he noted, "Patients' trust is my greatest motivation, and patients' recovery is my greatest encouragement." After years of medical practice, Dr. Zhong was still energetic, and he stayed on the clinical front line.

Dr. Zhong was truly deserving of the award. His name was closely associated with China's public health. After the SARS crisis, he took the initiative to be the spokesperson for public health emergencies, daring to speak out, deliver the truth, and stabilize people through public scares such as haze and influenza A. In particular, in less than ten years, he had changed the global modern medical community's belief that COPD could not be prevented. From then on, the world had a reference standard for "early intervention in COPD, similar to that of hypertension and diabetes." Through further follow-up and intervention studies, he hoped to change the WHO's guidelines for the diagnosis and treatment of COPD.

He clarified his attitude, saying, "Research should be both advanced and pragmatic. Advanced means seizing the international frontier and urgent national projects, and pragmatic means solving people's practical problems and developing safe, effective, inexpensive, and convenient medicines and devices. If the advanced research cannot be pragmatic and cannot relieve patients' pain, its significance will be discounted."

In May 2018, Dr. Zhong made another amazing move that surprised everyone. He made an appearance as the chairman of GIR (Guangzhou Institute of Respiratory) Medicine Company Limited, carrying the banner of industry-academia-research transformation. His goal was to strengthen medicine through science and technology for the benefit of the nation. Since 2009, Dr. Zhong's team had successfully built the industry-academia-research system of the State Key Laboratory of Respiratory Diseases and set up a number of associated project companies, covering medical innovation diagnosis centers, medicine innovation research centers and others. Everything was coming together at the right time.

He enjoined young students, "The striving spirit should be maintained. Striving does not mean to create an atmosphere, but instead requires perseverance and real effort." He hoped to strive for another twenty years to build up the largest heart-lung respiratory research center in Asia, an industry-academia-research center that would include scientific research, training, and treatment of intractable diseases.

On the morning of March 9, 2020, in Guangzhou, Foshan City's Nanhai District and the Guangzhou IRH signed a cooperation agreement to jointly promote the transformation of health science and technology achievement projects, which aimed to focus on five aspects of cooperation: big health industry venture capital funds, big health innovation project-special funds, pharmaceutical technology transformation service centers, big health industrial parks, and international medical complexes. It strove to create a benchmark for the development of big health industry in Guangdong-Hong Kong-Macao Greater Bay Area.

Dr. Zhong noted, "We previously focused more on scientific research and technology development, and we have not done enough in the transformation of scientific results." He said that products including prevention and control devices for infectious diseases had been deployed almost immediately after the SARS crisis, and much basic research was done, but how to transform these research results into products that everyone could use was still being explored. "How to organically connect scientific research and economic construction is indeed a key problem," he said. He went on to note that China had two scientific research directions for respiratory diseases, the international frontier and national urgent needs. Alongside being innovative and leading in the world, developing simple, inexpensive, safe and effective medicines and devices in the future was also desired, so that the general public could afford to buy and use them.

The weather in Guangzhou in December 2018 was refreshingly cool and slightly chilly, making the northerners who arrived there feel very comfortable. As the 70th anniversary of the founding of the People's Republic of China approached, I was asked by the *People's Daily · Overseas Edition* to interview Zhong Nanshan for an article about one of the most unforgettable events in his memory, sharing the same fate with the nation. At 5:00 pm, the office was still busy, as it always was. Dr. Zhong looked up a few times and glanced at me as I sat, waiting. Each time, he apologized and said, "Please give me a while."

Having known him for more than a decade, I knew the fine-print plaid shirt was his regular attire, with only slight variation in color. The dark blue shirt best complemented his earnest, clear, quiet temperament, just as it revealed the strength he maintained from his constant strength training exercise.

Although it was just after his 82nd birthday, did not consider himself an old man when it came to his work. In fact, even if a person was young and strong, their intensity of work could not have matched his. No one who had come into contact with him could doubt this. The agility of his thinking alone was not lagging behind young people, so no one took him as an old man.

He listened quietly to my interview questions, then carefully decided on a story from fifteen years earlier that seemed like it had happened just yesterday. It was an incident he told me about ten years before, which had taken place in the same season. He had spoken out for his country then, telling the world that China had made enormous contributions in the fight against SARS.

The whole process of that incident was engraved in his heart. He retold the story earnestly. After a busy day, he was not tired at all, and his account was almost an electronic manuscript without revision. How many people could do that? He said.

On May 18, 2003, I attended the annual International Conference of the American Thoracic Society (ATS) in Seattle, USA. The *US News & World Report* on the first-floor news reading board had a big headline which read, "SARS is China's Weapon to Destroy the World." It shocked me. Moreover, next to it was a copy of *Time* magazine, which bore a bright red Chinese flag on the cover, and the background of the flag was a human lung. The article was so full of distortions that reading it was unbearable.

I knew that from March to April 2003, some Western media, including *The Washington Post, The New York Times,* CNN, and BBC Radio, had published many distorted reports and made false accusations about SARS in China.

What I saw was truly appalling! I couldn't imagine that some press in the US and the rest of the West would vilify China and incite global anti-Chinese sentiment for the sake of political propaganda.

From the time I was invited to the conference, it had been twenty days in total. I was already worn out from my busy work schedule and the long flight. However, my determination to refute these rumors with facts filled me with courage and confidence.

There were experts in thoracic medicine from various countries and regions all over the world at the conference. The topic of my speech was SARS in China. Originally, I planned to introduce the real situation in China's fight against SARS to the world. After seeing such propaganda, I could not contain my indignation, and I decided that I had to clarify with truth to win the world's respect and understanding for China.

The order and content of the speeches for the entire conference had been arranged by the conference organizer a year earlier. In order to insert my speech, which was of worldwide interest, they set aside time at noon, and I was given a large conference room to deliver my speech.

Soon after my speech started, the room was filled up. The aisles were full of people, and the area outside the room was crowded with people too. The staff had to pull a line for live TV from the fourth floor where the conference room was located to the second floor, so that more people could watch my speech.

My speech received high praise from many international experts, including those in the US. An official from the US Center for Disease Control and

Prevention then invited me to hold a press conference on SARS. At the press conference, American journalists raised questions, and I answered with easy, humorous expressions, which brought me closer to the journalists. They began to look at me and our country with a sense of affection.

Subsequently, I was interviewed by media agencies, such as Deutsche Presse-Agentur and Associated Press, and the interviews were published.

More than eighty Chinese students came from different states of the US to attend the conference. They didn't leave after the conference, but stayed with me until late. They were very proud that China had made a great contribution to the prevention and control of SARS, winning the recognition and respect of the world. Our motherland was truly amazing.

I was strongly aware that explaining the real SARS situation to one more country or region would correct more bad influence and win more honor for our country, so I went to more than dozen countries, including Australia, Denmark, the US, Japan, Singapore, Malaysia, the Netherlands, Switzerland, and Sweden, as well as Hong Kong and Macau in China, to do my best to explain to the world the truth and the contribution made by China's fight against SARS.

Now in my 80s, I have experienced numerous ups and downs with our country. I always love these song lyrics because they speak to my heart:

"China catches my heart, no one can pull us apart"

PART 3

AN EXTRAORDINARY LIFE

1

HIS PARENTS: GREAT DOCTORS WITH A CONSCIENCE

An old gentleman drew his head near the desk, almost pressing his entire face to the table due to severely reduced eyesight caused by cataracts. He had to cover one of his eyes while writing, because he also suffered from diplopia. Eventually, he managed to finish a monograph on medical science, totaling over 400 thousand Chinese characters. This was a typical profile of someone cultivated in a family of doctors.

The old man was Dr. Zhong Shifan, a famous pediatrician in China. He and his wife, Dr. Liao Yueqin, were both from Xiamen, and they were both medical experts who had studied in the US. Dr. Liao was one of the co-founders of Huanan Cancer Center (now Sun Yat-sen University Cancer Center). Dr. Zhong Shifan and Dr. Liao Yueqin were Dr. Zhong Nanshan's parents.

Zhong Shifan was a man of few words, while Liao Yueqin was always seen with a gentle smile. Dr. Zhong Shifan rarely said much about his childhood to his son. Zhong Shifan was born in Xiamen in 1901, and he was raised by his uncle. When speaking about it later, Dr. Zhong Nanshan only vaguely remembered that his father was an orphan. After his parents passed away, Zhong Shifan had followed his uncle's path and received his education in Xiamen at a very young age. Graduating from secondary school with flying colors, he was admitted to the Peking Union Medical College. In 1924, the Peking Union Medical College only admitted forty new students. It was very hard to get in.

In 1932, Zhong Shifan graduated from the Peking Union Medical College, acquiring his MD from the University of Cincinnati in the US. When he returned to Guangzhou in 1946, Dr. Zhong Shifan worked as the Director and Head of the Pediatrics Department of the Central Hospital of Guangzhou, as well as a Professor of Pediatrics at the Medical School of Lingnan University. In 1949, he was hired by the WHO as a medical expert. In 1953, after the disciplinary adjustment of tertiary institutions in China, Dr. Zhong Shifan became the Professor and Dean of Pediatrics at the Sun Yat-sen University Zhongshan School of Medicine. He was a committee member of the Chinese Pediatric Society of the Chinese Medical Association, editor of the *Chinese Journal of Pediatrics,* and director of the Pediatric Society of the Guangdong Medical Association. At the same time, he was also a member of the Chinese People's Political Consultative Conference of Guangdong Province.

Despite the fact that his father had long been gone, when Dr. Zhong Nanshan talked about the elder Dr. Zhong, his tone was always respectful, loving, and obedient, as if his father were still alive. He took great pride in his father, a respect he held not merely due to his father's prestige and fame, but more because of his tireless pursuit of truth and high moral standards as a doctor.

From 1924 to 1932, Dr. Zhong Shifan studied in the Peking Union Medical College, which applied an "elimination" mechanism. Among the forty students in the class, only eight managed to graduate. Dr. Zhong Shifan was among these excellent students. He was a typical elite, born in the ivory tower. Both the prestigious dermatologist Dr. Hu Chuankui and the famous biochemist Dr. Liu Shihao were also among the eight graduates. Dr. Zhong Shifan was a pillar of pediatrics in China, with impeccable scholarship and medical ethics. Outstanding individuals that were discovered and cultivated during that period of time always possessed a certain quality of precision, rigidity and truthfulness. Dr. Zhong's father's speech and actions were always motivated by the truth, and this made a deep impact on Zhong Nanshan.

Dr. Zhong Shifan once worked at the Nanjing Central Hospital (now Nanjing General Hospital of the People's Liberation Army), a hospital directly under the Nanjing National Government of the Republic of China. He joined the Nationalist Party alongside his peers. In 1937, when the Japanese army occupied Nanjing, the Zhong family followed the hospital's retreat to Guizhou, where Dr. Zhong Shifan worked at the Guiyang Central Hospital. Nine years later, the family again relocated to Guangzhou with the hospital. He was later hired by Lingnan University as a professor of medical science.

In October 1949, two choices presented themselves to Dr. Zhong's family: departing to Taiwan or remaining in Mainland China. Dr. Zhong Shifan was a patriot, an honest doctor with a great conscience. Despising the corruption of the KMT, he decided to stay.

October 14, 1949, Guangzhou was on the verge of liberation. The roar of guns could be clearly heard within the city. Wang Zuxiang, the Director of the Department of Health, Ministry of the Interior of the Nationalist Government, anxiously paid Dr. Zhong Shifan frequent visits, attempting to mobilize him to bring the hospital's property worth USD$130,000 to Taiwan.

Dr. Zhong Shifan said firmly, "A true Chinese will stay here, not leave."

In fact, Dr. Zhong Shifan knew little about the Chinese Communist Party at the time, but he was determined not to go to Taiwan. He could have easily started a career in the US after he graduated from the university, but he did not want to leave his homeland. After the liberation of Guangzhou, he handed the $130,000 worth of property left by the Guangzhou Central Hospital to PLA's temporary Military Control Committee.

What challenges might a man face when holding fast to his conscience and sticking to his principle? The Zhong family encountered various obstacles, but Dr. Zhong Shifan never regretted his choice to stay in his homeland, and the patriotic flame within him never died. His spirit was a great inspiration to his successors. Zhong Nanshan not only learned his father's medical skills, but was also deeply imbibed in his perseverance.

Dr. Zhong Shifan spent his whole life unraveling mysteries. When virology began to develop in the 1940s, Dr. Zhong Shifan was in the US for his advanced studies in the discipline. He discovered that a bacteria's ability to preserve the virus's viability developed when the bacteria was actively reproducing. This discovery was taken seriously by A. B. Sabin, a virologist at the University of Cincinnati who believed that it was worth reporting. H. A. Howe, a virologist at Johns Hopkins University, also believed that this discovery was a great contribution to the field. At the same time, Dr. Zhong Shifan also discovered that fetal rats were an ideal growth medium for viruses.

In the 1950s, Dr. Zhong Shifan founded the Virology Laboratory of the Pediatrics Department of Zhongshan School of Medicine, Sun Yat-sen University, for the purpose of conducting studies on viruses and educating graduate students. This was one of the first clinical virology laboratories not only in Guangdong Province, but in all of China. The day before he passed away, Dr. Zhong Shifan was still teaching his son, the young Dr. Zhong Nanshan, to cut the liquid growth medium of virus using an electromagnetic field, so as to alter the virus. By doing so, he hoped to find a way to eliminate the virus. He was fully aware of his serious health condition while doing so. However, he remained calm in the face of death. He calmly instructed the young Dr. Zhong Nanshan, "Go source for an electromagnet and prepare for the next step of our experiment."

Oh his deathbed, he specifically reminded Dr. Zhong Nanshan not to organize a memorial service, so as not to waste other people's time. "Whenever I stood in front of him, I felt a sense of a reverence, as if my soul had reached a sublime state," commented Dr. Zhong Nanshan about his father many years later.

When Zhong Nanshan began to follow in his father's footsteps, working tirelessly in his medical career, he suddenly understood his father. What his father was seeking was beyond material gain, which prompted him use his personal funds to perform experiments at home.

Dr. Zhong Nanshan remembered vividly that when he was young, his father frequently left the house to treat patients that were not admitted into his hospital, rain or shine. Those who asked for his treatments came from every walk of life, and Dr. Zhong Shifan treated all of them equally.

Sometimes during his quiet reading time after dinner, people would hurry to the Zhongs' doorstep to ask for a doctor. There was once a patient from the School Guard whose children were all financially challenged and could not pay for a doctor. Dr. Zhong Shifan gladly went over to their place and treated the sick child.

Sometimes Dr. Zhong Shifan was reading or doing some urgent experiments when people knocked on his door. He would frown a little bit, like all humans do, but he would also treat the patients thoroughly. More importantly, most of Dr. Zhong's patients were completely cured. He received much praises and gratitude for his work.

During the Cultural Revolution, Dr. Zhong Shifan could not escape a dark fate. He was forced to attend criticism and struggle sessions, and worse, being a master pediatrician, he lost his job as a doctor and was appointed to wash the milk bottles in the hospital's pediatrics department. Being unable to treat patients or conduct research did not bother Dr. Zhong Shifan, but his wife Liao Yueqin's unjust death dealt a very heavy blow to him, making him almost lose hope in life.

Dr. Zhong Shifan constantly reminded his son that, regardless of the situation, one should always express his own ideas honestly and clearly. When Dr. Zhong Shifan marked his graduate students' essays and notes, he would cross the student's work if he found the quality dissatisfactory. As a student himself, the young Dr. Zhong Nanshan wondered whether this would hurt the students' feelings. Dr. Zhong Shifan said, "It is so bad that a strong impression has to be made."

Dr. Zhong Shifan always expressed his ideas frankly. The most important education Dr. Zhong Nanshan received from him was the value of integrity. "Speak only what your heart believes."

Dr. Zhong Shifan started writing *Erke Jibing Jianbie Zhenduan* (Diagnosing Pediatric Diseases) in 1975, when he was 74 years old. He took three years, finishing it in 1978. In Dr. Zhong Nanshan's mind, his father was determined to achieve his own goals, which prompted him to push for the development of medical science and preserve as much knowledge as he could, regardless of his situation. Only in that way could he believe that his life was not wasted.

Sometimes Zhong Nanshan would try to persuade his father, "Your eyes and your health are not in good shape. Let's not do more work now."

Dr. Zhong Shifan always replied, "What would you like me to do? Sit around and wait to die?"

Dr. Zhong Shifan never thought of earning remuneration with his writing. He only wanted to write something that would help medical workers. With this motivation in mind, he overcame many difficulties.

Few had the habit of visiting libraries in the old times, but this old man visited the library everyday early in the morning. Tears swelled in Dr. Zhong Nanshan's eyes when he recounted the scene. Dr. Wen in the Pediatrics Department of Zhongshan School of Medicine was so deeply touched by Dr. Zhong Shifan's deeds that he offered to help him transcribe the manuscript. As a result, Dr. Zhong Shifan's masterpiece *Erke Jibing Jianbie Zhenduan* was published on time.

His pediatrics monograph of 400 thousand words took three years of tireless writing, and the final remuneration was 3,000 yuan. He gave 1,500 yuan to Dr. Wen as a token of appreciation, and 1,000 to those who had helped him find reference materials, leaving only 500 for himself. He spent his 500 yuan on copies of his own book, *Erke Jibing Jianbie Zhenduan*, and distributed them to others. In the end, he did not leave any money for himself. During that time, it was no more than any true scholar would do. *Erke Jibing Jianbie Zhenduan* was sold out upon publication, and it was reprinted multiple times. The total circulation was some hundred thousand copies.

Dr. Zhong Shifan nurtured countless students who went on to work in different parts of China and throughout the world. He had a graduate student named Shen Jieping. Shen was very fond of his professor. Even when he was over 80 years old, every year during the Qingming Festival when Chinese families worship their deceased relatives, he went to the Dr. and Mrs. Zhong's tomb with the Zhong family.

Dr. Zhong Nanshan's mother, Liao Yueqin, was born in 1911. She was from the same hometown as Zhong Shifan, Xiamen. She was the daughter of a business man and lived with her family on Gulangyu Island. The Liao family was so prestigious that everyone on Gulangyu knew their name.

Liao Yueqin's great grandfather, Liao Zongwen, started the family business from scratch. He had four children, Liao Qingxia, Liao Yuefa, Liao Tianci, and Liao Tianfu. His second child, Liao Yuefa, was Liao Cuifeng's father, and later became Lin Yutang's father-in-law.

In those days, the entire Liao family lived together. The third branch of the family was led by Liao Tianci, father of Liao Chaoxi and grandfather of Liao Yueqin. Liao Chaoxi and Liao Cuifeng were cousins, and they grew up under the same roof. Liao Chaoxi was a businessman, and he was very openminded. Liao Cuifeng's mother, Xie Shuyuan, also came from a grand family. She was gentle, kind, and sensible. Born in such a family, Liao Yueqin was extremely elegant and refined, a woman who would stand out in any situation.

The ladies born to the Liao family all married extraordinary men and gave birth to extraordinary children. Their children were raised to become great pianists, musicians, and doctors. The Liaos were truly a family of elites. The Liaos of Gulangyu Island especially nurtured a wealth of talent.

Liao Yueqin had three sisters. When she was young, she studied at a local school, the Yude Girl's High school, and then went on to study in the Advanced Nursing program of the Affiliated High School of the Peking Union Medical College. During her time, girls born to wealthy families did not want to become nurses, because it was regarded as a serving job, and how could a refined lady do a servant's job?

However, Liao Yueqin had her own aspirations, and she was not swayed by others' words, whether that be regarding her career choice, or her marriage choice. During her studies in Union Medical, she met the love of her life, Zhong Shifan. Zhong Shifan was an outstanding student at Union Medical, but he came from a poor family and was ten years older than Liao Yueqin. Their social backgrounds did not match, but Liao Yueqin was determined to marry Zhong Shifan. In 1934, after Liao graduated, she married Zhong Shifan at the age of 23.

When they first started their family, they lived in adversity. As the main bread-winner, Zhong Shifan was overwhelmed by his career. He rarely had time for his family, so Liao Yueqin took on all the household chores. Though she had been a girl who lived in comfort and been quite pampered, she adapted extremely well to her new life in the Zhong family. She never complained but faced all the difficulties that came to them with a calm mind.

After Liao's graduation, the Nationalist Government's Department of Health sent her to Boston to further her studies in Advanced Nursing. She was later one of the co-founders of Huanan Cancer Center (now Sun Yat-sen University Cancer

Center), where she made exceptional contributions to medical science in China. She had to go for night school and read many books in anatomy and oncology, in order to do well in her job. The young Zhong Nanshan was concerned about his mother, who was then almost forty years old. He asked, "What's the point of learning all this?" Dr. Liao replied lovingly, "Your mother is going to be the dean of a cancer hospital! I have to at least know what cancer is. You have to love the things you do, and at the same time you need to understand the things you love." Dr. Liao's words and practice left a profound mark on Dr. Zhong Nanshan.

Dr. Liao was kind and compassionate. She loved to help others. Later In life, Dr. Zhong Nanshan remembered what his mother told him and his sister about her past when he was little. "I still remember how my mother treated those in need," he said. "My empathy and sense of responsibility were inherited from my mother."

When the young Zhong Nanshan enrolled in the Peking Medical University in 1955, a classmate asked him if he could borrow some money. Zhong told his mother, who fell silent. They had already spent all their money on Zhong's education, and to do that they had had to cut down on their living expenses even further.

His mother was troubled, "Nanshan, you might not know this, but we already had some difficulties preparing for your school expenses, so we really don't have the means to help your classmate."

To his surprise, his mother handed him a few crumbled 20 yuan notes and asked him to be sure to deliver the money to the classmate who was in need. Dr. Zhong Nanshan later recalled, "The 20 yuan did not come easily. It was almost two months of our family's living expense."

In Zhong's memory, his mother was always a typical lady. She had beautiful double eyelids, and she always smiled. Her clothes were always simple and well presented. During festivals, at most, she wore white clothes with some floral patterns. "She was a fantastic listener. Whenever I spoke, she listened intently. When she expressed her opinion or criticism, she did so obliquely."

The young Zhong Nanshan admired his mother's trustworthiness. Once she promised him something, no matter how small or difficult the promise was, she always kept to her word. This quality influenced Dr. Zhong Nanshan deeply. When he had his own children, he kept all his promises to them. "I do not make a promise easily, but once I do, I make sure that I accomplish it," he observed.

Dr. Liao Yueqin became a very responsible Dean of the Nursing School. While preparing for the Huanan Cancer Center, Dr. Liao was appointed Vice Dean of this hospital. The Dean was Dr. Xie Zhiguang, a master radiologist. At the founding of the Cancer Center, Dr. Liao put her heart and soul into it.

When she was 54 years old, she suffered from myocardial infarction. She had a family history of the disease, as her elder sister lost her life at the age of 62 because from it. Her younger sister had died at a very young age due to tuberculosis. When Dr. Liao suffered from MI and was hospitalized, the young Zhong Nanshan was still in Beijing, knowing nothing of his mother's condition. When he went back to Guangzhou and learned of her situation, he rushed to the hospital immediately.

In July 1966, as Vice Dean of the Huanan Cancer Center, Dr. Liao Yueqin was very responsible in her work. In order to prevent patients from getting infected, she placed a huge emphasis on the cleanliness of the wards. Once, the Publicity Department of the hospital wanted to put up some slogans in the wards, but Dr. Liao strongly objected, worrying that patients undergoing chemotherapy would get infected. Because of her stand, she was accused and criticized as an "anti-Maoist" during the Cultural Revolution. Dr. Liao would have rather died than living in dishonor. She could not stand the Red Guards' torture, and so she drowned herself in the river. In 1964, Zhong Nanshan graduated from university. He went back to Guangzhou to visit his parents. He never imagined that it would be the last time he would ever see his mother.

Both of Zhong's parents come from Xiamen, which gave him a natural affinity for the city. "People from Xiamen have a very good character. They are sincere and passionate, just like my mother," he often said.

In Zhong Nanshan's mind, Gulangyu Island was always beautiful and romantic. A vast sea surrounded the island, and the waves were like songs. It was an attractive, euphonious island, with some six or seven hills and mountains, the most famous being Riguang Yan (Sunshine Rock). Flowers and trees were the island's most splendid resource, and they lined the beaches and the sea. The sea breeze and the waves chanted day and night throughout the year. Since ancient times, people on the island had made their living by fishing and farming. They woke when the sun rose and rested when the sun set.

What Dr. Zhong Nanshan remembered about his grandmother's family was that all the people of Xiamen who lived on Gulangyu Island were cultivated and cultured. Every household on the island had a piano, no matter their financial background, even though the piano was still a luxurious instrument for a normal home in China. The piano was almost regarded as a must for a family on Gulangyu. Most people knew how to play the piano. Through the generations, a superb family and island culture had developed.

Dr. Zhong Nanshan was always very fond of his parents. He said that his character was smoother, so he was able to integrate into society. That was different from his parents, who were traditional literati with strong principles. Dr. Zhong Nanshan's life philosophy was that one had to integrate into the society they lived in, but not at the expense of their principles.

His parents' life experiences, to Dr. Zhong Nanshan, were a precious spiritual wealth. After being seasoned by all the difficulties he encountered, he came out even wiser. "One has to first be able to survive in society. Both justice and injustice are present in society. As long as we stick up for our basic principles, we will be fine. If we do not bend at all, then we lose flexibility. Luckily, I am more flexible than my parents," he observed.

He gave an example. When his father first started writing the medical masterpiece, *Erke Jibing Jianbie Zhenduan,* he had not been entirely redressed politically. However, he insisted that no quotations from Chairman Mao should be added into his work, especially not in the most eye-catching preface. At the time, it was difficult to publish a work without a quote from Chairman Mao. However, Dr. Zhong Shifan said without hesitation, "This is a medical monograph, not political propaganda." This was Dr. Zhong Shifan, an upright man.

As for Dr. Zhong Nanshan's mother, Dr. Liao Yueqin, she even resolved to commit suicide in protest against the injustice and to answer to all the wrongful accusations leveled at her. This became the greatest emotional trauma in Zhong Nanshan's life.

On June 22, 1987, at his deathbed, Dr. Zhong Shifan said with his last breath that his children should mingle his and Liao Yueqin's ashes and spread them into the ocean. He wanted to show his pain and remorse over the loss of his beloved wife in this way.

As we spoke, Dr. Zhong Nanshan indulged in his memories. He was so calm that he appeared distant, like a pedestrian walking hurriedly across a street he had known for many years.

"I'm different from my parents. I see both the light and the darkness in society. But at the end of the day, I have seen the light." When he talked about this painful topic, his tone was surprisingly peaceful, as if he was talking to an old friend.

He even appeared positive while talking about such a heavy topic. "Especially now," he said, "Our country is getting better and better. Although many things are still not up to our expectations, we can still see constant progress. China is still rising. That's why I said I am better at integrating into society. But at the same time, I do not lose my principles."

His principles have always been to stick to and tell the truth.

2

A PLAYFUL CHILD

On October 20, 1936, in Nanjing, Dr. Zhong Shifan, pediatric expert of the Central Hospital, and his loving wife, Dr. Liao Yueqin, welcomed their son into the world. Their first child was born safely in the Central Hospital.

Lying weakly on the hospital bed after labor, Liao was happy and content. Her first baby, a lovely son, was waiting for his father to rush over from the pediatric ward to name him.

Dr. Zhong, who had just finished examining a young patient, hurried to his wife and son and held his newborn son in his arm. The Zhong family finally had a successor. Dr. Zhong Shifan was overjoyed. They were living in war time, and it was foreseeable that life would get harder in the future, but this little baby brought him courage and hope.

How should they name this little unexpected guest? The Central Hospital was located south of the Zhong Mountain of Nanjing. Therefore, Dr. Zhong Shifan decided to name this child based on the location where he was born, Nanshan, literally meaning "south of the mountain." Dr. Zhong Shifan thought that the name sounded majestic, and Dr. Liao Yueqin gladly agreed. Who would have guessed that this newborn would lead such a legendary life and become a firm figure in history, solid as a mountain?

Little Nanshan's childhood was filled with the shrill of the air defense alert and the deafening sound of bombs. Shortly after he was born, Japanese invaders bombed Nanjing, leaving the city in shambles. He almost died in the ruins. The Zhongs house was destroyed by the bombs. Little Nanshan's elderly grandmother and mother took a long time to dig him out of the ruins, crying and screaming in fear. His tiny face turned purple-black, and for a long while he could not cry. His mother and grandmother were in shock. Had they found little Nanshan just a little later, he would have died.

Zhong's grandmother was a petite woman. She always tied her hair into a bun and wore a pair of small glasses. She could speak both Hokkien and Mandarin. When she wrote, she did not write Chinese characters, but she romanized Hokkien. During that time, being able to write in romanized Hokkien was considered as fashionable, as it resembled English.

In 1949, after the People's Republic of China was founded, Zhong Nanshan visited his grandmother with his parents back in their hometown in Xiamen. When he arrived at grandmother's house, he saw her looking up at him through her tiny glasses. Hunching slightly, she said, "Sweetie, come over here, Granny made you *ngoh hiang* (spiced pork)."

Zhong Nanshan's grandmother was diligent and always kept herself clean, even in the late years of her life.

In December, 1937, before Nanjing fell into the Japanese occupation, Nanjing Central Hospital quickly retreated and relocated thousands of miles to Guiyang, Guizhou.

In Guiyang, there was a popular jingle: *The weather doesn't remain sunny for three whole days. The ground can't remain flat for three square feet. The people won't keep three cents in their pocket.* The shadow of war loomed over Guiyang as well.

In 1942, 6-year-old Nanshan started primary school. A naughty, playful boy, he often made Dr. Zhong Shifan shake his head and sigh. He was busy with work, but when he got home at night, he still had to help Nanshan with his homework. The boy had a short attention span, and whenever he had to focus for too long, he got impatient and yelled, "I need to pee!" And then he ran off.

When Dr. Zhong Nanshan recounted his own childhood, he smiled and shook his head. With a sigh, he said, "I was very very naughty when I was young." When he was in primary school, he was not a good student. He skipped school often, and he loved to wander out of school to buy snacks. When teachers asked the students to pay a certain amount of money as food expenses, little Nanshan often kept the money his mother gave him and bought food from the streets instead of giving it to the teacher.

Once, when a semester was about to end, Liao Yueqin asked, "Was there any money left after you paid the food fee at school?" Nanshan rolled his eyes playfully and dodged the question. "You can ask the school yourself," he said. To his surprise, his mother actually took him to the school to ask the teachers. Nanshan had no choice but to tell the truth before they reached the school. "I spent all the food money." He could not face his teacher in such a state.

His mother's reaction was not what he expected. She did not reprimand him too harshly after speaking privately with his teachers. Instead, she exhorted, "What you did was dishonest." Dr. Zhong Shifan, who was always stern and reticent, said, "Please reflect on this. Why did you lie?"

At the beginning of 2009, Dr. Zhong Nanshan was set to celebrate his 73rd birthday in October. Even then, he vividly remembered this event from his childhood, and he repeated what his father said word-for-word.

In 1945, the US army was stationed in Guiyang as the Nationalist Army's ally. American soldiers could be seen everywhere on the street. In the 11-year-old Nanshan's view, the Americans were arrogant and cold. They drove recklessly on the road, and he witnessed a middle-aged Chinese woman being hit by one of their cars. One of her legs was torn off at the thigh. "I remember very clearly that the woman's leg was torn off. She was in great pain, very miserable." The American soldiers picked her up from the ground and left her at the hospital, and they were never seen again. That was the American version of "humaneness." Infuriated, Nanshan thought, "How could the American soldiers be such bullies?"

When Nanjing was bombed by the Japanese invaders, the Zhongs place was completely destroyed. It took them a while to get back on their feet, but before long, their hard-earned new belongings, especially their much cherished medical books, were devoured by the fires of war again and buried under the ruins.

In Guiyang, it was counted a luxury for the Zhong family to even a meal with a cube of fermented tofu. As the war situation heightened, starvation ran rampant across the land. It was completely disheartening.

At the end of 1945, the Zhong family again relocated with the hospital to Guangzhou. The family traveled on a bus for eight days and nights. The hostels along the way were infested with bedbugs and mosquitoes. Nanshan's two-year-old sister, Zhong Qianjun, had an allergic predisposition. She had to spray DDT that had been made in the US all over her body in order to sleep well. But there were too many bedbugs and mosquitoes, and early in the morning, she would wake up itching all over again.

They rode the hospital's ambulance. As the hospital relocated to Guangzhou, the ambulance had to be driven there as well. Since Dr. Zhong Shifan was the Vice-Dean of the hospital, he was given the special treatment, and his family was allowed to ride in the ambulance.

On the morning of the 9th day, the ambulance finally entered Guangzhou. They saw the Pearl River, Haizhu Bridge, and Aiqun Tower. They had finally reached Guangzhou! Everything seemed so strange and new. Nanshan and Qianjun were overjoyed. Guangzhou looked like heaven to them. Unlike Guiyang, Guangzhou was showered by bombs. Guiyang was a military choke point, and it underwent some of the most horrifying battles during the Anti-Japanese War. As a result, the city of Guiyang was much more shattered than Guangzhou.

Right before the War of Liberation, the Nationalist Government planned a Total Destruction mission, intending to destroy the Haizhu Bridge and turn Guangzhou into ruins. The reason they intended to bomb the river was to prevent the Liberation Army from pursuit, allowing the Nationalist Army to retreat smoothly to Hainan.

October 14, 1949, the unstoppable Liberation Army marched into the city of Guangzhou. The Commander in Chief of the Nationalist Army in Guangzhou, Li Jilan, sent troops and plainclothes agents to deliver around 100 boxes of yellow explosives, placing them at the junction of the Haizhu Bridge pier and beam. At the time, the Haizhu Bridge was the only bridge that connected the banks of Pearl River. When they were delivering the explosives, the bridge was under an order of martial law, and no vehicle or pedestrian was allowed on it. After the explosives were implemented, martial law was lifted.

Pedestrians and vehicles were already backed up at the bridge, waiting for passage. Once martial law was lifted, cars, horses, and pedestrians flocked onto the bridge. According to historical records, at 17:50 that day, the bridge collapsed in an ear-splitting roar, without any warning. Dead bodies, blood, and broken pieces of rock and metal were suddenly flew in all directions within a few kilometer radius of the Haizhu Bridge.

It was the rainy season in Guangzhou, and the line between the sky and the river blurred in the rain. The stream of cars on the street moved slowly forward. The veil of rain shrouded the hustle and bustle of the city, pushing the noises further away. The brown-colored Aiqun Hotel, built by patriotic overseas Chinese merchant Chen Zhuopin some 80 years earlier, was the tallest skyscraper in Guangzhou for thirty years. It stood out in the forest of steel and cement. Having witnessed over seventy years of history after the founding of the People's Republic of China, the rebuilt Haizhu Bridge stood silently in the rain, a blue-black outline. Nearly a century of past events seemed to be quietly replay.

Standing in front of the window, Dr. Zhong Nanshan watched the Haizhu Bridge and the bustling flow of people and vehicles on it. He pointed to Yanjiang Road, an east-west running thoroughfare to the north of the bridge.

When the bridge was exploded, Zhong Nanshan's family lived on the campus of the private Lingnan University (now Sun Yat-sen University) on the west side of the road, five or six kilometers away from the Haizhu Bridge. The sound of the explosion was so loud that it could be heard ten kilometers away, and the nearby houses were destroyed. His house remained intact, but all the glass windowpanes shattered. The bridge collapsed in the middle, and the cross-section was like two hanging heads, leaving a deep mark in Dr. Zhong's memory.

The Nationalist Party's propaganda said that when the Communists were fighting, they always first drove the common people to the front line so that the Nationalist troops would not be able to shoot. The Communist generals always used this method to siege cities. The destruction of civilian lives at the Haizhu Bridge debunked this lie.

Another deep impression that was left on little Nanshan's young mind was that before the Nationalist Party retreated, it issued a huge amount of golden yuan notes, causing serious inflation. Once, he carried a whole sack of yuan notes on his back just to get a haircut.

When Guangzhou was liberated, he was among the first batch of teenagers to join the Young Pioneers of China. He was only 13 years old at the time. There were troops stationed in Lingnan University, and every afternoon, Liberation Army soldiers taught them how to sing, do the Yangko dance, and play the waist drum.

Like those around him, Nanshan did not know much about the Liberation Army before they moved in, but after they arrived, Nanshan found, to his great delight, that they were very kind. "They taught us a lot. I was really happy. There was a real difference between the Liberation Army and the Nationalist Army."

He saw that when the Liberation Army soldiers sat alongside the people, they always performed the military salute. This made him think that the Liberation soldiers were respectful and not scary at all. He had a very good impression of these soldiers.

Dr. Zhong Shifan bought some guinea pigs for experiment purposes, which changed young Nanshan's playful character once and for all. He was especially interested in these guinea pigs, and he loved to observe their changes. He thought that what his father did to these guinea pigs for experiment was mysterious. Dr. Zhong killed them, took out their brains, and conducted cellular examinations, Nanshan did not know that his father had paid for these guinea pigs from his own salary. He observed their birth and growth, how they moved, and how they competed for food. He observed them every day and found that they were so swift and adorable. He also drew the conclusion that the guinea pigs were selfish. When they competed for food, they never left any for their friends. He loved to tease the guinea pigs when they ate.

Dr. Liao Yueqin was especially sympathetic to the weak, including small animals, and she taught Nanshan not to hurt the guinea pigs. As a result of her instruction, he never abused small animals, but has a strong sense of love and sympathy for them since he was a child. This quality lasted into his old age.

Life in Guangzhou was vastly different from that in Guizhou. In Guangzhou, Nanshan could actively watch many intriguing American movies. He especially loved martial arts movies, to the extent that he was addicted. The more he watched, the more he wanted to mimic the vigilantes: raising his arms and legs in hopes of flying. He thought of opening an umbrella and jumping out of the building, imagining that he would first glide for a while, then land slowly. The gliding part would be especially exciting. How exhilarating! He got more and more excited. He was only 11 years old, innocent, fearless.

He took out a firm cloth umbrella, went up to the third floor of his house when his parents were not home, pushed the window open, and opened the umbrella carefully. As he did this, he envisioned an imaginary vigilante floating in front of him. He imagined that the umbrella in his hand would sustain him in the air, and land slowly.

He jumped out.

The umbrella immediately overturned. He crashed to the ground like a rock. Fortunately, there was grass below the window. He could not even talk when he regained consciousness. His parents were at work, and it took him an hour or so to drag himself up.

"Ha! I would have died if my head landed first." Dr. Zhong Nanshan recalled, "I was really naughty when I was young."

There was a very tall bamboo outside Nanshan's house, which he learned many skills. The bamboo was so tall that it reached the windowsill of the third floor. Little Nanshan often climbed on the bamboo like a monkey, then slid down. Sometimes, he slid down to the first floor from the drainpipe on the exterior wall.

When he was young, he was often bullied by the rich kids. As soon as he turned fourteen or fifteen, his physique became taller and stronger. He thought it was time to seek his revenge.

Finally, one day, he asked his "enemies" for a "duel" in the bamboo forest. His classmates leaked this carefully wrought plan to the "enemy's" father, who came to Dr. Zhong Shifan to reason with him. Dr. Zhong warned Nanshan seriously, "You want to fight, even 'duel'? You must remain at home for the whole day tomorrow. If not, you'll never call me your father again!"

What Dr. Zhong said really scared the young Nanshan. However, the "white glove" had been thrown. It would really be shameful if he did not appear on time. He could not think of a way out, no matter how hard he tried.

On the next day, a few loyal friends came to Nanshan's house to cheer him on. Nanshan's parents said that he was not home. The "duel" was called off.

To Dr. Zhong Nanshan, his parents are very traditional. They were the typical "strict father and gentle mother."

Little Nanshan was the eldest son, therefore he was a "bully." He received count-less punishments as a result. For example, when the family was dining together, he always asked for the biggest portion of eggs. If there was meat on the table, he always picks the biggest chunk. At first, Dr. Zhong Shifan only frowned upon this behavior. However, after a few times of such misconduct, he could not hold back anymore. *Swat!* He slapped Nanshan's hand, and the chopsticks fell onto the table. "Think about others. How will others eat if you do this?" reprimanded Dr. Zhong Shifan. Nanshan's face suddenly turned red, and he never did that again.

Nanshan gave his parents a hard time in his academics as well. He was retained twice, the first time purely because he hated school. He was in Grade 4 when he moved to Guangzhou, but he still wanted to play all day every day.

Of course, he had just reached Guangzhou, where most people spoke Cantonese, so the language barrier was an obstacle for him. But when I suggested that possibility during our interview, he immediately debunked this interpretation of his delinquency in the most sincere manner. "Language wasn't the main problem. I just wanted to play." He was retained in Grade 4 when he was supposed to get promoted to Grade 5.

The second retainment happened during his studies in Peking Medical University, when he had to attend the training camp for the National Games. This time it, was for a valid reason.

Dr. Zhong Nanshan said that his way of doing things and his logic were shaped by his childhood education. His middle school, the Affiliated Middle School of Lingnan University, placed an emphasis on the holistic development of its students. This was the scientific way of education.

Dr. Zhong Nanshan believed that he had learned to develop holistically since a young age in such an environment. In the US, universities like Yale and Harvard also placed heavy emphasis on the students' holistic development. It was this mindset that meant Barack Obama could play basketball well and Bill Clinton could play the saxophone.

Zhong Nanshan later enrolled in the Affiliated Middle School of South China Normal College. He loved the education he received there. Naturally, family education, especially the parents' examples by practice, also played an important role in Zhong Nanshan's upbringing.

3

SETTING A GOAL DURING HIS TEENAGE YEARS

Zhong Nanshan finally woke up from daydreaming and started chasing the wind. He started out in a muddle, but he eventually fought his way towards excellence.

In 1949, after he graduated from Grade 6, Nanshan was admitted to the Affiliated Middle School of Lingnan University. In Grade 7, he was surrounded by positive influences. The typical view of a good student was not someone who was simply good at studying. At the time, many of his classmates had good academic results, but only those who were also good at physical and aesthetics education could become role models for everyone. The students were taught to attend speech contests and participate in voluntary labor from a young age, which left a deep impression on the young Zhong Nanshan.

There were many American professors at Lingnan University. Being in its Affiliated Middle School, Zhong Nanshan's impression of the American professors was different from the one he had formed of the American soldiers. He felt that the American professors were polite and knowledgeable.

When Zhong Nanshan was 12 years old, one of his good friends from his class came from a wealthier family. One day, the young Nanshan told his mother that this important friend of his would visit his house and have lunch with him. Liao Yueqin took Nanshan's words seriously, and she prepared a big meal for them.

After lunch, they went out to play. The friend took Nanshan to his own house. When the friend got home, he started having lunch again, and they ate sausages, something Nanshan had never seen before. A family like Nanshan's could not even dream to have such sausages.

The young Nanshan suddenly felt sad. We treated him to the best of our ability, yet he was not full and had to eat more when he got home. The food he is having now is something we could not provide. We cooked the best food we had, but we could not treat him with sausages.

His self-esteem was pricked. *We cannot compare to them,* he thought.

That was the first time he realized that his family was poor. After their house was bombed, it took them some time to reacquire all the household necessities. Dr. Zhong Shifan was a professor, but he was not wealthy.

The reason why Zhong Nanshan was admitted to the Affiliated Middle School of Lingnan University was not only because of his mother Liao Yueqin's loving, patient education, but also because of the encouragement and praise he received from his primary school teachers. One of his essays was especially well received by his teachers. Nanshan wrote about one of his classmates in this essay. The classmate loved to exercise and had bulging muscles. Nanshan admired that. He was much older than Nanshan, and he came from a financially challenged background. He was hired by the school guard, and his father was an auditor. Regardless of his background, he was well-read and loved music.

Once, a classmate's money was stolen, and some suspected the boy from the poor family. He was infuriated, declaring that he would never do such a thing. He asked Nanshan if he believed him, and Nanshan said he did. I believe you. Nanshan wrote about this event in his essay. The teacher felt that the content was very authentic and conveyed sincere feelings for a classmate from an ordinary family.

The teacher wrote many comments on the composition, praising Nanshan's writing, calling it authentic and full of emotion, but there was no score assigned. Nanshan looked for the teacher. "You did not grade my essay," he said.

"Oh, I forgot about it," replied the teacher apologetically, and he gave Nanshan five marks. Nanshan thought, "My teacher wrote so many positive comments. She wanted to give me five marks, but she forgot about it."

This reassurance from the teacher played a definite role in Nanshan's mind. He realized that he was capable of being a good student. Liao Yueqin also encouraged him, saying that if he studied hard and got into the middle school, she would give him a bicycle. This promise was a huge temptation to the young Nanshan. He studied hard in Grade 6, bidding farewell to playfulness and naughtiness. His academic performance skyrocketed, and he was successfully admitted to the Affiliated Middle School of Lingnan University.

Liao Yueqin kept her promise and bought Nanshan the bicycle that he had longed for. Nanshan learned that if he did things seriously and diligently and achieved good results, he could win the respect of others.

In 1951, when Zhong Nanshan was in Grade 8, his academic performance was outstanding, but his relationship with his classmates was not very good. Sometimes, when his classmates asked him for help or gave him any constructive feedback, he appeared unhappy. Later, a classmate pointed out frankly that Zhong Nanshan did not care about the collective and was sometimes selfish. That dealt a heavy blow on the young Nanshan. He could not comprehend this comment at first. A few days later, he changed tremendously. He started to think for the others, and he soon won his classmates' respect.

He was not content with the current situation, and he wanted to skip Grade 9. In hopes of getting straight into Grade 10, he studied through the entire summer holiday. He attained good results on the test, and he became overly confident. Who would have expected that his request was immediately rejected by his teacher? That made the young Nanshan rather upset. The teacher paid him a visit at home and told Dr. Zhong Shifan that Nanshan was too young and skipping grade might be detrimental to his development. Nanshan could not understand that, and he was very sad. He had to continue with Grade 9, since neither his teacher nor his parents agreed that he should skip a grade.

Nanshan was always the top of his class during his three years at the Affiliated Middle School of Lingnan. From Grade 9, he was directly admitted to the Affiliated High School due to his academic excellence, alongside the wealthy friend who had looked down on his family's treat. This time, Nanshan was truly proud of himself. He also began to understand his teacher and classmates' sincere help.

Liao Yueqin rewarded him again. "She gave me a trip to Beijing. I took a train there with one of my best friends," he said. It was 1952, and it was his first trip to Beijing.

The education Zhong Nanshan received in the Affiliated Middle School of Lingnan University was unforgettable. During a Chinese lesson, the teacher asked a question, and Nanshan actively responded. The teacher was very satisfied with Nanshan's answer. He sagely remarked, "One should not only live in reality, but also in dreams. Without a dream, one will focus on the unimportant and dwell on trivial things. Everything else will appear small when compared to one's ultimate goal."

These simple words were engraved on the heart of young Nanshan.

At the age of 75, Dr. Zhong Nanshan gleamed with happiness when he recalled his teenage years. He stroked the naturally curly hair at back of his head and said, "I used to have bad grades, but then I gradually grasped my teacher's words. One has to chase after some higher things in life. I have lived long and experienced much. Many events were incredibly difficult, but I managed to pull through. How did I manage? It was because I had a higher goal. Without this goal, I would not have overcome the obstacles, because they were certainly very hard!"

During High School, like other outstanding youths of the time, Zhong Nanshan fell in love with Soviet Russian literature. In the 1950s China, Soviet Russian literature heavily inspired millions of passionate young people in China. Pavel Korchagin's words in *How the Steel Was Tempered* became Zhong Nanshan's motto. *There is nothing more precious than one's life. When a person looks back, they should not feel ashamed by their mediocracy.*

The story in *Far from Moscow* purified his soul, shining on him like rays of the sun. Zhong Nanshan also liked Soviet Russian music. Although life was poor and rough, the romantic revolutionary education from the Soviet Union at that time penetrated Zhong Nanshan's soul. Such a generation, or even two generations, were deeply inspired by these masterpieces. Decades later, Zhong Nanshan felt that his generation was well nurtured and educated. Back then, education came first. The nation was always the top priority, followed by the collective, and lastly the individual. Everyone thought that was the natural order of things.

Zhong Nanshan always strove for excellence, a trait that formed during his participation in sports competitions since Grade 6. Through participation in sports, he cultivated the courage to overcome difficulties and the spirit of fighting. The most important influence in his life aside from his parents was sports, especially competitive sports.

When he was in Grade 10, his performance in school was mediocre. Yet he was not content with the situation. "I must buck up!" he said. In Grade 11, he managed to catch up.

At first, the young Nanshan participated in the 1954 Sports Competitions of the Affiliated Middle School of South China Normal College, and he obtained the 4th place in the 400 meter sprint. He had formerly participated in the non-professional training of the provincial track and field team in Guangdong, and he improved quickly. In the early spring of 1995, when he was in Grade 12, he participated in the Guangdong Provincial Track and Field Competition, where he won second place in the 400 meter sprint, breaking the provincial record. After that, he represented the

Guangdong Province in the National Track and Field Competition held in Shanghai, and he won third place in the 400 meter sprint at the national level.

The Central University of Physical Education (now Beijing Sport University) sent him a letter asking if he would join the national team's training. Nanshan discussed the idea with his father, but Dr. Zhong wanted him to continue on the path of academics, because one could only be a professional athlete for a limited number of years, while medical research and treatment could be done for life. Dr. Zhong Shifan believed that being a doctor was a more suitable career for Nanshan.

The High School Graduation Examinations were coming in June, and the young Nanshan still had to prepare for the University Entrance Examinations (the Gaokao). He studied hard to make up for the classes he missed during his training. In the end, he became one of the five students who was admitted to Peking Medical University. Some of the student leaders in his class went to Peking and Tsinghua Universities, with 98% of the students in his class managing to get into a university.

The cut-off point for Peking Medical University was rather high. Zhong Nanshan said, "I was not very satisfied with my Gaokao results. Other subjects were OK, but I only obtained 60 marks for mathematics. There were five questions, and I only got three correct. Well, at least it was a pass." At first, he thought there was no chance for him to get into the university, but he received the offer from PKMU at last.

Dr. Zhong Shifan's usual way of expressing his idea was through action. He rarely expressed his feelings to his son. When Nanshan got into high school, he was no longer an ignorant child. When Dr. Zhong Shifan saw that his own son had grown to become a young adult with passion and aspiration, he nodded and patted his son on the shoulder and said, "One has to leave the world with something meaningful to say that they have truly lived."

These words left a profound impression on Zhong Nanshan. When he was young, his father taught him to be useful and contribute to society, so as not to spend his life in vain. By contribution, Dr. Zhong Shifan meant academic progress. This subtle teaching paved the way for Zhong Nanshan to ultimately choose a career in medicine.

4

LIFE AT PEKING MEDICAL UNIVERSITY

He was in Beijing at Peking Medical University at last. Zhong Nanshan's dream had come true, and he felt great joy. His heart was full of dreams.

Though his dream of getting into PMU had come true, the political turmoil led to great upheaval in his life. As long as he lived, he would never forget his days in PMU.

Initially, Dr. Zhong Shifan wanted his son to study in South China Medical University, but there was no high school graduate who did not believe that the universities in Beijing were the best, who did not dream of studying in the capital city. As such, young Nanshan set his mind on PMU, and his effort was repaid. This was a pleasant surprise for his parents.

However, Nanshan realized that he was not as outstanding as his classmates. He soon learned that all his classmates from around China were better than him. At first, he thought he could be considered as one of the top students, but after getting to know his classmates, he found that they were all very strong in speech and organization skills, certainly much better than him.

"I believed that I needed to learn from my classmates. They excelled in academics. I still remember the class leaders' performance during important events," Dr. Zhong later recalled. He thought, these classmates, especially the class leaders, possessed strong organization skills during literary and artistic events, as well as during voluntary labors. They were strategic, and he needed to learn from them.

Indeed, PMU students were the crème de la crème, but Nanshan remained as competitive as when he was in high school. *I have to catch up!* he thought.

These subconscious comparisons were rather crucial to Zhong Nanshan's life. In the face of these differences, he strove to catch up with his classmates, pursuing those whom he deemed outstanding. In his sophomore year, he became the top of his class.

Dr. Zhong Shifan was pleased with his son's performance. He often asked about Nanshan's studies.

In 1956, during the second semester of Nanshan's freshman year, the university received exciting news. Premier Zhou Enlai was going to meet the Merit Students of Beijing. Everyone at PMU rejoiced at this news.

There were around 600 students in Nanshan's level, but only two or three students could be selected for this honor. In terms of academics, Nanshan was as outstanding as his peers, however, he was also a high-achiever in sports, being the champion of the Inter-College Games. He was thus fortunate enough to be selected to meet the Premier.

"I was overjoyed!" Dr. Zhong Nanshan could not help but smile, as he told me, even after so many years.

During his freshman year, there were 230 students in his class, and he was in Group 2. Wang Debing, who later became the President of PMU, was in his class. Wang specialized in Medical Education, and when PMU merged with Peking University in 2000, he became the Party Secretary of PKU, then later resigned in 2002.

In Zhong Nanshan's student days, the President of PMU was Dr. Hu Chuankui and Dr. Ma Xu. In 2008, when Dr. Ma Xu celebrated his 94th birthday, he still lived on campus at PMU. His mind was as clear as before, and he still remembered Dr. Zhong Nanshan. During the Cultural Revolution, PMU's faculty members and students were divided into two camps: The Flag Camp and the United Headquarters Camp. Zhong Nanshan belonged to the United Headquarters Camp. After graduation, Zhong stayed at PMU as a lecturer for the new department, Medical Radiology, studying the harm to the human body of radiation emitted by an atomic bomb detonation. During the Cultural Revolution, students conducted heated criticism of the cadres among the university's faculty staff. As a lecturer, Zhong tried to protect the old cadres numerous times, hoping to prevent them from getting beaten up by the students.

In that situation, as a lecturer, he pretended to follow orders and allow the students to conduct Public Criticism Sessions while also trying to protect the older cadres who were criticized.

In addition to Ma Xu and others who were protected by Zhong Nanshan during that difficult period, Qian Xinzhong, a well-known public health expert who later served as the Minister of Health, also received support from Dr. Zhong. At the 23rd National Meeting of the Chinese Medical Association held in April 2005, Dr. Qian, who was then in his 90s, recognized Zhong Nanshan at once. "I remember you. You protected me!" Dr. Qian exclaimed. Many other old cadres remembered Zhong Nanshan's protection as well.

During those years of frenzy and hysteria, when right and wrong were overturned, Zhong Nanshan calmly took both the cadres and his students into consideration. He needed to protect his students, so that later there would be no record of participation and contribution to Public Criticisms in the students' files. In this way, he helped the old cadres, while at the same time regulating his students.

In 1958, when Zhong Nanshan was in his third year of university, he was selected for the training camp held by Beijing Sports Team for the preparation of the first National Games. This was both a sudden opportunity and an unprecedented challenge. Zhong Nanshan, who was unyielding by nature, put unprecedented effort into achieving this goal. He had already become an outstanding student in both his class and his university. Now, he developed the habit of running on campus every day after class at 5:30 pm, only buying his dinner at the community shop outside of the school after sunset, because the school canteen was closed by then. The training became more intensive when he entered the training camp, but Zhong Nanshan, determined as he has always been, managed to pull through.

The actual competition was getting closer and closer. To his surprise, he was not shortlisted for the National Games after the selection stage, despite his hard work. This unexpected setback dealt a heavy blow to him. He became upset and discouraged, and he almost lost his fighting spirit completely.

Would his 300 days and nights of hard work go to waste? He told himself, *I will never give up! I will not yield to this defeat at this critical moment.*

In the final preparation stage, he challenged himself again, and he finally defeated himself. In August 1959, in the qualifiers for the first National Games, Zhong Nanshan broke the national record of 54.6 seconds in the men's 400 meter hurdles, with a time of 54.2 seconds. In February 1960, PMU held a grand celebration for Zhong Nanshan's achievement in the National Games.

Zhong Nanshan only attended 3.5 years of university. He started university in 1955, attended the training camp for the National Games, and subsequently the actual games in 1958, when he was in Year 3. After the end of the games, the Beijing Municipal Sports Commission proposed that Zhong Nanshan stay on the team. After thorough consideration, he made the difficult yet decisive choice to dedicate his entire life to the medical profession.

Given this chance to pursue a sports career, he calmly thought that if he was to go on this path, his goal would be the world championship. However, he thought that his physical condition was not good enough, that he was neither strong enough nor tall enough. After weighing these two options, he decided to go back to school.

In 1960, Zhong Nanshan went back to school and immediately entered the practical stage, which meant he only had 3.5 years of university, a fact he regretted. Because of his shortened studies, he missed much content on clinical medicine. He had a difficult time early in his career after he went back to Guangzhou because he did not have the chance to complete his studies in the university.

More than thirty years later, in 1999, Zhong Nanshan was one of the six Outstanding Alumni nominated by Peking Medical University. Decades later, Dr. Zhong used his fighting spirit to inspire generations of young people on many occasions.

Dr. Zhong observed, "Why do I still love sports? Because sports nurture three areas of a positive spirit in a person. The first is the spirit of competition, the will to fight your way to the top, the second is the spirit of teamwork, and the third is the spirit of efficiency, completing a task with high efficiency in a given amount of time, just like the 400 meters hurdles. I trained for a whole year to improve my result by three seconds. Each second was precious. Most importantly, the spirit of sports can be applied to work and studies." He leveraged the occasion presented by various conferences, especially the publicity of the media, to repeat this valuable experience. He also suggested that his subordinates and friends should cultivate their children to love sports, so as to develop their competitive and cooperative abilities, which would be very important to their lives. He even used himself as an example to promote this idea.

Whenever he mentioned his impressive achievements, Zhong Nanshan reiterated the spirit of sports that he advocated.

5

YOUNG LOVE

It was often said in China that things never happen at the same time, but it seemed that heaven had given Zhong Nanshan sugar in his left hand and filled his right with honey. In 1955, good things happened all at once for Zhong Nanshan. As soon as he was admitted to Peking Medical University, he stumbled upon the love of his life.

Zhong Nanshan and Li Shaofen entered into a happy marriage on December 31, 1963. They first met in 1955, not because of sports, but because of his visit to a relative. Nanshan's grandaunt lived in Beijing, and he started to visit her often after he started studying in the city. His grandaunt had a bosom friend from church who stayed with her, since they were both young ladies and had remained unmarried throughout their lives. His grandaunt was a doctor, and this sister of hers, a pianist, had a grandniece named Li Shaofen, who was the same age as Zhong Nanshan. Li had come to Beijing in 1953, after being recruited by the National Sports Team as a basketball player. She visited her own grandaunt often too. She came from Huadu, Guangdong, making both her and Zhong Nanshan Cantonese people living in the north. Both visited their grandaunts, and both have similar backgrounds and hobbies. It was a match made in heaven. They were both glad and surprised when they met, and it seemed quite natural that they started dating.

Li was part of the first group of players on the China Women's National Basketball Team at the age of 15. In November 1963, right before her marriage to Zhong Nanshan, she set off for the first Games of the New Emerging Forces (GANEFO), held in Jakarta, Indonesia.

In the late 1950s, the first sports-themed film in the People's Republic of China premiered and quickly gained popularity. It was the color feature film, *Woman's Basketball Player No. 5*. China's first women's basketball team in the movie drew inspiration from the first Chinese women's basketball team, founded in 1952. Li Shaofen was one of its main players, and as one of the key members of the team from Guangdong, Li Shaofen's sports career was filled with wonderful stories. Her favorite photo in her album was the one of her as the flag bearer in the Chinese delegation during the first GANEFO.

During the time when the Two Camps were still in opposition, the GANEFO were as significant as the Olympics. Li led the group sports team. The other flag bearer was Zheng Fengrong, a women's high jump athlete, who represented the individual sports team. The China Women's Basketball Team won the first GANEFO, making a striking figure.

At the time Zhong and Li fell in love, society was really conservative. They dated for eight years, beginning in 1955. During this period, they practiced strict abstinence, which was quite common in China at the time, Li Shaofen was often in training camps or overseas participating in competitions when she was in the National Team, so the couple rarely met, instead spending most of the time missing each other fondly.

When Li first joined, the National Team responded actively to Premier Zhou and He Long, the Head of National Sports Commission's advocacy. They were determined to debunk the derogatory nickname "Sick Man of Asia" through their outstanding performance on the sports field. The Soviet Union was China's "Big Brother" back then, so Chinese athletes were sent to the USSR for immersion training. At the same time, the Soviet Union sent over a National Level Honorary Coach to train Chinese athletes.

From 1954 to 1958, Li and her teammates went to the Soviet Union to study while also participating in consecutive sessions of the Universiade and the World Festival of Youth and Students. By 1958, the competitive level of China Woman's Basketball had improved tremendously.

While competing overseas, Li received a special invitation from France. A basketball club controlled by a French arms dealer offered extremely attractive terms for her. She was promised a high salary and a chance to tour the world while taking part in competitions. Attractive and romantic as it sounded, Li rejected the offer because she did not want to fail her homeland, and she did not want to make Zhong Nanshan, whom she loved and who loved her, feel sad and disappointed.

In September 1959, when Li was competing on international fields, Zhong Nan-shan was studying in PMU. He attended the first National Games and broke national record in the Men's 400 meters hurdles during the selection stage, and in 1961, he also won second place in the decathlon at the Beijing Municipal Games.

On December 31, 1963, after years of waiting, Zhong Nanshan finally married his dream bride. Li Shaofen returned home with honor, and with many medals and champion trophies as well. They ended the eight years of a dating marathon and entered the sacred hall of marriage.

The soon-to-be couple joyfully took wedding photos. Li had shoulder-length hair with little curls. At that time, this hair style could cause trouble because it was deemed "bourgeois." As soon as the photos were done, the National Sports Commission commanded Li Shaofen to cut her curly hair short, so as not to "advocate for a bourgeois lifestyle."

Li and Zhong's house was allocated by the Sports Commission, a small studio of less than 10 square meters. Once they put in a small bed and some simple household furniture, it was filled up.

Their wedding could not have been simpler. There was no wedding gown or suit. They merely wore a set of new clothes and opened sweets for each guest.

In 1964, the China Women's Basketball Team was unstoppable in the invitational tournament held in Switzerland and France, winning a big victory. Li Shaofen was at the peak of her personal sports career. After getting married, she served three more years in the National Team, totaling 13 years of service.

In 1966, Li Shaofen insisted on going back to Guangdong, giving up her opportunity to be a coach in the National Team, because she wanted to take care of her foster mother and her parents-in-law. After getting back to Guangdong, she continued to play for the provincial team before retiring completely in 1973, when she was 37 years old. After retirement, Li served as the coach of the Guangdong Women's Basketball Team, Vice Captain of the Provincial Sports Brigade, Vice Dean of the Provincial Institute of Sports Technique, Vice President of the Chinese Basketball Association, and Vice President of the Guangdong Provincial Basketball Association. Even when she was over 80 years old, Li contributed to China's sports development as a consultant of the Guangzhou Municipal Basketball Association.

In their late years, Dr. Zhong and Auntie Li's happy family was well-known for both their sports and medical heritage. Their daughter, Zhong Weiyue, was an outstanding swimmer in the 1990s. She won the FINA World Swimming Championships for the women's 100 meter butterfly and broke the world record for short course butterfly in 1994. Their son, Zhong Weide, was a urologist of the Guangzhou First Municipal People's Hospital and one of the main players of the hospital's basketball team. Zhong Weiyue's husband, Mr. Finley, was also a basketball fan.

∞ 6 ∞

TEMPERED STEEL

Dr. Zhong suffered greatly during the political movement because of his family background. From the end of 1964 to early 1966, he participated in the Socialist Education Movement (the Four Cleanups Movement). He was sent from PMU to Rushan County, Shandong on the Jiaodong Peninsula to experience rural life, during which he dined, lived, and worked with the farmers. Before his departure, he submitted his application to join the Party, and it was determined that he had stood the tests during the Four Cleanups and strives to join the Communist Party of China. As he often said, he always saw the positive, optimistic side of everything, even those that hurt him the most.

Along with other cadres who had been sent down, he shared the suffering of the farmers every day. Dr. Zhong Nanshan recalled, "I think the farmers' enthusiasm taught me a profound lesson. The farmers believed that we were sent by Chairman Mao, so they always treated us with what they thought was the best, but at that time, they only had the opportunity to eat buns made by wheat flour twice a year. Dumplings were a luxury. They could only have meat once per year. During the Lunar New Year, the farmers cooked a big pot of meat. That was the happiest meal of the year."

In the countryside, Zhong Nanshan lived in a typical farming house. A farmer's life in Northern China was much harder than Zhong Nanshan could have imagined. He did not sleep on the same *kang* as the farmers, but on an unheated brick bed in a freezing cold room infested by bedbugs and lice.

During the cold winter, Zhong Nanshan woke up in the middle of the night, shivering in the unforgiving coldness, even though he had already put on all his winter clothes. When he slept, he could not lie on the bed. He had to kneel on the bed, curl into a ball, and put everything that could provide him with warmth on his body until dawn broke. He had to do this every night just to survive the winter nights.

He lived on the verge of starvation. The year's rations usually depleted in March, so he had to start eating locust leaves. Dried sweet potatoes were regarded as a delicacy. He did the same amount of labor as the farmers every day, raking, growing sweet potatoes, and weeding. He also had to attend meetings at night. When the cadres gathered for meetings, everyone spread a layer of straw on the ground and slept together.

This experience of being sent down touched Zhong Nanshan to the core of his being. Years later, he could not help but think that there were still people living such a life in China. Life was hard, but they treated their guests like family. They were passionate and pure.

Zhong Nanshan formed a strong emotional bond with the farmers in Rushan County. They still wrote to him when he was in his 40s, hoping that he would "come back for a visit."

The lice bit Zhong Nanshan's ankle, and it was unbearably itchy. The scratched wound began to fester, and then it became more swollen. During the freezing winter, the big pustule swelled like a ball to a diameter of 6 inches. Zhong Nanshan could not even tie his shoelaces when he put on his cotton shoes. The knot could not even be covered by the leg of his pants. He could only bare it in the cold as he limped to work every day.

During the Spring Festival in the New Year, the Commune was closed for ten days. When the village cadres told Zhong Nanshan that he could go home for a few days, he finally got the chance to heal the pustule while he was in the city. He was very worried that the pustule was serious, and once osteomyelitis developed, he would have to have the foot amputated, making him disabled for the rest of his life. He would not be able to be an athlete or a doctor, and if he was disabled. Whenever he thought about it, he felt as if there was a huge boulder pressing against his shoulders. He was afraid that he would not be able to keep his foot any longer, so he borrowed money from a friend and immediately flew back to Guangzhou via Zhengzhou for medical treatment. Fortunately, after careful treatment, his foot was saved.

Another problem that Zhong Nanshan faced was his application to the Communist Party of China. At that time, applicants had to go through an extremely careful background check before joining the Party. Zhong Nanshan's father, Dr. Zhong Shi-fan, had joined the Nationalist Party before, and this could be a strike against him. He knew that there was no point being anxious. All he could do was to wait patiently while behaving to the best of his ability.

In March 1966, Zhong Nanshan was praised by the farmers because he showed perseverance in doing labor despite his illness. With their backing, he finally joined the Party, as he wished.

When Zhong Nanshan returned from Rushan County, he was still required to continue with his labor. He was the best performing member, but no matter how hard he tried, he could not become a Role Mode. This was because his family background determined his fate. At the time, he could not figure it out, but he refused to yield. He wanted to prove to everyone through his own efforts that one can be a good, positive person despite their family's political background. At the time, because he had been an athlete himself was in good physical condition, because he could not return to the teaching and researching for the time being, and because he had to continue to undergo labor reform, he decided to perform even better to prove himself the Party. While farming, when others carried one basket per turn, he would carry two.

He was overjoyed that he was appointed as PMU's Maoism Instructor. At just this time, though, the unprecedented Cultural Revolution swept across the country overnight, and set off an unbelievable upheaval at the university.

During the Cultural Revolution, Zhong continued to work hard to prove his positivity and responsibility. With the Party's emphasis on "Revolution and Productivity," most teachers had already returned to their teaching and researching posts, but Zhong Nanshan was still not trusted. The Party asked him to continue with the labor work and stay away from teaching. He endured in silence, with the firm belief that everything would be over soon.

7

SUFFERING, BUT UNYIELDING

During the Cultural Revolution, Zhong Nanshan protected numerous old experts and cadres when they were criticized. At the same time, he received the sad news that Liao Yueqin, his mother, had committed suicide in the face of injustice. To prove that he loved the Party and strove for positive progress, Zhong signed up to donate blood, but he almost died beside the boiler. Pain, torture, love, sadness, and all sorts of emotions threatened to drive him crazy.

In deep sorrow, Zhong Nanshan and his students traveled the path of the Red Army's Long March again. Later, he served for half a year as the PMU News editor, and then as a student instructor. In 1968, he worked in the boiler room for half a year. He recounted the times of upheaval and his difficult life.

In 1967, he tried his very best to return to Guangzhou and meet his wife Li Shaofen. Li conceived their first baby and gave birth to their son, Zhong Weide in 1968.

Before she went into labor, Li went to the train station with her father-in-law, Dr. Zhong Shifan, to pick up Zhong Nanshan, who had returned to Guangzhou from Beijing. There were still two weeks until her due date. Zhong Nanshan brought more than a dozen tins of milk powder back from Beijing. Li Shaofen gave birth to their son the morning after picking her husband up at the train station. She had been tired out standing at the crowded train station for too long. Their son, Zhong Weide, only weighed 2.5 kg when he was born.

Because of Zhong Nanshan's outstanding performance, the Revolutionary Committee of PMU assigned him the most "revolutionary" job: the boilerman. Although Zhong Nanshan longed to go back to his teaching post and dreamed of being a doctor, he knew that he was quite fortunate to be a boilerman during that time.

The boiler was an 8 connecters type. It was huge, and it consumed enormous amounts of coal each day. The boilerman had to keep shoveling coal into the combustion chamber. The boiler was extremely hot, and the temperature of the boiler room was barely tolerable, but Zhong Nanshan managed to get used to it. However, he had to clean the combustion chamber every day and scrape off the burnt slag with an iron pick. He could not stand the temperature there. It felt as if heat waves were pushing him away with the smoke and coal powder.

As a boilerman, he had to shovel dozens of kilograms of coal into the burning combustion chamber. This action had to be repeated countless times every day. Zhong Nanshan could already feel his stamina draining after a few days of work. This "Revolutionary" job challenged the limits of his body.

At that time, the annual Blood Donation Drive started. Registration was voluntary, but few people chose to volunteer, because malnutrition was rampant, and many were already weak even when they did not donate their blood. After blood donation, there was no guarantee that they would receive enough nutrition to compensate for their loss of blood.

Zhong Nanshan volunteered to donate blood. He watched 400 ml of blood flow from his body. According to the rules, he could take a few days of leave to rest, but he still reported for his night shift in the boiler room on the day he donated blood.

He did not expect that he would no longer be in control of his body. The empty shovel was too heavy for him to hold. He could no longer support his weak body, and he fainted in front of the boiler. The shovel handle knocked against his lower back the moment he threw the coal into the combustion chamber. Fortunately, he did not manage to get the coal into the chamber, otherwise the fire would have consumed him, causing serious burn injuries.

Since Li Shaofen gave birth to their son, Zhong Nanshan had tried very hard to go home and visit his family in 1969 and 1970, but the best he could do was to visit once per year.

Zhong Nanshan saw a child in the countryside who had a kidney problem and blood in the urine. When he returned home, he wanted his father, Dr. Zhong Shifan, to feel that he was improving, so he took the courage to "show off in front of the expert" and told Zhong Shifan what he knew about the treatment of renal tuberculosis. But the first thing Dr. Zhong Shifan said was, "How do you know it was renal tuberculosis?" There were many diseases that could manifest as blood in the urine. Renal tuberculosis might indeed lead to blood in the urine, but not all cases of blood in the urine point to this one disease.

Zhong Shifan corrected one of the most fundamental ideas of his son, who had just embarked on the path of medicine. This benefited him for the rest of his life. Dr. Zhong Shifan was always succinct. He emphasized to Zhong Nanshan repeatedly, "You must speak from evidence. This attitude toward medical practice became a lifelong exhortation to Zhong Nanshan.

"To speak for the truth" was a principle that had been infused into Zhong Nanshan's mind since he was young, and it shaped his life philosophy. In politics, speaking against truth would harm the interests of others. In medical science, it might cost actual human lives. Therefore, regardless of the field, politics or academics, whenever Zhong Nanshan wanted to convince others, he showed his supporting evidence.

Zhong Nanshan's truth-telling was mainly influenced by his father, and Dr. Zhong Shifan's image shed light on his whole life's journey. To speak the truth was to respect the facts and remain scientific. To speak the truth was to avoid distorting the standards of right and wrong.

Dr. Zhong's truthfulness was woven into every detail. The most typical example came during his lessons. When he taught his students, he emphasized, "To justify an idea, you must be careful to stay grounded and not simply repeat what others say." He also pointed out that this philosophy applied to social interactions. When he heard someone speak, he asked, "What's your reason for this?" He believed that this attitude was beneficial in many endeavors. "This is the foundation of my thinking, and it acts as one of my most important guiding principles."

In 1969, when Zhong Weide was a year old, Zhong Nanshan went to Kuancheng, Hebei with the decentralized medical team.

His classmate and best friend passed away only a few days after they reached the county. They were in the same medical team. When the team was trying to cross the river, his classmate, who was an excellent swimmer, thought that he could swim across the river. However, when he was about to reach the other side of the river, he screamed, "I can't grasp hold of anything!" He was then devoured by the waves.

There was a waterfall 200 meters away from the location. The current was strong, and the waters were rough. The medical team tried to find him. They sat in a small boat, which constantly swayed in the water. It seemed as if it would capsize at any time. A few days passed, but the classmate was never found again. The incident made

Zhong Nanshan particularly sad. He lamented that fate was ruthless and life was fragile.

The villagers in the county lacked a doctor and medicine. The situation was dire when they had an emergency or caught a serious illness. When Zhong Nanshan's medical team visited a village thirty kilometers away from the county, a farmer suffered from severe stomach pain and needed to find a doctor. At that time, Zhong Nanshan had joined the medical team as a cadre. He was inexperienced in clinical medicine, and thus could not treat this patient. The team had to bring Wang Haiyan, the team leader who came from the First Affiliated Hospital of PMU, from the county capital, but that was around 15 km away on an unfamiliar mountain path. The sun was about to set. What should they do? Zhong Nanshan, too worried about the patient to think too much, got onto an old clunky bicycle and rode to the county capital.

A section of the mountain path was extremely narrow, with a cliff right below. Zhong Nanshan later recalled that he must have been very blessed, or he would have died several times. When Wang Haiyan saw Zhong Nanshan, she took a look at the bicycle and got worried. It was so worn out, and they had to travel on the mountain. To make matters worse, she was quite plump. Zhong Nanshan said, "Don't worry. Sit at the back of the bike. I'll bring you there."

Zhong did not know where the mustered the strength from, but one thing for sure was that he was really worried that the patient might die any time. The next morning at around 2:00 am, they arrived and immediately treated the patient. But it was too late. The patient died later that morning. Zhong Nanshan blamed himself, saying, "Why couldn't I treat him?"

Decades later, when Zhong Nanshan met Dr. Wang Haiyan again, they talked about this incident. Wang Haiyan said that their lives really hung by a thread that night. A slight bit of carelessness would have caused both of their deaths that night. In hindsight, Zhong was fearful. He rode on that bumpy mountain path for sixty kilometers, back and forth, and it took him more than six hours.

When Zhong was sent to Kuancheng, Hebei, Li Shaofen was also sent to San-shui, Guangzhou for her countryside immersion. They only met once a year, and it was difficult to reach out to each other. They did not know if and when they would see each other at the end of the year. It seemed as if someone intentionally prevented them from meeting. Zhong had no sense of security, and he felt hopeless.

Dr. Zhong Shifan never asked if he had enough money or how much he earned. He cared about the progress in his career, he also helped his son financially, but in secret.

During the Cultural Revolution, Li Shaofen's maiden family also had its property confiscated. Both the Zhong and Li families were stripped clean, and they still had a little son to raise.

Finally, there came a piece of good news. At that time, the Guangdong Provincial Sports Team was led by the Military Administration Commission dispatched by the Provincial Military Area of Command. It reestablished the provincial basketball representative team. For the sake of her little son and the elders in her family, Li Shaofen, who was then 34 years old, put on her sports shoes again and restarted her basketball career. In this way, she managed to leave the countryside and return to Guangzhou.

During his recounting of these events, Zhong Nanshan did not indulge in the pain and sorrow of the past. For him, it seemed to be a normal experience. As he observed, talking about something that was not related to work counted as a break for him.

As he spoke, he rubbed his eyes, which were sore from overworking, and pinched his nose, which was sensitive to air conditioning. He also pressed his ears, seemingly relaxed.

From 1967 to 1971, Zhong Nanshan tried his best to visit his family once a year, but his heart was broken every time he left his house. When would he be back again? Everything seemed uncertain. His son Weide was so cute, so adorable. At home, apart from raising her child, Li Shaofen had to battle against all the pressure of supporting her parents and her in-laws.

In 1971, a heavy blow was dealt to Zhong Nanshan. It was this incident that caused him to leave Beijing.

In that year, PMU started to push for Revolution and Productivity. They started to recall the decentralized staff who had performed well and assigned them to teaching and research. That was good news for those in distress. Zhong Nanshan had been working very hard, but to his disappointment, because of the problem of his family's political background, his application to return to normal teaching and research was not approved. Zhong Nanshan had striven to perform well in his work, and he now felt as if he had fallen into an icy hole. When he was feeling hopeless, an accident happened to Li Shaofen. She was injured in one of her competitions, resulting in a concussion, and she had to stay at home and rest. The whole family was stranded, and her son and elders could not be taken care of. At that time, Hou Xiantang, Deputy Commander of Guangdong Military Area of Command and Party Secretary of Guangdong Sports Commission, who loved to nurture talent, went to visit Li Shaofen. He saw that there was only elderly folks and a child at home, and he asked Li Shaofen, "Where is your husband?"

"In Beijing," she replied.

Hou Xiantang immediately asked, "Why don't you ask your husband to come back? How can you always be separated like this?"

Li Shaofen, though still bed-ridden, was overjoyed. She nodded gratefully.

The military transfer order has to be obeyed. Zhong Nanshan loved Beijing very much, and he loved his colleagues who had worked together for more than ten years. However, after his experience in Beijing, he did not hesitate. He returned to Guangzhou the day after he received the transfer order.

He could not accept this defeat. How could he yield and retreat like this? That was not him.

When he looked back, there was so much joy, so many dreams. He chose to stay in Beijing, the heart of China, hoping to realize his ambition. However, in the end, his dream was lost, his wallet was empty, and his mind was shaken. He was too ashamed to meet his strict father, his loving wife, and his adorable son.

From the time of his marriage until he returned to Guangzhou in 1971, Zhong Nanshan had hardly done anything related to clinical work. That was eight years gone to waste. These eight years could have been the golden period for a man to achieve outstanding results.

Beijing was a place he both loved and hated.

8

STARTING HIS MEDICAL CAREER

The train slowly began to travel to its faraway destination. Zhong Nanshan sank into his memories. He thought of the teachers and students who were so sad to see him go, the friends who had been through all the obstacles with him, the career had been on an 8-year hiatus. Zhong Nanshan felt sorrow flushing through his heart like a turbulent river.

Eight years, all for nothing! He had achieved nothing.

When he returned to his hometown thousands of miles away and was faced with a new challenge – a hospital that could not have been more dilapidated – he did not retreat. Instead, he fought for change.

Guangzhou in early winter was so full of life and full of greenery. Facing this view, Zhong Nanshan subconsciously let down all his burdens.

Li Shaofen froze. Was that her dearest Nanshan, the man that she had been missing day and night? She could not say a single word. He was back? Was it real? They would never be apart again? She looked closely at her husband. He seemed to be ten years older than his actual age. He was dark and thin. His clothes had patches on top of patches, and he could not have looked any shabbier. His big eyes had once filled her heart with love and happiness, but now, full of misery. The only thing that remained unchanged was the light of persistence.

Zhong Nanshan looked so softly at his wife, who had dominated the sports field in her youth. She was still young, but life's ups and downs had left their mark on her face. She was burdened by fear, chores, and the responsibility of taking care of the family. And Zhong Nanshan knew that she bore all of these things for him.

Tears rolled down his face as he took his son from his wife's embrace. He suddenly felt a stream of energy rushing into his heart, making him feel warm and strong.

Dr. Zhong Shifan, who was now 70 years old, was extremely happy. He woke up early in the morning and changed into his best set of clothes. He stood in front of his son like a pine tree. He had spent all of his time writing his book.

Zhong Nanshan brought back his belongings. Piles of books in bags of varied sizes. They brought the books back from the train station on a tricycle and stored them in their relative's house, because their property was still at risk of another round of confiscation.

At night, Zhong Nanshan chatted with his father until late, telling him all the things he did and all he had seen while he was away. His father listened intently, then asked abruptly, "How old are you now?"

"I'm 35," replied Zhong Nanshan immediately.

"You're already 35? That's scary!" Dr. Zhong Shifan fell back into silence. Zhong Nanshan spent the whole night thinking about what his father said. He believed that his father meant, *You're already 35 years old, and you've achieved nothing,* but he was too nice to point it out directly. Even when he was 73 years old, Zhong Nanshan could not forget this reserved exhortation. Years later, when he was an accomplished doctor himself, Zhong Nanshan always said that his medical career only started when he was 35 years old.

Dr. Zhong pulled himself back from memories and pointed at something outside of the window. "Look at that construction site for the skyscraper. Three levels have been built." Half a kilometer from his window, the new 30-level Guangzhou Institute of Respiratory Diseases (now Guangzhou Institute of Respiratory Health) was taking shape. That was in the summer of 2009. At the end of 2009, the First Affiliated Hospital of Guangzhou Medical University and the Institute of Respiratory Health relocated into the new skyscraper from its previous tiny location.

But Dr. Zhong was not pointing at this new building. Instead, he indicated the hospital behind it, the old Guangzhou No. 4 People's Hospital. That was where he first started his medical career in 1971.

Every day, every moment of 1971 had been a test for Zhong Nanshan, being a new comer to the scene. He stumbled along his way, and he eventually managed to stand on his own two feet and stride forward with determination.

The Guangzhou No. 4 People's Hospital was the smallest, most dilapidated hospital in Guangzhou at the time. When Zhong Nanshan returned to Guangzhou, the Military Commander of Guangzhou asked him to pick the workplace that he preferred. He thought that Sun Yat-sen University Zhongshan School of Medicine was the best choice, but his father was working there. Furthermore, his father was still publicly denounced because of his political background, so it would be inappropriate for Zhong Nanshan to go there. His second choice was Guangdong General Hospital, an excellent hospital with good working conditions. However, the General Hospital was organizing for its doctors' decentralized countryside immersion. Zhong Nanshan and Li Shaofen had already been through too many separations and countryside immersions, so they did not want to do that all over again. They went through all of their options. In the end, Li Shaofen pointed randomly at this hospital a block away from their house, which had the smallest area and the worst conditions.

On his first day at work, Dr. Zhong Nanshan went down a small alley to the old, dilapidated Guangzhou No. 4 People's Hospital. The director of thoracic surgery wanted him to go to his department, and Zhong Nanshan wanted to be a surgeon. However, Dr. Sun Ping, Director of the Revolutionary Committee, said, "Zhong, you are too old to do surgery!"

Dr. Sun had read through Dr. Zhong's resume. He had never done clinical work and only went through three and a half years of university, and then started to work in a new biophysics department. Dr. Zhong knew nothing about clinical medicine. To put it frankly, he would be useless to any department that took him in. Although Dr. Sun chose not to be frank, his facial expression said a thousand words. Dr. Zhong would have preferred that he said it directly.

Nevertheless, Dr. Zhong had to be assigned to a post once he got into the hospital. Dr. Sun Ping planned to assign him to the medical department as an administrative secretary. Fortunately, two of Dr. Zhong's friends from the Internal Medicine department tried to persuade Dr. Sun. "Let's not do that," they said. "Don't make him do administrative work. We know he can't make it to the surgical department. Let's try him out in the internal medicine department." That's how Dr. Zhong was assigned to Internal Medicine.

He felt a great sense of disappointment when he reached the Internal Medical Clinic. There were only a few worn out stools in the clinic which doctors could sit on to see their patients. As he looked up, a wavering ceiling fan seemed to have been overworked for its entire life, and he thought it might fall any minute. Everything was shabby.

Dr. Zhong thought, *Is this place where I will end up? An old and worn out hospital? Do I have to learn a whole new discipline when I am already thirty-plus years old? And to learn that I had to be a disciple of another doctor. No! I will not yield to this situation! I have to achieve something greater and change this place!*

Since the day he left school and went to work, Zhong Nanshan had drawn valuable lessons from the wisdom he had been taught by his parents. Both of his parents would rather break than bend. He benefited from a good family upbringing, and he gained inspiration from his parents' life experiences. He has to adapt to society first, then he would be able to change it.

Throughout his life, he had never rested on his laurels or bowed to difficulties. This was a distinctive trait of Zhong Nanshan.

9

A LIFE LESSON

From the beginning of his working years, he yearned to be a doctor, but he was mercilessly mocked by the realities of life. He started to learn from scratch, like an elementary school student learning to read and write. At night, he drew his curtains and read his books slowly, as if he was enchanted by the knowledge.

Dr. Zhong said that in other countries, one could do the things they loved, work hard for it, and then contribute through effort. However, in China at that time, it was hard to do so. Dr. Zhong Nanshan was educated to work hard toward whatever goal the Party assigned to him, and he was indeed someone who would do just that.

Many people in China at that time accepted their job passively, forced themselves to become interested, and started from scratch. After two or three months in Internal Medicine, Dr. Zhong found the work too boring for him. All he could do was to prescribe some medicine. He asked to be transferred to the Emergency Room. Life in the ER was challenging. When he first transferred over, he knew nothing about the procedures, but he was willing to challenge himself.

One day, less than two weeks after Dr. Zhong transferred to the ER, the director of his unit, Dr. You Suzhen, asked him to go on ambulance duty. He was required to fetch a patient from Luogang, a suburb of Guangzhou. At that time, the hospital's ambulance was very slow; moreover, it was raining that day, and it took three hours to drive the twenty-odd kilometers to get to the patient.

The patient was an old tuberculosis patient who had to be brought to the hospital in the city. It was supposed to be a simple task, so Dr. You asked Dr. Zhong to deal with it. When he arrived, he saw blood around the patient's mouth. He did the usual treatment to stop the bleeding and carried the patient to the ambulance.

Halfway back to the city, about an hour and a half later, the patient started spitting blood again. Dr. Zhong took a look at the blood and saw that it was dark red. He rehydrated the patient and sent him to the tuberculosis ward located at Yuexiu District of Guangzhou.

Dr. You praised him when she saw him, "Good job."

Dr. Zhong left this patient in the ward and went home. It was already late, but he was happy, because that was the first time he had finished his task independently, and it went rather smoothly.

However, Dr. You approached him first thing in the morning and reprimanded him. "What kind of patient did you admit yesterday?"

Dr. Zhong said, "A tuberculosis patient."

"Wrong! Head to the ward now and get him back. He was vomiting blood, not coughing blood!"

It turned out that the patient was having gastrointestinal bleeding, instead of haemoptysis. Zhong Nanshan hurriedly transported the patient to the ER. The situation was dire, the patient started to spit huge amounts of blood when he reached the ER. The blood was bright red. His blood pressure was dropping to zero. Dr. Zhong was very nervous. He looked for a surgeon, who started to treat the patient immediately.

On the operating table, the patient's blood pressure was zero. The doctor pumped blood directly into the aorta to raise his blood pressure a little, then immediately began surgery.

The patient was also named Zhong, and he was about 40 years old. His abdominal cavity was opened, and it was found that a fish bone was lodged in a tiny artery, which was still bleeding. The patient was saved because emergency treatment measures were taken in time.

On the third day, someone complained to Dr. You that doctors like Zhong Nanshan should not be allowed to stay in the ER. He should be expelled.

During the Cultural Revolution, doctors talked and acted carefully to avoid getting "criticized and self-criticized," which might lead to exposure, denunciation, and criticism of each other. As such, Dr. You spoke to Dr. Zhong obliquely.

She said, "Dr. Zhong, you seem tired out from the work in the ER. Would you prefer that we transferred you to the outpatient clinic?"

Dr. Zhong Nanshan said anxiously, "I'm not tired, not at all. I think I am fine. There's no problem."

Dr. You could only smile bitterly. Dr. Zhong only learned later that Dr. You had to look out for him every day. The work in ER was too dangerous for Dr. Zhong to handle alone. She was afraid that a mistake from Dr. Zhong would cost the patients their lives.

Dr. Zhong was devastated. He had become a doctor, but he lacked the most basic medical common sense. He could not even differentiate gastrointestinal bleeding from haemoptysis. Haemoptysis was bleeding of the respiratory tracts, while gastrointestinal bleeding happened in the digestive system. They could be easily told apart from the color of the blood. The latter manifested as dark red blood, while the former was bright red. Dr. Zhong did not undergo clinical medical training, so he did not even know such basic things. This became a harsh lesson for him.

After that, Dr. Zhong started to learn with the humblest manner. He was attached to Dr. Yu, the Internal Medicine practitioner who helped him to save the patient to learn and study. Every time Dr. Yu treated a patient, Dr. Zhong paid careful attention to see how and why she treated the patients, as well as what kind of check-ups she prescribed to them. After learning from Dr. Yu, he went home and studied more. Because of the basic medical training he received, Dr. Zhong could understand why Dr. Yu prescribed certain tests. Dr. Zhong took notes on what each patient's examination indicated, why Dr. Yu made a diagnosis, what treatment plan she used, and so on.

In this way, Dr. Zhong studied diligently for three months, like a hardworking elementary school student, accumulating several large, thick books of notes and making very detailed records of each patient's treatment process. He improved very quickly, because he took it seriously. About three months later, he had gained some experience because, although the conditions of the patients in the ER were urgent, there were only a few types of illnesses: gastric bleeding, hypertension, cerebrovascular accident, and respiratory failure being the main ones. He soon noticed the pattern.

Three months later, the head nurse who had laughed at him said, "Dr. Zhong, you are much better now! You're at the level of a primary physician, aren't you?"

After that lesson, Dr. Zhong did make substantial progress.

Every afternoon after work, he borrowed the key from the technician. To see the electrocardiogram, he opened the door of the electrocardiogram room, drew the curtains, studied carefully, and gained the knowledge. Gradually, he learned to analyze the x-ray image, and he learned to diagnose.

When he began to do well in the ER, he asked to get into the wards, so that he could learn more. The Head of Internal Medicine told Dr. Zhong that they were full at the moment. If he got in, another doctor named Guo Nanshan would have to leave. The staff in Internal Medicine strongly disagreed. The two Nanshans were totally different! This Nanshan was useless, while Guo Nanshan was the backbone of the department. How could they switch him out? They were all against the idea that Dr. Zhong Nanshan move to the Internal Medicine wards. This incident was a slap to Dr. Zhong, making him dizzy and teary.

But he held on. He told himself that his colleagues could not be blamed for underestimating him. He could only blame his own incompetence.

He cheered himself up and continued to work hard in the ER. He was so careful and responsible that before long, he was regarded as a great doctor. He gradually gained his colleagues' appreciation and trust, and they started to entrust him with more independent tasks. But Dr. Zhong still longed to get into the wards.

FIRST STEPS IN MEDICAL EXPLORATION

There had been studies in the field of respiratory medicine in China on the physiology and pathology of lung function and heart and even the entire respiratory system in pigs, and the results had confirmed that the characteristics of pigs' respiratory system resembled that of human. This was the discovery of Dr. Zhong and his respiratory research team, and it kick-started Dr. Zhong and his team's climb in the field of respiratory medicine.

In the early 1970s, the level of respiratory disease research in China was very backward and did not receive the attention it deserved. There was not a single reputable research institution in this field in the country. In 1971, Premier Zhou Enlai recruited specialists from all over the country to treat respiratory diseases when Chairman Mao Zedong suffered from one. However, there was no such specialist in China at that time, and many large hospitals did not yet have specialized respiratory departments. As a result, Premier Zhou called on the national medical system to conduct research on group prevention and treatment of chronic bronchitis. It was at this time that Dr. Zhong took his first step in his glorious medical career.

The instructions from the central government came, but it was not clear who should be assigned for this job. No one wanted to do it, because everyone knew that the research on chronic bronchitis was futile. There was nothing to study, and no results would be produced.

A common saying at the time was, "Treat the cough instead of the asthma. If you try to treat the asthma, you'll never get promoted." The common belief at the times was that the chronic bronchitis could not be cured.

The Revolutionary Committee of Guangzhou No. 4 People's Hospital responded positively to the call from the higher levels, and they started organizing the establishment of a relevant department. An old professor, Dr. Hou Shu, was responsible for the treatment of chronic bronchitis patients at that time. Dr. Sun Ping, Head of the Revolutionary Committee, asked for one more person in the outpatient clinic, but no one wanted to go. In the end, he appointed Dr. Zhong, who had recently applied for an attachment in the Internal Medicine Outpatient Clinic.

It was true that Dr. Zhong had dreamed of being immersed in the Internal Medicine Department, but he didn't expect to be assigned to the Chronic Bronchitis Prevention and Treatment Team. Facing an "opportunity" like this, he hesitated.

But the hospital issued a transfer order. As a member of the Party, Dr. Zhong had to obey. Dr. Zhong always believe that when life gave him lemon, he could make lemonade. Since he had been transferred to this department, he would cultivate his interest and not give up. He chose to face obstacles with a challenging stance, as if the challenge was an opportunity bestowed by Heaven.

Who would have expected that this would become Dr. Zhong Nanshan's life pursuit? It had never been his intention.

Everything had to start from scratch. Dr. Zhong Nanshan's inquiry antenna reached into a variety of areas related to the treatment of respiratory diseases. It was during this period that he finally had the opportunity to learn about the therapies and theories of Chinese medicine and took any interest in them.

Once he transferred to the Respiratory Team, he found out through careful observation that the sputum of each patient was different. Some was yellow, some green, some foamy, and some sticky. He often squatted without thinking about it, allowing him to observe the sputum patients spat out.

Thanks to the biophysics discipline he worked on when he first graduated from university, he had experience in designing biochemical experiments. As such, he conducted a biochemical decomposition of the patient's sputum to gain understanding of its composition. Through this experiment, he learned that patients' secretions had different compositions, even though they suffered from the same disease, chronic bronchitis. Dr. Zhong thought that different treatments might be needed to deal with different conditions. At that time, they maintained contact with the TCM department and learned the comprehensive approach to the regulation of the internal organs of some Chinese medicines.

During this experience, Dr. Zhong learned the TCM approach to the treatment of respiratory diseases, and he developed his own understanding to the theories. Most importantly, he utilized these theories in his work.

Most important was the understanding he gained of the analysis of asthenia, excess, cold, and heat syndromes. In addition, he gained insight into the analysis of the *zang* and the *fu* (the Chinese categorization of internal organs). Chronic bronchitis was related to three organs, the lungs, spleen, and kidneys. To elaborate further, there were three types of chronic bronchitis caused by deficiencies in the lungs, spleen, and kidneys, and they had different manifestations.

Dr. Zhong combined TCM treatment with Western medicine's local symptom treatments, and he learned from his elderly mentor, Dr. Hou Shu. Based on Dr. Hou's research, Dr. Zhong adopted an herb, rhododendron amesiae, to facilitate the combined treatment. This approach proved to be more than 50% effective, an outstanding achievement.

While Dr. Hou, Dr. Yu Zhen, and Dr. Zhong were engaged in the research on the prevention and treatment of respiratory diseases, especially chronic bronchitis, in October 1976, the Central Party released the news that the Gang of Four had been toppled. The whole nation celebrated this news. The people and the Liberation Army organized grand gatherings and parades to celebrate this significant victory.

In 1977, a Delegation of Traditional Medicine from the WHO visited China. When they arrived in Guangzhou, they began to learn about TCM, and they came to the chronic bronchitis team of which Dr. Zhong was a part. Dr. Zhong and his teammates were knowledgeable about the combined Chinese-Western treatment of chronic bronchitis. They seized the opportunity and gave a thorough presentation to the delegation. After the presentation, the experts gave their results a high evaluation. The Guangdong Provincial Health Department began to look at the No. 4 People's Hospital in a new light. The hospital was small, but it had a group of able professionals.

This was an opportunity bestowed on Dr. Zhong by fate. Who could have imagined that this would prove to be such a grand opportunity? In fact, for most people, the assignment to the bronchitis team was an omen of defeat, not a sign of good fortune. But Dr. Zhong's lifelong career was established there.

After the WHO's visit, the Provincial Health Department suggested that the Respiratory Team could form a research institute. At the time, they belonged to a work unit called the New Medicine Department, which referred to a department that combined Chinese and Western approaches to medical treatment.

A ray of light finally fell on Dr. Zhong, the first since he returned to Guangzhou.

He realized the value he expected through his own hard work. He was very proud of this achievement.

The early conditions were difficult. Dr. Zhong recalled that they once resuscitated a patient with respiratory failure. They could not afford an imported ventilator, so they could only get a ventilator made domestically, either in Anshan or Tianjin. At that time, ventilators made in China broke down easily, sometimes failing to work after an hour, which required doctors to operate manually. At night, Dr. Zhong, Dr. Hou, and Dr. Yu rotated shifts. Dr. Zhong also became a good ventilator repairman.

Sometimes, at night, he would open the lid of the ventilator that has just started working "to see if there was any problem to deal with." This became Dr. Zhong's mantra. In fact, what he meant was, if there was a problem, he could quench his thirst for problem solving. Or rather, he was constantly expecting an opportunity to conduct further studies.

When the patients were asleep at night, the ventilator delivered air to them. If the air flow sounded even, that meant the ventilator was operating normally. Dr. Zhong would jump up from his chair beside the patient's bed to repair the ventilator as soon as he heard anything unusual in the sound of the air flow. That was the conditions in which they had to treat patients then. They once had to resuscitate a patient suffering from myasthenia gravis for seven whole days and nights, and they managed to nurse him back to good health. At that time, Zhong Nanshan and his team held the idea that they could not always rest on the status quo of stability and only seeing ordinary patients.

In such conditions, it was a miracle that Dr. Zhong was able to come up with new ideas every day. He thought their scope would be much-too narrow if they only treated chronic bronchitis. They needed to expand their treatments to emphysema, respiratory failure, and pulmonary heart disease, so that they could learn more things. He knew that his field of knowledge was too narrow, because he knew very little of clinical medicine. Later, in the course of his work, he met countless patients. Whether they were from respiratory medicine or internal medicine, Dr. Zhong paid much attention to the pathology of their diseases.

In order to broaden the field of their research and treatment and move beyond the specialization of chronic bronchitis, Dr. Zhong's team started to search for an animal that had a similar physical structure to the human. They found out that the heart of a pig most closely resembles that of the human heart, and the lungs of pigs were similar to human lungs. Most importantly, pigs could also develop pulmonary heart disease. They thus sourced for a very large pig and conducted their own experiments to study the physiological changes of pulmonary heart disease.

It cost some 200 yuan to buy a pig. Dr. Zhong and his colleagues managed to gather some money, and the hospital provided them with some funding as well. Through research on the pig, the future Institute of Respiratory Health started to take shape. This research played a large role in guiding future medical research. This small chronic bronchitis research team started to lead the most advanced level of scientific research in China at that time, and they made some of the most updated medical discoveries in the country.

Initially, they conducted observational studies of heart and pulmonary vascular function and changes in active mediators in the blood after hypoxia, and they had to anesthetize the pigs before intubating them. Dr. Zhong and his team slowly mastered these technical skills through experiments on the pig.

According to Dr. Zhong, this kind of research broadened the horizon of what was previously just a simple treatment of chronic bronchitis, and it inspired research on the whole respiratory system. Of course, the research level at that time was not advanced enough, and they hardly dared to dream of reaching world class levels, but they had, in fact, caught up and surpassed the highest levels in any related field in China. Dr. Zhong, Dr. Hou, and Dr. Yu had to rotate shifts at night and see patients in the day. Their only option for managing their work was to carefully divide the tasks between them. Once they had checked the wards, they conducted experiments on the pig when they were free.

The experiments on the pig were a milestone on their scientific journey. Others had rarely done such work, but Dr. Zhong had insisted on doing these experiments.

Dr. Zhong said that the key was that, through the experiments on the pig, they discovered the pattern of changes in the pulmonary artery based on different degrees of hypoxia. In addition, they observed changes in some mediators under hypoxia, like histamines and prostaglandins. Histamines were a chemical transmitter in the body that could affect many cellular responses, including allergies, inflammatory responses, and gastric acid secretion. It could also affect nerve conduction in the brain and cause diseases like pulmonary vascular hypertension. Histamines could be found in mast cells and also inside the mucosal tissues of the lungs, liver, and stomach. They played a very important role in the regulation of respiratory tract inflammation.

The research results were outstanding. At the National Conference on Respiratory Diseases held four years later, the results presented by Zhong Nanshan's research team were highly evaluated by experts. Several reports of the research results were subsequently published in national academic journals.

In March 1978, Chinese intellectuals ushered in the spring of science. With the support of the Party and the effort of scientific workers, the National Science

Conference was ceremoniously opened in Beijing. Dr. Zhong participated in this historical event as a representative of Guangdong Province. "Diagnosis and Treatment of Chronic Bronchitis by Integrating Chinese and Western Medicine and Typology," a paper co-authored by Dr. Zhong and Dr. Hou, won the Achievement Award at the National Scientific Conference. The congress was a summary of 22 years of scientific achievements (more than 7,600 awards, another 860 awards for progressive collectives, and 1,200 awards for progressive individuals) since the first nationwide scientific prize was awarded in 1956. Awards were not graded because the evaluation mechanism had not yet been established. Later, it was called the National Scientific Conference Achievement Award.

Most of the outstanding practitioners in the field of science and technology gathered in this conference. Since everyone was scattered in different corners of China due to their work, many scientists were very moved when they saw their old friends. During the conference, the scientists denounced the misdeeds of the Gang of Four and elaborated on the importance of science to the country and nation. Everyone enthusiastically expressed their confidence in the future development and progress of science and technology in China.

During the conference, Dr. Zhong read the documentary literature, "Goldbach's Conjecture," written by the renowned author Xu Chi. He was deeply touched by the spirit of the person featured in the book, Chen Jingrun, a mathematician who was enterprising, hardworking, dedicated, and unyielding, and who had been highly recognized in the field of mathematics. More impressively, Chen sat among the representatives of the National Scientific Conference.

Dr. Zhong could not settle in for a long time after the Conference ended. Chen Jingrun's thin but spirited image left him an impression so deep that he would never forget it.

11

FOUNDING THE INSTITUTE OF RESPIRATORY HEALTH

Assessing the broken and dilapidated equipment and rudimentary consultation rooms, Dr. Zhong came up with a surprising idea. He wanted to provide a one-stop solution to laboratories, wards, outpatient clinics, and a medical treatment base of chronic bronchitis. His colleagues were initially stunned, but soon, their eyes started to brighten. In fact, at first, the team only wanted to have a proper environment for their scientific research, but in fact, they were laying the foundation for a modern hospital. This period of their life was arduous, yet happy, and it must be mentioned here.

Guangzhou IRH traveled a long path, transforming from a small team dedicated for the treatment and prevention of chronic bronchitis into a laboratory of great national importance. In 1981, Dr. Yu Zhen left the IRH when her family relocated. Her life in the IRH became a fond memory for her, and she opened a private clinic in Macau. Dr. Yu Zhen was slightly older than Dr. Zhong Nanshan. As a well-read, affectionate woman who loved to write, she was the closest witness of the birth of Guangzhou Institute of Respiratory Health. This chapter was written by Dr. Yu Zhen in Macao in December 2000. It is presented here some slight modifications and citations, with great care taken to ensure it retains its truthfulness and friendliness. The team's experiences at that time have been brought to life back in her narration.

"I can't narrate the full process of the development of our IRH, but I can jot down some fragments of the history of its inception. I'd like to preserve this history and leave it for our subsequent generations, so that these anecdotes won't be forgotten when our generation passes on," the manuscript began. Dr. Yu gave the manuscript to Dr. Zhong at New Year, 2001. Since Dr. Zhong was certain to be remembered by history, Dr. Yu recorded this memoir mainly from his point of view. There are two sides of things, and often it takes many years before people can make a fair judgment of them. Dr. Yu firmly believed this.

Dr. Zhong Nanshan, the Director of the IRH, is well-known both in and outside the industry. He spent most of this life nurturing this institute, and although it might be too early to say, "I think it is not too much to give him the title of the Lifelong Honorary Director."

Dr. Zhong Nanshan was born into a medical family and graduated from the medical faculty of Beijing Medical College in 1960. After graduation, he stayed on for a period of time to do basic research and was transferred to the No. 4 People's Hospital in Guangzhou in 1971 to work as a clinician. I was one of the first who worked with Dr. Zhong after he started his medical career in Guangzhou.

Dr. Zhong came to work at the Guangzhou No. 4 People's Hospital and was assigned to the Internal Medicine clinic as an outpatient physician. At the morning meeting with his colleagues, where they first met, he humbly introduced himself, saying, "I used to work in the basic department, with little clinical exposure, and I was sat to the front line of the outpatient clinic quite suddenly, so I expect to run into many difficult problems. I would like to thank you all in advance for your kind help and guidance."

Dr. You Suzhen, who was in charge of the outpatient clinic, replied sagely, "Clinical experience needs to be accumulated through practice. In the past, you lacked some knowledge in this field, but you have more knowledge in other areas. This is your unique advantage. From now on, we can complement each other's strengths and weaknesses, learning from each other. I believe that we can do things even better."

It was a formality for new colleagues to introduce themselves. People were tired of the same old introductory lines. However, these two lines of improvised dialogue feel like they were said just yesterday to me. There are two reasons. First, it was unusual for someone to be transferred from a basic department to a clinical department, and second, this conversation did not turn into empty words, as proven by the subsequent events.

The words that Zhong Nanshan said as part of his introduction were not an attempt to appear humble. They were sincere, and they came out of a deep self-understanding.

Two months into his new job, Dr. Zhong's dark, strong, athletic physique shrank by more than a size. A lively man with a round face, shining eyes, and a smiling expression became a stern, gaunt man who appeared pensive even as he walked. His white coat, which was once tight on him, started to hang loosely. He began to look like an unearthly doctor.

Outsiders did now know what happened. They kept asking us whether there was something wrong with his health. However, those who paid attention could see that, in addition to going to work on time, Dr. Zhong spent most of his time off in the X-Ray room, ECG room, library, and other similar places in an effort to absorb more knowledge and grow into a mature clinician as quickly as he could.

Some might not know that Dr. Zhong, a graduate of PMU, was the athlete that broke the national record in the Men's 400 Meter Hurdles in the qualifying stage of the first National Games in 1959. His motto was, *Wake up as soon as the rooster wakes up, and train as soon as you open your eyes.* He woke up early each morning and never procrastinated. During this period of rapid transition in his work, from Beijing to Guangzhou and beyond, he continued to follow this motto. He never gave himself a chance to rest.

Apart from being diligent, he was always active in his thinking. He sought new ideas, stayed open-minded, and was proactive in asking questions whenever he was in doubt. To him, he always had to search for an answer for his questions. He was good at finding the merits of others, so as to trigger his own inspiration and improve himself. Looking back at the opening statement of his first day in the outpatient clinic, the truthfulness of his words is evident.

Moreover, his "unique advantage," as mentioned by Dr. You, was maximized by Dr. Zhong. It can be concluded that this unique advantage helped him become one of the core figures of IRH.

After a year of working in the outpatient clinic, he was transferred to the Chronic Bronchitis Prevention and Treatment Team, which later developed into the Guangzhou IRH. The founder and the first director of the team was Dr. Hou Shu, so we still call Dr. Hou Shu the founder of IRH.

In 1972, the team lead by Dr. Hou started to gain its prestige in building the animal research model of chronic bronchitis and experimental therapy. Nearing the end of the Cultural Revolution, the Education and Healthcare system started to optimize their organizational structure and improve the level of science and technology. The group was able to increase its manpower, expand its organization, and strengthen itself by virtue of this opportune wind.

After joining this team, Dr. Zhong immediately drafted a grand plan in line with the trend of the times. To begin with, the research and treatment of chronic bronchitis, emphysema and pulmonary heart disease were to be integrated. In addition, the animal experimental research and clinical research would be integrated. And finally, the laboratory, wards, outpatient clinics, and a medical base for chronic bronchitis in the suburbs of the city were to be integrated. This meant additional manpower, equipment, and space for development. Probably any enterprising person, including Dr. Hou, would have had these ideas, but they would have likely given up sooner or later, given how difficult it was to achieve anything in China during that time. But Dr. Zhong did not give up. He kept going until the end, which was why he succeeded.

He made full use of his favorable conditions, including his Party membership and his polished interpersonal network. He lobbied for people, goods, and houses, though monetary issues only came in later, because they were not very useful at first.

He first presented the advantages and disadvantages to his superiors and eventually got support for the plan. Then, thanks to the fact that the Cultural Revolution was coming to an end, the East No. 1 Medical Zone, which had held study classes for many years, was vacated. That was a must-have place for hospitals, so it was not readily available.

As such, the Chronic Bronchitis Prevention and Treatment Team finally had its independent outpatient clinic and wards, and they could finally start its clinical research. It was small, yet complete.

The opening of the ward required a good deal of manpower and material resources. Many people contributed ideas the team's critical points. A few months after Dr. Zhong was transferred to the team, someone unofficially told Dr. Yu Zhen that she would be transferring to another team to do research work. This confused her. "Who am I? Not long ago, I was regarded as a 5.16 Member To-Be and was reviewed repeatedly." Dr. Yu's file had always stated that she was a "problematic person" to be used only carefully. Although she was a skilled physician with more than ten years of experience in internal medicine and a versatile woman who was often jokingly referred to as a talent, who would dare to transfer her to that position? She had no experience in research work. There was no proof that she could make any achievement. Should she fail, it would not only damage the reputation of this newly established team, but the referrer would be accused of favoritism and harboring the "black sheep" as well. At the very least, he would be accused of fatuity and improper use of human resources.

Dr. Yu never learned who transferred her to the team, and no one mentioned anything about it to her. With profound respect and humility, she began her research on respiratory disease and became a specialist in pulmonary heart disease.

When her old colleagues from the Department of Internal Medicine saw her, they always smiled and said, "My dear expert, why have you lost so much weight? You are under a lot of stress, right?"

That was indeed the most stressful period in Dr. Yu's life. The pressure not only came from her work, but also her own expectations. The pressure was intangible, and it came from someone else – the anonymous person who transferred her to this team out of good will.

During the Cultural Revolution, Dr. Yu lived in the cowshed, isolated with her family and without a salary. When she first moved to Macau, she was without a job. At the beginning of her career in Macau, her income was unstable and her future was uncertain, but not of this made her feel the heavy pressure that she felt when she was in the Chronic Bronchitis Prevention and Treatment Team, because it is easy for one to be in debt to oneself, but heavy to be indebted to someone else, especially someone who had expectations of you. "I felt like a horse that has been bet on, having to keep all four hooves busy." Yu Zhen often said, laughing at the metaphor of herself being a soldier crossing a river – one who could only move desperately forward. It was not until a decade later, after Dr. Yu left the IRH, that she learned that her referrer was none other than Dr. Zhong Nanshan.

"Now that I look back, how did he find the courage to recommend me?" Dr. Yu pondered. She had only been a colleague with Dr. Zhong Nanshan in the outpatient clinic for a year. She was assigned to him for political education. Dr. Zhong knew Dr. Yu's background well, but he was not one to stereotype. Dr. Zhong knew how to use talent, and he discovered many talented individuals for the IRH.

It should be said that the success of this stage mainly resulted from the harmony of the people, and the key to this harmony was Dr. Zhong Nanshan's open-mindedness and his ability to handle complicated matters. "That's why I said that Dr. Zhong was a 'giant red umbrella' who protected me well," Dr. Yu said years later, recalling her strongest impression of Dr. Zhong Nanshan.

12

CHARTING THE UNKNOWN

Leading his Respiratory Team, Zhong Nanshan started with nothing, but in the simplest environment and the shortest amount of time, he conducted a solid exploration and achieved the amazing result of founding a respiratory department with a basic medical research environment in China. The founding of the IRH was a systematic process and a real-life legend, because it was built from nothing, but became one of many.

With Dr. Zhong as the umbrella, Dr. Hou and Dr. Yu were able to avoid many distractions and concentrate on their research. The achievements of this period of time were conducted by this trio, and they had the same mind and worked hard together.

Dr. Hou Shu and Dr. Yu Zhen were very aware of the pressure Dr. Zhong was under during this period. If it were someone else, he might have retreated and given up. Without his persistence, in those days, there would be no IRH today, but those who did not experience that era might feel difficult to understand what it was like.

When the team was first founded, everything needed to be built from scratch. Being an all-rounder, as he always had been, Dr. Zhong aptly positioned himself as a jack-of-all-trades and master of all-rounders. He filled whichever post needed him, and his relatively deeper basic medical knowledge came in handy.

To engage in respiratory disease research, the first priority was experimental data on lung function. In the Chronic Bronchitis Prevention and Treatment Team, Dr. Hou found an obsolete spirometer in the warehouse, which could roughly yield data on pulmonary ventilation function. When it came to further information on the patient's blood oxygen level and partial pressure of carbon dioxide, additional equipment was necessary. At that time, the global standard was to use automatic micro blood-gas analyzers, which were convenient and accurate. However, they had to be imported, and they were incredibly expensive, so only a few were available in China. Although Dr. Zhong Nanshan and the others had great ambitions, thinking that they would eventually be able to use something expensive as this, for the time being, they could not put out a nearby fire using distant water.

In 1973, when the National Pulmonary Heart Disease Conference was set to start, the fledgling group had to come up with a paper of significant value in order to situate themselves in the forefront of national research. At that time, without advanced equipment, it was difficult to talk about research breakthroughs, and they urgently needed to conduct triglyceride analysis. Fortunately, they found another broken oximeter in the warehouse.

With great enthusiasm, Dr. Zhong went to Shanghai a few times with this broken machine to visit Dr. Li Huade, an expert in respiratory medicine. After several eventful trips, Dr. Li was persuaded to help, and they fixed the machine, though it was very difficult to do so. When Dr. Zhong returned with this treasured item in his arms, they felt like they had won a huge battle. They were so happy that they cried and laughed, but when they thought of the more significant battle on the following day, the laughter stopped.

From fixing the machine to testing the data, the laboratory did a series of work before attempting clinical use of the oximeter. All of this work was the basis for the establishment of the respiratory laboratory, and without Dr. Zhong's pioneering work, there would have been no clinical research.

A similar thing happened with the establishment of the carbon dioxide partial pressure measurement method. At that time, almost all pulmonary research units were struggling with the lack of relevant instruments. Zhong Nanshan and his team could not sit and wait. Dr. Zhong and Dr. Hou painstakingly studied the evolutionary history of the spirometer and decided to use past approaches to tackle present challenges, borrowing the method of repeated respiratory gas analysis to calculate the partial pressure of arterial blood carbon dioxide. This method required several key instruments. One was a gas analyzer to analyze the carbon dioxide content of the patient's exhaled gas. The other was an oxygen bag and a three-way switch connected to the patient's airway. Unfortunately, these were not readily available.

If it was not for Dr. Zhong's understanding of basic medicine, these problems could not have been solved by clinical knowledge alone. He searched around and ended up borrowing a gas analyzer no longer in use by a basic laboratory at the Guangzhou Medical College, and he put much effort into modifying it to suit their measurement needs. With the help of the mechanical room and a machine shop with which he was acquainted, after repeated design and modification, Dr. Zhong managed to create a three-way copper connector that could adapt to frequent changes in temperature and humidity without rusting and without lubricant, and which could change its switching mode smoothly.

While other hospitals were hindered from new research progress due to the lack of blood gas analyzers, Dr. Zhong and his team took advantage of this obsolete method to write a series of research papers on pulmonary heart disease that provided blood gas information. Although their method was questioned by the growing trend of promoting new sophisticated foreign machines, their originality and self-reliance under the conditions of the time made their group highly visible in the Guangzhou area. Moreover, although they had been preceded by the research groups of the First Affiliated Hospital of Sun Yat-sen University Zhongshan School of Medicine and Guangdong Provincial People's Hospital in terms of seniority, their group eventually stood out because of their diligence in research. When the Guangzhou provincial government intended to develop a municipal respiratory disease research institute, the opportunity finally came to this group of people who had worked so hard to prepare themselves. It was at this point that Dr. Zhong began his years-long work in coordination.

In terms of arranging research topics, both Dr. Zhong and Dr. Hou paid close attention to domestic and international trends and did their best to catch up. They were the first in the Guangzhou area to use the fibrinoscope and to use it for the treatment of respiratory diseases. From applying for foreign exchange to ordering, from traveling to Hangzhou to learn how to use it to setting up the fibrinoscopy room, Dr. Zhong did everything himself. As for the long-awaited automatic micro triglyceride analyzer, the new spirometer that Dr. Hou Shu dreamed of and the new respiratory machine that was updated with each generation, not a single one failed to be obtained by Dr. Zhong Nanshan, all with great effort and eloquent persuasion. Things then were very different from what they are today, when it is easy to purchase anything as long as the funds are allocated from the government. It is hard to imagine how these things could have been obtained without Dr. Zhong's persistence.

With solid work with clinical and scientific research sitting like two wings on either side of them, Dr. Zhong and his colleagues were able to write a number of high-quality scientific papers. At that time, medical journals had just started to resume normal publication, and there were many rules and regulations. Dr. Zhong and his team were the first to publish two papers in the *National Medical Journal of China* and the *Chinese Journal of Internal Medicine* in 1974 and 1975, filling the gap in which no papers had been published in national-level medical journals in Guangzhou for many years.

According to Dr. Yu's recollection, the IRH had matured a long time before it was officially listed. After the listing, Zhong Nanshan was appointed as the Director, and Dr. Hou Shu was named Deputy Director.

Before that, Dr. Hou was the administrative head. Although Dr. Zhong did not have an administrative position, he was in effect the soul of the organization. Besides taking care of all the chores of upward and outward liaisons and being placed in charge of laboratory operations, he also went on rounds in the ward, rescued critically ill patients, worked the night shift, and discussed difficult cases. Dr. Zhong Nanshan observed relatively early on that among the comorbidities of respiratory failure was the phenomenon of diffuse intravascular coagulation and two different manifestations of pulmonary encephalopathy, acidosis and alkalosis. Observing patterns from these clinical phenomena required patience, keen observation, and critical thinking skills. These were summarized by Dr. Zhong, who gathered wisdom from many schools of thought.

Numerous respiratory failure patients were successfully resuscitated, and Dr. Zhong was always involved in the process. In particular, during the fibrinoscopy of a patient with a persistent cough suspected to be lung cancer, after careful observation, Dr. Zhong removed a few chicken bones from his right main bronchus, thus curing the disease that had plagued the patient for years. This was a pioneering use of fibrinoscopy for treatment in China.

Many people did not understand the inside story and thought that Dr. Zhong had little clinical experience and that the clinical achievements of the IRH had little to do with him. In fact, he also devoted himself to clinical work, and he achieved many things. At the time that he took on the role of director, there was no doubt that he was more than competent in both the basic and clinical fields.

Before concluding her memoir, Dr. Yu said she wished she could collect the early artifacts of the IRH and establish a museum. It was probably a very old-fashioned thing to "recount the hardships and think of the sweetness," but with the relentless forward progress of history, those who work in research today are very different from those who did so decades ago, and recalling the lessons of these pioneers can help today's medical workers anticipate the future.

Dr. Wu Hua joined the Guangzhou No. 4 People's Hospital in the 1970s and was transferred to the Department of Respiratory Medicine (today's GRS) in 1995.

Like Dr. Yu, she was Dr. Zhong's old work partner, colleague, and friend.

As a member of the Chronic Bronchitis Prevention and Treatment Team who joined later than Dr. Yu Zhen, Dr. Wu spoke in her interview about the founding of IRH. She said that they wanted to do some research in the beginning, but "there was really no place." Later, they started doing experiments in the doctor's office, and they had to move stools and tables away to make space.

Everyone shared the same office, and they had specific duties, assigning who needed to collect what kind of data and what they needed to do. It was very difficult, and they always had to stay up late, go home late, and return to work as usual during the day, without extra allowances, bonuses, or overtime pay. It was a tiring yet happy time.

When Dr. Zhong led his team, he often used his own money to buy food for everyone to eat and soda for everyone to drink. They were happy, because they were still very young, energetic, and idealistic, and they wanted to achieve something in their career.

Usually, the hospital canteen served meals, and they ate there together. There was a stall next to the hospital that sold a very famous, delicious snack, and they loved to buy it. Whenever there was an animal experiment, they pooled their funds to buy something special. That was indeed a period of pure happiness, when they were a united collective. Even if Dr. Zhong had not paid for the meal, others were willing to pay. They were happy together. Dr. Wu observed, "In retrospect, it was really hard at that time, and the environment was poor, but surprisingly, we survived."

Under these conditions, Dr. Zhong attached great importance to the cultivation of talent. For example, in order to encourage scientific research, regardless of the fact that the bonuses of laboratory personnel in other hospitals were much lower than those of doctors, he advocated for the same bonuses for scientific researchers to those of clinicians, the same for laboratory directors as those of clinical department directors, and the same technicians as those of attending doctors in their collective. That has remained the case for many years since.

13

TRAVELING TO THE UNITED KINGDOM

The international train raced from the north of Beijing toward Moscow like a thick black pencil trace. Nine days after its departure, Dr. Zhong Nanshan arrived in England. He had been sent to England for further studies abroad. As the train entered the Federal Republic of Germany, all passengers had to be checked, and the laundry powder carried by Dr. Zhong's party was suspected of being heroin.

Dr. Zhong was the leader of this group of sixteen Chinese students. It was the 1970s. The train rocked slowly, and the carriages were filled with the smell of diesel fuel. As much as he felt uneasy as he left his motherland to head for a strange place, Dr. Zhong also felt that his horizons had broadened greatly with his first international trip.

The train left Beijing, entered Inner Mongolia, crossed the Mohe, and passed Lake Baikal. Amid the serene snowy weather, the train went past lake after lake. On October 20, 1979, Dr. Zhong celebrated his 43rd birthday. He rejoiced. When he thought about it, there had been more than a decade that he did not feel this kind of pure happiness. His fellow friends celebrated his birthday and held a party on the train.

Dr. Zhong was scheduled to study at the Royal Infirmary of Edinburgh (ERI) in the UK. The sixteen students had been sent abroad by the government after the beginning of Reform and Opening Up. They came from a wide range of fields. One was the dean of an aeronautics institute, some were mathematicians, and some were atomic scientists. Many of them became academicians of the Chinese Academy of Sciences or Chinese Academy of Engineering. China was experiencing a tight financial situation, so they did not fly, but instead took international trains.

In Moscow, the train stopped for half a day so that everyone could visit Lenin's Mausoleum. The train then entered Poland and Germany. It entered East Germany, the German Democratic Republic, first, and then crossed the Berlin Wall, preparing to enter West Germany, the Federal Republic of Germany. Suddenly, all the passengers on the train were told to get off for immediate inspection.

The sixteen Chinese students had too much luggage with them. Because of their financial constraints, they were worried about their living costs abroad. Each of them brought a good deal of tissue paper, and their huge luggage bags were stuffed with laundry powder. They carried several large bags, each with a tightly fastened zipper, and were all locked. As the leader of the group, Dr. Zhong helped everyone to stuff their huge bags into the luggage rack, under the bed, and in every corner where a piece of luggage could fit.

As soon as the doors opened, tall, fierce police dogs jumped up and sniffed. It was so nerve-wracking that the air seemed to have frozen. The Germans feared that some passengers were smuggling heroin, and they checked their luggage.

It was surprising that the Chinese had brought so much laundry powder, and Dr. Zhong had brought the most. The sixteen Chinese students were immediately detained.

The Germans could not understand Chinese, and none of the students could speak German. The sixteen of them froze, not knowing what to do. The train would depart in a few minutes. The German train captain and policeman stared at them suspiciously.

The laundry powder was torn open packet by packet, and the Germans questioned them over and over. Dr. Zhong was anxious and apprehensive. He could not imagine how heavy a blow he would face if this trip failed. Moreover, this was not only his personal business! Nervously, Dr. Zhong said loudly in his inarticulate English, "Washing powder!"

"Washing powder?" The German policeman, with piercing eyes, examined Dr. Zhong, who looked very sincere. He dipped his index finger into the white laundry powder, held it next to his lips, and shook his head. "Washing powder." He repeated the phrase in an approving tone.

The train was about to depart. The laundry powder was scattered all over the place.

"We desperately stuffed the scattered laundry powder back into our bags and dragged them onto the train. I was overwhelmed because I was in charge," said Dr. Zhong.

The train made across West Germany and then to the Netherlands. After that, they took a ship across the English Channel.

They were greeted by staff from the Embassy of the People's Republic of China in the United Kingdom of Great Britain and Northern Ireland. Dr. Zhong, who was in the best of health, fell ill at their destination because of the unusual shock and exertion he had endured. The other fifteen students with him were particularly grateful to him. They maintained close contact with him even many years later.

The first thing the sixteen of them did after arriving in London was not to meet with experts, but to study English at Ealing College in West London for about three months.

Ealing College, now named as Ealing, Hammersmith and West London College, was founded in 1843, a history of almost 200 years. It was one of the largest and best attended institutions of higher education in the UK and the world, training countless professionals, scholars, and business elites who exerted a huge influence in various fields all around the world.

At that time, Dr. Zhong and his fellow students knew almost nothing. A specialist who studied with him and later worked at the Cancer Hospital of the Chinese Academy of Medical Sciences, Yin Weibo, was a radiotherapist and could speak English a bit more fluently than the rest. Together, they learned to listen, speak, and express themselves. Although they had undergone intensive English training at home, they were still unable to speak well when they first arrived in the UK.

The teacher liked Zhong Nanshan and Yin Weibo best because they were the most doctorly and caring, and when they saw that the teacher was not feeling well, they advised him what medicine to take. It was arranged for Dr. Zhong to stay in the house of an old English lady, living and dining together with the English people. What they normally ate was simple Western food, which Dr. Zhong Nanshan was not used to. The other student who stayed with Dr. Zhong in the old lady's house was Fan Mingwu, an expert in atomic energy research.

Normally, Dr. Zhong always hoped to introduce some of his successful experiences to other doctors and to society at large, so that more people could take the quickest path to success. He said over and over that Chinese students should not take learning English as a daunting chore. He used himself as an example, saying that he was bad at listening when he first arrived in the UK. However, the most important thing if he hoped to learn English was to be able to listen, and only after learning to listen could he communicate with others, so listening was the most critical ability. He spent an hour every night listening to English tapes. Afterwards, he wrote down every sentence he heard. If there were sentences that he really could not understand, he would ask a friend or colleague to help translate the meaning of the words. He filled up three thick notebooks with notes. After three months of hard work on his listening, he finally made great progress.

Later, he wrote a special article about his experience in learning English, which was published in Hong Kong's *Ta Kung Pao.* He said that the biggest problem of Chinese people faced when learning English was that they were afraid to speak up, to ask questions, and communicate, making them come across as very introverted. Dr. Zhong dared to speak up and had the courage to push himself to the front even under unfavorable circumstances. For example, every time he discussed a patient case, he saw his courage to ask questions as a victory. In this way, he slowly ascended in a short time and became a fluent English speaker who could communicate with the world.

A MOVING SPEECH

Who would have thought that Dr. Zhong Nanshan, who was not good at English, would quickly become a master speaker? While taking his English course, he wrote a letter to his mentor, Professor David Flenley, expressing his hopes of getting his supervision. Flenley was a famous chronic disease specialist in the UK. Dr. Zhong had never met him, but had read his articles and admired him very much. However, after a month or so, there was no reply from Flenley.

He finally received a response. The letter read, "As according to the law in the UK, Chinese medical qualifications are not recognized. Therefore, you are not allowed to see patients alone when you come to the hospital for further training. You can only observe the laboratory and the wards. Based on this, it is obvious that the two years you want to further your training with us is too long. We can take you on for at most eight months. Any time longer than that is not appropriate for you or for us. You should contact the British Cultural and Educational Association and consider where to go after eight months."

Dr. Zhong felt a bucket of cold water had been poured on him, and he was immediately overwhelmed by its coldness. Judging from Professor Flenley's tone, it seemed that there was no room for negotiation. According to the UK view, when a Chinese doctor traveled to the UK, they were merely coming for a visit. Further, Dr. Zhong read between the lines that Flenley was very suspicious of his research methods.

Zhong Nanshan sat down and analyzed the situation calmly. Professor Flenley do not know enough about China, and he could not understand the articles Dr. Zhong had written in Chinese. Therefore, it was important to not get discouraged.

After further consideration, Zhong Nanshan decided to pay Flenley a visit in person.

It was snowing heavily in Edinburgh. For someone in a relaxed mood, the snowflakes in a foreign country would have appeared romantic and passionate, but Dr. Zhong felt nothing but extreme coldness and a heavy mental burden that was almost too much to bear.

Just after New Year's Day in 1980, Dr. Zhong took a train from London to Edinburgh. Another Chinese student, Ma Jianquan from Sun Yat-sen University in Guangzhou, who had been studying in Edinburgh for more than a month, went to the train station to pick him up. Although it was the first time they met, Ma Jianquan kindly took him to his rented room. The next day, they arranged for an appointment with Flenley.

The appointment with Professor Flenley was at 10:00 am. Zhong and Ma arrived at 9:30, and Flenley's secretary, Alice, gave them a seat and asked them to wait.

When they were shown in, Flenley sat opposite them in a tall-backed executive chair. He did not turn around. Dr. Zhong could sense the characteristic arrogance of this Englishman. There was a dead silence as Flenley kept making his own coffee, his back facing them.

"Doctor Zhong," asked Flenley with confusion, still not turning back, "what do you want from me?"

Dr. Zhong froze for a moment and spoke to the professor's back about his plan. Before coming to Edinburg, Dr. Zhong Nanshan had rehearsed his request. Flenley replied, "Spend a month observing our wards and laboratories before you plan for anything." The implication was that Dr. Zhong was there to visit. What else could he hope to do?

Although the conversation was short, the wise Dr. Flenley sensed the persistence of the Chinese man behind him. He wanted to achieve his purpose of doing research in the UK. He said something that helped Dr. Zhong tremendously. "You have a friend from China. You might look for him." He was talking about was Dr. Zhu Junlong, who came to advance his studies under the WHO's sponsorship.

Through the seven or eight minute meeting, Zhong Nanshan felt that he had received a gift from Professor Flenley: His suggestion that Dr. Zhong meet the Chinese man who came to advance his studies under the WHO's sponsorship was a valuable one.

British experts might be arrogant, but in the face of science, they harbored no racial prejudice. On January 5, 1980, Professor Flenley saw Dr. Zhong in the classroom, and Dr. Zhong hurried forward to greet him. Flenley grew suddenly thoughtful. He looked at Dr. Zhong with gleaming eyes and asked, "Could you talk about healthcare in China?"

Dr. Zhong understood every word that Flenley said. "OK!" he replied almost instantaneously. The depression and anxiety in his heart seemed to have dissipated.

However, what followed was the heavy pressure to prepare for a speech in less than a month. What should he prepare for? Chinese medicine and treatment was a combination of TCM and modern medicine, so where should he start? Further, the knowledge system was so vast and profound, so what should he introduce? Even worse, his English level was not up to the task of giving such an important lecture in front of fifty to sixty people. But could he say no? Never! That was not who he was. No matter how much pressure he had to bear, he could not give up in the face of a challenge. That was not the way of Zhong Nanshan.

"I did not know why I had so much courage. He asked me to talk, so I did. This is who I am. If you give me an opportunity, I will take it." Looking back, Dr. Zhong was still full of confidence.

But in the moment, he was unsure if he could do it. Usually, a person would not have accepted a request, such as Flenley's because the pressure would be unbearable. But Dr. Zhong was motivated by a single belief. He could not let foreigners underestimate the Chinese, and he needed to introduce the advantages and practicalities of traditional Chinese medicine to them.

The initial draft of his speech had about 8,000 words. He prepared slides that focused on the characteristics of respiratory diseases in China and their treatments, including Chinese medicine. He also asked Mr. Zhu, who lived in the same dormitory as him at the time, to correct and revise the draft for him. Mr. Zhu was a lecturer in the English Department of Fudan University in Shanghai. Mr. Zhu carefully corrected the grammatical errors and said to him with some concern, "You have to write the draft well first, indeed. But the key is to speak in a way that others can understand."

Dr. Zhong adopted a "stupid" method – he tried, as far as he could, to recite all 8,000 words. He never stopped reciting his draft. He did it while he ate, before he slept, and during his bathroom breaks. He did not waste a single second.

About a month later, on the eve of Chinese New Year, Dr. Zhong's speech began. The classroom was full of teachers and students. Professor Flenley introduced Dr. Zhong to the audience, saying, "Let's welcome Dr. Zhong Nanshan, a doctor from China. He will be speaking to us about the current state of healthcare in China."

Dr. Zhong took the slides and lecture notes he had made and walked to the podium. He couldn't help but feel nervous. His hands shook a little.

The presentation started from traditional Chinese medicine. He talked about the similarity in diagnostic methods of Chinese medicine and Western respiratory medicine, how TCM physicians observed the patient's tongue, and theories of how TCM and western medicine were similar. He said that when a patient with pulmonary heart disease had an acute attack, and in the absence of an arterial triglyceride analysis of the patient, one could borrow a diagnostic method from TCM, observing the color of the patient's tongue as a way to determine the patient's hypoxia and acid base balance. He also explained other aspects, such as the ancient Chinese practice of acupuncture anesthesia, which was a uniquely Chinese medical practice that had long been used in clinical treatment in China.

Dr. Zhong had recited his speech day and night before the event, so he knew it by heart. He soon relaxed from the initial nervousness when he saw that everyone was captivated by his speech. The more he spoke, the more confident he became. Half an hour passed before he knew it. When he finished speaking, the whole room resounded with thunderous applause.

The doctors participated actively in a Q&A session, asking questions regarding the presentation. Sir Crofton, an emeritus professor, took the initiative to go to Dr. Zhong and said, "Dr. Zhong, you gave a very good presentation. When may I invite you over to my house for a discussion?"

Dr. Zhong happily agreed. He felt as if he had won a big battle. His hard work had not been in vain.

In this presentation, all of the research done by the IRH came in handy. From 1971 to 1978, he studied the treatment of chronic respiratory diseases and respiratory failure of the Chinese people. Why did Dr. Zhong dare to talk about his research in front of these British experts? Even if he had memorized the speech, it might merely be showing off a shallow knowledge before experts.

The reason he was so bold was that he remembered one thing. A few days before his presentation, Dr. Zhong had been given the opportunity to visit the wards. When he reached the wards for tracheal diseases, a doctor named Chartraw was performing fiberoptic bronchoscopy on a patient. He asked Dr. Zhong, "Have you seen this?"

Dr. Zhong replied humbly, "Yes, I have."

Dr. Chartraw went on to introduce the benefits of fiberoptic bronchoscopy to Dr. Zhong, assuming that he had never seen a fiberoptic bronchoscope at all. Moreover, Dr. Chartraw's introduction was tinted with self-appreciation, saying that he had done fiberoptic bronchoscopy for more than 400 patients, so he was very familiar with the procedure. Dr. Zhong smiled and felt confident, because he had already done 1,500 cases of fiberoptic bronchoscopy before he arrived in the UK and was very skilled at it as well.

"He thought that we came from under a rock," a student from São Paulo, Brazil, who had also come to the UK for advanced trainings, said to Dr. Zhong so humorously. "They think we don't know anything."

The reason Dr. Zhong spoke about tongue diagnosis in TCM was because there was a discussion about a case. A British patient suffering from pulmonary heart disease took diuretics for a few days, and the swelling subsided, but he became very hyperactive. Dr. Zhong took a look at the patient's tongue and found that it was magenta-red, meaning his symptoms belonged to what Chinese medicine often called a yin deficiency and fire exuberance. When he was working at the IRH Institute, he had encountered patients like this. He knew that such a patient might have an imbalance of the body's PH value due to the use of too many alkaline diuretics, and that was why the tongue was reddish in color. He told the British professor in charge of this patient, "This patient must have hypokalemia and needs potassium supplements." He went on to explain, "The patient lost a lot of potassium after taking too much diuretics, so he has developed metabolic alkalosis."

His British colleagues found it strange. Why would the Chinese doctor think this way?

The English professor then said, "Sure, let's measure his arterial triglycerides and potassium." The triglycerides showed alkalosis and the potassium level really was low. After the patient was supplemented with potassium, his situation improved after two days. The British professor was very happy and said to Dr. Zhong, "It seems that you are quite knowledgeable after all." His words were affirmative, yet his tone was still condescending.

Dr. Zhong's diagnosis made the British professor interested in Chinese medical practices. He did not expect that a tongue diagnosis would help so much. In his subsequent treatment of the patient, Dr. Zhong also used a modern treatment from Chinese medicine that made the British doctor even more amazed: acupuncture anesthesia. Acupuncture anesthesia was a new achievement in the inheritance and development of Chinese medicine. It was less effective in the pain relief of thoracic surgeries, but it had proven effective on the pain relief of thyroid surgery.

A THRILLING HUMAN EXPERIMENT

If what happened to Dr. Zhong earlier was surprising, then what followed was completely beyond comprehension for his arrogant British counterparts at the Royal Infirmary of Edinburgh: he repaired a medical instrument that was completely broken. Even more shockingly, he experimented on his own body to prove a medical conundrum, inhaling carbon monoxide with a concentration equal to that of 60 cigarettes, even though he had always avoided smoking.

After arriving at the Royal Infirmary of Edinburgh in January 1980, Dr. Zhong felt that to the British experts, everyone was equal in the field of knowledge. They highly valued the abilities of their peers, respecting those who were capable, regardless of their nationality or background.

After graduating from Beijing Medical College, Dr. Zhong had stayed in the college as a lecturer, and he was engaged in biochemical research. At that time, his operational skills were better than ordinary doctors, which proved helpful for his later studies in the UK.

The respiratory biochemistry laboratory at the Royal Infirmary of Edinburgh had an aerotonometer that had been sitting idle for over a year. The hospital's doctors, of course, did not use it for their experiments, but Dr. Zhong had to use it for his. The director of the laboratory, Mr. Walker, had no use for the aerotonometer and was about to apply for a grant to purchase a new one.

"Let me try it," Dr. Zhong said. When Walker heard that the Chinese doctor, Zhong Nanshan, was trying to recycle this instrument, he gave this instrument to Dr. Zhong as a sort of plaything for his amusement.

The two years of training would pass by quickly, so Dr. Zhong did not want to waste a single second of it. He wanted to make use of an instrument like this as soon as possible, but the aerotonometer needed to be tested once it was repaired, and blood was needed for the test.

Dr. Zhong drew blood from his own veins from the test, 20 or 30 ml at a time. He kept drawing blood while testing. After more than 30 rounds of testing, he drew out 800 ml of blood. This time he succeeded. The dashboard of the aerotonometer started to indicate readings in an orderly way, as if it had been awakened from a deep sleep.

"That was £3,000 saved!" Mr. Walker was surprised.

Standing beside him, Dr. Morgan said in confusion, "Dr. Zhong, have you repaired such instruments in China?"

"Oh, no. The first time I saw this kind of instrument was after I came to the Royal Infirmary," replied Dr. Zhong truthfully. He had only heard of an aerotonometer before.

Dr. Morgan marveled, "That's incredible!"

The repair of the instrument was only the first step. The second step was to start conducting the experiment. Dr. Zhong had begun preparing for his experiments from the moment he arrived at this hospital, and it was a very challenging experiment, a study of the effect of carbon monoxide on the dissociation curve of human haemoglobin.

After browsing through a vast amount of reference materials, Dr. Zhong found that studying the effect of carbon monoxide on human hemoglobin was not only in line with his own research on respiratory diseases, but also a project that Professor Flenley was looking forward to carrying out as well. Dr. Zhong studied day and night and finally finished designing this experiment.

Professor Flenley read Dr. Zhong's design doubtfully. But after reading it, he praised it, saying, "OK, Doctor Zhong." For the first time, he took Dr. Zhong's hand. "Great minds think alike! I support you!"

After this, many smokers instantly became friends of Dr. Zhong, a non-smoker, including everyone from international students to Chinese restaurant owners. He sought them out as his experiment subjects to analyze the effect of carbon monoxide on the hemoglobin dissociation curve when inhaling different concentrations of cigarette smoke. However, after doing so, Dr. Zhong felt that the information they had gathered was rather fragmented.

A systematic observation was required to ensure that there was enough evidence. Dr. Zhong came up with a reliable method. He conducted the experiment on his own body. This was a thrilling human experiment. Dr. Zhong inhaled air containing carbon monoxide, while allowing his peers draw blood from him according to the inhalation condition from time to time to draw blood. When the concentration of carbon monoxide in the blood reached 15%, that was equivalent to smoking 50 to 60 cigarettes continuously. Dr. Zhong was rarely exposed to cigarettes before this.

"It's too dangerous! Stop it!" his colleagues yelled in shock.

Dr. Zhong judged from his own experience that this concentration had not yet brought the dissociation curve of hemoglobin to the equilibrium section. He shook his head. "Please continue."

He continued inhaling carbon monoxide until the concentration in his haemoglobin reached 22%. By this time, he felt dizzy.

The experiment finally yielded satisfactory results. His British colleagues were deeply touched. Later, because of this experiment, Dr. Zhong was invited to make a presentation at the Academy of Medical Sciences (United Kingdom) in 1980.

The Chinese research on chronic bronchitis was refreshing to the medical experts, who were awed by the courage of the Chinese doctor. The presentation by Dr. Zhong provided a challenging conclusion. Although the experiment proved the formula and conclusion derived by Flenley in 1975 using mathematics, they were only half correct, while the other half stood to be corrected.

The air in Edinburgh in May was exceptionally fresh. Dr. Zhong rejoiced in his long lost relaxation. Even the experiment, which always seemed cold, had a sense of cordiality. Alice happily handed Dr. Zhong a letter, which was written to him by Professor Flenley. In the letter, Flenley said, "Next week, representatives of the Royal Air Force and the President of the Scottish Medical Council are coming to visit our laboratory. At stake is our ability to secure a substantial financial sponsorship for the construction of the laboratory building. I would like you to make a presentation that day on the effect of various factors on the hemoglobin dissociation curve."

The fact that the Royal Infirmary of Edinburgh placed such trust in a foreign scholar was something Dr. Zhong had not expected. His painstaking efforts were rewarded, his skills were recognized, and his 800 ml of blood had not been drawn in vain.

CHALLENGING AUTHORITY

Dr. Zhong had boldly corrected the experiment results of an authoritative figure of the Royal College of Physicians. After this incident, twelve experts asked him twelve questions.

Professor Truman from the Royal Infirmary of Edinburgh wanted Dr. Zhong to conduct an experiment. For the experiment, patients with respiratory failure would be subjected to artificial respiration, and the concentration of oxygen supplied would gradually increase while observing the shunting within the patients' lungs. He asked Dr. Zhong to reproduce a research project previously conducted by Professor Alexander Crampton Smith, the Director of the Department of Anesthesia at John Radcliffe Hospital, a teaching hospital of Oxford University. Crampton Smith's conclusion was that as the concentration of oxygen went up, shunting would increase.

Dr. Zhong conducted the same experiments on some patients that were given artificial respiration under the hospital's care. He found that Crampton Smith's results could not be validated via his experiments. Following Truman's advice, he repeated the experiment several times with no significant changes in results. By this point, Dr. Zhong had started to wonder if Crampton Smith had drawn the wrong conclusion. Truman asked Dr. Zhong why he deemed the conclusion to be wrong. Dr. Zhong explained that he had been carefully observing the oxygen electrodes. He noticed that when the concentration of oxygen rose above 70%, the data collected by those electrodes contained large errors, and the shunting must be calculated based on the revised numbers. In Dr. Zhong's numerous attempts, the results all pointed to the same conclusion: as the concentration of oxygen rose, the shunting was either stable or decreased, instead of increasing, as per Crampton Smith's results.

Truman was very pleased with Dr. Zhong's results. He told Dr. Zhong, "Great! You should write a paper based on your discovery and send it to the Royal College of Anaesthetists."

Not long after, Dr. Zhong drafted his report and sent it to the college. It was accepted in August 1980.

The 1980 Annual Anaesthesia Conference of the UK was held at Cambridge University. Attending members were all authoritative figures in the field of anesthesia from all over the UK. Such conferences were considered a great chance for knowledgeable doctors to showcase their research. Dr. Zhong was the first speaker.

With his findings being completely opposite from that of an authoritative scholar, Dr. Zhong knew his research would be controversial. But fortunately, his courage aligned with the rigorous, objective, truthful, and fair style of UK scientific researchers.

With a slide presentation, he first explained Crampton Smith's statements on the subject and followed it up with the results of his own experiments, proposing a different theory while questioning Crampton Smith's conclusions. In the end, he showed the correct curve that was drafted based on the revised data, further proving the errors in Crampton Smith's conclusions. Seeing that Dr. Zhong's conclusion was the polar opposite of that of the authoritative Crampton Smith, all the experts stared at the Chinese doctor.

As Dr. Zhong finished his demonstration, many experts in the audience, including some of Crampton Smith's assistants, came up with twelve questions, eleven of which had been anticipated by Dr. Zhong. In the end, the then President of the Association of Anaesthetists of Great Britain and Ireland, Cyril Scurr stood up and said, "We have conducted similar experiments, and we think that Dr. Zhong's methodology is correct." He proceeded to ask the members of the Royal College of Anaesthetists, who were sitting in front rows, "What do you think?" Everyone at the venue raised their hands in approval, showing that they agreed with Dr. Zhong's results.

This article of Dr. Zhong's was later published in the 1983 issue of the *British Journal of Anaesthesia,* spanning 13 pages.

Zhong Nanshan said, "Truman and I were ecstatic, like we had just won a war. That night, we drank beer together and rowed a boat on the River Cam. It was a grand celebration." Recalling these old times, Dr. Zhong Nanshan could not help but smile, even after so many years.

In 2009, the Royal Infirmary of Edinburgh invited Dr. Zhong back to Edinburgh, where he met Truman again. Truman fervently embraced Dr. Zhong Nanshan, his student and old friend. Talking about old times, they had a great time together.

While Dr. Zhong looked back on his time in Edinburgh with much fondness, he also admitted that the period of time was rather difficult for him, given the challenges in his work and his financial situation. In July 1980, when Dr. Zhong was facing the greatest difficulties in his experiments, he wanted to request assistance from Peter Claverley, an outstanding researcher of COPD. Dr. Zhong contacted him multiple times in hope of acquiring his help, but he always refused "due to his busy schedule." Dr. Zhong did not have much money at the time, but he decided to invite Claverley for a beer, so that he could ask him some questions. Deeming it rude to turn it down, Claverley accepted the invitation. However, Claverley offered his explanation in only a few minutes, leaving behind a very confused Dr. Zhong.

Every student conducting advanced studies at the Royal Infirmary of Edinburgh needed to report their progress at certain stages, and their reporting was done at a Beer Seminar, where experts sipped beer as they listened to the students' reports. Every student was given a chance to speak. Dr. Zhong's turn came in September 1980. The title of his report was "The Effect of Carbon Monoxide on the Oxygen Transport Capacity of Blood." During the speech, Dr. Zhong conducted a comprehensive analysis on Flenley's mathematical process on the oxygen transport capacity of blood, and utilized Flenley's math to interpret the results of his experiments. While the Beer Seminar seemed like a relaxed event, it was actually a very tense situation, and the speaker had to speak with utmost rigorousness.

As Dr. Zhong concluded his speech, multiple respiratory specialists, anesthesiologists, and endocrinologists applauded and congratulated him for his achievements. This time, Claverley took the initiative to shake Dr. Zhong's hand. "A fantastic speech, and a fantastic job, Dr. Zhong."

From then on, Claverley no longer treated Dr. Zhong with the same aloofness. The change in attitude brought great joy to Dr. Zhong. Late into that night, when everyone had gone home, Dr. Zhong continued to sit on a bench in the Royal Infirmary of Edinburgh, all alone. He was intoxicated by the sense of excitement. "Finally, they approve of me, my work, and my skills."

Following his success at the UK Conference of Medical Research in September 1980, he traveled to Vienna as an invited guest at the European Congress of Immunology. There, he met the Director of the Thoracic Department of St Bartholomew's Hospital, Robert Davies, who fervently invited him to participate in a collaborative project in St Bartholomew's Hospital. Dr. Zhong decided to conduct research on the inflammatory mediators of asthma with Dr. Davies. Dr. Zhong was very excited.

In April 1981, the sunshine at Edinburgh was filled with a sense of sadness. In two days' time, Dr. Zhong's research work at Edinburgh would come to an early end, as he would be taking his advanced studies to St. Bartholomew Hospital with the University of London.

Professor Flenley was away at an academic conference in the US, so Dr. Zhong could only say his goodbyes to Flenley's wife and children. Dr. Zhong arrived on time at Flenley's home. As the door opened, a crowd of guests appeared in front of him, accompanied by the melody of a Scottish folk song. Seeing Flenley's wife, Alice, Dr. Zhong rushed over to apologize. "So sorry that I've interrupted your party. I'll just quickly say goodbye."

With a big smile, Alice took Dr. Zhong's hand and said, "No, no, no! This party is for you! Come in!"

Glasses of champagne and dishes filled the table, while guests crowded every corner of the room. The respiratory specialists, anesthetists, radiologists, and nurses were all there. It was a farewell party Mrs. Flenley hosted for Dr. Zhong. Raising her glass, Alice proposed a toast. "Come, friends! Let's all share a happy drink before we shake Dr. Zhong's hands and bid him goodbye."

Everyone was warm and friendly, and their smiles surrounded him. Clearly touched by the scene, Dr. Zhong bowed to everyone. "You have my most sincere gratitude! As a doctor from China, I hope that one day you can all visit China," Dr. Zhong raised his voice, "and get to know the real China!" He bowed again, "My deepest thanks for everyone!"

Showered with the warmth of friendship, every handshake brought intense emotions to Dr. Zhong's heart. One by one, the guests took out gifts for Dr. Zhong. He was overwhelmed. How could he possibly return the favor? He didn't know what to do. Seeing Dr. Zhong's thoughts, Cetro proposed another toast. "Cheers, for Dr. Zhong's success!"

Chief Cardiologist Dr. Matthews and the director of the computer lab Blasch gave him a beautiful Scottish tapestry. Deputy Chief Respiratory Specialist Dr. Cetro prepared a bracelet for Dr. Zhong's wife, while Mrs. Flenley prepared books and toys for his children. As Dr. Zhong's sixteen months with the Royal Infirmary of Edinburgh came to an end, everyone was sad to see him go.

17

THE RETURN OF A SCHOLAR

Edinburgh bid him a final farewell, as his friend Professor Flenley heaped praises on him that brought tears to his eyes. It was time for Dr. Zhong to embark on his next journey.

In the early 1980s, everyone in China admired people who traveled overseas. To them, travelers were almost mythical creatures. Dr. Zhong was given every chance to stay overseas at that time. His love for his country and his people was not just a notion, but an idea backed by action. Like a pine tree on the top of a mountain, Dr. Zhong grew his roots into the land of China. Neither storm nor earthquake could extinguish his burning patriotism. Turning adversities into miracles, he found strength as he faced life's difficulties, a strength that pushed him forward, and that pushed him toward change.

Dr. Zhong said that many of his relatives and friends jumped at any opportunities to go abroad, leaving him rather alone in China. After their departure, most of them acquired a good life in foreign countries. If wealth were the only factor in the quality of life, many of them were enjoying far superior lives to Dr. Zhong. Many expressed their admiration. In their mind, Dr. Zhong might have achieved a better life if he had left China. But Dr. Zhong felt that he enjoyed the richness of mind far more than wealth and material comforts. To Dr. Zhong, a sense of achievement in his work and a sense of fulfilment in his spirit were all that was needed.

On November 18, 1981, Dr. Zhong ended his advanced studies after 25 months in the UK, and he returned to China from London. Two years earlier, his fellow international students celebrated his 43rd birthday on a train to the UK, and now, he had just celebrated his 45th.

Holding Dr. Zhong in its embrace, the zephyr of Edinburgh was trying to keep Dr. Zhong from leaving. All the experts and medical workers of the Royal Infirmary of Edinburgh came to bid him farewell. With great sadness in his heart, Dr. Zhong embarked on his journey home. Flenley, the man who had once disappointed Dr. Zhong, had completely changed his attitude toward the Chinese doctor after just two years. Now, he considered Dr. Zhong his partner and one of his closest friends.

In that two years, Dr. Zhong put forth great effort that yielded great results. He simply couldn't wait to return to China and bring the good news back to everyone. With six important research projects on respiratory diseases, seven academic papers, four of which were published in the Medical Research Council, the Association of Anaesthetists of Great Britain and Ireland, and the UK Diabetes Association, and the titles of Honorary Scholar and Honorary Member from St. Bartholomew Hospital and the Mexico World Allergy Association, the achievements of Dr. Zhong kept piling up. He hoped that his father would finally be satisfied with him.

On the journey home, he brought more than just luggage. The Embassy of the People's Republic of China in the United Kingdom of Great Britain and Northern Ireland forwarded a letter to Dr. Zhong. It was from his mentor, Professor Flenley. It was just as concise as the first letter Dr. Zhong received from him, but with a completely different tone. In the letter, Flenley wrote, "I have worked with scholars from many countries in my academic career. But frankly, I have never met any scholar as diligent, as cooperative, and as fruitful as Dr. Zhong."

Hearing this, even the Iron Man Dr. Zhong couldn't help but shed a few tears. All that happened during the previous two years flooded his mind. "In the end, I had done something to show them what I was made of." He was proud and pleased.

As a British scholar with an explorative and practical mindset, Flenley had been a great teacher for Dr. Zhong. All of his achievements and researches would not have been possible without Flenley's teaching and cooperation. Beyond that, Flenley's demeanor left a lasting impression on Dr. Zhong as well, affecting his medical career.

But what excited Dr. Zhong Nanshan the most, was probably the fact that Dr. Zhong Shifan finally praised him. According to his memory, it was the first time in 45 years that he received praise from his father. Even when he got into PMU, Zhong Shifan only congratulated him, but this time he praised Dr. Zhong with a great sense of gravity. "You showed the foreigners with your actions. You showed them that we Chinese people are not useless," his father said.

Many years later, when Dr. Zhong mentioned his studies in the UK to his students, he would always say, "One day, you all will travel around the world. I would like to remind you that even though science does not have a nationality, scientists do."

From Edinburgh to Beijing, and back to Guangzhou, bags of medical reference books were always beside Dr. Zhong. To him, these books worth more than their weight in gold.

The two years in the UK was only a brief period of Dr. Zhong's life, yet the education he received from the University of Edinburgh would accompany him for his life. To Dr. Zhong, the best thing he acquired in the UK was the customary truthfulness. He learned two of his most treasured lessons in the University of Edinburgh. First, always ensure that you have a firm foothold before you take the next step. Even a matter of little to no importance still deserves great diligence. Second, never blindly believe what authoritative figures say. Instead, trust the truth that you see with your own eyes.

When Dr. Zhong conducted experiments, he never proceeded to the second step without perfecting the first. Influenced by the rigorous style of the British, he gradually adopted this practice into his daily work. Regardless of the nature of his work, Dr. Zhong always approached his work with this attitude. He said, "Such methods may seem slower, but they will turn out to be faster in the end."

When he first arrived in the UK, this style was a shock to Dr. Zhong, who was more accommodated to the Chinese way of doing things. The Cultural Revolution had just ended, and in that political atmosphere, people still had many concerns when they tried to work, but the requirements put on them were usually extremely vague and numerous. This led to a rather chaotic working attitude. Shifting from "vague, generic, and pointless" to "truthfulness," Dr. Zhong couldn't help but exclaim, "We Chinese people will have to change a lot and suffer a great deal before we can eliminate such terrible impetuousness."

Dr. Zhong saw the diligent, rigorous ways of the British experts. Any action, no matter how insignificant, must be conducted to fulfill a specific goal.

Dr. Zhong concluded, "The British experts always did things step by step. Their experiments might not seem ambitious on the surface, yet they carried everything out with a great sense of purpose and diligence. As I returned to China, my style and attitude regarding work had completely changed. I owe this change to those British experts." Such truthfulness and rigorousness were the prime qualities of a scientific worker.

Before Dr. Zhong returned to China, one of Flenley's experiments yielded great results, unveiling a great learning opportunity for Dr. Zhong. The experiment was related to at-home oxygen treatment of COPD patients with hypoxemia. The patients were subjected to eight hours of oxygen supply each day. The goal of the experiment was to observe if such treatment could increase the patient's survival rates or general quality of life. The Medical Research Council allocated five years for Flenley to complete this simple experiment.

The methodology was rather straightforward. One group of patients would receive oxygen during the night, while the other group would not. From the first year all the way to the third, the mortality rates remained the same for both groups. It was suggested that the experiment might had been a waste of time, and some even proposed to end it. But Flenley refused, claiming that the full five years were necessary for the experiment.

Surprisingly, the mortality rates began to diverge in the fourth year. By the end of the fifth year, a significant gap could be observed between the rates of the two groups.

In the end, 60% of the patients who received the oxygen supply survived, while the ratio was only 30% for those who did not. The difference stood as the undeniable proof of the importance of carrying out the experiment over five years.

Finally, the report was published in *The Lancet*, as the experiment proved that oxygen treatment during the night could indeed improve the patients' survival rate and quality of life. Flenley and his team conducted five years of research on this small problem. This was a matter of attitude, and it taught Dr. Zhong some very important lessons.

Primarily, he was amazed by the rigorous attitude of UK medical workers in their pursuit of science, but he was also impressed by the administrative supervision of British society. The British Medical Association Medical Ethics Committee was very strict in its supervision. Medical workers had to adhere to the relevant laws while maintaining objectivity and integrity. Failure to do so or any other fraudulent behaviors was met with heavy punishment.

Dr. Zhong once worked with Professor Robert Davies, a renowned expert on asthma. A few years later, Davies suddenly went off the grid. Another two or three years had passed before Dr. Zhong learned from a friend that his qualifications had been revoked by the BMA Medical Ethics Committee. For the sake of acquiring further funding, he committed academic fraud and falsified data and results from an animal experiment regarding asthma. While going over the details of the experiment, a student found this unacceptable and recorded his instructions. Later, the student submitted the recording to the Medical Ethics Committee as evidence against Davies.

Dr. Zhong continues to contemplate this incident even today. "In China, the science community is still suffering from impetuousness." He noted that many researchers took their results for granted, conducting very little actual work before calling it a day and moving on to the next step. But every step of scientific research needed to be treated with great care. Rigorousness was one of Dr. Zhong's favorite qualities. He observed that the reason China was now encouraging its medical workers to publish their work in established foreign periodicals was that such periodicals always treat their work with utmost rigorousness. Only articles that were creative, clear, and truthful in their academic research would be published.

Many of Dr. Zhong's colleagues at the Chinese Medical Association and the IRH published their work on numeral foreign periodicals. This brought Dr. Zhong great comfort. "That means we are competent at what we do," he observed.

18

APPOINTED AS AN ACADEMICIAN

Dr. Zhong had made impressive progress in the field of medical research since the 1970s. One of his most influential achievements came at the end of the 1980s. By utilizing the bronchial responsive test method he created and epidemiological investigation techniques, he became the first person in the world to prove and improve the concept of Cough Variant Asthma. In addition, he explored the part played by the imbalance of nitric oxide and endothelin in the lungs and the abnormal expression of proto-oncogene in the development of hypoxic pulmonary hypertension. Under his guidance, his postgraduate students created the testing methods of moving diaphragm functions. He proved that among COPD patients, including those in early to medium stages, 60% suffered from protein-energy malnutrition, and he created the modified formula for their energy consumption, while developing the nutrition supplement specifically designed for Chinese, Youtelisheng. In medical practice, he also raised the rescue success rate of respiratory failure to above 85%.

For these impressive achievements, Dr. Zhong was listed as the Chinese representative in the UN's effort to create the Global Initiative for Asthma. He was named a medical consultant of the WHO and elected as an academician of the Chinese Academy of Engineering. It was through these astonishing achievements that the confident Dr. Zhong Nanshan that led the war against SARS emerged. In 1993, Dr. Zhong also became a member of the Eighth National Committee of the Chinese People's Political Consultative Conference.

Despite the shining list of achievements, Dr. Zhong still did not consider applying to become an academician of the Chinese Academy of Engineering, as he felt that he was not qualified. While he submitted his application, he did not get his hopes up. It was even more surprising to him that he was elected with an impressive vote count. All Academicians of the Chinese Academy of Engineering had undergo rigorous inspection and screening, and it was extremely rare for anyone to be elected with a high vote count.

At the end of the 1980s, Dr. Zhong became the first person in the world to propose the concept of Cough Variant Asthma. He made the proposal based on one of his critical findings.

The reason he discovered CVA was that he needed to solve a technical problem. Before the concept was known, when doctors checked patients for Airway Hyper Reactivity (AHR) for asthma diagnosis, they always needed to deploy the Bronchial Challenge Test. The test itself required complicated techniques and advanced technologies, with every set of instruments costing US$ 5,000–6,000. Such prices were impossible for Chinese patients and hospitals at the time, which led to many difficulties in the diagnosis of asthma.

In 1984, Dr. Zhong simplified the process by developing a smaller and simpler instrument for such tests. He utilized multiple self-made glass bottles for the nebulization of reactive agents of different concentrations. As AHR was a very significant sign for asthma, diagnosis could be completed by conducting a Maximum Peak Flow test using a peak flow meter to check if the patient had AHR.

Just like that, an instrument that cost thousands of US dollars was replaced by the peak flow meter. Such inventions might not be necessary in developed countries, but it was much needed in China, and it showed the traditional medical ideals of Dr. Zhong: simplicity, convenience, accessibility, and practicality. Such developments allowed Chinese doctors to cure patients with cheaper materials and simpler methods.

The simple yet effective instrument was finished in 1986, and it became the first TAR Type I Histamine Bronchial Challenge Test Instrument. With the help of this equipment, Dr. Zhong managed to conduct bronchial challenge tests on a massive scale. With such accessibility, many patients who had AHR but had yet to show asthmatic symptoms were diagnosed at relatively early stages. This brought Dr. Zhong an immense sense of encouragement.

Dr. Zhong published an article in a major journal of thoracic medicine in the USA in 1992. The article focused on two things, the first being a discussion of whether AHR alone should be treated as an indication of CVA, and the second being the track record of young patients with AHR over two years. According to his research, 20%

of those patients developed asthma within two years, despite having only AHR and no other asthmatic symptoms.

Although Dr. Zhong had already posted the concept of CVA in authoritative international thoracic medical journals, the idea did not receive sufficient attention from most of the medical community. Five years later, a Canadian scholar finally decided to conduct further research on the concept. They posted their theories and follow-up results in the British journal *Thorax* in 1977, claiming that asymptomatic AHR patients had a higher chance of developing symptomatic asthma, which proved Dr. Zhong's theory.

Finally, after sixteen years, the authoritative medical journal *The Lancet* published a paper citing Dr. Zhong's conclusion that "CVA patients do exist." Integrating numerous discoveries by the Canadian scholar, the paper concluded that 14%–58% of asymptomatic AHR patients would develop asthma. By this point, CVA finally had become a widely recognized concept.

Dr. Zhong's paper was published in 1992. Further supporting proof was published five years later. However, it was not until 2008 that the idea was recognized. The 16-year wait for such a medical conclusion that could save so many from suffering was frustrating to Dr. Zhong. It was only from that point on that the long-awaited theory began to be adopted by many countries. For the sake of safety, AHR patients could finally receive treatment from doctors, even when they did not show asthmatic symptoms. The concept of CVA was one of Dr. Zhong's most significant achievements in the earlier stages of his medical career.

The significance of the concept lay in the possibility it provided for early detection and prevention of the disease. It was very similar to the detection of early stage diabetes. While the patient might be asymptomatic, doctors could still monitor their blood sugar levels, finding patients that were prone to develop diabetes in the process. It could also be compared to the detection of early stage high blood pressure. While the patient might be asymptomatic, their blood pressure levels could still be indicative. And how could it be determined whether someone had asthma, when they showed no symptoms at all? The answer is easy: a simple test could diagnose them. Like the illnesses listed above, CVA was easily preventable; it just did not receive enough attention. Even today, this major achievement of Dr. Zhong is still utilized in respiratory medicine research and respiratory illness diagnoses, not only in China, but all over the world. CVA is also known as asymptomatic asthma. By definition, even if the patient is not showing asthmatic symptoms, they can still be diagnosed. In the respiratory medicine community, this was a revolutionary idea at the time. Before its emergence, the conclusion that was widely accepted throughout the world was that asthma patients must have related symptoms. However, Dr. Zhong discovered that asymptomatic patients could still develop symptomatic asthma. A seemingly iron-clad medical conclusion was thus modified.

Unlike foreign patients, COPD patients in China generally also suffered from malnutrition. The medical term for this phenomenon was protein calorie malnutrition, the definition of which in China was significantly different from that of the world. In China, around 60% of COPD patients suffered from protein calorie malnutrition. Dr. Zhong surmised that early-stage treatment for these patients should also be different from those of foreign patients, supplying more protein and fat.

Chinese COPD patients were usually thinner, while COPD patients in other countries were usually heavier. After some tests, Dr. Zhong noticed this issue. Due to high consumption of energy, these patients were suffering from protein insufficiency. Academically speaking, Dr. Zhong's discovery led to more specific nutrition treatments for COPD patients, and on the practical level, discovery led to the development of specific nutrition plans for COPD patients, which provided new means and directions for the nutrition treatment meant for COPD patients.

In 1990, Dr. Zhong received an official notification saying that the Standing Committee of the Guangdong Provincial Committee of the CPC had decided to issue commendations to two persons, Hung Sin Nui and Zhong Nanshan. He had not had the slightest idea this was happening beforehand.

Hung Sin Nui was the Deputy Director of Guangdong Cantonese Opera Theater and the Chief Arts Director of Guangzhou Cantonese Opera Troupe. She was elected as Vice Chairman of the Guangdong Provincial Musician's Association, member of the Second CPPCC National Committee, and deputy of the Third, Fourth, Seventh, Eighth, and Ninth NPC. She started studying theatrics in 1938. In her decades-long acting career, she was featured in almost a hundred Cantonese Opera shows, along with over ninety movies. She was very innovative in her arts, creating many famous Hong Qiang songs in her career.

In 1994, officials arranged for Dr. Zhong to apply to become an academician of the Chinese Academy of Engineering. By then, he had never imagined that his application would succeed, so it was not a big deal to him.

In 1995, then Director of the Guangzhou Municipal Personnel Bureau Sheng Nanfang talked to Dr. Zhong three times, in the hope of convincing him to apply for the position of academician of the Chinese Academy of Engineering. Dr. Zhong replied with utmost sincerity that he was far from qualified for the position. However, as this was mandated as an official order, he had to fill in the application form.

In Dr. Zhong's mind, those who could be elected as academicians were all older and had a long list of shining achievements. Being awarded only a Third Prize in the National Science and Technology Progress Award, Dr. Zhong thought he had no chance of being elected as an academician. Fortunately for Dr. Zhong, a new policy came out that at least one third of newly admitted academicians must be below the age of 60. Later, Dr. Zhong joked about his admission as an academician, saying, "This policy benefited me greatly. They asked for people younger than 60 years of age, when I just happened to be 59."

An academician of the CAE, Dr. Hou Yunde, worked in the National Institute for Viral Disease at the Chinese Center for Disease Control and Prevention. He was the Director of the Division of Medicine and Health of the CAE, serving as the leader of the Academician Election Committee. One day, he called up two professors in the Guangzhou Medical University that were well known for having high standards, and he asked, "What do you think of this Dr. Zhong Nanshan? I want to know about his academic skills and personal qualities."

The election of Academicians of the Chinese Academy of Engineering relied heavily on the candidate's personal qualities. One of the professors, Prof. Liang answered, "Do you mean *that* Dr. Zhong? He is a good fellow. He works very hard, and he is very nice to us older professors." As a result, Dr. Hou grew fonder of the "young man" Zhong Nanshan.

While Dr. Zhong did not receive many international awards, the articles that he published on international platforms were widely recognized and appreciated by his peers due to their innovative discoveries. For example, the CVA theory suggested that some asthma patients were not aware of their own situation, as they were asymptomatic. Dr. Zhong not only proposed the theory, but also attached an investigation proving that these patients, after a few years, might develop symptomatic asthma. He also proposed a way to detect and diagnose CVA patients.

By 1989 and 1990, Dr. Zhong had published multiple papers in some renowned international journals. Moreover, he was also elected as the Chinese representative, participating in international conferences held by the WHO and the creation of Global Initiative for Asthma. Such an event was very rare in China at that time, and it was quite impactful among China's medical community.

There was another critical factor that came into play. Since 1983, Dr. Zhong had served as the personal doctor for many officials from local and central government departments. The CAE Election Committee was thus well aware of Dr. Zhong's medical skills. Many officials came to see Dr. Zhong when they were in Guangzhou, knowing that he was famous for his professional skills. Dr. Zhong also often went to Beijing for joint consultation. To the members of the Election Committee, these aspects all demonstrated Dr. Zhong's actual capabilities.

In addition, Dr. Zhong had quite the reputation among his patients, as they were all very satisfied with his work. The *Yangcheng Evening News* once had a senior commentator called Wei Yin, who was the creator of many fierce editorials. They also wrote some commentary pieces about Dr. Zhong, praising him for his kindness and noble medical ethics. Dr. Zhong first attracted the attention of the press in 1981. The journalist who interviewed Dr. Zhong, Wang Huaji, later became the Deputy Editor-in-Chief of the *Yangcheng Evening News*. The title of his interview piece was "The Story of a Fighting Man." The article detailed Dr. Zhong's experience and struggles when he studied in the UK. At that time, the Chinese men's football team had just lost to New Zealand in the 1982 World Cup Qualifiers, and the public was feeling rather depressed. With such nuanced timing, Wang Huaji specifically named his article "The Story of a Fighting Man," using Dr. Zhong as an example to tell the public that even if the Chinese football team had lost to their opponents, the Chinese people were still standing strong. The interview piece made quite an impact.

While Dr. Zhong was elected as a CAE Academician with an impressive vote count, Guangzhou Medical College held a celebration. With everyone urging him to give a speech, Dr. Zhong made a point, but not about himself, his joy, or his pride. "Ours is rather small local university, and not exactly prestigious. However, even a small university like ours can still produce academicians," he said.

What he was trying to say was that universities needed to face their own short-comings, but they also needed to try their best to overcome them. With this mindset, great success could come, even for small institutions.

"It is critical for one to acknowledge their own shortcomings. It is not a bad thing, because that's how we overcome them. Do not fret because you are faced with bad conditions. Instead, create a favorable condition for yourself with what you have." He said, "If I had to point to a recurring theme in my life, this would be it."

THE GREATEST HAPPINESS

In December 2008, the weather in Guangzhou was quite pleasant. Through the window, rays of sunlight poured into the dilapidated office. It was only 220 square feet, and apart from the two desks and a sofa, books and reference materials filled the room. Looking over the materials on his desk, Dr. Zhong was working hard. Raising one hand, he combed his hair backwards, a subconscious movement when he read. His hands were not particularly big, but they seemed strong thanks to his habit of physical exercise. Somewhat grey, his hair looked soft and curly. Although his hair was thinning at the back of his head, it was barely noticeable. During SARS, his hair suddenly became grey, but it returned to black over time.

His secretary walked in, with a file in their hand. "Director, they're requesting an interview with you again."

It was the crew from the Guangdong Television Station. They were trying to make a documentary for "30 Influential Figures in the 30 Years of Reform and Opening Up."

It had been quite a while since the SARS crisis was brought back into his life and mentioned so many times for various reasons, causing a slight disturbance in his mind. He told his secretary to inform the crew that he would be available for the interview in the evening.

On a series of blue folders resting on the windowsill were some of his favorite photos. One was of himself walking out of a pool, one was of him standing next to the President of China, Mr. Hu Jintao, one was of him during the SARS crisis, full of courage, and another was taken recently, of him smiling in his lab coat, standing underneath the blue sky.

On the wall near the door was a plaque. Inscribed with *Zhong Nanshan the Brave Warrior,* it was a gift from the students of the Guangzhou Nursing School.

He walked out of the office. The hall was barely over three feet wide. The building was constructed in the 1990s, with some unimportant things that he could not throw away piled at the entrance to both the northern and southern room. It was cluttered. In every room, various equipment, instruments, and reference materials filled up every inch. During the fight against SARS, the sixth, seventh, and eighth floors of this building had been converted into isolation wards. The room on the northern side was Dr. Zhong's Expert Consultation Room. There was a plaque on the wall, which read, *Practice medicine to save the world, and spread happiness among the people.* It was a hand-written gift from a famous Guangdong calligrapher, Lu Youguang.

Behind this plaque, the now-renovated wall had witnessed quite a bad situation during the fight against SARS. "Sewage is coming down again! Move!" Directly above the room was a ward for SARS patients. For days, excrement and sewage had flowed through the initially small crack on the wall. The wall was soaked.

"Move it! The plastic bag is full. Get a new one!"

The secretary spoke with great anxiety. "We need to fix this right now. The officials and the press will be here any minute. We cannot let them see this!"

The repairman finally came. "Well, if the sewage keeps dripping down, I have no way to fix it either."

The sewage system of the floor above was fine before, and it had to happen now, at such a bad time. No one knew how to fix it.

Once SARS passed, the plumbing issue was soon fixed, and the wall that the plaque was now attached to had been renovated.

Outside the north-facing window of this office stood the newer inpatient building that was nearing its completion. The run down environment of the First Affiliated Hospital of Guangzhou Medical College and the Institute of Respiratory Health would soon become ancient history.

Despite its 3A rating, the affiliated hospital was tiny, with a land size of only 2.5 acres. It was not initially a specialist hospital for infectious diseases. The IRH was located on the fifth, sixth, seventh, and eighth floors of the building. Having its own laboratories, wards, and offices, it was around 32,000 square feet.

Numerous medical workers moved between the rooms, greeting Dr. Zhong as they walked past him. At the end of the hall were two wooden benches, which dated back to the 1970s. They were there for patients and visitors to rest on, should the medical workers not be able to tend to them right away.

During the SARS crisis, these benches were never empty. Anxious families of the patients would sit silently, as if they were waiting for angles to come and save them. For the patients and their families, these shabby benched held all the weight of their prayers.

Dr. Zhong never missed his weekly consultation session. He always walked at a fast pace. Unless he was intentionally waiting for someone, others often needed to jog a little just to keep up with him. He walked toward his consultation room. Due to the waiting time, using the lift was slower than walking. Like Dr. Zhong, his staff usually didn't use the lift at all. In his younger years, Dr. Zhong always walked up the stairs, taking two or three stairs at a time, and he continued to do so even as an old man.

The consultation hall had many seats, most of which were filled with waiting patients. Being very fit, Dr. Zhong quickly walked through all the people and the aisles. Before long, the crowd started whispering in admiration. "It's Dr. Zhong." Among the voices were some speaking Cantonese, while others did not.

In the consultation room, his students, assistants, and interns waited for him. Every week, someone complained about the fact that they could not reach Dr. Zhong, as he never picked up his phone during this period. During the sessions, he dedicated all of his attention to the patients.

The room was around 400 square feet, with examination cubicles located on both sides. The desk was placed under the window, next to two examination beds. On the opposite wall hung the X-ray lightbox. It was no different from the consultation room of any other doctor, except for the little sign on his table with his name written on it, Zhong Nanshan. It was a simple desk, coupled with a simple office chair. They hadn't been changed in many years.

Before I entered the consultation room, an IRH staff member said to me, "Just take one look and you will know how it is. All of our superiors would simply shake their heads at how bad it is." They also told me, "It was even worse before. As the old building was demolished, he was moved into this new building, and that's how he got this semi-decent room."

Dr. Zhong rarely sat when he waited for patients to come in. As soon as they entered, they saw Dr. Zhong standing in front of them, smiling. Many said that as they saw Dr. Zhong, they felt a wave of relaxation, and the tense emotions that came with "seeing a doctor" mostly went away.

Soon, the first patient came in. It was a thin and sickly woman in her fifties from rural Gansu. Supported on both sides by her family members, her face was very pale.

"How are you? Come, please sit down."

The woman whispered calmly, as if asking about someone else's health. No pain or sadness could be observed in her expression. "Doctor, please tell me, how long do I have?" It was only when she caught a glimpse of Dr. Zhong's face and his smile that a tiny spark of hope lit up her eyes.

"Don't worry. You need to relax first."

Observing her tongue and throat, Dr. Zhong once again demonstrated what she should do, opening his mouth wide. "Ah—" Following his example, the patient slowly opened her mouth.

Dr. Zhong's hands wrapped around his stethoscope, heating the chest piece. "Come, let me listen to your breathing." He reached out his right hand and supported her body, adjusting her position and easing her nerves. She lifted up her shirt, and Dr. Zhong started to listen with his stethoscope.

Despite the strong smell of disinfectant in the room, a rather unpleasant odor still seeped through. Dr. Zhong's full attention remained on the stethoscope, listening as if trying to find an echo in a valley. The patient was very sick with lung illness. She had traveled a long way to see Dr. Zhong, as she knew his reputation.

Supporting the patient with his arm, Dr. Zhong accompanied her to the examination bed and closed the white curtains. With one arm supporting her neck and shoulders, he helped the patient lie down. As the examination concluded, he helped her back up. He poured his heart and soul into every patient, and this one was no exception.

The assistants rushed to work, setting up tests and X-ray appointments for the patient. Dr. Zhong instructed his assistants to begin processing the paperwork for admission to the inpatient wing.

The clock on the wall ticked away. Calculating from the time when the patient entered the room, Dr. Zhong had spent 55 minutes in total conducting the inquiry, auscultation, and palpation and providing analysis of the X-rays she brought.

Usually, Dr. Zhong provided consultations for around ten patients during a half-day session, working from 2:30 pm to past 6 pm. Sometimes the number would exceed ten, and he started early at 2:00 and ended the session even later.

The second patient entered the room.

"Hey, it's you, Mr. Zhang! Have you been feeling better?" Dr. Zhong greeted his regular patient like an old friend.

Mr. Zhang was an elderly chronic bronchial patient. He was in his sixties, and he lived in a suburb of Guangzhou. He was here for a follow-up consultation under Dr. Zhong's instructions. A huge smile appeared on his face. "I've been feeling much better, thanks to you, Dr. Zhong!" He reached out his hands and grabbed onto Dr. Zhong's hands tightly in gratitude.

Dr. Zhong conducted auscultation and palpation on him and talked about his condition for another 15 minutes. The consultation with Mr. Zhang lasted for around thirty minutes, which was the shortest of the consultations Dr. Zhong conducted that day.

The last time Mr. Zhang was here, he had been very frustrated and devastated. He told Dr. Zhong, "I couldn't even breathe." As he delved deeper into his concerns for his children and his sick wife, he felt increasingly hopeless. "What if something happens to me? What will become of my family then?" Conducting examinations and talking about his family at the same time, Dr. Zhong told him, "Mr. Zhang, I am more than ten years older than you. My workload is very heavy every day, but I am still happy with my life. This is because I have all the things in my day planned out."

And that was how Mr. Zhang learned from Dr. Zhong that even if we have our own limitations, as long as we achieve something and solve some problems during our day, we would make ourselves and those around us a lot happier. As Mr. Zhang left the room, he laughed and said, "Eh? Why does my breathing feel easier?"

It was as if even a simple conversation with Dr. Zhong could ease their illness. For many patients, this really was the case. "It's called 'conversation therapy,'" Dr. Zhong said.

The assistant came back, carrying the test results for the first patient. Holding the newly-taken X-ray in his hand, Dr. Zhong took another closer look. As it turned out, she had to be admitted to an inpatient ward immediately. The assistant told Dr. Zhong that the ward had already set the process in motion.

Dr. Zhong said to the assistant, "Please follow through with them. With this response, I fear that something might go wrong."

Dr. Zhong's patients were not all middle-aged or elderly folks. There were children as well. A pair of siblings came in. The sister was ten, and the little brother was six. They had red dots on their hands. They were from Jieyang, Guangdong. Their father had told them that the doctor they would be seeing was the famous Dr. Zhong. As they entered the room, they shouted, "Grandpa Zhong!" The boy was very outgoing and unafraid, and he even began playing with the various objects on Dr. Zhong's desk. Seeing this, his father started to scold him, but Dr. Zhong laughed, pulling the boy into an embrace. To Dr. Zhong, without his patients, all his effort would mean nothing.

Exactly how many patients in China were hoping they could have a consultation with Dr. Zhong? One could only imagine. The same was true for the number of people who were hoping to meet him. For the working staff at the IRH, one of the major tasks was to read all the inquiring letters that came from all over the country.

When Dr. Zhong entered the consultation room, he stopped responding to phone calls, despite the fact that there were still many matters for him to attend to. To him, his consultation time belonged only to his patients, and he poured his heart out tending to them. In the extremely rare circumstance where he could not conduct any consultations on a given day, his assistants would inform the patients in advance. For Dr. Zhong, seeing a patient recover from illnesses under his care was his greatest happiness.

TRUE BEAUTY

When a country had the courage to face reality and speak the truth, there would be no difficulty that it could not conquer. In this regard, Dr. Zhong was a true hero.

In China, as a doctor, he had won the love of the people by virtue of his personal credibility. The Chinese people were proud of him. In Guangdong, the people even saw Dr. Zhong as a role model.

On August 31, 2019, Dr. Zhong was on a China Southern Airlines flight from Singapore to Guangzhou. He had just finished a conference in Singapore. As usual, the cabin became his office in the air. During the flight, a 9-year-old boy could no longer tolerate the itching he was suffering from, and the boy's father had to call the flight attendant for urgent help. Although the cabin temperature was lowered and ice was brought to cool the boy, he still had an unbearable itch, and his face and body started to become red and swollen.

Dr. Zhong got up and walked to the boy. Some of the more observant Cantonese people started to whisper, "Zhong Nanshan!" Dr. Zhong waved to the passengers in a friendly manner. The child's father was very surprised to see him. Dr. Zhong examined the child carefully and said, "It looks like hives caused by a food allergy." He reassured the boy's father that there would be no danger. The father said, "I never imagined I would be on the same plane as Dr. Zhong, not to mention that he could do the checkup himself." He said, "I was relieved when I heard Dr. Zhong said that my child was not in danger." This incident immediately trended on the Internet. An ordinary Cantonese person would be able to tell the story of Dr. Zhong Nanshan as if it were a common tale.

In 2013, Dr. Zhong said, "Atmospheric pollution is scarier than SARS." In 2015, he said, "If a fish grows big and fat in a very short time, it might have been fed certain antibiotics. It is not scientific to farm and feed fish in this way." He also said, "Some hospitals and doctors do not speak of medical ethics. They make illicit income. A heart doctor did coronary angiography for a patient and found out that he had no big problem, but he eventually installed five stents for the patient."

Zhong Nanshan, had almost become a household name. His story was fondly remembered and recounted by the people again and again. The reason Dr. Zhong was named the "most beautiful warrior" was that he was always closely connected with public health in China. People would never forget that in early 2003, when the SARS epidemic came out of nowhere, as a scientist, he defended the truth, sought truth and pragmatism, disregarded his personal safety, faced pressure from all sides, responded to the epidemic without fear, and worked around the clock to save lives.

After the SARS crisis, he was not beaten down by pressure from different sources, nor did he sit on his accolades. Instead, he did his best to make suggestions, actively promoted the construction of a public health emergency system, advocated for cooperation with international health organizations, and presided over the formulation of guidelines for the diagnosis and treatment of acute infectious diseases such as SARS in China. He was the first to formulate the Clinical Diagnostic Criteria for SARS. The Three Early and Three Reasonable Treatment Plan established by him took the lead across the world to form prevention and treatment guidelines with obvious efficacy. This effort was recognized by the WHO and considered to be of guiding significance for the fight against SARS worldwide. His contributions became great contributions of China to the world's battle against SARS.

Over the years, he stayed on the front line of the fight against different epidemics, carrying the crisis of national public health emergencies on his shoulders. He was outspoken on public events such as haze control, indoor air pollution, and influenza A prevention and control. He was never afraid to speak out, deliver true knowledge, and calm people's hearts.

Dr. Zhong led his team to explore the establishment of a prevention and control system for major respiratory infectious diseases in line with China's national conditions, and he established an advanced chain management system of prevention – treatment – control of new and special major respiratory infectious diseases. These efforts played an important role in promoting the establishment of a public health emergency prevention and control system in China, improving the capacity and efficiency of surveillance of major epidemics and strengthening the formation of emergency teams. Dr. Zhong also played an important role in the successful response of H5N1, H1N1, H7N9, H5N6, MERS, and other outbreaks.

People were always curious about how Dr. Zhong always remained spirited and hardworking. Journalists tended to idolize him and depict him from a certain vantage point during their interviews, however his reply was always down to "what exactly I am doing." He did not drift along with trends and fashions. Instead, he had a long-term goal, and everything that he had done was to accomplish a checkpoint on the way to his ultimate pursuit.

When he was asked about his title, "the most beautiful warrior," he said with utmost sincerity, "When I was awarded this honorary title, the first thing I thought of was my team and the people that fought alongside me for decades. I did not fight alone. The 'warrior' refers to a team, a group of like-minded people who overcame countless obstacles together. This title belongs to all of us."

Dr. Zhong said he was emotional participating in such a grand conference, and there were many people and deeds worthy of his admiration. One of the most important reasons Dr. Zhong's struggle had been called the Nanshan Spirit was that selflessness and fearlessness had become an instinct, a daily habit, for him. He felt the need to sacrifice for the greater good just like ordinary people felt the need to eat every day. Progressive figures are often praised for their spirit of sacrifice, and for such people, it seems as if they came to be in this world with a mission to sacrifice. Dr. Zhong is one such person, the pride of China, and an example for all of us to learn from.

On the night of September 25, 2019, after the recognition ceremony, Dr. Zhong Nanshan got off the bus in front of his hotel to take the elevator back to his room and rest, together with other awardees of the title "most beautiful warriors." When he approached the entrance of the elevator, he slowed down to give way to others, especially to the awardees who were older than him.

Not a single sign of complacency was shown on his face, instead, he appeared serious. "I learned a lot today," he exclaimed when he talked about the other awardees' deeds. "They are truly amazing."

His words, along with the suit he wore only on formal occasions, exuded an aura of solemnity.

CHRONOLOGY OF DR. ZHONG'S MAJOR LIFE EVENTS

1936   Born in Nanjing on October 20

1937   Moved to Guiyang with his parents in November

1946   Moved to Guangzhou with his parents in January

1949   Entered the Affiliated Middle School of Lingnan University

1952   Entered the Affiliated High School of South China Normal College (now South China Normal University)

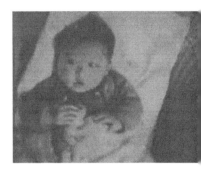

1955   Entered Peking Medical College (later renamed as Peking Medical University, subsequently merged into Peking University as its Department of Medical Science)

1959   Broke national record in Men's 400 Meters Hurdle in the qualifier of the first National Games

1960   Stayed in Peking Medical College to work after graduating from college

1963   Married Li Shaofen on December 31

1965 — Sent to Rushan, Shandong, to participate in the Four Cleanups Movement

1966 — Joined the Communist Party of China in March

1971 — Transferred to Guangzhou No. 4 People's Hospital to work as a doctor

1972 — Joined the Chronic Bronchitis Prevention and Treatment Team

1978 — Participated in the National Science Conference, won the National Scientific Conference Achievement Award with his team's research project on the Diagnosis and Treatment of Chronic Bronchitis by Integrating Chinese and Western Medicine and Typology

Qualified for state-financed overseas advanced education in October

1979 — Started his advanced studies in the Respiratory Department of the Royal Infirmary of Edinburgh in October

1981 — Started his advanced studies in the Respiratory Department in the St Bartholomew Hospital in April

In September, attended the Annual Anesthesia Conference of UK in September, where his paper received the award of distinction, attained 7 scientific research achievements during his course of his overseas studies

Returned to China in November

1982 — Appointed as the Director of Guangzhou IRH

1985 — Became a member of FCCP

1986 — Became a professor of the Respiratory Department in Guangzhou Medical College and a mentor of master students

1987 — Became the President of the First Affiliated Hospital of Guangzhou Medical College

1991 — First proposed the CVA theory

1992 — Became the Secretary of the Guangzhou Medical College Branch of the Party, the President of the Guangzhou Medical College, Member of the Standing Executive Committee of the Global Alliance Against Chronic Respiratory Disease, elected as a member of the Commission of Guangzhou Municipal Committee of the Communist Party of China

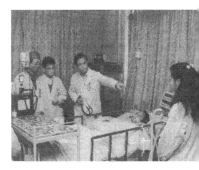

1993 — Became the Member of the 8th CPPCC, started instructing doctoral candidates of Guangzhou Medical College

1994 — Took part in the formulation of the Global Initiative for Asthma of the WHO as the only Chinese scientist representative

1996 — Became the Academician of CAE

1997 — Elected as a Representative of the 15th National Congress of the Communist Party of China

1998 — Became the Member of the 9th CPPCC

1999 — Nominated as one of the six Outstanding Alumni of the Peking Medical University, became the President of Guangzhou Association for Science and Technology

2000 — Became the Director of Respiratory Society of the Chinese Medical Association

2002 — Vice Chairman of Guangdong Association for Science and Technology

2003   Elected as the Member of the 10th CPPCC, became the Leader of the Guangdong Provincial SARS Prevention and Treatment Clinical Expert Team, received the May 1st Labor Medal, nominated as an Outstanding Member of the Communist Party of China, a Progressive Worker of China, a Progressive Individual in the National Healthcare System against SARS, an Outstanding Scientist in the Prevention and Treatment of SARS in China, a Model Party Member of the Guangdong Province, a Role Model of Medical Ethics of the Guangdong Province with a Special Class Merit in the Battle against SARS in the Guangdong Province, an Outstanding Party Member of the Guangzhou Province, a Progressive Worker in the Construction of Guangzhou Municipal Cultural-Ethical Standards, a Role Model in the Battle Against SARS of Guangzhou. Won the *Banyue Tan* (China Comment) Award for Innovation in Ideological and Political Work, the Ho Leung Ho Lee Foundation Prize for Scientific and Technological Progress (Medicine), became a Medical Consultant of the Global Alliance Against Chronic Respiratory Disease and a member of the Influenza Programme of the WHO

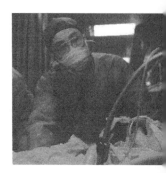

2004   Nominated by CCTV as one of the 10 Inspirational Role Models of China in 2003, received the National Bethune Medal from the Ministry of Health, the Chinese Doctor Prize from the Chinese Medical Doctor Association, nominated as one of the 10 Outstanding Chinese Figures by the Overseas Chinese Affairs Office. Received the Special Class of Guangdong Provincial Science and Technology Award, nominated as an Outstanding Teacher of Southern Canton, one of the 10 Role Models in the Construction of Guangzhou Municipal Cultural-Ethical Standards, received the Outstanding Contribution Award from the Guangzhou Medical College, received the Special Class of the 6th National Book Prize

2005   Nominated a National Role Model of Laborers, his
book, *Jiedu Jixing Chuanranxing Feidianxing Feiyan
– Yufang Yu Duice*, received the Special Class of the
First Guangdong Provincial Popular Science Book
Prize, received the Special Class of Guangdong
Provincial Science and Technology Prize for
Individuals, nominated as an Outstanding Party
Member in the Guangzhou Municipal Education
System, nominated as an Outstanding Party
Member of the Guangzhou Medical College

2005   Became a member of FRCPIRE

2006   Won Respiratory Doctor of China Award, Wuyang
Award (Special Contribution)

2007   Nominated as a National Role Model in Ethics
and Morality (Professionalism), one of the 10
Outstanding Scientific and Technological Talents
of China, became the Ambassador of Guangzhou
Municipal Volunteers, awarded Hon Doctor in
Medical Science of the University of Edinburgh

2008   Received the Special Contribution Award to
Guangdong Provincial Science and Technology,
Guangzhou Overseas Chinese Entrepreneur
Honorary Award, nominated as an Inspirational
Figure of Guangdong since the Reform and
Opening Up, received the title as an Honorary
Member of the European Respiratory Association

2009   Elected as a member of the 11th CPPCC, received
the Lancet Paper of the Year 2008 Award, the 5th
Outstanding Teacher in the Tertiary Institutions of
China Award, nominated as one of the 100 Most
Inspirational Figures since the Founding of the
People's Republic of China

2011   Became a member of the Royal College of
Physicians of Edinburgh, Doctor of Science in the
University of Birmingham

2013 ○ Elected as a member of the 12ᵗʰ CPPCC, became
the Director of Guangzhou IRH, became the
Leader of Guangdong Provincial H7N9 Prevention
and Control Team, published a series of his studies
on H7N9 on *The New England Journal of Medicine*,
making significant contributions to the prevention
and control of the disease

2014 ○ Received Hon Doctor of Science from Hong Kong
Chinese University

2015 ○ Successfully cured the first known case of H5N6 in
Guangzhou

2016 ○ Received the highest honor in the field of
Engineering in China – the 11ᵗʰ Guanghua
Engineering Technology Achievement Award – on
June 1

2016 ○ Received the title HKU Centennial Distinguished
Chinese Scholar

2018 ○ Selected as one of 100 outstanding contributors
to reform and opening up, awarded the title of
Reform Pioneer by the Party Central Committee
and the State Council, and awarded the Important
Promoter of Public Health Emergency Response
System Construction

2019 ○ Nominated as the "Most Beautiful Warrior," listed
in 70 Outstanding Chinese Figures Who Came
Back from Overseas in the Past 70 Years

2020 ○ In January, geared up again at the age of 84 to fight
in the front line of the COVID-19 Pandemic, now
the Director of the China Clinical Research Center
for Respiratory Disease, Leader of the Senior
Experts Team of the National Health Commission
of the People's Republic of China

On August 11, awarded the Medal of the Republic

On September 4, rated as the National Model for
Teaching and Educating People in 2020

SELECTED WORKS OF DR. ZHONG NANSHAN

A) Chinese Books and Chapters

Lu, Zaiying 陆再英, and Zhong Nanshan 钟南山, eds. *Neike Xue* 内科学. Renmin Weisheng Chubanshe, 2008.

Zhong, Nanshan 钟南山, ed. *Jiaxing H1N1 Liugan Fangzhi Zhishi* 甲型H1N1流感防治知识. Guangdong Jiaoyu Chubanshe, 2009.

———. *Linchuang Zhenliao Zhinan—Huxibing Xue Fence* 临床诊疗指南——呼吸病学分册. Renmin Weisheng Chubanshe, 2009.

———. *Zhiming Yixue Zhuanjia Jin Nongjia Congshu* 知名医学专家进农家丛书. Kexue Chubanshe, 2008.

———. *Zhiqiguan Xiaochuan—Jichu Yu Linchuang* 支气管哮喘——基础与临床. Renmin Weisheng Chubanshe, 2006.

———. *Chuanran Xing Feidianxing Feiyan Linchuang Zhenduan Yu Zhiliao* 传染性非典型肺炎临床诊断与治疗. Guangdong Jiaoyu Chubanshe, 2003.

Zhong, Nanshan 钟南山, and Liu Youning 刘又宁, eds. *Huxibing Xue* 呼吸病学. Renmin Weisheng Chubanshe, 2012.

Zhong, Nanshan 钟南山, and Wang Chen 王辰, eds. *Huxi Neike Xue* 呼吸内科学. Renmin Weisheng Chubanshe, 2008.

Zhong, Nanshan et al. 钟南山等, eds and trans. *Ying Zhong Ri Tujie Yixue Cidian* 英中日图解医学辞典. Wanli Shudian, 1985.

B) English Books and Chapters

Zhong, N. S. "Management of Asthma in Developing Countries." In *Asthma*, edited by P. J. Barnes, 1869–1882, Philadelphia: Lippincott Raven Publishers, 1997.

———. "Diagnosis and Classification (Asthma)." In *Global Strategy for Asthma Management and Prevention*, 48–61, WHLBI/WHO workshop (GINA), 1995.

C) Journal Articles

Asher, I., A. Boner, A. Chuchalin, N. S. Zhong, et al. "Prevention of Allergy and Asthma: Interim Report." *Allergy* 55, no. 11 (2000): 1069–1088.

Chen, Aihuan 陈爱欢, Zhang Chunqing 张纯青, and Zhong Nanshan 钟南山. "*Erbingsuanbeilusong Xiru Liaofa Dui Xiaochuan Ertong Xiaqiunao–Chuiti–Shenshangxianzhou Gongneng De Yingxiang* 二丙酸倍氯松吸入疗法对哮喘儿童下丘脑—垂体—肾上腺轴功能的影响." *Zhonghua Erke Zazhi* 中华儿科杂志 2, no. 55 (1998): 55.

Li, Jing 李靖, Zheng Jingping 郑劲平, Zhong Nanshan 钟南山, et al. "The Protective Effect of a Bacterial Extract Against Acute Exacerbation in Patients with Chronic Bronchitis Accompanied by Chronic Obstructive Pulmonary Disease." *Chinese Medical Journal* 6 (2004): 28–34.

Li, Shiyue 李时悦, and Zhong Nanshan 钟南山. "*Jing Xianzhijing Jubu Zhushe Yiliuxian (Immusyn) Zhiliao Feiai Linchuang Guancha (Fu 9 Li Baogao)* 经纤支镜局部注射抑瘤仙 (Immusyn) 治疗肺癌临床观察(附9例报告)." *Guangzhou Yixueyuan Xuebao* 广州医学院学报 4 (1997): 35–37.

Mo, Hongying 莫红缨, Zhong Nanshan 钟南山, Zheng Jingping 郑劲平, and Long Qicai 龙启才. "*N–Yixianbankuangansuan Dui Jixmanxing Xiyan Dashu Feizuzhi He Feipao Guanxiye Zhong Heyinzi – KB Biaoda De Yingxiang* N–乙酰半胱氨酸对急慢性吸烟大鼠肺组织和肺泡灌洗液中核因子—KB表达的影响." *Zhongguo Linchuang Yaolixue Yu Zhiliaoxue* 中国临床药理学与治疗学 2 (2001): 103–106.

Tan, Yaxia 谭亚夏, Han Wenling 韩文玲, Zhong Nanshan 钟南山, et al. "Chemokine–like Factor 1, a Novel Cytokine, Contributes to Airway Damage, Remodeling and Pulmonary Fibrosis." *Chinese Medical Journal* 8 (2004): 3–9.

Xu, Jun 徐军, and Zhong Nanshan 钟南山. "EDRF *He Neipisu Zai Diyang Feidongmai Gaoya Xingcheng Zhong De Zuoyong* EDRF和内皮素在低氧肺动脉高压形成中的作用." *Beijing Yike Daxue Xuebao* 北京医科大学学报 1 (1994): 233–235.

Xu, J., and Zhong N. S. "Interaction of TNF–A and ET–l on the Pathogenesis of the Animal Asthmatic Model." *Clinical & Experimental Allergy* 27 (1997): 568–573.

———. "Mechanisms of Bronchial Hyperresponsiveness: The Interaction of Endothelin–1 and other Cytokines." *Respirology* 4, no. 4 (1999): 413–417.

Zhang, Y. C., and Zhong N. S. "COPD and Noninvasive Ventilation." *RT International* 4 (1995): 99–106.

Zheng, J. P., and Zhong N. S. "Risk Factors of the Environment and Occupation on Lung Diseases in China." *Enviro Med* 1, no. 2 (1999): 359–382.

Zhong, Nanshan. "Fighting SARS in Grand Collaboration: Our Strategies." *Chinese Medical Journal* 6 (2003): 5–6.

———. "Consensus for the Management of Severe Acute Respiratory Syndrome." *Chinese Medical Journal* 11 (2003): 5–38.

Zhong, N. S. "Atopic Diseases in the Chinese Community." *Clinical & Experimental Allergy* 24 (1994): 297–298.

Zhong, N. S., et al. "Bronchial Hyperresponsiveness in Young Students in China, in Relation to Respiratory Symptoms, Diagnosed Asthma and Risk Factors." *Thorax* 45 (1990): 860–865.

———. "Is Asymptomatic Bronchial Hyperresponsiveness an Indication of Potential Asthma?" *Chest* 102 (1992): 1104–1109.

EPILOGUE

An amazing figure appeared in my empty heart. When he carried the poorest and weakest of the sick in his arms, I learned how greatness came from the ordinary. I began to admire his name and learn about his spirit. I sincerely feel that his golden heart belonged to the people, to the country, and to justice.

Research, politics, consultations, and conferences made his phone ring non-stop every day, and often his doorbell as well. He met with different kinds of people very often.

The heavy load of reality befell him every day as soon as he woke up. Yet, it was in his nature to turn pressure into motivation. His efficiency was his secret weapon in accomplishing his tasks.

His work was almost his entire life. Roughly 65% of his day was dedicated to all kinds of urgent work matters, and his only rest was when he slept and when he ate three meals each day. He always wished that he was able to make a choice, that even for one day, or even half a day, he might be undisturbed by sudden matters, so that he could stay quiet and concentrate on medical research. "If that were the case, I believe I could produce more results," he said. He always valued scientific research most. The confidence and calmness in him, an 84-year-old man, was truly admirable.

He was admired for always being able to remain so calm, like a vast, serene lake. He was swift like the wind, calm like the mountain, and tolerant like the sea. The demeanor of a great doctor was reflected in even the minor details of his life. He lived a simple life and always carried two items in his pocket: a pen and a stack of his name cards. The name cards would be given to any patient seeking medical treatment at any time. "This is my phone number. My assistant will convey your situation to me," he would say as he gave the card away.

If his kindness resembled clear, gentle water, his humor was a piece of jade in the water. When I really got close to him and came to understand and perceive him, I realized that I felt the same as the people around him who cared for him. We all hoped that experts like Dr. Zhong could remain healthy and energetic, because so many critical, difficult patients from all over the country needed to be rescued, and many complex medical problems were waiting to be studied. In our mind, his health was invaluable.

The media interviewed me regarding my writings about Dr. Zhong. How did I get along with him? How long had I been interviewing him?

I made the following analogy: how could a glass that was almost empty understand a glass that was full of water? Does time really matter? How would it matter? Could the vast difference in mindset be bridged by time?

With my level of energy being like a glass that was almost empty, I was trying to reflect Dr. Zhong Nanshan from my perspective. The image would inevitably be distorted. It was my wish to construct a truthful image of him, because only through a truthful image could anyone understand his greatness.

I always waited silently for him to accept my interview requests, because he was traveling in foreign countries to win academic awards for our country, or he was speaking in the lecture hall, nurturing the doctors of tomorrow, or he was sitting in the consultation room, answering questions and speaking the truth. The word self was never part of his vocabulary, and there was always some demand on him.

He experienced decades of wind and rain, and he was misunderstood, wronged, and isolated. None of the difficulties left a mark on his sharp mind. He was only concerned with the concrete, actual truth, instead of vanity and fame. More than one friend sincerely reminded me that I had to remain objective because he was a cannon who never hesitated to speak the truth, so he would always be controversial.

Even so, he has a bright light in the scale of justice and conscience. It has been my honor to be inspired by such a spirit during my pursuit of spiritual values. Upon getting to know Dr. Zhong, any conscientious person could only reflect on themselves with him as a role model. Looking back, what is the value of our own personal losses, gains, loves, and hates? If I met someone like Dr. Zhong in my life and did not write about him, how could I ever claim that I had a heart of humanism?

Only when the time passes and the present becomes history can we better understand Dr. Zhong's remarkable achievements. We read about him carefully now, and we aspire to attain the inspiration he has bestowed on us for our future generations.

In fact, who am I to write about him? Many people of great talent have offered to help over the years. In this world, no one dares to claim that they are the best of the best. Would there really be someone that was talented enough for this task?

I have sincerely stated that it is everyone's wish to write well about Dr. Zhong. If other people's works are more vivid than mine and can better inspire society, is that not also my wish? Dr. Zhong reassured me, "Ye Yi, I have appointed you. This decision will not change."

Religions encourage us to offer our compassion to those who need it the most. Dr. Zhong offers opportunities to ordinary people who value hard work. I am ordinary, yet I've been fortunate enough to be honored by Dr. Zhong's esteem.

During my cooperation with my publisher, I admired the seriousness of the editors in charge. With this book's publication, the imperfections in my narrative have become marks of remorse. This remorse is like a boulder that sinks to the bottom of my heart. It will stay with me for life, and I will not be able to let go of it. I should have done better. I should have written more about the real Zhong Nanshan.

I have done my best and devoted all my energy to this book's publication. Dr. Zhong has been humble enough to cooperate with me and help me with the completion of this book when he has had time. His time is much too precious for me to bother him too often.

Dr. Zhong hopes that the narratives of this book are truthful and not exaggerated. A man of legendary experience and peace of mind has no interest in getting praise or glory. Furthermore, he is already well-known in China. He does not lack admirers, even on the international level, in the field of medicine and beyond. He is quite famous.

Vivid and expressive, he does not have any specific feelings about the labels of "greatness" and "extraordinary" that have been showered to him. Only when he is faced with truth, justice, distress, and the plight of the ordinary people will his deeds shine through the darkness and his voice pierce through the mist. When I began writing this book, he confessed to me, "In fact, I am nothing but a doctor who treats patients."

I pointed to the plaque given to him that reads, *A Treasured Doctor, A Gift to the World,* and praised him for living up this name. To my surprise, his expression like that of a primary school student, he asked me the question that matters to him the most, "Oh, does that mean you think that I have a sense of responsibility?" In Dr. Zhong's mind, the responsibility of a doctor weighs more than a mountain.

During the months-long interview process and writing, Mr. Cheng Donghai, Secretary of the Guangzhou IRH Party Branch, gave his full support and collaborated with me. My company allowed me ample time to complete this work, which was really not easy for them.

A candle will burn to the last of its moment. Dr. Zhong is destined to be a candle. Therefore, I fully understand that many people, like me, admire him, respect him, and wish him well, only because we know him.

No words are needed to praise him except the words of truth, because it is already in his instinct to share the burden of the country and serve the people.

YE YI

A MIND-CLEANSING READING EXPERIENCE

We are used to getting along with him every day, and it seems to be a common experience, but his gracious, respectable, powerful, and spiritually inspiring image motivates us and moves those of us who are much younger than him. He is our revered mentor, charming leader, and trusted friend.

History always moves forward along a twisting path, and the times make heroes. The SARS crisis in 2003 made Zhong Nanshan a memorable figure. He saved people with the heart of a doctor and helped the world with the courage of an admonisher. He demonstrated the moral and historical responsibility of intellectuals.

In 2020, at the age of 84, he told the public not to go to Wuhan unless there were special circumstances during the dangerous outbreak of Covid-19, while he boarded the high-speed rail and traveled back to Wuhan himself. He issued a shocking warning that there was human-to-human transmission of the virus.

Doctors are benevolent. They help the world and save the people. No matter how life-threatening the situation is, doctors will go plunge into the fray.

The famous Chinese writer Lu Xun once said, "Since ancient times, there have been people who work hard, people who strive to overcome difficulties, and people who sacrifice their lives for truths." This truth has been passed down from generation to generation of Chinese people: each era has its own backbone and the backbone has its own noble spirit. In today's world, the most basic, cherished values of human beings – loyalty, dedication, courage, and conscience – are even more rare and commendable.

These indelible spiritual qualities shine in Zhong Nanshan.

Firm and Persistent Ideals and Beliefs

Ideals and beliefs are spiritual motivation and rational self-awareness. Life's road always twists. It is complicated and full of thorns. Only with firm ideals and beliefs can people withstand difficulties and setbacks and not lose the way forward in a tough, complex environment. Zhong Nanshan's life path fluctuated, but he always upheld the ideal and belief of "love the country and serve the people." In his youth, he was not discouraged by the unjust treatment of his family. Instead, he always believed that "the cause of the Party always rushes forward and is unstoppable."

In the early 1980s, he didn't long for the superior conditions abroad, but politely declined when his mentor asked him to stay. In the 1990s, he insisted on "doing big business in a small hospital," and he united and led the team to gradually develop the Guangzhou IRH into a first-class research institution in China. During the battle against SARS in 2003, he was indignant at the demonization of China by a small group of foreign forces. He took every possible opportunity to introduce the correct measures taken by the Chinese government to his foreign counterparts and the media, safeguarding China's reputation and playing a positive role in helping the international community correctly understand the epidemic in China.

During the battle against Covid-19 in 2020, he was resolute against the hypocritical faces of some overseas media who disregarded their conscience, kicked China when it was down, concocted insulting anti-China remarks, and applied double standards. He spoke with the voice of hundreds of millions of Chinese people, saying, "Chinese people have never been afraid of being berated or insulted. We will still go the right way." With the way Chinese people are used to speaking with their actions, he and countless others who fought against the pandemic were fully committed, being the first to stop the spread of the pandemic, making the land the safest and warmest home in the world, and letting those who had unspeakable motives end in disappointment. Throughout his growth process, Zhong Nanshan's firm, persistent ideals and beliefs were the prerequisite for his growth and success.

The Aim of Serving the People Wholeheartedly

His worldview, life perspective, and values center on selfless dedication for the benefit of the people. Over the past sixty years of medical practice, Zhong Nanshan has always adhered to one principle: life is priceless, and the patients' interests are above all. Growing from his role as an ordinary doctor to become an academician of the Chinese Academy of Engineering, his heart remained as clear as the moon. In winter, before examining a patient, he always first rubs his hands to warm them, and when he goes to the ward, no matter how sick, unsightly, or smelly the patient is, he will kindly hold their hand and greet them, leaning forward to listen carefully to what the patient says. It is like a son listening to his mother's ramblings, or a father listening to his child tell a story. There is never an impatient look on his face.

His volunteered request of "transfer to the critical patients" during SARS or "going backwards" during Covid-19 were not done on a whim, but came from a call from within. He said that the people were the real force for national development, national revitalization, and social progress. The value of medical personnel was reflected in serving society and the public. Only by obtaining strong support and drawing wisdom from the masses could they continue to grow. Over the years, from the height of maintaining the health of the people, he had paid attention to the problems of it being "difficult to see a doctor" and "medical care being expensive." He called on the government to strengthen its effort in healthcare, advocated the development of community medical care, and promoted the return of public hospitals to public benefit. In his work, he constantly urged and implemented "prevention-oriented" policy, adhered to the advanced, pragmatic academic research paradigm based on the national conditions, and strove to develop simple, effective, safe, and inexpensive medical treatments to benefit society.

The Scientific Spirit of Seeking Truth from Facts

Zhong Nanshan's reason and academic qualities as a scientist are impressive. During the SARS outbreak in 2003, through his clinical practice, he publicly explained to society at the early stages of the epidemic that SARS was "preventable, controllable, and curable." His foresight as a scientist helped the people correctly understand the disease and restore their mental stability.

With a sense of responsibility for the health of the people and the persistent pursuit of the truth, he did not take the easy way out in discerning the pathogen for SARS. Instead, he respected the facts and courageously challenged the authority's judgment that "the SARS pathogen is chlamydia."

According to his judgment of the epidemic, he believed that when the pathogen was still unknown, the term "effective control" was misleading, and the term "effective containment" was more scientific. This sounded the alarm on the prevailing optimism and provided a scientific basis for the government's more appropriate decision.

Despite the criticism, he strongly advocated and promoted the collaboration of science and technology both inside and outside the country so that it was possible to deal with the SARS epidemic together. His generous scientific mind and humanistic concern stemmed from his profound global vision and in-depth understanding of the development of science and technology.

Self-Conscious Moral Pursuit and Personality Building

Zhong Nanshan has always been strict with himself and generous with others. He leads by example in all matters and is rich in affinity. Whether in leadership positions, in the fight against epidemics, or in teaching and education, he always sets an example for his students and subordinates, insisting that "the greatest politics is to do our jobs well." He leads by example, gathers the wisdom and strength of the team, and pushes the cause forward. Especially in the face of major tests such as SARS and Covid-19, he has not been afraid of death, but has taken the lead to make significant contributions in virus tracing, pathogenesis, clinical and laboratory diagnosis, treatment plans, effective medicines, and vaccine research and development, fully demonstrating his professionalism as an academician, the courage of a warrior, and the undertakings of national talent. When people criticized the experts who made the judgment that "the pathogen of SARS is chlamydia," he insisted that "academic differences need not be politicized," and opposed overemphasizing it. Collectivism, leading by example, and treating others with generosity are all integral parts of the moral personality of Zhong Nanshan.

The four value dimensions of ideals and beliefs, worldview and life perspective, methodology, and moral character constitute the complete connotation of the Nanshan Spirit. The book *A Tribute to Zhong Nanshan* has as its distinctive feature an insistence that historical events and figures be evaluated with a materialistic view of history, excavating the rich, colorful spiritual world of Zhong Nanshan. In reading the book, we can enter Zhong Nanshan's spiritual world, and we can also cleanse our own hearts and enrich our own spiritual worlds.

This is the value of reading *A Tribute to Zhong Nanshan*.

CHENG DONGHAI

INDEX

ABOUT THE AUTHOR

YE YI, a famous Chinese writer, poet, and journalist, has published many works in *People's Daily*, *People's Literature*, and China National Radio. She has followed and reported on Mr. Zhong Nanshan for more than ten years and was authorized by Mr. Zhong as the only biographer in China. She has published ten books, including *Biography of Zhong Nanshan* and *Interviews with Zhong Nanshan*. She also served as the chief writer of *Zhong Nanshan*, a documentary by Guangdong T.V. Now, she is a director of the China Popular Science Writers Association, dedicated to children's science education.